Bernard Shaw was born in Dublin in 1856. Essentially shy, he created the
persona of G.B.S., the showman, satirist, controversialist, critic, pundit,
wit, intellectual buffoon and dramatist. Commentators brought a new
adjective into English: Shavian, a term used to embody all his brilliant
qualities.

After his arrival in London in 1876 he became an active Socialist and a
brilliant platform speaker. He wrote on many social aspects of the day; on
Commonsense about the War (1914), *How to Settle the Irish Question* (1917) and
The Intelligent Woman's Guide to Socialism and Capitalism (1928). He under-
took his own education at the British Museum and consequently became
keenly interested in cultural subjects. Thus his prolific output included
music, art and theatre reviews, which were collected into several volumes,
such as *Music in London 1890–1894* (3 vols., 1931); *Pen Portraits and Reviews*
(1931); and *Our Theatres in the Nineties* (3 vols., 1931). He also wrote five
novels.

He conducted a strong attack on the London theatre and was closely
associated with the intellectual revival of British theatre. His many plays
fall into several categories: 'Plays Unpleasant'; 'Plays Pleasant'; comedies; chronicle-plays; 'metabiological Pentateuch' (*Back to Methuselah*, a
series of plays) and 'political extravaganzas'. G.B.S. died in 1950.

Bernard Shaw

SELECTED
SHORT PLAYS

DEFINITIVE TEXT
under the editorial supervision of
Dan H. Laurence

PENGUIN BOOKS

PENGUIN BOOKS

Published by the Penguin Group
Penguin Books Ltd, 27 Wrights Lane, London W8 5TZ, England
Penguin Books USA Inc., 375 Hudson Street, New York, New York 10014, USA
Penguin Books Australia Ltd, Ringwood, Victoria, Australia
Penguin Books Canada Ltd, 2801 John Street, Markham, Ontario, Canada L3R 1B4
Penguin Books (NZ) Ltd, 182–190 Wairau Road, Auckland 10, New Zealand

Penguin Books Ltd, Registered Offices: Harmondsworth, Middlesex, England

All business connected with Bernard Shaw's plays is in the hands of The Society of Authors, 84 Drayton Gardens, London SW10 9SB (Telephone: 071–373 6642), to which all inquires and applications for licences to perform should be addressed and performing fees paid. Dates and places of contemplated performances must be precisely specified in all applications.
Applications for permission to give stock and amateur performances of Bernard Shaw's plays in the United States of America and Canada should be made to Samuel French Inc., 45 West 25th Street, New York, New York 10010.

❧ CONTENTS ❧

The Admirable Bashville

or Constancy Unrewarded

being the novel of Cashel Byron's Profession
done into a stage play in three
acts and in blank verse

WITH

Preface

Composition begun January 1901; completed manuscript sent to publisher 2 February 1901. Published in *Cashel Byron's Profession* (revised edition), 1901. First collected in *Translations and Tomfooleries*, 1926. Revised preface in Collected Edition, 1930. Copyright reading at the Victoria Hall (Bijou Theatre), London, on 13 March 1901. First presented by amateurs at the Pharos Club, London, on 14 December 1902. First professional performance presented by the Stage Society at the Imperial Theatre, London, on 7 June 1903; repeated on 8 June.

Lydia Carew   *Henrietta Watson*
Cashel Byron   *Ben Webster*
Bob Mellish   *William Wyes*
Lucian Webber   *Charles Quartermaine*
Bashville   *J. Farren Soutar*
Cetewayo   *James Hearn*
Paradise   *W. Pilling*
Lord Worthington   *Douglas Gordon*
Master of the Revels   *A. Lingham Power*
A Policeman   *C. Aubrey Smith*
Adelaide Gisborne   *Fanny Brough*

Period – Spring and Summer 1882

FIRST TABLEAU: Scene 1: *A Glade in Wiltstoken Park*
Scene 2: *London. A Room in Lydia's House*
Scene 3: *Islington. The Agricultural Hall*

SECOND TABLEAU: *Wiltstoken. A Room in the Warren Lodge*

✤ PREFACE ✤

It may be asked why I wrote The Admirable Bashville in blank verse. My answer is that the operation of the copyright law of that time (now happily superseded) left me only a week to write it in. Blank verse is so childishly easy and expeditious (hence, by the way, Shakespear's copious output), that by adopting it I was enabled to do within the week what would have cost me a month in prose.

Besides, I am fond of blank verse. Not nineteenth century blank verse, of course, nor indeed, with a very few exceptions, any post-Shakespearean blank verse. Nay, not Shakespearean blank verse itself later than the histories. I am quite sure that anyone who is to recover the charm of blank verse must go back frankly to its beginnings, and start a literary pre-Raphaelite Brotherhood. I like the melodious sing-song, the clear simple one-line and two-line sayings, and the occasional rhymed tags, like the half closes in an eighteenth century symphony, in Peele, Kyd, Greene, and the histories of Shakespear. Accordingly, I poetasted The Admirable Bashville in the primitive Elizabethan style. And lest the literary connoisseurs should declare that there was not a single correct line in all my three acts, I stole or paraphrased a few from Marlowe and Shakespear (not to mention Henry Carey); so that if any man dared quote me derisively, he should do so in peril of inadvertently lighting on a purple patch from Hamlet or Faustus.

I also endeavored in this little play to prove that I was not the heartless creature some of my critics took me for. I observed the established laws of stage popularity and probability. I simplified the character of the heroine, and summed up her sweetness in the one sacred word: Love. I gave consistency to the heroism of Cashel. I paid to Morality, in the final scene, the tribute of poetic justice. I restored to Patriotism its usual place on the stage, and gracefully acknowledged The Throne as the fountain of social honor. I paid particular attention to the construction of the play, which will be found equal in this respect to the best contemporary models.

And the result was that the British playgoer, to whom Elizabethan English is a dead language, only half understood nine-tenths of the play, and applauded the other tenth (the big speeches) with a seriousness that was far funnier than any burlesque.

The play, by the way, should be performed on an Elizabethan stage, with traverses for the indoor scenes, and with only one interval after the second act.

On reading over the above after a lapse of thirty years I am not quite so sure as I was that Elizabethan English may not again become a living language to the ordinary playgoer. To people who never read anything but newspapers and popular magazines, a good deal of Shakespear's more euphuistic blank verse is hardly more intelligible than classical Greek. Even actors may be heard repeating it by rote with an air that persuades the public that they understand what they are saying; but it cannot impose any such illusion on a professionally skilled listener.

Then there are the people who do not go to Protestant churches nor read anything at all, and consequently understand no English except modern vernacular English. This class is by no means a negligible one even in the theatre; for it includes a large body of intelligent manual and open air workers and sportsmen who, though after their day's exertions they fall asleep in less than a minute if they sit down with an open book in their hands, can be kept awake and alert very effectually in the theatre by a play. Only, it must be a play in the vernacular. Otherwise it does not exist for them except as an incomprehensible bore.

There was a time when not only the theatres but the newspapers addressed themselves to the literate alone. Hunt up an old melodrama (say Sweeny Todd the Demon Barber of Fleet Street) or an old newspaper file; and you will at once see that the writers of the play and of the contemporary leading articles, though they may have been the seediest of Bohemians, had learnt Latin grammar and read books written by persons similarly schooled. They had literally the benefit of clergy, and wrote accordingly. With the advent of compulsory education sixty years ago, and the creation thereby of a class which could read and write, but had no Latin and less Greek, newspapers and plays alike soon came to be written by illiterate masters of the vernacular; and I myself welcomed the change and discarded my early very classical style for a vernacular one. Nowadays, when I read typewritten plays by young authors, as I sometimes have occasion to do, I find in them such illiteracies as He exits, She exits, They exit etc. etc. Chapman, who wrote all his stage directions in Latin, or Ben Jonson, who deplored the slenderness of Shakespear's classical education, would have risen up and roared for a birchrod to castigate such execrable solecisms. By the end of the nineteenth century the press and the theatre had lost all their Latinity; and this was why, whenever The Admirable Bashville was performed, men of letters like Maurice Hewlett would chuckle delightedly over it almost line by line, whilst the ordinary playgoers would listen with a puzzled and troubled stare, wondering what on earth it was all about and how they ought to take it, and the unfortunate persons who had been forced to 'get up Shakespear' as part of an academic course on English literature, sat with a scowl of malignant hatred that poisoned the atmosphere. When Bashville was followed by a piece in the vernacular the relief of the audience was so great that there was always a burst of applause at the very first sentence.

And yet, whenever the meaning of the words was clear, the listeners shewed unmistakably that they liked hyperbolical rhetoric and deliberately artificial language. My parodies of the Elizabethan mannerism, and funny echoes of pet lines from the Elizabethan playwrights were, as such, quite lost on them; but Ben Webster brought down the house with Cashel Byron's declamatory repudiation of the name of gentleman, and James Hearn's lamentation over the tragedy of Cetewayo came off, not as a mockery, but as genuine tragedy, which indeed it also is. It was the literary fun that proved a mere puzzle, in spite of the acting of casts which included such accomplished comedians as Charles Quartermaine, William Wyes, Lennox Pawle, Henrietta Watson, Marie Lohr, and Fanny Brough.

Another significant fact pointed in the same direction. In no country is the worship of the old authorized version of the Bible carried to greater lengths than in the United States of America. To alter a single word of it was, it was believed, to incur the curse in the last chapter of Revelations. Even in England the very timid official revision of 1885 shocked our native Fundamentalists (a ridiculous but convenient name not then invented). Yet it was in the United States that the ministers of religion first found themselves compelled to produce versions in modern vernacular and journal-ese under stress of the flat fact that their flocks often could not understand the old authorized version, and always found the style so artificial that though it could produce an unintelligent reverence it brought no intimate conviction to the reader.

Sometimes, however, the simple and direct passages were not sentimental enough to satisfy people whose minds were steeped in modern literary sob stuff. For instance, such bald statements about Barabbas as that he was a robber, or that he had killed a certain man in a sedition, quite failed to interest anyone in him; but when Marie Corelli expanded this concise information into a novel in her own passionate and richly colored style it sold like hot cakes.

I must make a personal confession in this matter. Though I was saturated with the Bible and with Shakespear before I was ten years old, and the only grammar I ever learned was Latin gram-mar, so that Elizabethan English became a mother tongue to me, yet when I first read such vivid and unaffected modern versions as Dr James Moffatt's New Translation of the New Testament I at once got from them so many lights on the Bible narratives which I had missed in the authorized version that I said to myself 'Some day I will translate Hamlet into modern vernacular English.' But indeed if the alienation of our young from Elizabethan English continues it will be necessary to produce revised versions not only of Shakespear but of Sir Walter Scott and even of my own early novels.

Still, a revival of Elizabethan literature may be possible. If I, as an Irish child in the eighteen-sixties, could without enforced study become so familiar with it that I had some difficulty as a journalist later on in getting rid of it, it must be possible for the same thing to occur to an English child in the nineteen-sixties. The Elizabethan style has many charms for imaginative children. It is bloody, bombastic, violent, senselessly pretentious, barbarous and chil-dish in its humor, and full of music. In short, the taste for it, as anyone can observe at the Old Vic or the Stratford Festivals, is essentially half childish, half musical. To acquire it, all that is necessary is access to it. Now the opportunities for such access are enormously wider than they used to be. Of course as long as we persist in stuffing Shakespear and the Bible down our children's throats with threats of condign punishment if they fail to answer silly questions about them, they will continue to be loathed as they very largely are at present. But if our children, when they have been simply taught to read, have plenty of dramatically illustrated Bibles and Shakespears left in their way, with the illustrated passages printed under the pictures, it will soon be possible to find a general audience which can laugh at The Admirable Bashville as heartily as Maurice Hewlett did, and for repertory theatres to amuse themselves and their congregations with occasional performances of Carey's Chrononhotonthologos, Fielding's Tom Thumb, and even Bombastes Furioso.

I shall not here raise the question of whether such a revival is desirable. It would carry me too far and plunge me too deep for a volume of trifles and tomfooleries. But as the Elizabethan style is unquestionably both musical and powerful, I may at least say that it is better to have a sense of it and a fancy for it than to have no sense of style or literary fancy at all.

❧ ACT I ❧

A glade in Wiltstoken Park. Enter LYDIA.

LYDIA. Ye leafy breasts and warm protecting wings
    Of mother trees that hatch our tender souls,
    And from the well of Nature in our hearts
    Thaw the intolerable inch of ice
    That bears the weight of all the stamping world,
    Hear ye me sing to solitude that I,
    Lydia Carew, the owner of these lands,
    Albeit most rich, most learned, and most wise,
    Am yet most lonely. What are riches worth
    When wisdom with them comes to shew the purse bearer
    That life remains unpurchasable? Learning
    Learns but one lesson: doubt! To excel all
    Is, to be lonely. Oh, ye busy birds,
    Engrossed with real needs, ye shameless trees
    With arms outspread in welcome of the sun,
    Your minds, bent singly to enlarge your lives,
    Have given you wings and raised your delicate heads
    High heavens above us crawlers.
    [*A rook sets up a great cawing; and the other birds chatter loudly as a gust
    of wind sets the branches swaying. She makes as though she would shew
    them her sleeves.*

                    Lo, the leaves
    That hide my drooping boughs! Mock me – poor maid! –
    Deride with joyous comfortable chatter
    These stolen feathers. Laugh at me, the clothed one.
    Laugh at the mind fed on foul air and books.
    Books! Art! And Culture! Oh, I shall go mad.
    Give me a mate that never heard of these,
    A sylvan god, tree born in heart and sap;
    Or else, eternal maidhood be my hap.

[*Another gust of wind and bird-chatter. She sits on the mossy root of an oak and buries her face in her hands. Cashel Byron, in a white singlet and breeches, comes through the trees.*]

CASHEL. Whats this? Whom have we here? A woman!

LYDIA [*looking up*]   Yes.

CASHEL. You have no business here. I have. Away!
Women distract me. Hence!

LYDIA.   Bid you me hence?
I am upon mine own ground. Who are you?
I take you for a god, a sylvan god.
This place is mine: I share it with the birds,
The trees, the sylvan gods, the lovely company
Of haunted solitudes.

CASHEL.   A sylvan god!
A goat-eared image! Do your statues speak?
Walk? heave the chest with breath? or like a feather
Lift you – like this?   [*He sets her on her feet.*

LYDIA [*panting*] You take away my breath!
Youre strong. Your hands off, please. Thank you. Farewell.

CASHEL. Before you go: when shall we meet again?

LYDIA. Why should we meet again?

CASHEL.   Who knows? We shall.
That much I know by instinct. Whats your name?

LYDIA. Lydia Carew.

CASHEL.   Lydia's a pretty name.
Where do you live?

LYDIA.   I' the castle.

CASHEL [*thunderstruck*]   Do not say
You are the lady of this great domain.

LYDIA. I am.

CASHEL.   Accursed luck! I took you for
The daughter of some farmer. Well, your pardon.
I came too close: I looked too deep. Farewell.

LYDIA. I pardon that. Now tell me who you are.

CASHEL. Ask me not whence I come, nor what I am.
You are the lady of the castle. I
Have but this hard and blackened hand to live by.

LYDIA. I have felt its strength and envied you. Your name?
I have told you mine.

CASHEL.   My name is Cashel Byron.

LYDIA. I never heard the name; and yet you utter it

As men announce a celebrated name.
Forgive my ignorance.

CASHEL.   I bless it, Lydia.
I have forgot your other name.

LYDIA.   Carew.
Cashel's a pretty name too.

MELLISH [*calling through the wood*] Coo-ee! Byron!

CASHEL. A thousand curses! Oh, I beg you, go.
This is a man you must not meet.

MELLISH [*further off*]   Coo-ee!

LYDIA. He's losing us. What does he in my woods?

CASHEL. He is a part of what I am. What that is
You must not know. It would end all between us.
And yet there's no dishonor in't: your lawyer,
Who let your lodge to me, will vouch me honest.
I am ashamed to tell you what I am –
At least, as yet. Some day, perhaps.

MELLISH [*nearer*]   Coo-ee!

LYDIA. His voice is nearer. Fare you well, my tenant.
When next your rent falls due, come to the castle.
Pay me in person. Sir: your most obedient.

                                   [*She curtsies and goes.*

CASHEL. Lives in this castle! Owns this park! A lady
Marry a prizefighter! Impossible.
And yet the prizefighter must marry her.

Enter MELLISH

Ensanguined swine, whelped by a doggish dam,
Is this thy park, that thou, with voice obscene,
Fillst it with yodeled yells, and screamst my name
For all the world to know that Cashel Byron
Is training here for combat.

MELLISH.   Swine you me?
Ive caught you, have I? You have found a woman.
Let her shew here again, I'll set the dog on her.
I will. I say it. And my name's Bob Mellish.

CASHEL. Change thy initial and be truly hight
Hellish. As for thy dog, why dost thou keep one
And bark thyself? Begone.

MELLISH.   I'll not begone.
You shall come back with me and do your duty –

Your duty to your backers, do you hear?
You have not punched the bag this blesséd day.

CASHEL. The putrid bag engirdled by thy belt
Invites my fist.

MELLISH [*weeping*] Ingrate! O wretched lot!
Who would a trainer be? O Mellish, Mellish,
Trainer of heroes, builder-up of brawn,
Vicarious victor, thou createst champions
That quickly turn thy tyrants. But beware:
Without me thou art nothing. Disobey me,
And all thy boasted strength shall fall from thee.
With flaccid muscles and with failing breath
Facing the fist of thy more faithful foe,
I'll see thee on the grass cursing the day
Thou didst forswear thy training.

CASHEL.   Noisome quack
That canst not from thine own abhorrent visage
Take one carbuncle, thou contaminat'st
Even with thy presence my untainted blood.
Preach abstinence to rascals like thyself
Rotten with surfeiting. Leave me in peace.
This grove is sacred: thou profanest it.
Hence! I have business that concerns thee not.

MELLISH. Ay, with your woman. You will lose your fight.
Have you forgot your duty to your backers?
Oh, what a sacred thing your duty is!
What makes a man but duty? Where were we
Without our duty? Think of Nelson's words:
England expects that every man —

CASHEL.   Shall twaddle
About his duty. Mellish: at no hour
Can I regard thee wholly without loathing;
But when thou playst the moralist, by Heaven,
My soul flies to my fist, my fist to thee;
And never did the Cyclops' hammer fall
On Mars's armor — but enough of that.
It does remind me of my mother.

MELLISH.   Ah,
Byron, let it remind thee. Once I heard
An old song: it ran thus. [*He clears his throat*] Ahem,
  Ahem!

[*Sings*] – They say there is no other
    Can take the place of mother –

I am out o' voice: forgive me; but remember:
Thy mother – were that sainted woman here –
Would say, Obey thy trainer.
CASHEL.   Now, by Heaven,
Some fate is pushing thee upon thy doom.
Canst thou not hear thy sands as they run out?
They thunder like an avalanche. Old man:
Two things I hate, my duty and my mother.
Why dost thou urge them both upon me now?
Presume not on thine age and on thy nastiness.
Vanish, and promptly.
MELLISH.   Can I leave thee here
Thus thinly clad, exposed to vernal dews?
Come back with me, my son, unto our lodge.
CASHEL. Within this breast a fire is newly lit
Whose glow shall sun the dew away, whose radiance
Shall make the orb of night hang in the heavens
Unnoticed, like a glow-worm at high noon.
MELLISH. Ah me, ah me, where wilt thou spend the night?
CASHEL. Wiltstoken's windows wandering beneath,
Wiltstoken's holy bell hearkening,
Wiltstoken's lady loving breathlessly.
MELLISH. The lady of the castle! Thou art mad.
CASHEL. Tis thou art mad to trifle in my path.
Thwart me no more. Begone.
MELLISH.   My boy, my son,
I'd give my heart's blood for thy happiness.
Thwart thee, my son! Ah no. I'll go with thee.
I'll brave the dews. I'll sacrifice my sleep.
I am old – no matter: ne'er shall it be said
Mellish deserted thee.
CASHEL.   You resolute gods
That will not spare this man, upon your knees
Take the disparity twixt his age and mine.
Now from the ring to the high judgment seat
I step at your behest. Bear you me witness
This is not Victory, but Execution.
[*He solemnly projects his fist with colossal force against the waistcoat of*

Mellish, who doubles up like a folded towel, and lies without sense or motion.
And now the night is beautiful again.

> [*The castle clock strikes the hour in the distance.*

Hark! Hark! Hark! Hark! Hark! Hark! Hark! Hark! Hark!
  Hark!
It strikes in poetry. Tis ten o'clock.
Lydia: to thee!
[*He steals off towards the castle. Mellish stirs and groans.*

❦ ACT II ❦

SCENE I

London. A room in Lydia's house. Enter LYDIA *and* LUCIAN.

LYDIA. Welcome, dear cousin, to my London house.
　　Of late you have been chary of your visits.
LUCIAN. I have been greatly occupied of late.
　　The minister to whom I act as scribe
　　In Downing Street was born in Birmingham,
　　And, like a thoroughbred commercial statesman,
　　Splits his infinitives, which I, poor slave,
　　Must reunite, though all the time my heart
　　Yearns for my gentle coz's company.
LYDIA. Lucian: there is some other reason. Think!
　　Since England was a nation every mood
　　Her scribes with adverbs recklessly have split,
　　But thine avoidance dates from yestermonth.
LUCIAN. There is a man I like not haunts this house.
LYDIA. Thou speakst of Cashel Byron?
LUCIAN. 　　　　　　　　　　　　　Aye, of him.
　　Hast thou forgotten that eventful night
　　When as we gathered were at Hoskyn House
　　To hear a lecture by Herr Abendgasse,
　　He placed a single finger on my chest,
　　And I, ensorceled, would have sunk supine
　　Had not a chair received my falling form.
LYDIA. Pooh! That was but by way of illustration.
LUCIAN. What right had he to illustrate his point
　　Upon my person? Was I his assistant
　　That he should try experiments on me
　　As Simpson did on his with chloroform?
　　Now, by the cannon balls of Galileo
　　He hath unmanned me: all my nerve is gone.

This very morning my official chief,
Tapping with friendly forefinger this button,
Levelled me like a thunderstricken elm
Flat upon the Colonial Office floor.

LYDIA. Fancies, coz.

LUCIAN.   Fancies! Fits! the chief said fits!
Delirium tremens! the chlorotic dance
Of Vitus! What could anyone have thought?
Your ruffian friend hath ruined me. By Heaven,
I tremble at a thumbnail. Give me drink.

LYDIA. What ho, without there! Bashville.

BASHVILLE [*without*]   Coming, madam.

Enter BASHVILLE

LYDIA. My cousin ails, Bashville. Procure some wet.

                                        [*Exit* BASHVILLE.

LUCIAN. Some wet!!! Where learnt you that atrocious word?
This is the language of a flower-girl.

LYDIA. True. It is horrible. Said I 'Some wet'?
I meant, some drink. Why did I say 'Some wet'?
Am I ensorceled too? 'Some wet'! Fie! fie!
I feel as though some hateful thing had stained me.
Oh, Lucian, how could I have said 'Some wet'?

LUCIAN. The horrid conversation of this man
Hath numbed thy once unfailing sense of fitness.

LYDIA. Nay, he speaks very well: he's literate:
Shakespear he quotes unconsciously.

LUCIAN.   And yet
Anon he talks pure pothouse.

Enter BASHVILLE

BASHVILLE.   Sir: your potion.

LUCIAN. Thanks. [*He drinks*]. I am better.

A NEWSBOY [*calling without*]   Extra special Star!
Result of the great fight! Name of the winner!

LYDIA. Who calls so loud?

BASHVILLE.   The papers, madam.

LYDIA.   Why?
Hath ought momentous happened?

BASHVILLE.   Madam: yes.

                                    [*He produces a newspaper.*

All England for these thrilling paragraphs
A week has waited breathless.

LYDIA.   Read them us.

BASHVILLE [*reading*] 'At noon today, unknown to the police,
Within a thousand miles of Wormwood Scrubbs,
Th' Australian Champion and his challenger,
The Flying Dutchman, formerly engaged
I' the mercantile marine, fought to a finish.
Lord Worthington, the well-known sporting peer,
Was early on the scene.'

LYDIA.   Lord Worthington!

BASHVILLE. 'The bold Ned Skene revisited the ropes
To hold the bottle for his quondam novice;
Whilst in the seaman's corner were assembled
Professor Palmer and the Chelsea Snob.
Mellish, whose epigastrium has been hurt,
Tis said, by accident at Wiltstoken,
Looked none the worse in the Australian's corner.
The Flying Dutchman wore the Union Jack:
His colors freely sold amid the crowd;
But Cashel's well-known spot of white on blue –'

LYDIA. Whose, did you say?

BASHVILLE.   Cashel's, my lady.

LYDIA.   Lucian:
Your hand – a chair –

BASHVILLE.   Madam: youre ill.

LYDIA.   Proceed.
What you have read I do not understand;
Yet I will hear it through. Proceed.

LUCIAN.   Proceed.

BASHVILLE. 'But Cashel's well-known spot of white on blue
Was fairly rushed for. Time was called at twelve,
When, with a smile of confidence upon
His ocean-beaten mug –'

LYDIA.   His mug?

LUCIAN [*explaining*]   His face.

BASHVILLE [*continuing*] 'The Dutchman came undaunted to the
    scratch,
But found the champion there already. Both
Most heartily shook hands, amid the cheers
Of their encouraged backers. Two to one

Was offered on the Melbourne nonpareil;
And soon, so fit the Flying Dutchman seemed,
Found takers everywhere. No time was lost
In getting to the business of the day.
The Dutchman led at once, and seemed to land
On Byron's dicebox; but the seaman's reach,
Too short for execution at long shots,
Did not get fairly home upon the ivory;
And Byron had the best of the exchange.'

LYDIA. I do not understand. What were they doing?

LUCIAN. Fighting with naked fists.

LYDIA.   Oh, horrible!
I'll hear no more. Or stay: how did it end?
Was Cashel hurt?

LUCIAN [to Bashville] Skip to the final round.

BASHVILLE. 'Round Three: the rumors that had gone about
Of a breakdown in Byron's recent training
Seemed quite confirmed. Upon the call of time
He rose, and, looking anything but cheerful,
Proclaimed with every breath Bellows to Mend.
At this point six to one was freely offered
Upon the Dutchman; and Lord Worthington
Plunged at this figure till he stood to lose
A fortune should the Dutchman, as seemed certain,
Take down the number of the Panley boy.
The Dutchman, glutton as we know he is,
Seemed this time likely to go hungry. Cashel
Was clearly groggy as he slipped the sailor,
Who, not to be denied, followed him up,
Forcing the fighting mid tremendous cheers.'

LYDIA. Oh stop – no more – or tell the worst at once.
I'll be revenged. Bashville: call the police.
This brutal sailor shall be made to know
There's law in England.

LUCIAN.   Do not interrupt him:
Mine ears are thirsting. Finish, man. What next?

BASHVILLE. 'Forty to one, the Dutchman's friends exclaimed.
Done, said Lord Worthington, who shewed himself
A sportsman every inch. Barely the bet
Was booked, when, at the reeling champion's jaw
The sailor, bent on winning out of hand,

Sent in his right. The issue seemed a cert,
When Cashel, ducking smartly to his left,
Cross-countered like a hundredweight of brick —'
LUCIAN. Death and damnation!
LYDIA.   Oh, what does it mean?
BASHVILLE. 'The Dutchman went to grass, a beaten man.'
LYDIA. Hurrah! Hurrah! Hurrah! Oh, well done, Cashel!
BASHVILLE. 'A scene of indescribable excitement
    Ensued; for it was now quite evident
    That Byron's grogginess had all along
    Been feigned to make the market for his backers.
    We trust this sample of colonial smartness
    Will not find imitators on this side.
    The losers settled up like gentlemen;
    But many felt that Byron shewed bad taste
    In taking old Ned Skene upon his back,
    And, with Bob Mellish tucked beneath his oxter,
    Sprinting a hundred yards to show the crowd
    The perfect pink of his condition' — [a knock].
LYDIA [turning pale]   Bashville,
    Didst hear? A knock.
BASHVILLE.   Madam: tis Byron's knock.
    Shall I admit him?
LUCIAN.   Reeking from the ring!
    Oh, monstrous! Say youre out.
LYDIA.   Send him away.
    I will not see the wretch. How dare he keep
    Secrets from ME? I'll punish him. Pray say
    I'm not at home. [Bashville turns to go]. Yet stay. I am afraid
    He will not come again.
LUCIAN.   A consummation
    Devoutly to be wished by any lady.
    Pray, do you wish this man to come again?
LYDIA. No, Lucian. He hath used me very ill.
    He should have told me. I will ne'er forgive him.
    Say, Not at home.
BASHVILLE.   Yes, madam.   [Exit.
LYDIA.   Stay —
LUCIAN [stopping her]   No, Lydia;
    You shall not countermand that proper order.
    Oh, would you cast the treasure of your mind,

The thousands at your bank, and, above all,
Your unassailable social position
Before this soulless mass of beef and brawn.
LYDIA. Nay, coz: youre prejudiced.
CASHEL [*without*]   Liar and slave!
LYDIA. What words were those?
LUCIAN.   The man is drunk with slaughter.

Enter BASHVILLE *running: he shuts the door and locks it*

BASHVILLE. Save yourselves: at the staircase foot the champion
Sprawls on the mat, by trick of wrestler tripped;
But when he rises, woe betide us all!
LYDIA. Who bade you treat my visitor with violence?
BASHVILLE. He would not take my answer; thrust the door
Back in my face; gave me the lie i' th' throat;
Averred he felt your presence in his bones.
I said he should feel mine there too, and felled him;
Then fled to bar your door.
LYDIA.   O lover's instinct!
He felt my presence. Well, let him come in.
We must not fail in courage with a fighter.
Unlock the door.
LUCIAN.   Stop. Like all women, Lydia,
You have the courage of immunity.
To strike you were against his code of honor;
But me, above the belt, he may perform on
T' th' height of his profession. Also Bashville.
BASHVILLE. Think not of me, sir. Let him do his worst.
Oh, if the valor of my heart could weigh
The fatal difference twixt his weight and mine,
A second battle should he do this day:
Nay, though outmatched I be, let but my mistress
Give me the word: instant I'll take him on
Here – now – at catchweight. Better bite the carpet
A man, than fly, a coward.
LUCIAN.   Bravely said:
I will assist you with the poker.
LYDIA.   No:
I will not have him touched. Open the door.
BASHVILLE. Destruction knocks thereat. I smile, and open.

[*Bashville opens the door. Dead silence. Cashel enters, in tears. A solemn pause.*

CASHEL. You know my secret?

LYDIA.   Yes.

CASHEL.   And thereupon
You bade your servant fling me from your door.

LYDIA. I bade my servant say I was not here.

CASHEL [*to Bashville*] Why didst thou better thy instruction, man?
Hadst thou but said, 'She bade me tell thee this,'
Thoudst burst my heart. I thank thee for thy mercy.

LYDIA. Oh, Lucian, didst thou call him 'drunk with slaughter'?
Canst thou refrain from weeping at his woe?

CASHEL [*to Lucian*] The unwritten law that shields the amateur
Against professional resentment, saves thee.
O coward, to traduce behind their backs
Defenceless prizefighters!

LUCIAN.   Thou dost avow
Thou art a prizefighter.

CASHEL.   It was my glory.
I had hoped to offer to my lady there
My belts, my championships, my heaped-up stakes,
My undefeated record; but I knew
Behind their blaze a hateful secret lurked.

LYDIA. Another secret?

LUCIAN.   Is there worse to come?

CASHEL. Know ye not then my mother is an actress?

LUCIAN. How horrible!

LYDIA.   Nay, nay: how interesting!

CASHEL. A thousand victories cannot wipe out
That birthstain. Oh, my speech bewrayeth it:
My earliest lesson was the player's speech
In Hamlet; and to this day I express myself
More like a mobled queen than like a man
Of flesh and blood. Well may your cousin sneer!
What's Hecuba to him or he to Hecuba?

LUCIAN. Injurious upstart: if by Hecuba
Thou pointest darkly at my lovely cousin,
Know that she is to me, and I to her,
What never canst thou be. I do defy thee;
And maugre all the odds thy skill doth give,
Outside I will await thee.

LYDIA. I forbid.
Expressly any such duello. Bashville:
The door. Put Mr Webber in a hansom,
And bid the driver hie to Downing Street.
No answer: tis my will.

[*Exeunt* LUCIAN *and*
BASHVILLE.

And now, farewell.
You must not come again, unless indeed
You can some day look in my eyes and say:
Lydia: my occupation's gone.

CASHEL. Ah no:
It would remind you of my wretched mother.
O God, let me be natural a moment!
What other occupation can I try?
What would you have me be?

LYDIA. A gentleman.

CASHEL. A gentleman! Cashel Byron, stoop
To be the thing that bets on me! the fool
I flatter at so many coins a lesson!
The screaming creature who beside the ring
Gambles with basest wretches for my blood,
And pays with money that he never earned!
Let me die broken hearted rather!

LYDIA. But
You need not be an idle gentleman.
I call you one of Nature's gentlemen.

CASHEL. Thats the collection for the loser, Lydia.
I am not wont to need it. When your friends
Contest elections, and at foot o' th' poll
Rue their presumption, tis their wont to claim
A moral victory. In a sort they are
Nature's M.P.s. I am not yet so threadbare
As to accept these consolation stakes.

LYDIA. You are offended with me.

CASHEL. Yes I am.
I can put up with much; but – 'Nature's gentleman'!
I thank your ladyship of Lyons, but
Must beg to be excused.

LYDIA. But surely, surely,
To be a prizefighter, and maul poor mariners
With naked knuckles, is no work for you.

CASHEL. Thou dost arraign the inattentive Fates
    That weave my thread of life in ruder patterns
    Than these that lie, antimacassarly,
    Asprent thy drawing room. As well demand
    Why I at birth chose to begin my life
    A speechless babe, hairless, incontinent,
    Hobbling upon all fours, a nurse's nuisance?
    Or why I do propose to lose my strength,
    To blanch my hair, to let the gums recede
    Far up my yellowing teeth, and finally
    Lie down and moulder in a rotten grave?
    Only one thing more foolish could have been,
    And that was to be born, not man, but woman.
    This was thy folly, why rebuk'st thou mine?
LYDIA. These are not things of choice.
CASHEL.   And did I choose
    My quick divining eye, my lightning hand,
    My springing muscle and untiring heart?
    Did I implant the instinct in the race
    That found a use for these, and said to me,
    Fight for us, and be fame and fortune thine?
LYDIA. But there are other callings in the world.
CASHEL. Go tell thy painters to turn stockbrokers,
    Thy poet friends to stoop oer merchants' desks
    And pen prose records of the gains of greed.
    Tell bishops that religion is outworn,
    And that the Pampa to the horsebreaker
    Opes new careers. Bid the professor quit
    His fraudulent pedantries, and do i' the world
    The thing he would teach others. Then return
    To me and say: Cashel: they have obeyed;
    And on that pyre of sacrifice I, too,
    Will throw my championship.
LYDIA.   But tis so cruel.
CASHEL. Is it so? I have hardly noticed that,
    So cruel are all callings. Yet this hand,
    That many a two days bruise hath ruthless given,
    Hath kept no dungeon locked for twenty years,
    Hath slain no sentient creature for my sport.
    I am too squeamish for your dainty world,
    That cowers behind the gallows and the lash,

The world that robs the poor, and with their spoil
Does what its tradesmen tell it. Oh, your ladies!
Sealskinned and egret-feathered; all defiance
To Nature; cowering if one say to them
'What will the servants think?' Your gentlemen!
Your tailor-tyrannized visitors of whom
Flutter of wing and singing in the wood
Make chickenbutchers. And your medicine men!
Groping for cures in the tormented entrails
Of friendly dogs. Pray have you asked all these
To change their occupations? Find you mine
So grimly crueller? I cannot breathe
An air so petty and so poisonous.

LYDIA. But find you not their manners very nice?

CASHEL. To me, perfection. Oh, they condescend
With a rare grace. Your duke, who condescends
Almost to the whole world, might for a Man
Pass in the eyes of those who never saw
The duke capped with a prince. See then, ye gods,
The duke turn footman, and his eager dame
Sink the great lady in the obsequious housemaid!
Oh, at such moments I could wish the Court
Had but one breadbasket, that with my fist
I could make all its windy vanity
Gasp itself out on the gravel. Fare you well.
I did not choose my calling; but at least
I can refrain from being a gentleman.

LYDIA. You say farewell to me without a pang.

CASHEL. My calling hath apprenticed me to pangs.
This is a rib-bender; but I can bear it.
It is a lonely thing to be a champion.

LYDIA. It is a lonelier thing to be a woman.

CASHEL. Be lonely then. Shall it be said of thee
That for his brawn thou misalliance mad'st
Wi' the Prince of Ruffians? Never. Go thy ways;
Or, if thou hast nostalgia of the mud,
Wed some bedoggéd wretch that on the slot
Of gilded snobbery, *ventre à terre*,
Will hunt through life with eager nose on earth
And hang thee thick with diamonds. I am rich;
But all my gold was fought for with my hands.

LYDIA. What dost thou mean by rich?

CASHEL.   There is a man,
Hight Paradise, vaunted unconquerable,
Hath dared to say he will be glad to hear from me.
I have replied that none can hear from me
Until a thousand solid pounds be staked.
His friends have confidently found the money.
Ere fall of leaf that money shall be mine;
And then I shall possess ten thousand pounds.
I had hoped to tempt thee with that monstrous sum.

LYDIA. Thou silly Cashel, tis but a week's income.
I did propose to give thee three times that
For pocket money when we two were wed.

CASHEL. Give me my hat. I have been fooling here.
Now, by the Hebrew lawgiver, I thought
That only in America such revenues
Were decent deemed. Enough. My dream is dreamed.
Your gold weighs like a mountain on my chest.
Farewell.

LYDIA. The golden mountain shall be thine
The day thou quitst thy horrible profession.

CASHEL. Tempt me not, woman. It is honor calls.
Slave to the Ring I rest until the face
Of Paradise be changed.

                        Enter BASHVILLE

BASHVILLE.   Madam, your carriage,
Ordered by you at two. Tis now half-past.

CASHEL. Sdeath! is it half-past two? The king! the king!

LYDIA. The king! What mean you?

CASHEL   I must meet a monarch

This very afternoon at Islington.

LYDIA. At Islington! You must be mad.

CASHEL.   A cab!
Go call a cab; and let a cab be called;
And let the man that calls it be thy footman.

LYDIA. You are not well. You shall not go alone.
My carriage waits. I must accompany you.
I go to find my hat.   [*Exit.*

CASHEL.   Like Paracelsus,
Who went to find his soul [*To Bashville*] And now, young man,

How comes it that a fellow of your inches,
So deft a wrestler and so bold a spirit,
Can stoop to be a flunkey? Call on me
On your next evening out. I'll make a man of you.
Surely you are ambitious and aspire —

BASHVILLE. To be a butler and draw corks; wherefore,
By Heaven, I will draw yours.

                              [*He hits Cashel on the nose, and runs out.*

CASHEL [*thoughtfully putting the side of his forefinger to his nose, and
     studying the blood on it*] Too quick for me!
There's money in this youth.

Re-enter LYDIA, *hatted and gloved*

LYDIA.   O Heaven! you bleed.

CASHEL. Lend me a key or other frigid object,
That I may put it down my back, and staunch
The welling life stream.

LYDIA [*giving him her keys*] Oh, what have you done?

CASHEL. Flush on the boko napped your footman's left.

LYDIA. I do not understand.

CASHEL.   True. Pardon me.
I have received a blow upon the nose
In sport from Bashville. Next, ablution; else
I shall be total gules.   [*He hurries out.*

LYDIA.   How well he speaks!
There is a silver trumpet in his lips
That stirs me to the finger ends. His nose
Dropt lovely color: tis a perfect blood.
I would twere mingled with mine own!

Enter BASHVILLE

                                        What now?

BASHVILLE. Madam, the coachman can no longer wait:
The horses will take cold.

LYDIA.   I do beseech him
A moment's grace. Oh, mockery of wealth!
The third class passenger unchidden rides
Whither and when he will: obsequious trams
Await him hourly: subterranean tubes
With tireless coursers whisk him through the town;
But we, the rich, are slaves to Houyhnhnms:

We wait upon their colds, and frowst all day
Indoors, if they but cough or spurn their hay.
BASHVILLE. Madam, an omnibus to Euston Road,
And thence t' th' Angel —

Enter CASHEL

LYDIA.   Let us haste, my love:
The coachman is impatient.
CASHEL.   Did he guess
He stays for Cashel Byron, he'd outwait
Pompei's sentinel. Let us away.
This day of deeds, as yet but half begun,
Must ended be in merrie Islington.
                        [*Exeunt* LYDIA *and* CASHEL.
BASHVILLE. Gods! how she hangs on's arm! I am alone.
Now let me lift the cover from my soul.
O wasted humbleness! Deluded diffidence!
How often have I said, Lie down, poor footman:
She'll never stoop to thee, rear as thou wilt
Thy powder to the sky. And now, by Heaven,
She stoops below me; condescends upon
This hero of the pothouse, whose exploits,
Writ in my character from my last place,
Would damn me into ostlerdom. And yet
Theres an eternal justice in it; for
By so much as the ne'er subduéd Indian
Excels the servile negro, doth this ruffian
Precedence take of me. '*Ich dien.*' Damnation!
I serve. My motto should have been, 'I scalp.'
And yet I do not bear the yoke for gold.
Because I love her I have blacked her boots;
Because I love her I have cleaned her knives,
Doing in this the office of a boy,
Whilst, like the celebrated maid that milks
And does the meanest chares, Ive shared the passions
Of Cleopatra. It has been my pride
To give her place the greater altitude
By lowering mine, and of her dignity
To be so jealous that my cheek has flamed
Even at the thought of such a deep disgrace
As love for such a one as I would be

For such a one as she; and now! and now!
A prizefighter! O irony! O bathos!
To have made way for this! Oh, Bashville, Bashville:
Why hast thou thought so lowly of thyself,
So heavenly high of her? Let what will come,
My love must speak: twas my respect was dumb.

SCENE II

The Agricultural Hall in Islington, crowded with spectators. In the arena a throne, with a boxing ring before it. A balcony above on the right, occupied by persons of fashion: among others, Lydia and Lord Worthington.

Flourish. Enter LUCIAN *and* CETEWAYO, *with Chiefs in attendance.*

CETEWAYO. Is this the Hall of Husbandmen?

LUCIAN.   It is.

CETEWAYO. Are these anæmic dogs the English people?

LUCIAN. Mislike us not for our complexions,
 The pallied liveries of the pall of smoke
 Belched by the mighty chimneys of our factories,
 And by the million patent kitchen ranges
 Of happy English homes.

CETEWAYO.   When first I came
 I deemed those chimneys the fuliginous altars
 Of some infernal god. I now perceive
 The English dare not look upon the sky.
 They are moles and owls: they call upon the soot
 To cover them.

LUCIAN.   You cannot understand
 The greatness of this people, Cetewayo.
 You are a savage, reasoning like a child.
 Each pallid English face conceals a brain
 Whose powers are proven in the works of Newton
 And in the plays of the immortal Shakespear.
 There is not one of all the thousands here
 But, if you placed him naked in the desert,
 Would presently construct a steam engine,
 And lay a cable t' th' Antipodes.

CETEWAYO. Have I been brought a million miles by sea
 To learn how men can lie! Know, Father Webber,
 Men become civilized through twin diseases,
 Terror and Greed to wit: these two conjoined
 Become the grisly parents of Invention.

Why does the trembling white with frantic toil
Of hand and brain produce the magic gun
That slays a mile off, whilst the manly Zulu
Dares look his foe i' the face; fights foot to foot;
Lives in the present; drains the Here and Now;
Makes life a long reality, and death
A moment only; whilst your Englishman
Glares on his burning candle's winding-sheets,
Counting the steps of his approaching doom,
And in the murky corners ever sees
Two horrid shadows, Death and Poverty:
In the which anguish an unnatural edge
Comes on his frighted brain, which straight devises
Strange frauds by which to filch unearnéd gold,
Mad crafts by which to slay unfacéd foes,
Until at last his agonized desire
Makes possibility its slave. And then —
Horrible climax! All-undoing spite! —
Th' importunate clutching of the coward's hand
From wearied Nature Devastation's secrets
Doth wrest; when straight the brave black-livered man
Is blown explosively from off the globe;
And Death and Dread, with their white-livered slaves,
Oer-run the earth, and through their chattering teeth
Stammer the words 'Survival of the Fittest.'
Enough of this: I come not here to talk.
Thou sayest thou hast two white-faced ones who dare
Fight without guns, and spearless, to the death.
Let them be brought.
LUCIAN.   They fight not to the death,
But under strictest rules: as, for example,
Half of their persons shall not be attacked;
Nor shall they suffer blows when they fall down,
Nor stroke of foot at any time. And, further,
That frequent opportunities of rest
With succor and refreshment be secured them.
CETEWAYO. Ye gods, what cowards! Zululand, my Zululand:
Personified Pusillanimity
Hath taen thee from the bravest of the brave!
LUCIAN. Lo the rude savage whose untutored mind
Cannot perceive self-evidence, and doubts

That Brave and English mean the self-same thing!
CETEWAYO. Well, well, produce these heroes. I surmise
They will be carried by their nurses, lest
Some barking dog or bumbling bee should scare them.

CETEWAYO *takes his state. Enter* PARADISE

LYDIA. What hateful wretch is this whose mighty thews
Presage destruction to his adversaries.
LORD WORTHINGTON. Tis Paradise.
LYDIA.   He of whom Cashel spoke?
A dreadful thought ices my heart. Oh, why
Did Cashel leave us at the door?

Enter CASHEL

LORD WORTHINGTON.   Behold!
The champion comes.
LYDIA.   Oh, I could kiss him now
Here, before all the world. His boxing things
Render him most attractive. But I fear
Yon villain's fists may maul him.
WORTHINGTON.   Have no fear.
Hark! the king speaks.
CETEWAYO.   Ye sons of the white queen:
Tell me your names and deeds ere ye fall to.
PARADISE. Your royal highness, you beholds a bloke
What gets his living honest by his fists.
I may not have the polish of some toffs
As I could mention on; but up to now
No man has took my number down. I scale
Close on twelve stun; my age is twenty-three;
And at Bill Richardson's Blue Anchor pub
Am to be heard of any day by such
As likes the job. I dont know, governor,
As ennythink remains for me to say.
CETEWAYO. Six wives and thirty oxen shalt thou have
If on the sand thou leave thy foeman dead.
Methinks he looks full scornfully on thee.
[*To Cashel*] Ha! dost thou not so?
CASHEL.   Sir, I do beseech you
To name the bone, or limb, or special place
Where you would have me hit him with this fist.

CETEWAYO. Thou hast a noble brow; but much I fear
    Thine adversary will disfigure it.
CASHEL. Theres a divinity that shapes our ends
    Rough hew them how we will. Give me the gloves.
THE MASTER OF THE REVELS. Paradise, a professor.
    Cashel Byron,   [*They spar.*
    Also professor. Time!
LYDIA.   Eternity
    It seems to me until this fight be done.
CASHEL. Dread monarch: this is called the upper cut,
    And this is a hook-hit of mine own invention.
    The hollow region where I plant this blow
    Is called the mark. My left, you will observe,
    I chiefly use for long shots: with my right
    Aiming beside the angle of the jaw
    And landing with a certain delicate screw
    I without violence knock my foeman out.
    Mark how he falls forward upon his face!
    The rules allow ten seconds to get up;
    And as the man is still quite silly, I
    Might safely finish him; but my respect
    For your most gracious majesty's desire
    To see some further triumphs of the science
    Of self-defence postpones awhile his doom.
PARADISE. How can a bloke do hisself proper justice
    With pillows on his fists?
    [*He tears off his gloves and attacks Cashel with his bare knuckles.*
THE CROWD.   Unfair! The rules!
CETEWAYO. The joy of battle surges boiling up
    And bids me join the mellay. Isandhlana
    And Victory!   [*He falls on the bystanders.*
THE CHIEFS. Victory and Isandhlana!
    [*They run amok. General panic and stampede. The ring is swept away.*
LUCIAN. Forbear these most irregular proceedings.
    Police! Police!
    [*He engages Cetewayo with his umbrella. The balcony comes down with a crash. Screams from its occupants. Indescribable confusion.*
CASHEL [*dragging Lydia from the struggling heap*] My love, my love,
    art hurt?
LYDIA. No, no; but save my sore oermatchéd cousin.
A POLICEMAN. Give us a lead, sir. Save the English flag.

Africa tramples on it.

CASHEL.   Africa!
Not all the continents whose mighty shoulders
The dancing diamonds of the seas bedeck
Shall trample on the blue with spots of white.
Now, Lydia, mark thy lover.   [*He charges the Zulus.*

LYDIA.   Hercules
Cannot withstand him. See: the king is down;
The tallest chief is up, heels over head,
Tossed corklike oer my Cashel's sinewy back;
And his lieutenant all deflated gasps
For breath upon the sand. The others fly.
In vain: his fist oer magic distances
Like a chameleon's tongue shoots to its mark;
And the last African upon his knees
Sues piteously for quarter. [*Rushing into Cashel's arms*] Oh, my
   hero:
Thoust saved us all this day.

CASHEL.   Twas all for thee.

CETEWAYO [*trying to rise*] Have I been struck by lightning?

LUCIAN.   Sir, your conduct
Can only be described as most ungentlemanly.

POLICEMAN. One of the prone is white.

CASHEL.   Tis Paradise.

POLICEMAN. He's choking: he has something in his mouth.

LYDIA [*to Cashel*] Oh Heaven! there is blood upon your hip.
Youre hurt.

CASHEL. The morsel in yon wretch's mouth
Was bitten out of me.
   [*Sensation. Lydia screams and swoons in Cashel's arms.*

❧ ACT III ❧

Wiltstoken. A room in the Warren Lodge. Lydia at her writing-table.

LYDIA. O Past and Present, how ye do conflict
　　As here I sit writing my father's life!
　　The autumn woodland woos me from without
　　With whispering of leaves and dainty airs
　　To leave this fruitless haunting of the past.
　　My father was a very learnéd man.
　　I sometimes think I shall oldmaided be
　　Ere I unlearn the things he taught to me.

Enter POLICEMAN

POLICEMAN. Asking your ladyship to pardon me
　　For this intrusion, might I be so bold
　　As ask a question of your people here
　　Concerning the Queen's peace?
LYDIA. 　　　　　　　　　My people here
　　Are but a footman and a simple maid;
　　And both have craved a holiday to join
　　Some local festival. But, sir, your helmet
　　Proclaims the Metropolitan Police.
POLICEMAN. Madam, it does; and I may now inform you
　　That what you term a local festival
　　Is a most hideous outrage gainst the law,
　　Which we to quell from London have come down:
　　In short, a prizefight. My sole purpose here
　　Is to inquire whether your ladyship
　　Any bad characters this afternoon
　　Has noted in the neighborhood.
LYDIA. 　　　　　　　　　No, none, sir.
　　I had not let my maid go forth today
　　Thought I the roads unsafe.
POLICEMAN. 　　　　　　Fear nothing, madam:
　　The force protects the fair. My mission here

Is to wreak ultion for the broken law.
I wish your ladyship good afternoon.
LYDIA. Good afternoon.   (*Exit* POLICEMAN.
                         A prizefight! O my heart!
Cashel: hast thou deceived me? Can it be
Thou hast backslidden to the hateful calling
I asked thee to eschew?
                         O wretched maid,
Why didst thou flee from London to this place
To write thy father's life, whenas in town
Thou mightst have kept a guardian eye on him —
Whats that? A flying footstep —

Enter CASHEL

CASHEL.   Sanctuary!
The law is on my track. What! Lydia here!
LYDIA. Ay: Lydia here. Hast thou done murder, then,
That in so horrible a guise thou comest?
CASHEL. Murder! I would I had. Yon cannibal
Hath forty thousand lives; and I have taen
But thousands thirty-nine. I tell thee, Lydia,
On the impenetrable sarcolobe
That holds his seedling brain these fists have pounded
By Shrewsb'ry clock an hour. This bruiséd grass
And cakéd mud adhering to my form
I have acquired in rolling on the sod
Clinched in his grip. This scanty reefer coat
For decency snatched up as fast I fled
When the police arrived, belongs to Mellish.
Tis all too short; hence my display of rib
And forearm mother-naked. Be not wroth
Because I seem to wink at you: by Heaven,
Twas Paradise that plugged me in the eye
Which I perforce keep closing. Pity me,
My training wasted and my blows unpaid.
Sans stakes, sans victory, sans everything
I had hoped to win. Oh, I could sit me down
And weep for bitterness.
LYDIA.   Thou wretch, begone.
CASHEL. Begone!
LYDIA.   I say begone. Oh, tiger's heart

Wrapped in a young man's hide, canst thou not live
In love with Nature and at peace with Man?
Must thou, although thy hands were never made
To blacken other's eyes, still batter at
The image of Divinity? I loathe thee.
Hence from my house and never see me more.

CASHEL. I go. The meanest lad on thy estate
Would not betray me thus. But tis no matter.

                                        [*He opens the door.*
Ha! the police. I'm lost.   [*He shuts the door again.*
                    Now shalt thou see
My last fight fought. Exhausted as I am,
To capture me will cost the coppers dear.
Come one, come all!

LYDIA.   Oh, hide thee, I implore:
I cannot see thee hunted down like this.
There is my room. Conceal thyself therein.
Quick, I command.   [*He goes into the room.*
                    With horror I foresee,
Lydia, that never lied, must lie for thee.

Enter POLICEMAN, *with* PARADISE *and* MELLISH
in custody, BASHVILLE, constables, *and others*

POLICEMAN. Keep back your bruiséd prisoner lest he shock
This wellbred lady's nerves. Your pardon, maam;
But have you seen by chance the other one?
In this direction he was seen to run.

LYDIA. A man came here anon with bloody hands
And aspect that did turn my soul to snow.

POLICEMAN. Twas he. What said he?

LYDIA.   Begged for sanctuary.
I bade the man begone.

POLICEMAN.   Most properly.
Saw you which way he went?

LYDIA.   I cannot tell.

PARADISE. He seen me coming; and he done a bunk.

POLICEMAN. Peace, there. Excuse his damaged features, lady:
He's Paradise; and this one's Byron's trainer,
Mellish.

MELLISH. Injurious copper, in thy teeth
I hurl the lie. I am no trainer, I.

My father, a respected missionary,
Apprenticed me at fourteen years of age
T' the poetry writing. To these woods I came
With Nature to commune. My revery
Was by a sound of blows rudely dispelled.
Mindful of what my sainted parent taught
I rushed to play the peacemaker, when lo!
These minions of the law laid hands on me.

BASHVILLE. A lovely woman, with distracted cries,
In most resplendent fashionable frock,
Approaches like a wounded antelope.

Enter ADELAIDE GISBORNE

ADELAIDE. Where is my Cashel? Hath he been arrested?
POLICEMAN. I would I had thy Cashel by the collar:
He hath escaped me.
ADELAIDE.   Praises be for ever!
LYDIA. Why dost thou call the missing man thy Cashel?
ADELAIDE. He is mine only son.
ALL.   Thy son?
ADELAIDE.   My son.
LYDIA. I thought his mother hardly would have known him,
So crushed his countenance.
ADELAIDE.   A ribald peer,
Lord Worthington by name, this morning came
With honeyed words beseeching me to mount
His four-in-hand, and to the country hie
To see some English sport. Being by nature
Frank as a child, I fell into the snare,
But took so long to dress that the design
Failed of its full effect; for not until
The final round we reached the horrid scene.
Be silent all; for now I do approach
My tragedy's catastrophe. Know, then,
That Heaven did bless me with an only son,
A boy devoted to his doting mother –
POLICEMAN. Hark! did you hear an oath from yonder room?
ADELAIDE. Respect a broken-hearted mother's grief,
And do not interrupt me in my scene.
Ten years ago my darling disappeared
(Ten dreary twelvemonths of continuous tears,

Tears that have left me prematurely aged;
For I am younger far than I appear).
Judge of my anguish when today I saw
Stripped to the waist, and fighting like a demon
With one who, whatsoe'er his humble virtues,
Was clearly not a gentleman, my son!

ALL. O strange event! O passing tearful tale!

ADELAIDE. I thank you from the bottom of my heart
For the reception you have given my woe;
And now I ask, where is my wretched son?
He must at once come home with me, and quit
A course of life that cannot be allowed.

Enter CASHEL

CASHEL. Policeman: I do yield me to the law.

LYDIA. Oh no.

ADELAIDE.   My son!

CASHEL.   My mother! Do not kiss me.
My visage is too sore.

POLICEMAN.   The lady hid him.
This is a regular plant. You cannot be
Up to that sex. [*To Cashel*] You come along with me.

LYDIA. Fear not, my Cashel: I will bail thee out.

CASHEL. Never. I do embrace my doom with joy.
With Paradise in Pentonville or Portland
I shall feel safe: there are no mothers there.

ADELAIDE. Ungracious boy —

CASHEL.   Constable: bear me hence.

MELLISH. Oh, let me sweetest reconcilement make
By calling to thy mind that moving song:—
                    [*Sings*] They say there is no other —

CASHEL. Forbear at once, or the next note of music
That falls upon thine ear shall clang in thunder
From the last trumpet.

ADELAIDE.   A disgraceful threat
To level at this virtuous old man.

LYDIA. Oh, Cashel, if thou scornst thy mother thus,
How wilt thou treat thy wife?

CASHEL.   There spake my fate:
I knew you would say that. Oh, mothers, mothers,
Would you but let your wretched sons alone

Life were worth living! Had I any choice
In this importunate relationship?
None. And until that high auspicious day
When the millennium on an orphaned world
Shall dawn, and man upon his fellow look,
Reckless of consanguinity, my mother
And I within the self-same hemisphere
Conjointly may not dwell.
ADELAIDE.   Ungentlemanly!
CASHEL. I am no gentleman. I am a criminal,
Redhanded, baseborn —
ADELAIDE.   Baseborn! Who dares say it?
Thou art the son and heir of Bingley Bumpkin
FitzAlgernon de Courcy Cashel Byron,
Sieur of Park Lane and Overlord of Dorset,
Who after three months wedded happiness
Rashly fordid himself with prussic acid,
Leaving a tearstained note to testify
That having sweetly honeymooned with me,
He now could say, O Death, where is thy sting?
POLICEMAN. Sir: had I known your quality, this cop
I had averted; but it is too late.
The law's above us both.

Enter LUCIAN, *with an Order in Council*

LUCIAN.   Not so, policeman.
I bear a message from The Throne itself
Of fullest amnesty for Byron's past.
Nay, more: of Dorset deputy lieutenant
He is proclaimed. Further, it is decreed,
In memory of his glorious victory
Over our country's foes at Islington,
The flag of England shall for ever bear
On azure field twelve swanlike spots of white;
And by an exercise of feudal right
Too long disused in this anarchic age
Our sovereign doth confer on him the hand
Of Miss Carew, Wiltstoken's wealthy heiress.
                                        [*General acclamation.*
POLICEMAN.Was anything, sir, said about me?

LUCIAN. Thy faithful services are not forgot:
In future call thyself Inspector Smith

[*Renewed acclamation.*

POLICEMAN. I thank you, sir. I thank you, gentlemen.
LUCIAN. My former opposition, valiant champion,
Was based on the supposed discrepancy
Betwixt your rank and Lydia's. Heres my hand.
BASHVILLE. And I do here unselfishly renounce
All my pretensions to my lady's favor.   [*Sensation.*
LYDIA. What, Bashville! didst thou love me?
BASHVILLE.   Madam: yes.
Tis said: now let me leave immediately.
LYDIA. In taking, Bashville, this most tasteful course
You are but acting as a gentleman
In the like case would act. I fully grant
Your perfect right to make a declaration
Which flatters me and honors your ambition.
Prior attachment bids me firmly say
That whilst my Cashel lives, and polyandry
Rests foreign to the British social scheme,
Your love is hopeless; still, your services,
Made zealous by disinterested passion,
Would greatly add to my domestic comfort;
And if—
CASHEL. Excuse me. I have other views.
Ive noted in this man such aptitude
For art and exercise in his defence
That I prognosticate for him a future
More glorious than my past. Henceforth I dub him
The Admirable Bashville, Byron's Novice;
And to the utmost of my mended fortunes
Will back him gainst the world at ten stone six.
ALL. Hail, Byron's Novice, champion that shall be!
BASHVILLE. Must I renounce my lovely lady's service,
And mar the face of man?
CASHEL.   Tis Fate's decree.
For know, rash youth, that in this star crost world
Fate drives us all to find our chiefest good
In what we can, and not in what we would.
POLICEMAN. A post-horn—hark!
CASHEL.   What noise of wheels is this?

*Lord Worthington drives upon the scene
in his four-in-hand, and descends*

ADELAIDE. Perfidious peer!
LORD WORTHINGTON.   Sweet Adelaide —
ADELAIDE.   Forbear,
  Audacious one: my name is Mrs Byron.
LORD WORTHINGTON. Oh, change that title for the sweeter one
  Of Lady Worthington.
CASHEL.   Unhappy man,
  You know not what you do.
LYDIA.   Nay, tis a match
  Of must auspicious promise. Dear Lord Worthington,
  You tear from us our mother-in-law —
CASHEL.   Ha! True.
LYDIA. — but we will make the sacrifice. She blushes:
  At least she very prettily produces
  Blushing's effect.
ADELAIDE.   My lord: I do accept you.
                              [*They embrace. Rejoicings.*
CASHEL [*aside*] It wrings my heart to see my noble backer
  Lay waste his future thus. The world's a chessboard,
  And we the merest pawns in fist of Fate.
  [*Aloud*] And now, my friends, gentle and simple both,
  Our scene draws to a close. In lawful course
  As Dorset's deputy lieutenant I
  Do pardon all concerned this afternoon
  In the late gross and brutal exhibition
  Of miscalled sport.
LYDIA [*throwing herself into his arms*] Your boats are burnt at last.
CASHEL. This is the face that burnt a thousand boats,
  And ravished Cashel Byron from the ring.
  But to conclude. Let William Paradise
  Devote himself to science, and acquire,
  By studying the player's speech in Hamlet,
  A more refined address. You, Robert Mellish,
  To the Blue Anchor hostelry attend him;
  Assuage his hurts, and bid Bill Richardson
  Limit his access to the fatal tap.
  Now mount we on my backer's four-in-hand,
  And to St George's Church, whose portico

Hanover Square shuts off from Conduit Street,
Repair we all. Strike up the wedding march;
And, Mellish, let thy melodies trill forth
Broad oer the wold as fast we bowl along.
Give me the post-horn. Loose the flowing rein;
And up to London drive with might and main.

[*Exeunt.*

How He Lied
to Her Husband

Composition begun 13 August 1904; completed 16 August 1904. First published in German translation as *Wie er ihren Mann belog*, in the *Berliner Tageblatt*, 28 November 1904. Published in *John Bull's Other Island, How He Lied to Her Husband, Major Barbara*, 1907. Revised text in Collected Edition, 1930. Copyright reading at the Victoria Hall (Bijou Theatre), London, on 27 August 1904. First presented at the Berkeley Lyceum Theatre, New York, on 26 September 1904.

Her Lover [Henry Apjohn]   *Arnold Daly*
Her Husband [Teddy Bompas]   *Dodson Mitchell*
Herself [Aurora Bompas]   *Selene Johnson*

Period – The Present
Scene: *Her Flat in the Cromwell Road*

Like many other works of mine, this playlet is a *pièce d'occasion*. In 1904 it happened that the late Arnold Daly, who was then playing the part of Napoleon in The Man of Destiny in New York, found that whilst the play was too long to take a secondary place in the evening's performance, it was too short to suffice by itself. I therefore took advantage of four days continuous rain during a holiday in the north of Scotland to write How He Lied To Her Husband for Daly. In his hands, it served its turn very effectively.

Trifling as it is, I print it as a sample of what can be done with even the most hackneyed stage framework by filling it in with an observed touch of actual humanity instead of with doctrinaire romanticism. Nothing in the theatre is staler than the situation of husband, wife, and lover, or the fun of knockabout farce. I have taken both, and got an original play out of them, as anybody else can if only he will look about him for his material instead of plagiarizing Othello and the thousand plays that have proceeded on Othello's romantic assumptions and false point of honor.

It is eight o'clock in the evening. The curtains are drawn and the lamps lighted in the drawing room of Her flat in Cromwell Road. Her lover, a beautiful youth of eighteen, in evening dress and cape, with a bunch of flowers and an opera hat in his hands, comes in alone. The door is near the corner; and as he appears in the doorway, he has the fireplace on the nearest wall to his right, and the grand piano along the opposite wall to his left. Near the fireplace a small ornamental table has on it a hand mirror, a fan, a pair of long white gloves, and a little white woollen cloud to wrap a woman's head in. On the other side of the room, near the piano, is a broad, square, softly upholstered stool. The room is furnished in the most approved South Kensington fashion: that is, it is as like a shop window as possible, and is intended to demonstrate the social position and spending powers of its owners, and not in the least to make them comfortable.

He is, be it repeated, a very beautiful youth, moving as in a dream, walking as on air. He puts his flowers down carefully on the table beside the fan; takes off his cape, and, as there is no room on the table for it, takes it to the piano; puts his hat on the cape; crosses to the hearth; looks at his watch; puts it up again; notices the things on the table; lights up as if he saw heaven opening before him; goes to the table and takes the cloud in both hands, nestling his nose into its softness and kissing it; kisses the gloves one after another; kisses the fan; gasps a long shuddering sigh of ecstasy; sits down on the stool and presses his hands to his eyes to shut out reality and dream a little; takes his hands down and shakes his head with a little smile of rebuke for his folly; catches sight of a speck of dust on his shoes and hastily and carefully brushes it off with his handkerchief; rises and takes the hand mirror from the table to make sure of his tie with the gravest anxiety; and is looking at his watch again when She comes in, much flustered. As she is dressed for the theatre; has spoilt, petted ways; and wears many diamonds, she has an air of being a young and beautiful woman; but as a matter of hard fact, she is, dress and pretensions apart, a very ordinary South Kensington female of about 37, hopelessly inferior in physical and spiritual distinction to the beautiful youth, who hastily puts down the mirror as she enters.

HE [*kissing her hand*] At last!

SHE. Henry: something dreadful has happened.

HE. Whats the matter?

SHE. I have lost your poems.

HE. They were unworthy of you. I will write you some more.

SHE. No, thank you. Never any more poems for me. Oh, how could I have been so mad! so rash! so imprudent!

HE. Thank Heaven for your madness, your rashness, your imprudence!

SHE [*impatiently*] Oh, be sensible, Henry. Cant you see what a terrible thing this is for me? Suppose anybody finds these poems! what will they think?

HE. They will think that a man once loved a woman more devotedly than ever man loved woman before. But they will not know what man it was.

SHE. What good is that to me if everybody will know what woman it was?

HE. But how will they know?

SHE. How will they know! Why, my name is all over them: my silly, unhappy name. Oh, if I had only been christened Mary Jane, or Gladys Muriel, or Beatrice, or Francesca, or Guinevere, or something quite common! But Aurora! Aurora! I'm the only Aurora in London; and everybody knows it. I believe I'm the only Aurora in the world. And it's so horribly easy to rhyme to it! Oh, Henry, why didnt you try to restrain your feelings a little in common consideration for me? Why didnt you write with some little reserve?

HE. Write poems to you with reserve! You ask me that!

SHE [*with perfunctory tenderness*] Yes, dear, of course it was very nice of you; and I know it was my own fault as much as yours. I ought to have noticed that your verses ought never to have been addressed to a married woman.

HE. Ah, how I wish they had been addressed to an unmarried woman! how I wish they had!

SHE. Indeed you have no right to wish anything of the sort. They are quite unfit for anybody but a married woman. Thats just the difficulty. What will my sisters-in-law think of them?

HE [*painfully jarred*] Have you got sisters-in-law?

SHE. Yes, of course I have. Do you suppose I am an angel?

HE [*biting his lips*] I do. Heaven help me, I do – or I did – or [*he almost chokes a sob*].

SHE [*softening and putting her hand caressingly on his shoulder*] Listen to me, dear. It's very nice of you to live with me in a dream, and to love me, and so on; but I cant help my husband having disagreeable relatives, can I?

HE [*brightening up*]Ah, of course they are your husband's relatives: I forgot that. Forgive me, Aurora. [*He takes her hand from his shoulder and kisses it. She sits down on the stool. He remains near the table, with his back to it, smiling fatuously down at her*].

SHE. The fact is, Teddy's got nothing but relatives. He has eight sisters and six half-sisters, and ever so many brothers – but I dont mind his brothers. Now if you only knew the least little thing about the world, Henry, youd know that in a large family, though the sisters quarrel with one another like mad all the time, yet let one of the brothers marry, and they all turn on their unfortunate sister-in-law and devote the rest of their lives with perfect unanimity to persuading him that his wife is unworthy of him. They can do it to her very face without her knowing it, because they always have a lot of stupid low family jokes that nobody understands but themselves. Half the time you cant tell what theyre talking about; it just drives you wild. There ought to be a law against a man's sister ever entering his house after he's married. I'm as certain as that I'm sitting here that Georgina stole those poems out of my workbox.

HE. She will not understand them, I think.

SHE. Oh, wont she! She'll understand them only too well. She'll understand more harm than ever was in them: nasty vulgar-minded cat!

HE [*going to her*] Oh dont, dont think of people in that way. Dont think of her at all. [*He takes her hand and sits down on the carpet at her feet*]. Aurora: do you remember the evening when I sat here at your feet and read you those poems for the first time?

SHE. I shouldnt have let you: I see that now. When I think of Georgina sitting there at Teddy's feet and reading them to him for the first time, I feel I shall just go distracted.

HE. Yes you are right. It will be a profanation.

SHE. Oh, I dont care about the profanation; but what will Teddy think? what will he do? [*Suddenly throwing his head away from her knee*] You dont seem to think a bit about Teddy. [*She jumps up, more and more agitated*].

HE [*supine on the floor; for she has thrown him off his balance*] To me Teddy is nothing, and Georgina less than nothing.

SHE. Youll soon find out how much less than nothing she is. If you think a woman cant do any harm because she's only a scandal-mongering dowdy ragbag, youre greatly mistaken. [*She flounces about the room. He gets up slowly and dusts his hands. Suddenly she runs to him and throws herself into his arms*]. Henry: help me. Find a way out of this for me; and I'll bless you as long as you live. Oh, how wretched I am! [*She sobs on his breast*].

HE. And oh! how happy I am!

SHE [*whisking herself abruptly away*] Dont be selfish.

HE [*humbly*] Yes: I deserve that. I think if I were going to the stake with you, I should still be so happy with you that I should forget your danger as utterly as my own.

SHE [*relenting and patting his hand fondly*] Oh, you are a dear darling boy, Henry; but [*throwing his hand away fretfully*] youre no use. I want somebody to tell me what to do.

HE [*with quiet conviction*] Your heart will tell you at the right time. I have thought deeply over this; and I know what we two must do, sooner or later.

SHE. No, Henry. I will do nothing improper, nothing dishonorable. [*She sits down plump on the stool and looks inflexible*].

HE. If you did, you would no longer be Aurora. Our course is perfectly simple, perfectly straightforward, perfectly stainless and true. We love one another. I am not ashamed of that: I am ready to go out and proclaim it to all London as simply as I will declare it to your husband when you see – as you soon will see – that this is the only way honorable enough for your feet to tread. Let us go out together to our own house, this evening, without concealment and without shame. Remember! we owe something to your husband. We are his guests here: he is an honorable man: he has been kind to us: he has perhaps loved you as well as his prosaic nature and his sordid commercial environment permit-ted. We owe it to him in all honor not to let him learn the truth from the lips of a scandalmonger. Let us go to him now quietly, hand in hand; bid him farewell; and walk out of the house without concealment or subterfuge, freely and honestly, in full honor and self-respect.

SHE [*staring at him*] And where shall we go to?

HE. We shall not depart by a hair's breadth from the ordinary natural current of our lives. We were going to the theatre when the loss of the poems compelled us to take action at once. We shall go to the theatre still; but we shall leave your diamonds here; for we cannot afford diamonds, and do not need them.

SHE [*fretfully*] I have told you already that I hate diamonds; only Teddy insists on hanging me all over with them. You need not preach simplicity to me.

HE. I never thought of doing so, dearest: I know that these trivialities are nothing to you. What was I saying? – oh yes. Instead of coming back here from the theatre, you will come with me to my home – now and henceforth our home – and in due course of time, when you are divorced, we shall go through whatever idle legal ceremony you may desire. *I* attach no importance to the law: my love was not created in me by the law, nor can it be bound or loosed by it. That is simple enough, and sweet enough, is it not? [*He takes the flowers from the table*]. Here are flowers for you: I have the tickets: we will ask your husband to lend us the carriage to shew that there is no malice, no grudge, between us. Come!

SHE. Do you mean to say that you propose that we should walk right bang up to Teddy and tell him we're going away together?

HE. Yes. What can be simpler?

SHE. And do you think for a moment he'd stand it? He'd just kill you.

HE [*coming to a sudden stop and speaking with considerable confidence*] You dont understand these things, my darling: how could you? I have followed the Greek ideal and not neglected the culture of my body. Like all poets I have a passion for pugilism. Your husband would make a tolerable second-rate heavy weight if he were in training and ten years younger. As it is, he could, if strung up to a great effort by a burst of passion, give a good account of himself for perhaps fifteen seconds. But I am active enough to keep out of his reach for fifteen seconds; and after that I should be simply all over him.

SHE [*rising and coming to him in consternation*] What do you mean by all over him?

HE [*gently*] Dont ask me, dearest. At all events, I swear to you that you need not be anxious about me.

SHE. And what about Teddy? Do you mean to tell me that you are going to beat Teddy before my face like a brutal prizefighter?

HE. All this alarm is needless, dearest. Believe me, nothing will happen. Your husband knows that I am capable of defending myself. Under such circumstances nothing ever does happen. And of course *I* shall do nothing. The man who once loved you is sacred to me.

SHE [*suspiciously*] Doesnt he love me still? Has he told you anything?

HE. No, no. [*He takes her tenderly in his arms*]. Dearest, dearest: how agitated you are! how unlike yourself! All these worries belong to the lower plane. Come up with me to the higher one. The heights, the solitudes, the soul world!

SHE [*avoiding his gaze*] No: stop: it's no use, Mr Apjohn.

HE [*recoiling*] Mr Apjohn!!!

SHE. Excuse me: I meant Henry, of course.

HE. How could you even think of me as Mr Apjohn? I never think of you as Mrs Bompas: it is always Aurora, Aurora, Auro —

SHE. Yes, yes: thats all very well, Mr Apjohn [*he is about to interrupt again: but she wont have it*]: no: it's no use: Ive suddenly begun to think of you as Mr Apjohn; and it's ridiculous to go on calling you Henry. I thought you were only a boy, a child, a dreamer. I thought you would be too much afraid to do anything. And now you want to beat Teddy and to break up my home and disgrace me and make a horrible scandal in the papers. It's cruel, unmanly, cowardly.

HE [*with grave wonder*] Are you afraid?

SHE. Oh, of course I'm afraid. So would you be if you had any common sense. [*She goes to the hearth, turning her back to him, and puts one tapping foot on the fender*].

HE [*watching her with great gravity*] Perfect love casteth out fear. That is why I am not afraid. Mrs Bompas: you do not love me.

SHE [*turning to him with a gasp of relief*] Oh, thank you, thank you! You really can be very nice, Henry.

HE. Why do you thank me?

SHE [*coming prettily to him from the fireplace*] For calling me Mrs Bompas again. I feel now that you are going to be reasonable and behave like a gentleman. [*He drops on the stool; covers his face with his hands; and groans*]. Whats the matter?

HE. Once or twice in my life I have dreamed that I was exquisitely happy and blessed. But oh! the misgiving at the first stir of consciousness! the stab of reality! the prison walls of the bedroom! the bitter, bitter disappointment of waking! And this time! oh, this time I thought I was awake.

SHE. Listen to me, Henry: we really havnt time for all that sort of flapdoodle now. [*He starts to his feet as if she had pulled a trigger and straightened him by the release of a powerful spring, and goes past her with set teeth to the little table*]. Oh, take care: you nearly hit me in the chin with the top of your head.

HE [*with fierce politeness*] I beg your pardon. What is it you want me to do? I am at your service. I am ready to behave like a gentleman if you will be kind enough to explain exactly how.

SHE [*a little frightened*] Thank you, Henry: I was sure you would. Youre not angry with me, are you?

HE. Go on. Go on quickly. Give me something to think about, or I will – I will – [*he suddenly snatches up her fan and is about to break it in his clenched fists*].

SHE [*running forward and catching at the fan, with loud lamentation*] Dont break my fan – no, dont. [*He slowly relaxes his grip of it as she draws it anxiously out of his hands*]. No, really, thats a stupid trick: I dont like that. Youve no right to do that. [*She opens the fan, and finds that the sticks are disconnected*]. Oh, how could you be so inconsiderate?

HE. I beg your pardon. I will buy you a new one.

SHE [*querulously*] You will never be able to match it. And it was a particular favorite of mine.

HE [*shortly*] Then you will have to do without it: thats all.

SHE. Thats not a very nice thing to say after breaking my pet fan, I think.

HE. If you knew how near I was to breaking Teddy's pet wife and presenting him with the pieces, you would be thankful that you are alive instead of – of – of howling about fiveshillingsworth of ivory. Damn your fan!

SHE. Oh! Dont you dare swear in my presence. One would think you were my husband.

HE [*again collapsing on the stool*] This is some horrible dream. What has become of you? You are not my Aurora.

SHE. Oh, well, if you come to that, what has become of you? Do you think I would ever have encouraged you if I had known you were such a little devil?

HE. Dont drag me down – dont – dont. Help me to find the way back to the heights.

SHE [*kneeling beside him and pleading*] If you would only be reasonable, Henry. If you would only remember that I am on the brink of ruin, and not go on calmly saying it's all quite simple.

HE. It seems so to me.

SHE [*jumping up distractedly*] If you say that again I shall do something I'll be sorry for. Here we are, standing on the edge of a frightful precipice. No doubt it's quite simple to go over and have done with it. But cant you suggest anything more agree-able?

HE. I can suggest nothing now. A chill black darkness has fallen: I can see nothing but the ruins of our dream. [*He rises with a deep sigh*].

SHE. Cant you? Well, I can. I can see Georgina rubbing those poems into Teddy. [*Facing him determinedly*] And I tell you, Henry Apjohn, that you got me into this mess; and you must get me out of it again.

HE [*polite and hopeless*] All I can say is that I am entirely at your service. What do you wish me to do?

SHE. Do you know anybody else named Aurora?

HE. No.

SHE. Theres no use in saying No in that frozen pigheaded way. You must know some Aurora or other somewhere.

HE. You said you were the only Aurora in the world. And [*lifting his clasped fists with a sudden return of his emotion*] oh God! you were the only Aurora in the world for me. [*He turns away from her, hiding his face*].

SHE [*petting him*] Yes, yes, dear: of course. It's very nice of you; and I appreciate it: indeed I do; but it's not seasonable just at present. Now just listen to me. I suppose you know all those poems by heart.

HE. Yes, by heart. [*Raising his head and looking at her with a sudden suspicion*] Dont you?

SHE. Well, I never can remember verses; and besides, Ive been so busy that Ive not had time to read them all; though I intend to the very first moment I can get: I promise you that most faithfully, Henry. But now try and remember very particularly. Does the name of Bompas occur in any of the poems?

HE [*indignantly*] No.

SHE. Youre quite sure?

HE. Of course I am quite sure. How could I use such a name in a poem?

SHE. Well, I dont see why not. It rhymes to rumpus, which seems appropriate enough at present, goodness knows! However, youre a poet, and you ought to know.

HE. What does it matter – now?

SHE. It matters a lot, I can tell you. If theres nothing about Bompas in the poems, we can say that they were written to some other Aurora, and that you shewd them to me because my name was

Aurora too. So youve got to invent another Aurora for the occasion.

HE [*very coldly*] Oh, if you wish me to tell a lie –

SHE. Surely, as a man of honor – as a gentleman, you wouldnt tell the truth: would you?

HE. Very well. You have broken my spirit and desecrated my dreams. I will lie and protest and stand on my honor: oh, I will play the gentleman, never fear.

SHE. Yes, put it all on me, of course. Dont be mean Henry.

HE [*rousing himself with an effort*] You are quite right, Mrs Bompas: I beg your pardon. You must excuse my temper. I am having growing pains, I think.

SHE. Growing pains!

HE. The process of growing from romantic boyhood into cynical maturity usually takes fifteen years. When it is compressed into fifteen minutes, the pace is too fast; and growing pains are the result.

SHE. Oh, is this a time for cleverness? It's settled, isnt it, that youre going to be nice and good, and that youll brazen it out to Teddy that you have some other Aurora?

HE. Yes: I'm capable of anything now. I should not have told him the truth by halves: and now I will not lie by halves. I'll wallow in the honor of a gentleman.

SHE. Dearest boy, I knew you would. I – Sh! [*She rushes to the door, and holds it ajar, listening breathlessly*].

HE. What is it?

SHE [*white with apprehension*] It's Teddy: I hear him tapping the new barometer. He cant have anything serious on his mind or he wouldnt do that. Perhaps Georgina hasnt said anything. [*She steals back to the hearth*]. Try and look as if there was nothing the matter. Give me my gloves, quick. [*He hands them to her. She pulls on one hastily and begins buttoning it with ostentatious unconcern*]. Go further away from me, quick. [*He walks doggedly away from her until the piano prevents his going farther*]. If I button my glove, and you were to hum a tune, dont you think that –

HE. The tableau would be complete in its guiltiness. For Heaven's sake, Mrs Bompas, let that glove alone: you look like a pickpocket.

Her husband comes in: a robust, thicknecked, well groomed city man with a strong chin but a blithering eye and credulous mouth. He has a momentous air, but shews no sign of displeasure: rather the contrary.

HER HUSBAND. Hallo! I thought you two were at the theatre.

SHE. I felt anxious about you, Teddy. Why didnt you come home to dinner?

HER HUSBAND. I got a message from Georgina. She wanted me to go to her.

SHE. Poor dear Georgina! I'm sorry I havnt been able to call on her this last week. I hope theres nothing the matter with her.

HER HUSBAND. Nothing, except anxiety for my welfare – and yours. [*She steals a terrified look at Henry*]. By the way, Apjohn, I should like a word with you this evening, if Aurora can spare you for a moment.

HE [*formally*] I am at your service.

HER HUSBAND. No hurry. After the theatre will do.

HE. We have decided not to go.

HER HUSBAND. Indeed! Well, then, shall we adjourn to my snuggery?

SHE. You neednt move. I shall go and lock up my diamonds since I'm not going to the theatre. Give me my things.

HER HUSBAND [*as he hands her the cloud and the mirror*] Well, we shall have more room here.

HE [*looking about him and shaking his shoulders loose*] I think I should prefer plenty of room.

HER HUSBAND. So, if it's not disturbing you, Rory – ?

SHE. Not at all. [*She goes out*].

When the two men are alone together, Bompas deliberately takes the poems from his breast pocket; looks at them reflectively: then looks at Henry, mutely inviting his attention. Henry refuses to understand, doing his best to look unconcerned.

HER HUSBAND. Do these manuscripts seem at all familiar to you, may I ask?

HE. Manuscripts?

HER HUSBAND. Yes. Would you like to look at them a little closer? [*He proffers them under Henry's nose*].

HE [*as with a sudden illumination of glad surprise*] Why, these are my poems!

HER HUSBAND. So I gather.

HE. What a shame! Mrs Bompas has shewn them to you! You must think me an utter ass. I wrote them years ago after reading Swinburne's Songs Before Sunrise. Nothing would do me then but I must reel off a set of Songs to the Sunrise. Aurora, you know: the rosy fingered Aurora. Theyre all about Aurora. When

Mrs Bompas told me her name was Aurora, I couldnt resist the temptation to lend them to her to read. But I didnt bargain for your unsympathetic eyes.

HER HUSBAND [*grinning*] Apjohn: thats really very ready of you. You are cut out for literature; and the day will come when Rory and I will be proud to have you about the house. I have heard far thinner stories from much older men.

HE [*with an air of great surprise*] Do you mean to imply that you dont believe me?

HER HUSBAND. Do you expect me to believe you?

HE. Why not? I dont understand.

HER HUSBAND. Come! Dont underrate your own cleverness, Apjohn. I think you understand pretty well.

HE. I assure you I am quite at a loss. Can you not be a little more explicit?

HER HUSBAND. Dont overdo it, old chap. However, I will just be so far explicit as to say that if you think these poems read as if they were addressed, not to a live woman, but to a shivering cold time of day at which you were never out of bed in your life, you hardly do justice to your own literary powers — which I admire and appreciate, mind you, as much as any man. Come! own up. You wrote those poems to my wife. [*An internal struggle prevents Henry from answering*]. Of course you did. [*He throws the poems on the table; and goes to the hearthrug, where he plants himself solidly, chuckling a little and waiting for the next move*].

HE [*formally and carefully*] Mr Bompas: I pledge you my word you are mistaken. I need not tell you that Mrs Bompas is a lady of stainless honor, who has never cast an unworthy thought on me. The fact that she has shewn you my poems —

HER HUSBAND. Thats not a fact. I came by them without her knowledge. She didnt shew them to me.

HE. Does not that prove their perfect innocence? She would have shewn them to you at once if she had taken your quite unfounded view of them.

HER HUSBAND [*shaken*] Apjohn: play fair. Dont abuse your intellectual gifts. Do you really mean that I am making a fool of myself?

HE [*earnestly*] Believe me, you are. I assure you, on my honor as a gentleman, that I have never had the slightest feeling for Mrs Bompas beyond the ordinary esteem and regard for a pleasant acquaintance.

HER HUSBAND [*shortly, shewing ill humor for the first time*] Oh! Indeed! [*He leaves his hearth and begins to approach Henry slowly, looking him up and down with growing resentment*].

HE [*hastening to improve the impression made by his mendacity*] I should never have dreamt of writing poems to her. The thing is absurd.

HER HUSBAND [*reddening ominously*] Why is it absurd?

HE [*shrugging his shoulders*] Well, it happens that I do not admire Mrs Bompas – in that way.

HER HUSBAND [*breaking out in Henry's face*] Let me tell you that Mrs Bompas has been admired by better men than you, you soapy headed little puppy, you.

HE [*much taken aback*]There is no need to insult me like this. I assure you, on my honor as a –

HER HUSBAND [*too angry to tolerate a reply, and boring Henry more and more towards the piano*] You dont admire Mrs Bompas! You would never dream of writing poems to Mrs Bompas! My wife's not good enough for you, isnt she? [*Fiercely*] Who are you, pray, that you should be so jolly superior?

HE. Mr Bompas: I can make allowances for your jealousy –

HER HUSBAND. Jealousy! do you suppose I'm jealous of you? No, nor of ten like you. But if you think I'll stand here and let you insult my wife in her own house, youre mistaken.

HE [*very uncomfortable with his back against the piano and Teddy standing over him threateningly*] How can I convince you? Be reasonable. I tell you my relations with Mrs Bompas are relations of perfect coldness – of indifference –

HER HUSBAND [*scornfully*] Say it again: say it again. Youre proud of it, arnt you? Yah! youre not worth kicking.

Henry suddenly executes the feat known to pugilists as slipping, and changes sides with Teddy, who is now between Henry and the piano.

HE. Look here: I'm not going to stand this.

HER HUSBAND. Oh, you have some blood in your body after all! Good job!

HE. This is ridiculous. I assure you Mrs Bompas is quite –

HER HUSBAND.What is Mrs Bompas to you, I'd like to know. I'll tell you what Mrs Bompas is. She's the smartest woman in the smartest set in South Kensington, and the handsomest, and the cleverest, and the most fetching to experienced men who know a good thing when they see it, whatever she may be to conceited penny-a-lining puppies who think nothing good enough for them. It's admitted by the best people; and not to know it argues yourself unknown. Three of our first actor-managers have offered her a hundred a week if she'll go on the stage when they start a repertory theatre; and I think they know what theyre about as well as you. The only member of the present Cabinet that you might call a handsome man has neglected the business of the country to dance with her, though he dont belong to our set as a regular thing. One of the first professional poets in Bedford Park wrote a sonnet to her, worth all your amateur trash. At Ascot last season the eldest son of a duke excused himself from calling on me on the ground that his feelings for Mrs Bompas were not consistent with his duty to me as host; and it did him honor and me too. But [*with gathering fury*] she isnt good enough for you, it seems. You regard her with coldness, with indifference; and you have the cool cheek to tell me so to my face. For two pins I'd flatten your nose in to teach you manners. Introducing a fine woman to you is casting pearls before swine [*yelling at him*] before SWINE! d'ye hear?

HE [*with a deplorable lack of polish*] You call me a swine again and I'll land you one on the chin thatll make your head sing for a week.

HER HUSBAND [*exploding*] What!

He charges at Henry with bull-like fury. Henry places himself on guard in the manner of a well taught boxer, and gets away smartly, but unfortunately forgets the stool which is just behind him. He falls backwards over it, unintentionally pushing it against the shins of Bompas, who falls forward over it. Mrs Bompas, with a scream, rushes into the room between the sprawling champions, and sits down on the floor in order to get her right arm round her husband's neck.

SHE. You shant, Teddy: you shant. You will be killed: he is a prizefighter.

HER HUSBAND [*vengefully*] I'll prizefight him. [*He struggles vainly to free himself from her embrace*].

SHE. Henry; dont let him fight you. Promise me that you wont.

HE [*ruefully*] I have got a most frightful bump on the back of my head. [*He tries to rise*].

SHE [*reaching out her left hand to seize his coat tail, and pulling him down again, whilst keeping fast hold of Teddy with the other hand*] Not until you have promised: not until you both have promised [*Teddy tries to rise: she pulls him back again*]. Teddy: you promise, dont you? Yes, yes. Be good: you promise.

HER HUSBAND. I wont, unless he takes it back.

SHE. He will: he does. You take it back, Henry? — yes.

HE [*savagely*] Yes. I take it back. [*She lets go his coat. He gets up. So does Teddy*]. I take it all back, all, without reserve.

SHE [*on the carpet*] Is nobody going to help me up? [*They each take a hand and pull her up*]. Now wont you shake hands and be good?

HE [*recklessly*] I shall do nothing of the sort. I have steeped myself in lies for your sake; and the only reward I get is a lump on the back of my head the size of an apple. Now I will go back to the straight path.

SHE. Henry: for Heaven's sake —

HE. It's no use. Your husband is a fool and a brute —

HER HUSBAND. Whats that you say?

HE. I say you are a fool and a brute; and if youll step outside with me I'll say it again. [*Teddy begins to take off his coat for combat*]. Those poems were written to your wife, every word of them, and to nobody else. [*The scowl clears away from Bompas's countenance. Radiant, he replaces his coat.*] I wrote them because I loved her. I thought her the most beautiful woman in the world, and I told her so over and over again. I adored her: do you hear? I told her that you were a sordid commercial chump, utterly unworthy of her; and so you are.

HER HUSBAND [*so gratified, he can hardly believe his ears*] You dont mean it!

HE. Yes, I do mean it, and a lot more too. I asked Mrs Bompas to walk out of the house with me — to leave you — to get divorced from you and marry me. I begged and implored her to do it this very night. It was her refusal that ended everything between us. [*Looking very disparagingly at him*] What she can see in you, goodness only knows!

HER HUSBAND [*beaming with remorse*] My dear chap, why didnt you say so before? I apologize. Come! dont bear malice: shake hands. Make him shake hands, Rory.

SHE. For my sake, Henry. After all, he's my husband. Forgive him. Take his hand. [*Henry, dazed, lets her take his hand and place it in Teddy's*].

HER HUSBAND [*shaking it heartily*] Youve got to own that none of your literary heroines can touch my Rory. [*He turns to her and claps her with fond pride on the shoulder*]. Eh, Rory? They cant resist you: none of em. Never knew a man yet that could hold out three days.

SHE. Dont be foolish, Teddy. I hope you were not really hurt, Henry. [*She feels the back of his head. He flinches*]. Oh, poor boy, what a bump! I must get some vinegar and brown paper. [*She goes to the bell and rings*].

HER HUSBAND. Will you do me a great favor, Apjohn. I hardly like to ask; but it would be a real kindness to us both.

HE. What can I do?

HER HUSBAND [*taking up the poems*] Well, may I get these printed? It shall be done in the best style. The finest paper, sumptuous binding, everything first class. Theyre beautiful poems. I should like to shew them about a bit.

SHE [*running back from the bell, delighted with the idea, and coming between them*] Oh Henry, if you wouldnt mind?

HE. Oh, *I* dont mind. I am past minding anything.

HER HUSBAND. What shall we call the volume? To Aurora, or something like that, eh?

HE. I should call it How He Lied to Her Husband.

Passion, Poison and Petrifaction

or the Fatal Gazogene
A Brief Tragedy for Barns and Booths

Composition begun May 1905; completed 4 June 1905. Published in *Harry Furniss's Christmas Annual*, 1905. Privately printed for copyright in the United States, 1905. First collected in *Translations and Tomfooleries*, 1926. First presented in 'The Theatre Royal' (a 'tent booth' theatre) at the Theatrical Garden Party, Regent's Park, London, on 14 July 1905 (several performances were given, at intervals during the afternoon, in aid of the Actors' Orphanage Fund).

Lady Magnesia Fitztollemache   *Irene Vanbrugh*
Phyllis, her maid   *Nancy Price*
George Fitztollemache   *Eric Lewis*
Adolphus Bastable   *Cyril Maude*
The Landlord   *Lennox Pawle*
Police Constable   *Arthur Williams*
Doctor   *G. P. Huntley*
Choir of Invisible Angels   *Messrs. Mason, Tucker, Maney, Humphreys*

Period – Not for an age but for all time.

Scene: *A bed sitting-room in a fashionable quarter of London.*

This tragedy was written at the request of Mr Cyril Maude, under whose direction it was performed repeatedly, with colossal success, in a booth in Regent's Park, for the benefit of The Actors' Orphanage, on the 14th July 1905, by Miss Irene Vanbrugh, Miss Nancy Price, Mr G. P. Huntley, Mr Cyril Maude, Mr Eric Lewis, Mr Arthur Williams, and Mr Lennox Pawle.

As it is extremely difficult to find an actor capable of eating a real ceiling, it will be found convenient in performance to substitute the tops of old wedding cakes for bits of plaster. There is but little difference in material between the two substances; but the taste of the wedding cake is considered more agreeable by many people.

The orchestra should consist of at least a harp, a drum, and a pair of cymbals, these instruments being the most useful in enhancing the stage effect.

The landlord may with equal propriety be a landlady, if that arrangement be better suited to the resources of the company.

As the Bill Bailey song has not proved immortal, any equally appropriate ditty of the moment may be substituted.

In a bed-sitting room in a fashionable quarter of London a lady sits at her dressing-table, with her maid combing her hair. It is late; and the electric lamps are glowing. Apparently the room is bedless; but there stands against the opposite wall to that at which the dressing-table is placed a piece of furniture that suggests a bookcase without carrying any conviction. On the same side is a chest of drawers of that disastrous kind which, recalcitrant to the opener until she is provoked to violence, then suddenly come wholly out and defy all her efforts to fit them in again. Opposite this chest of drawers, on the lady's side of the room, is a cupboard. The presence of a row of gentleman's boots beside the chest of drawers proclaims that the lady is married. Her own boots are beside the cupboard. The third wall is pierced midway by the door, above which is a cuckoo clock. Near the door a pedestal bears a portrait bust of the lady in plaster. There is a fan on the dressing-table, a hatbox and rug strap on the chest of drawers, an umbrella and a bootjack against the wall near the bed. The general impression is one of brightness, beauty, and social ambition, damped by somewhat inadequate means. A certain air of theatricality is produced by the fact that though the room is rectangular it has only three walls. Not a sound is heard except the overture and the crackling of the lady's hair as the maid's brush draws electric sparks from it in the dry air of the London midsummer.

The cuckoo clock strikes sixteen.

THE LADY. How much did the clock strike, Phyllis?

PHYLLIS. Sixteen, my lady.

THE LADY. That means eleven o'clock, does it not?

PHYLLIS. Eleven at night, my lady. In the morning it means half-past two; so if you hear it strike sixteen during your slumbers, do not rise.

THE LADY. I will not, Phyllis. Phyllis: I am weary. I will go to bed. Prepare my couch.

Phyllis crosses the room to the bookcase and touches a button. The front of the bookcase falls out with a crash and becomes a bed. A roll of distant thunder echoes the crash.

PHYLLIS [*shuddering*] It is a terrible night. Heaven help all poor mariners at sea! My master is late. I trust nothing has happened to him. Your bed is ready, my lady.

THE LADY. Thank you, Phyllis. [*She rises and approaches the bed*].
Goodnight.

PHYLLIS. Will your ladyship not undress?

THE LADY. Not tonight, Phyllis. [*Glancing through where the fourth
wall is missing*] Not under the circumstances.

PHYLLIS [*impulsively throwing herself on her knees by her mistress's side,
and clasping her round the waist*] Oh, my beloved mistress, I know
not why or how; but I feel that I shall never see you alive again.
There is murder in the air. [*Thunder*]. Hark!

THE LADY. Strange! As I sat there methought I heard angels
singing, Oh, wont you come home, Bill Bailey? Why should
angels call me Bill Bailey? My name is Magnesia
Fitztollemache.

PHYLLIS [*emphasizing the title*] Lady Magnesia Fitztollemache.

LADY MAGNESIA. In case we should never again meet in this
world, let us take a last farewell.

PHYLLIS [*embracing her with tears*] My poor murdered angel
mistress!

LADY MAGNESIA. In case we should meet again, call me at
half-past eleven.

PHYLLIS. I will, I will.

> *Phyllis withdraws, overcome by emotion. Lady Magnesia switches off
the electric light, and immediately hears the angels quite distinctly. They
sing Bill Bailey so sweetly that she can attend to nothing else, and forgets to
remove even her boots as she draws the coverlet over herself and sinks to
sleep, lulled by celestial harmony. A white radiance plays on her pillow,
and lights up her beautiful face. But the thunder growls again; and a lurid
red glow concentrates itself on the door, which is presently flung open,
revealing a saturnine figure in evening dress, partially concealed by a
crimson cloak. As he steals towards the bed the unnatural glare in his eyes
and the broad-bladed dagger nervously gripped in his right hand bode ill for
the sleeping lady. Providentially she sneezes on the very brink of eternity;
and the tension of the murderer's nerves is such that he bolts precipitately
under the bed at the sudden and startling Atscha! A dull, heavy, rhythmic
thumping – the beating of his heart – betrays his whereabouts. Soon he
emerges cautiously and raises his head above the bed coverlet level.*

THE MURDERER. I can no longer cower here listening to the
agonized thumpings of my own heart. She but snoze in her sleep.
I'll do't. [*He again raises the dagger. The angels sing again. He cowers*]
What is this? Has that tune reached Heaven?

LADY MAGNESIA [*waking and sitting up*] My husband! [*All the colors *of the rainbow chase one another up his face with ghastly brilliancy*]. Why do you change color? And what on earth are you doing with that dagger?

FITZ [*affecting unconcern, but unhinged*] It is a present for you: a present from mother. Pretty, isnt it? [*he displays it fatuously*].

LADY MAGNESIA. But she promised me a fish slice.

FITZ. This is a combination fish slice and dagger. One day you have salmon for dinner. The next you have a murder to commit. See?

LADY MAGNESIA. My sweet mother-in-law! [*Someone knocks at the door*]. That is Adolphus's knock. [*Fitz's face turns a dazzling green*]. What has happened to your complexion? You have turned green. Now I think of it, you always do when Adolphus is mentioned. Arnt you going to let him in?

FITZ. Certainly not. [*He goes to the door*]. Adolphus: you cannot enter. My wife is undressed and in bed.

LADY MAGNESIA [*rising*] I am not. Come in, Adolphus [*she switches on the electric light*].

ADOLPHUS [*without*] Something most important has happened. I must come in for a moment.

FITZ [*calling to Adolphus*] Something important happened? What is it?

ADOLPHUS [*without*] My new clothes have come home.

FITZ. He says his new clothes have come home.

LADY MAGNESIA [*running to the door and opening it*] Oh, come in, come in. Let me see.

Adolphus Bastable enters. He is in evening dress, made in the latest fashion, with the right half of the coat and the left half of the trousers yellow and the other halves black. His silver-spangled waistcoat has a crimson handkerchief stuck between it and his shirt front.

ADOLPHUS. What do you think of it?

LADY MAGNESIA. It is a dream! a creation! [*she turns him about to admire him*].

ADOLPHUS [*proudly*] I shall never be mistaken for a waiter again.

FITZ. A drink, Adolphus?

ADOLPHUS. Thanks.

Fitztollemache goes to the cupboard and takes out a tray with tumblers and a bottle of whisky. He puts them on the dressing-table.

FITZ. Is the gazogene full?

LADY MAGNESIA. Yes: you put in the powders yourself today.

FITZ [*sardonically*] So I did. The special powders! Ha! ha! ha! ha! ha! [*his face is again strangely variegated*].

LADY MAGNESIA. Your complexion is really going to pieces. Why do you laugh in that silly way at nothing?

FITZ. Nothing! Ha, ha! Nothing, Ha, ha, ha!

ADOLPHUS. I hope, Mr Fitztollemache, you are not laughing at my clothes. I warn you that I am an Englishman. You may laugh at my manners, at my brains, at my national institutions; but if you laugh at my clothes, one of us must die.

   Thunder.

FITZ. I laughed but at the irony of Fate [*he takes a gazogene from the cupboard*].

ADOLPHUS [*satisfied*] Oh, that! Oh, yes, of course!

FITZ. Let us drown all unkindness in a loving cup. [*He puts the gazogene on the floor in the middle of the room*]. Pardon the absence of a table: we found it in the way and pawned it. [*He takes the whisky bottle from the dressing-table*].

LADY MAGNESIA. We picnic at home now. It is delightful.

   She takes three tumblers from the dressing-table and sits on the floor, presiding over the gazogene, with Fitz and Adolphus squatting on her left and right respectively. Fitz pours whisky into the tumblers.

FITZ [*as Magnesia is about to squirt soda into his tumbler*] Stay! No soda for me. Let Adolphus have it all – all. I will take mine neat.

LADY MAGNESIA [*proffering tumbler to Adolphus*] Pledge me, Adolphus.

FITZ. Kiss the cup, Magnesia. Pledge her, man. Drink deep.

ADOLPHUS. To Magnesia!

FITZ. To Magnesia! [*The two men drink*] It is done. [*Scrambling to his feet*] Adolphus: you have but ten minutes to live – if so long.

ADOLPHUS. What mean you?

MAGNESIA [*rising*] My mind misgives me. I have a strange feeling here [*touching her heart*].

ADOLPHUS. So have I, but lower down [*touching his stomach*]. That gazogene is disagreeing with me.

FITZ. It was poisoned!

   Sensation.

ADOLPHUS [*rising*] Help! Police!

FITZ. Dastard! you would appeal to the law! Can you not die like a gentleman?

ADOLPHUS. But so young! when I have only worn my new clothes once.

MAGNESIA. It is too horrible. [*To Fitz*] Fiend! what drove you to this wicked deed?

FITZ. Jealousy. You admired his clothes: you did not admire mine.

ADOLPHUS. My clothes [*his face lights up with heavenly radiance*]! Have I indeed been found worthy to be the first clothes-martyr? Welcome, death! Hark! angels call me. [*The celestial choir again raises its favorite chant. He listens with a rapt expression. Suddenly the angels sing out of tune; and the radiance on the poisoned man's face turns a sickly green*] Yah – ah! Oh – ahoo! The gazogene is disagreeing extremely. Oh! [*he throws himself on the bed, writhing*].

MAGNESIA [*to Fitz*] Monster: what have you done? [*She points to the distorted figure on the bed*]. That was once a Man, beautiful and glorious. What have you made of it? A writhing, agonized, miserable, moribund worm.

ADOLPHUS [*in a tone of the strongest remonstrance*] Oh, I say! Oh, come! No: look here, Magnesia! Really!

MAGNESIA. Oh, is this a time for petty vanity? Think of your misspent life –

ADOLPHUS [*much injured*] Whose misspent life?

MAGNESIA [*continuing relentlessly*] Look into your conscience: look into your stomach. [*Adolphus collapses in hideous spasms. She turns to Fitz*] And this is your handiwork!

FITZ. Mine is a passionate nature, Magnesia. I must have your undivided love. I must have your love: do you hear? LOVE! LOVE!! LOVE!!! LOVE!!!! LOVE!!!!!

He raves, accompanied by a fresh paroxysm from the victim on the bed.

MAGNESIA [*with sudden resolution*] You shall have it.

FITZ [*enraptured*] Magnesia! I have recovered your love! Oh, how slight appears the sacrifice of this man compared to so glorious a reward! I would poison ten men without a thought of self to gain one smile from you.

ADOLPHUS [*in a broken voice*] Farewell: my last hour is at hand. Farewell, farewell, farewell!

MAGNESIA. At this supreme moment, George Fitztollemache, I solemnly dedicate to you all that I formerly dedicated to poor Adolphus.

ADOLPHUS. Oh, please not poor Adolphus yet. I still live, you know.

MAGNESIA. The vital spark but flashes before it vanishes. [*Adolphus groans*]. And now, Adolphus, take this last comfort from the unhappy Magnesia Fitztollemache. As I have dedicated to

George all that I gave to you, so I will bury in your grave – or in your urn if you are cremated – all that I gave to him.

FITZ. I hardly follow this.

MAGNESIA. I will explain. George: hitherto I have given Adolphus all the romance of my nature – all my love – all my dreams – all my caresses. Henceforth they are yours!

FITZ. Angel!

MAGNESIA. Adolphus: forgive me if this pains you.

ADOLPHUS. Dont mention it. I hardly feel it. The gazogene is so much worse. [*Taken bad again*] Oh!

MAGNESIA. Peace, poor sufferer: there is still some balm. You are about to hear what I am going to dedicate to you.

ADOLPHUS. All I ask is a peppermint lozenge, for mercy's sake.

MAGNESIA. I have something far better than any lozenge: the devotion of a lifetime. Formerly it was George's. I kept his house, or rather, his lodgings. I mended his clothes. I darned his socks. I bought his food. I interviewed his creditors. I stood between him and the servants. I administered his domestic finances. When his hair needed cutting or his countenance was imperfectly washed, I pointed it out to him. The trouble that all this gave me made him prosaic in my eyes. Familiarity bred contempt. Now all that shall end. My husband shall be my hero, my lover, my perfect knight. He shall shield me from all care and trouble. He shall ask nothing in return but love – boundless, priceless, rapturous, soul-enthralling love, LOVE! LOVE!! LOVE!!! [*she raves and flings her arms about Fitz*]. And the duties I formerly discharged shall be replaced by the one supreme duty of duties: the duty of weeping at Adolphus's tomb.

FITZ [*reflectively*] My ownest, this sacrifice makes me feel that I have perhaps been a little selfish. I cannot help feeling that there is much to be said for the old arrangement. Why should Adolphus die for my sake?

ADOLPHUS. I am not dying for your sake, Fitz. I am dying because you poisoned me.

MAGNESIA. You do not fear to die, Adolphus, do you?

ADOLPHUS. N-n-no, I dont exactly fear to die. Still –

FITZ. Still, if an antidote –

ADOLPHUS [*bounding from the bed*] Antidote!

MAGNESIA [*with wild hope*] Antidote!

FITZ. If an antidote would not be too much of an anti-climax.

ADOLPHUS. Anti-climax be blowed! Do you think I am going to die to please the critics? Out with your antidote. Quick!

FITZ. The best antidote to the poison I have given you is lime, plenty of lime.

ADOLPHUS. Lime! You mock me! Do you think I carry lime about in my pockets?

FITZ. There is the plaster ceiling.

MAGNESIA. Yes, the ceiling. Saved, saved, saved!

All three frantically shy boots at the ceiling. Flakes of plaster rain down which Adolphus devours, at first ravenously, then with a marked falling off in relish.

MAGNESIA [*picking up a huge slice*] Take this, Adolphus: it is the largest [*she crams it into his mouth*].

FITZ. Ha! a lump off the cornice! Try this.

ADOLPHUS [*desperately*] Stop! Stop!

MAGNESIA. Do not stop. You will die. [*She tries to stuff him again*].

ADOLPHUS [*resolutely*] I prefer death.

MAGNESIA and FITZ [*throwing themselves on their knees on either side of him*] For our sakes, Adolphus, persevere.

ADOLPHUS. No: unless you can supply lime in liquid form, I must perish. Finish that ceiling I cannot and will not.

MAGNESIA. I have a thought – an inspiration. My bust. [*She snatches it from its pedestal and brings it to him*].

ADOLPHUS [*gazing fondly at it*] Can I resist it?

FITZ. Try the bun.

ADOLPHUS [*gnawing the knot of hair at the back of the bust's head: it makes him ill*] Yah, I cannot. I cannot. Not even your bust, Magnesia. Do not ask me. Let me die.

FITZ [*pressing the bust on him*] Force yourself to take a mouthful. Down with it, Adolphus!

ADOLPHUS. Useless. It would not stay down. Water! Some fluid! Ring for something to drink [*he chokes*].

MAGNESIA. I will save you [*she rushes to the bell and rings*].

Phyllis, in her night-gown, with her hair prettily made up into a chevaux de frise of crocuses with pink and yellow curl papers, rushes in straight to Magnesia.

PHYLLIS [*hysterically*] My beloved mistress, once more we meet. [*She sees Fitztollemache and screams*] Ah! ah! ah! A man! [*She sees Adolphus*] Men!! [*She flies; but Tollemache seizes her by the night-gown just as she is escaping*]. Unhand me, villain!

FITZ. This is no time for prudery, girl. Mr Bastable is dying.

PHYLLIS [*with concern*] Indeed, sir? I hope he will not think it unfeeling of me to appear at his deathbed in curl papers.

MAGNESIA. We know you have a good heart, Phyllis. Take this [*giving her the bust*]; dissolve it in a jug of hot water; and bring it back instantly. Mr Bastable's life depends on your haste.

PHYLLIS [*hesitating*] It do seem a pity, dont it, my lady, to spoil your lovely bust?

ADOLPHUS. Tush! This craze for fine art is beyond all bounds. Off with you [*he pushes her out*]. Drink, drink, drink! My entrails are parched. Drink! [*he rushes deliriously to the gazogene*].

FITZ [*rushing after him*] Madman, you forget! It is poisoned!

ADOLPHUS. I dont care. Drink, drink! [*They wrestle madly for the gazogene. In the struggle they squirt all its contents away, mostly into one another's face. Adolphus at last flings Fitztollemache to the floor, and puts the spout into his mouth*] Empty! Empty! [*with a shriek of despair he collapses on the bed, clasping the gazogene like a baby, and weeping over it*].

FITZ [*aside to Magnesia*] Magnesia: I have always pretended not to notice it; but you keep a siphon for your private use in my hat-box.

MAGNESIA. I use it for washing old lace; but no matter: he shall have it [*she produces a siphon from the hat-box, and offers a tumbler of soda-water to Adolphus*].

ADOLPHUS. Thanks, thanks, oh, thanks! [*he drinks. A terrific fizzing is heard. He starts up screaming*] Help! help! The ceiling is effervescing! I am BURSTING! [*He wallows convulsively on the bed*].

FITZ. Quick! the rug strap! [*They pack him with blankets and strap him*]. Is that tight enough?

MAGNESIA [*anxiously*] Will you hold, do you think?

ADOLPHUS. The peril is past. The soda-water has gone flat.

MAGNESIA and FITZ. Thank heaven!

Phyllis returns with a washstand ewer, in which she has dissolved the bust.

MAGNESIA [*snatching it*] At last!

FITZ. You are saved. Drain it to the dregs.

Fitztollemache holds the lip of the ewer to Adolphus's mouth and gradually raises it until it stands upside down. Adolphus's effort to swallow it are fearful, Phyllis thumping his back when he chokes, and Magnesia loosening the straps when he moans. At last, with a sigh of relief, he sinks back in the women's arms. Fitz shakes the empty ewer upside down like a potman shaking the froth out of a flagon.

ADOLPHUS. How inexpressibly soothing to the chest! A delicious numbness steals through all my members. I would sleep.

MAGNESIA }
FITZ   } [*whispering*] Let him sleep.
PHYLLIS }

   He sleeps. Celestial harps are heard; but their chords cease on the abrupt entrance of the landlord, a vulgar person in pyjamas.

THE LANDLORD. Eah! Eah! Wots this? Wots all this noise? Ah kin ennybody sleep through it? [*Looking at the floor and ceiling*] Ellow? wot you bin doin te maw ceilin?

FITZ. Silence, or leave the room. If you wake that man he dies.

THE LANDLORD. If e kin sleep through the noise you three mikes e kin sleep through ennythink.

MAGNESIA. Detestable vulgarian: your pronunciation jars on the finest chords of my nature. Begone!

THE LANDLORD [*looking at Adolphus*] Aw downt blieve eze esleep. Aw blieve eze dead. [*Calling*] Pleece! Pleece! Merder! [*A blue halo plays mysteriously on the door, which opens and reveals a policeman. Thunder*]. Eah, pleecmin: these three's bin an merdered this gent between em, an naw tore moy ahse dahn.

THE POLICEMAN [*offended*] Policeman, indeed! Wheres your manners?

FITZ. Officer —

THE POLICEMAN [*with distinguished consideration*] Sir?

FITZ. As between gentlemen —

THE POLICEMAN [*bowing*] Sir: to you.

FITZ [*bowing*] I may inform you that my friend had an acute attack of indigestion. No carbonate of soda being available, he swallowed a portion of this man's ceiling. [*Pointing to Adolphus*] Behold the result!

THE POLICEMAN. The ceiling was poisoned! Well, of all the artful — [*he collars the landlord*]. I arrest you for wilful murder.

THE LANDLORD [*appealing to the heavens*] Ow, is this jestice! Ah could aw tell e wiz gowin te eat moy ceilin?

THE POLICEMAN [*releasing him*] True. The case is more complicated than I thought. [*He tries to lift Adolphus's arm but cannot*]. Stiff already.

THE LANDLORD [*trying to lift Adolphus's leg*] An' precious evvy. [*Feeling the calf*] Woy, eze gorn ez awd ez niles.

FITZ [*rushing to the bed*] What is this?

MAGNESIA. Oh, say not he is dead. Phyllis: fetch a doctor. [*Phyllis runs out. They all try to lift Adolphus; but he is perfectly stiff, and as heavy as lead*]. Rouse him. Shake him.

THE POLICEMAN [*exhausted*] Whew! Is he a man or a statue? [*Magnesia utters a piercing scream*]. What's wrong, Miss?

MAGNESIA [*to Fitz*] Do you not see what has happened?

FITZ [*striking his forehead*] Horror on horror's head!

THE LANDLORD. Wotjemean?

MAGNESIA. The plaster has set inside him. The officer was right: he is indeed a living statue.

Magnesia flings herself on the stony breast of Adolphus. Fitztollemache buries his head in his hands; and his chest heaves convulsively. The policeman takes a small volume from his pocket and consults it.

THE POLICEMAN. This case is not provided for in my book of instructions. It dont seem no use trying artificial respiration, do it? [*To the landlord*] Here! lend a hand, you. We'd best take him and set him up in Trafalgar Square.

THE LANDLORD. Aushd pat im in the cestern an worsh it aht of im.

Phyllis comes back with a Doctor.

PHYLLIS. The medical man, my lady.

THE POLICEMAN. A poison case, sir.

THE DOCTOR. Do you mean to say that an unqualified person! a layman! has dared to administer poison in my district?

THE POLICEMAN [*raising Magnesia tenderly*] It looks like it. Hold up, my lady.

THE DOCTOR. Not a moment must be lost. The patient must be kept awake at all costs. Constant and violent motion is necessary.

He snatches Magnesia from the policeman, and rushes her about the room.

FITZ. Stop! That is not the poisoned person!

THE DOCTOR. It is you, then. Why did you not say so before?

He seizes Fitztollemache and rushes him about.

THE LANDLORD. Naow, naow, thet ynt im.

THE DOCTOR. What, you!

He pounces on the landlord and rushes him round.

THE LANDLORD. Eah! chack it. [*He trips the doctor up. Both fall*]. Jest owld this leoonatic, will you, Mister Horficer?

THE POLICEMAN [*dragging both of them to their feet*] Come out of it, will you. You must all come with me to the station.

Thunder.

MAGNESIA. What! In this frightful storm!

The hail patters noisily on the window.

PHYLLIS. I think it's raining.

The wind howls.

THE LANDLORD. It's thunderin and lawtnin.

FITZ. It's dangerous.

THE POLICEMAN [*drawing his baton and whistle*] If you wont come quietly, then —

He whistles. A fearful flash is followed by an appalling explosion of heaven's artillery. A thunderbolt enters the room, and strikes the helmet of the devoted constable, whence it is attracted to the waistcoat of the doctor by the lancet in his pocket. Finally it leaps with fearful force on the landlord, who, being of a gross and spongy nature, absorbs the electric fluid at the cost of his life. The others look on horror-stricken as the three victims, after reeling, jostling, cannoning through a ghastly quadrille, at last sink inanimate on the carpet.

MAGNESIA [*listening at the doctor's chest*] Dead!

FITZ [*kneeling by the landlord, and raising his hand, which drops with a thud*] Dead!

PHYLLIS [*seizing the looking-glass and holding it to the Policeman's lips*] Dead!

FITZ [*solemnly rising*] The copper attracted the lightning.

MAGNESIA [*rising*] After life's fitful fever they sleep well. Phyllis: sweep them up.

Phyllis replaces the looking-glass on the dressing-table; takes up the fan; and fans the policeman, who rolls away like a leaf before the wind to the wall. She disposes similarly of the landlord and doctor.

PHYLLIS. Will they be in your way if I leave them there until morning, my lady? Or shall I bring up the ashpan and take them away?

MAGNESIA. They will not disturb us. Goodnight, Phyllis.

PHYLLIS. Goodnight, my lady. Goodnight, sir.

She retires.

MAGNESIA. And now, husband, let us perform our last sad duty to our friend. He has become his own monument. Let us erect him. He is heavy; but love can do much.

FITZ. A little leverage will get him on his feet. Give me my umbrella.

MAGNESIA. True.

She hands him the umbrella, and takes up the boot-jack. They get them under Adolphus's back, and prize him up on his feet.

FITZ. Thats done it! Whew!

MAGNESIA [*kneeling at the left hand of the statue*] For ever and for ever, Adolphus.

FITZ [*kneeling at the right hand of the statue*] The rest is silence.

The Angels sing Bill Bailey. The statue raises its hands in an attitude of blessing, and turns its limelit face to heaven as the curtain falls. National Anthem.

ATTENDANTS [*in front*] All out for the next performance. Pass along, please, ladies and gentlemen: pass along.

The Glimpse of Reality

A Tragedietta

Composition begun 8 March 1909; completed 30 August 1910. Published in *Translations and Tomfooleries*, 1926. First presented by amateurs (Glasgow Clarion Players) at the Fellowship Hall, Glasgow, on 8 October 1927. First professional performance at the Arts Theatre Club, London, on 20 November, 1927.

Count Ferruccio (The Friar)   *Harcourt Williams*
Giulia   *Elissa Landi*
Squarcio   *Harold B. Meade*
Sandro   *Terence O'Brien*

Period – The Fifteenth Century

Scene – *An Inn on the edge of an Italian Lake*

THE GIRL. Father: were you sent here by a boy from —

THE FRIAR [*in a high, piping, but clear voice*] I'm a very old man. Oh, very old. Old enough to be your great grandfather, my daughter. Oh, very very old.

THE GIRL. But were you sent here by a boy from —

THE FRIAR. Oh yes, yes, yes, yes, yes. Quite a boy, he was. Very young. And I'm very old. Oh, very very old, dear daughter.

THE GIRL. Are you a holy man?

THE FRIAR [*ecstatically*] Oh, very holy. Very, very, very, very holy.

THE GIRL. But have you your wits still about you, father? Can you absolve me from a great sin?

THE FRIAR. Oh yes, yes, yes. A very great sin. I'm very old; but Ive my wits about me. I'm one hundred and thirteen years old, by the grace of Our Lady; but I still remember all my Latin; and I can bind and loose; and I'm very very wise; for I'm old and have left far behind me the world, the flesh, and the devil. You see I am blind, daughter; but when a boy told me that there was a duty for me to do here, I came without a guide, straight to this spot, led by St Barbara. She led me to this stone, daughter. It's a comfortable stone to me: she has blessed it for me.

THE GIRL. It's a cross, father.

THE FRIAR [*piping rapturously*] Oh blessed, blessed, ever blessed be my holy patroness for leading me to this sacred spot. Is there any building near this, daughter? The boy mentioned an inn.

THE GIRL. There is an inn, father, not twenty yards away. It's kept by my father, Squarcio.

THE FRIAR. And is there a barn where a very very old man may sleep and have a handful of peas for his supper?

THE GIRL. There is bed and board both for holy men who will take the guilt of our sins from us. Swear to me on the cross that you are a very holy man.

THE FRIAR. I'll do better than that, daughter. I'll prove my holiness to you by a miracle.

THE GIRL. A miracle!

THE FRIAR. A most miraculous miracle. A wonderful miracle! When I was only eighteen years of age I was already famous for my devoutness. When the hand of the blessed Saint Barbara, which was chopped off in the days when the church was persecuted, was found at Viterbo, I was selected by the Pope himself to carry it to Rome for that blessed lady's festival there; and since that my hand has never grown old. It remains young and warm and plump whilst the rest of my body is withered almost to dust, and my voice is cracked and become the whistling you now hear.

THE GIRL. Is that true? Let me see. [*He takes her hand in his. She kneels and kisses it fervently*] Oh, it's true. You are a saint. Heaven has sent you in answer to my prayer.

THE FRIAR. As soft as your neck, is it not? [*He caresses her neck*].

THE GIRL. It thrills me: it is wonderful.

THE FRIAR. It thrills me also, daughter. That, too, is a miracle at my age.

THE GIRL. Father –

THE FRIAR. Come closer, daughter. I'm very very old and very very very deaf: you must speak quite close to my ear if you speak low. [*She kneels with her breast against his arm and her chin on his shoulder*]. Good. Good. Thats better. Oh, I'm very very old.

THE GIRL. Father: I am about to commit a deadly sin.

THE FRIAR. Do, my daughter. Do, do, do, do, do.

THE GIRL [*discouraged*] Oh, you do not hear what I say.

THE FRIAR. Not hear! Then come closer, daughter. Oh, much much closer. Put your arm round my shoulders, and speak in my ear. Do not be ashamed, my daughter: I'm only a sack of old bones. You can hear them rattle. [*He shakes his shoulders and makes the beads of his rosary rattle at the same time*]. Listen to the old man's bones rattling. Oh, take the old old man to heaven, Blessed Barbara.

THE GIRL. Your wits are wandering. Listen to me. Are you listening?

THE FRIAR. Yes yes yes yes yes yes yes. Remember: whether I hear or not, I can absolve. All the better for you perhaps if I do not hear the worst. He! He! He! Well well. When my wits wander, squeeze my young hand; and the blessed Barbara will restore my faculties. [*She squeezes his hand vigorously.*] Thats right. Tha-a-a-a-ats right. Now I remember what I am and who you are. Proceed, my child.

THE GIRL. Father, I am to be married this year to a young fisherman.

THE FRIAR. The devil you are, my dear.

THE GIRL [*squeezing his hand*] Oh listen, listen; you are wandering again.

THE FRIAR. Thats right: hold my hand tightly. I understand, I understand. This young fisherman is neither very beautiful nor very brave; but he is honest and devoted to you; and there is something about him different to all the other young men.

THE GIRL. You know him, then!

THE FRIAR. No no no no no. I'm too old to remember people. But Saint Barbara tells me everything.

THE GIRL. Then you know why we cant marry yet.

THE FRIAR. He is too poor. His mother will not let him unless his bride has a dowry —

THE GIRL [*interrupting him impetuously*] Yes, yes: oh blessed be Saint Barbara for sending you to me! Thirty crowns — thirty crowns from a poor girl like me: it is wicked — monstrous. I must sin to earn it.

THE FRIAR. That will not be your sin, but his mother's.

THE GIRL. Oh, that is true: I never thought of that. But will she suffer for it?

THE FRIAR. Thousands of years in purgatory for it, my daughter. The worse the sin, the longer she will suffer. So let her have it as hot as possible. [*The girl recoils*]. Do not let go my hand: I'm wandering. [*She squeezes his hand*]. Thats right, darling. Sin is a very wicked thing, my daughter. Even a mother-in-law's sin is very expensive; for your husband would stint you to pay for masses for her soul.

THE GIRL. That is true. You are very wise, father.

THE FRIAR. Let it be a venial sin: an amiable sin. What sin were you thinking of, for instance?

THE GIRL. There is a young Count Ferruccio [*the Friar starts at the name*], son of the tyrant of Parma —

THE FRIAR. An excellent young man, daughter. You could not sin with a more excellent young man. But thirty crowns is too much to ask from him. He cant afford it. He is a beggar: an outcast. He made love to Madonna Brigita, the sister of Cardinal Poldi, a Cardinal eighteen years of age, a nephew of the Holy Father. The Cardinal surprised Ferruccio with his sister; and Ferruccio's temper got the better of him. He threw that holy young Cardinal out of the window and broke his arm.

THE GIRL. You know everything.

THE FRIAR. Saint Barbara, my daughter, Saint Barbara. *I* know nothing. But where have you seen Ferruccio? Saint Barbara says that he never saw you in his life, and has not thirty crowns in the world.

THE GIRL. Oh, why does not Saint Barbara tell you that I am an honest girl who would not sell herself for a thousand crowns.

THE FRIAR. Do not give way to pride, daughter. Pride is one of the seven deadly sins.

THE GIRL. I know that, father; and believe me, I'm humble and good. I swear to you by Our Lady that it is not Ferruccio's love that I must take, but his life. [*The Friar, startled, turns powerfully on her*]. Do not be angry, dear father: do not cast me off. What is a poor girl to do? We are very poor, my father and I. And I am not to kill him. I am only to decoy him here; for he is a devil for women; and once he is in the inn, my father will do the rest.

THE FRIAR. [*in a rich baritone voice*] Will he, by thunder and lightning and the flood and all the saints, will he? [*He flings off his gown and beard, revealing himself as a handsome youth, a nobleman by his dress, as he springs up and rushes to the door of the inn, which he batters with a stone*]. Ho there, Squarcio, rascal, assassin, son of a pig: come out that I may break every bone in your carcass.

THE GIRL. You are a young man!

THE FRIAR. Another miracle of Saint Barbara. [*Kicking the door*] Come out, whelp: come out, rat. Come out and be killed. Come out and be beaten to a jelly. Come out, dog, swine, animal, mangy hound, lousy – [*Squarcio comes out, sword in hand*]. Do you know who I am, dog?

SQUARCIO [*impressed*] No, your Excellency.

THE FRIAR. I am Ferruccio, Count Ferruccio, the man you are to kill, the man your devil of a daughter is to decoy, the man who is now going to cut you into forty thousand pieces and throw you into the lake.

SQUARCIO. Keep your temper, Signor Count.

FERRUCCIO. I'll not keep my temper. Ive an uncontrollable

temper. I get blinding splitting headaches if I do not relieve my temper by acts of violence. I'll relieve it now by pounding you to jelly, assassin that you are.

SQUARCIO [*shrugging his shoulders*] As you please, Signor Count. I may as well earn my money now as another time. [*He handles his sword*].

FERRUCCIO. Ass: do you suppose I have trusted myself in this territory without precautions? My father has made a wager with your feudal lord here about me.

SQUARCIO. What wager, may it please your Excellency?

FERRUCCIO. What wager, blockhead! Why, that if I am assassinated, the murderer will not be brought to justice.

SQUARCIO. So that if I kill you —

FERRUCCIO. Your Baron will lose ten crowns unless you are broken on the wheel for it.

SQUARCIO. Only ten crowns, Excellency! Your father does not value your life very highly.

FERRUCCIO. Dolt. Can you not reason? If the sum were larger your Baron would win it by killing me himself and breaking somebody else on the wheel for it: you, most likely. Ten crowns is just enough to make him break you on the wheel if you kill me, but not enough to pay for all the masses that would have to be said for him if the guilt were his.

SQUARCIO. That is very clever, Excellency. [*Sheathing his sword*]. You shall not be slain: I will take care of that. If anything happens, it will be an accident.

FERRUCCIO. Body of Bacchus! I forgot that trick. I should have killed you when my blood was hot.

SQUARCIO. Will your Excellency please to step in? My best room and my best cooking are at your Excellency's disposal.

FERRUCCIO. To the devil with your mangy kennel! You want to tell every traveller that Count Ferruccio slept in your best bed and was eaten by your army of fleas. Take yourself out of my sight when you have told me where the next inn is.

SQUARCIO. I'm sorry to thwart your Excellency; but I have not forgotten your father's wager; and until you leave this territory I shall stick to you like your shadow.

FERRUCCIO. And why, pray?

SQUARCIO. Someone else might kill your Excellency; and, as you say, my illustrious Baron might break me on the wheel for your father's ten crowns. I must protect your Excellency, whether your Excellency is willing or not.

FERRUCCIO. If you dare to annoy me, I'll handle your bones so that there will be nothing left for the hangman to break. Now what do you say?

SQUARCIO. I say that your Excellency over-rates your Excellency's strength. You would have no more chance against me than a grasshopper. [*Ferruccio makes a demonstration*]. Oh, I know that your Excellency has been taught by fencers and wrestlers and the like; but I can take all you can give me without turning a hair, and settle the account when you are out of breath. That is why common men are dangerous, your Excellency: they are inured to toil and endurance. Besides, I know all the tricks.

THE GIRL. Do not attempt to quarrel with my father, Count. It must be as he says. It is his profession to kill. What could you do against him? If you want to beat somebody, you must beat me. [*She goes into the inn*].

SQUARCIO. I advise you not to try that, Excellency. She also is very strong.

FERRUCCIO. Then I shall have a headache: thats all. [*He throws himself ill-humoredly on a bench at the table outside the inn. Giulia returns with a tablecloth and begins preparing the table for a meal*].

SQUARCIO. A good supper, Excellency, will prevent that. And Giulia will sing for you.

FERRUCCIO. Not while theres a broomstick in the house to break her ugly head with. Do you suppose I'm going to listen to the howling of a she-wolf who wanted me to absolve her for getting me killed?

SQUARCIO. The poor must live as well as the rich, sir. Giulia is a good girl. [*He goes into the inn*].

FERRUCCIO [*shouting after him*] Must the rich die that the poor may live?

GIULIA. The poor often die that the rich may live.

FERRUCCIO. What an honor for them! But it would have been no honor for me to die merely that you might marry your clod of a fisherman.

GIULIA. You are spiteful, Signor.

FERRUCCIO. I am no troubadour, Giuliaccia, if that is what you mean.

GIULIA. How did you know about my Sandro and his mother? How were you so wise when you pretended to be an old friar? you that are so childish now that you are yourself?

FERRUCCIO. I take it that either Saint Barbara inspired me, or else that you are a great fool.

GIULIA. Saint Barbara will surely punish you for that wicked lie you told about her hand.

FERRUCCIO. The hand that thrilled you?

GIULIA. That was blasphemy. You should not have done it. You made me feel as if I had had a taste of heaven; and then you poisoned it in my heart as a taste of hell. That was wicked and cruel. You nobles are cruel.

FERRUCCIO. Well! do you expect us to nurse your babies for you? Our work is to rule and to fight. Ruling is nothing but inflicting cruelties on wrong-doers: fighting is nothing but being cruel to one's enemies. You poor people leave us all the cruel work, and then wonder that we are cruel. Where would you be if we left it undone? Outside the life I lead all to myself – the life of thought and poetry – I know only two pleasures: cruelty and lust. I desire revenge: I desire women. And both of them disappoint me when I get them.

GIULIA. It would have been a good deed to kill you, I think.

FERRUCCIO. Killing is always sport, my Giuliaccia.

SANDRO'S VOICE [on the lake] Giulietta! Giulietta!

FERRUCCIO [calling to him] Stop that noise. Your Giulietta is here with a young nobleman. Come up and amuse him. [To Giulietta] What will you give me if I tempt him to defy his mother and marry you without a dowry?

GIULIA. You are tempting me. A poor girl can give no more than she has. I should think you were a devil if you were not a noble, which is worse. [She goes out to meet Sandro].

FERRUCCIO [calling after her] The devil does evil for pure love of it: he does not ask a price: he offers it. [Squarcio returns]. Prepare supper for four, bandit.

SQUARCIO. Is your appetite so great in this heat, Signor?

FERRUCCIO. There will be four to supper. You, I, your daughter, and Sandro. Do not stint yourselves: I pay for all. Go and prepare more food.

SQUARCIO. Your order is already obeyed, Excellency.

FERRUCCIO. How?

SQUARCIO. I prepared for four, having you here to pay. The only difference your graciousness makes is that we shall have the honor to eat with you instead of after you.

FERRUCCIO. Dog of a bandit: you should have been born a nobleman.

SQUARCIO. I was born noble, Signor; but as we had no money to maintain our pretensions, I dropped them. [*He goes back into the inn*].

Giulia returns with Sandro.

GIULIA. This is the lad, Excellency. Sandro: this is his lordship Count Ferruccio.

SANDRO. At your lordship's service.

FERRUCCIO. Sit down, Sandro. You, Giulia, and Squarcio are my guests. [*They sit*].

GIULIA. Ive told Sandro everything, Excellency.

FERRUCCIO. And what does Sandro say? [*Squarcio returns with a tray*].

GIULIA. He says that if you have ten crowns in your purse, and we kill you, we can give them to the Baron. It would be the same to him as if he got it from your illustrious father.

SQUARCIO. Stupid: the Count is cleverer than you think. No matter how much money you give the Baron he can always get ten crowns more by breaking me on the wheel if the Count is killed.

GIULIA. That is true. Sandro did not think of that.

SANDRO [*with cheerful politeness*] Oh! what a head I have! I am not clever, Excellency. At the same time you must know that I did not mean my Giulietta to tell you. I know my duty to your Excellency better than that.

FERRUCCIO. Come! You are dear people: charming people. Let us get to work at the supper. You shall be the mother of the family and give us our portions, Giulietta. [*They take their places*]. Thats right. Serve me last, Giulietta. Sandro is hungry.

SQUARCIO [*to the girl*] Come come! do you not see that his Excellency will touch nothing until we have had some first. [*He eats*]. See, Excellency! I have tasted everything. To tell you the truth, poisoning is an art I do not understand.

FERRUCCIO. Very few professional poisoners do, Squarcio. One of the best professionals in Rome poisoned my uncle and aunt. They are alive still. The poison cured my uncle's gout, and only made my aunt thin, which was exactly what she desired, poor lady, as she was losing her figure terribly.

SQUARCIO. There is nothing like the sword, Excellency.

SANDRO. Except the water, Father Squarcio. Trust a fisherman to know that. Nobody can tell that drowning was not an accident.

FERRUCCIO. What does Giulietta say?

GIULIA. I should not kill a man if I hated him. You cannot torment a man when he is dead. Men kill because they think it is what they call a satisfaction. But that is only fancy.

FERRUCCIO. And if you loved him? Would you kill him then?

GIULIA. Perhaps. If you love a man you are his slave: everything he says – everything he does – is a stab to your heart: every day is a long dread of losing him. Better kill him if there be no other escape.

FERRUCCIO. How well you have brought up your family, Squarcio! Some more omelette, Sandro?

SANDRO [*very cheerfully*] I thank your Excellency. [*He accepts and eats with an appetite*].

FERRUCCIO. I pledge you all. To the sword and the fisherman's net: to love and hate! [*He drinks: they drink with him*].

SQUARCIO. To the sword!

SANDRO. To the net, Excellency, with thanks for the honor.

GIULIA. To love, Signor.

FERRUCCIO. To hate: the noble's portion!

SQUARCIO. The meal has done you good, Excellency. How do you feel now?

FERRUCCIO. I feel that there is nothing but a bait of ten crowns between me and death, Squarcio.

SQUARCIO. It is enough, Excellency. And enough is always enough.

SANDRO. Do not think of that, Excellency. It is only that we are poor folk, and have to consider how to make both ends meet as one may say. [*Looking at the dish*] Excellency –?

FERRUCCIO. Finish it, Sandro. Ive done.

SANDRO. Father Squarcio.

SQUARCIO. Finish it, finish it.

SANDRO. Giulietta?

GIULIA [*surprised*] Me? Oh no. Finish it, Sandro: it will only go to the pig.

SANDRO. Then, with your Excellency's permission – [*he helps himself*].

SQUARCIO. Sing for his Excellency, my daughter.

Giulia turns to the door to fetch her mandoline.

FERRUCCIO. I shall jump into the lake Squarcio, if your cat begins to miaowl.

SANDRO [*always cheerful and reassuring*] No, no, Excellency: Giulietta sings very sweetly: have no fear.

FERRUCCIO. I do not care for singing: at least not the singing of peasants. There is only one thing for which one woman will do as well as another, and that is lovemaking. Come, Father Squarcio: I will buy Giulietta from you: you can have her back for nothing when I am tired of her. How much?

SQUARCIO. In ready money, or in promises?

FERRUCCIO. Old fox. Ready money.

SQUARCIO. Fifty crowns, Excellency.

FERRUCCIO. Fifty crowns! Fifty crowns for that black-faced devil! I would not give fifty crowns for one of my mother's ladies-in-waiting. Fifty pence, you must mean.

SQUARCIO. Doubtless your Excellency, being a younger son, is poor. Shall we say five and twenty crowns?

FERRUCCIO. I tell you she is not worth five.

SQUARCIO. Oh, if you come to what she is worth, Excellency, what are any of us worth? I take it that you are a gentleman, not a merchant.

GIULIA. What are you worth, Signorino?

FERRUCCIO. I am accustomed to be asked for favors, Giuliaccia, not to be asked impertinent questions.

GIULIA. What would you do if a strong man took you by the scruff of your neck, or his daughter thrust a knife in your throat, Signor?

FERRUCCIO. It would be many a year, my gentle Giuliaccia, before any baseborn man or woman would dare threaten a nobleman again. The whole village would be flayed alive.

SANDRO. Oh no, Signor. These things often have a great air of being accidents. And the great families are well content that they should appear so. It is such a great trouble to flay a whole village alive. Here by the water, accidents are so common.

SQUARCIO. We of the nobility, Signor, are not strict enough. I learnt that when I took to breeding horses. The horses you breed from thoroughbreds are not all worth the trouble: most of them are screws. Well, the horsebreeder gets rid of his screws for what they will fetch: they go to labor like any peasant's beast. But our nobility does not study its business so carefully. If you are a screw, and the son of a baron, you are brought up to think yourself a little god, though you are nothing, and cannot rule yourself, much less a province. And you presume, and presume, and presume –

GIULIA. And insult, and insult, and insult.

SQUARCIO. Until one day you find yourself in a strange place with nothing to help you but your own hands and your own wits –

GIULIA. And you perish –

SANDRO. Accidentally –

GIULIA. And your soul goes crying to your father for vengeance –

SQUARCIO. If indeed, my daughter, there be any soul left when the body is slain.

FERRUCCIO [*crossing himself hastily*] Dog of a bandit: do you dare doubt the existence of God and the soul?

SQUARCIO. I think, Excellency, that the soul is so precious a gift that God will not give it to a man for nothing. He must earn it by being something and doing something. I should not like to kill a man with a good soul. Ive had a dog that had, I'm persuaded, made itself something of a soul; and if anyone had murdered that dog, I would have slain him. But shew me a man with no soul: one who has never done anything or been anything; and I will kill him for ten crowns with as little remorse as I would stick a pig.

SANDRO. Unless he be a nobleman, of course –

SQUARCIO. In which case the price is fifty crowns.

FERRUCCIO. Soul or no soul?

SQUARCIO. When it comes to a matter of fifty crowns, Excellency, business is business. The man who pays me must square the account with the devil. It is for my employer to consider whether the action be a good one or no: it is for me to earn his money honestly. When I said I should not like to kill a man with a good soul, I meant killing on my own account: not professionally.

FERRUCCIO. Are you such a fool then as to spoil your own trade by sometimes killing people for nothing?

SQUARCIO. One kills a snake for nothing, Excellency. One kills a dog for nothing sometimes.

SANDRO [*apologetically*] Only a mad dog, Excellency, of course.

SQUARCIO. A pet dog, too. One that eats and eats and is useless, and makes an honest man's house dirty. [*He rises*]. Come,

Sandro, and help me to clean up. You, Giulia, stay and entertain his Excellency.

He and Sandro make a hammock of the cloth, in which they carry the wooden platters and fragments of the meal indoors. Ferruccio is left alone with Giulia. The gloaming deepens.

FERRUCCIO. Does your father do the house work with a great girl like you idling about? Squarcio is a fool, after all.

GIULIA. No, Signor: he has left me here to prevent you from escaping.

FERRUCCIO. There is nothing to be gained by killing me, Giuliaccia.

GIULIA. Perhaps; but I do not know. I saw Sandro make a sign to my father: that is why they went in. Sandro has something in his head.

FERRUCCIO [*brutally*] Lice, no doubt.

GIULIA [*unmoved*] That would only make him scratch his head, Signor, not make signs with it to my father. You did wrong to throw the Cardinal out of the window.

FERRUCCIO. Indeed: and pray why?

GIULIA. He will pay thirty crowns for your dead body. Then Sandro could marry me.

FERRUCCIO. And be broken on the wheel for it.

GIULIA. It would look like an accident, Signor. Sandro is very clever; and he is so humble and cheerful and good-tempered that people do not suspect him as they suspect my father.

FERRUCCIO. Giulietta: if I reach Sacromonte in safety, I swear to send you thirty crowns by a sure messenger within ten days. Then you can marry your Sandro. How does that appeal to you?

GIULIA. Your oath is not worth twenty pence, Signor.

FERRUCCIO. Do you think I will die here like a rat in a trap – [*his breath fails him*].

GIULIA. Rats have to wait in their traps for death, Signor. Why not you?

FERRUCCIO. I'll fight.

GIULIA. You are welcome, Signor. The blood flows freeest when it is hot.

FERRUCCIO. She devil! Listen to me, Giulietta –

GIULIA. It is useless, Signor. Giulietta or Giuliaccia: it makes no difference. If they two in there kill you it will be no more to me – except for the money – than if my father trod on a snail.

FERRUCCIO. Oh, it is not possible that I, a nobleman, should die by such filthy hands.

GIULIA. You have lived by them, Signor. I see no sign of any work on your own hands. We can bring death as well as life, we poor people, Signor.

FERRUCCIO. Mother of God, what shall I do?

GIULIA. Pray, Signor.

FERRUCCIO. Pray! With the taste of death in my mouth? I can think of nothing.

GIULIA. It is only that you have forgotten your beads, Signor [*she picks up the Friar's rosary*]. You remember the old man's bones rattling. Here they are [*she rattles them before him*].

FERRUCCIO. That reminds me. I know of a painter in the north that can paint such beautiful saints that the heart goes out of one's body to look at them. If I get out of this alive I'll make him paint St Barbara so that every one can see that she is lovelier than St Cecilia, who looks like my washerwoman's mother in her Chapel in our cathedral. Can you give St Cecilia a picture if she lets me be killed?

GIULIA. No; but I can give her many prayers.

FERRUCCIO. Prayers cost nothing. She will prefer the picture unless she is a greater fool than I take her to be.

GIULIA. She will thank the painter for it, not you, Signor. And I'll tell her in my prayers to appear to the painter in a vision, and order him to paint her just as he sees her if she really wishes to be painted.

FERRUCCIO. You are devilishly ready with your answers. Tell me, Giulietta: is what your father told me true? Is your blood really noble?

GIULIA. It is red, Signor, like the blood of the Christ in the picture in Church. I do not know if yours is different. I shall see when my father kills you.

FERRUCCIO. Do you know what I am thinking, Giulietta?

GIULIA. No, Signor.

FERRUCCIO. I am thinking that if the good God would oblige me by taking my fool of an elder brother up to heaven, and his silly doll of a wife with him before she has time to give him a son, you would make a rare duchess for me. Come! Will you help me to outwit your father and Sandro if I marry you afterwards?

GIULIA. No, Signor: I'll help them to kill you.

FERRUCCIO. My back is to the wall, then?

GIULIA. To the precipice, I think, Signor.

FERRUCCIO. No matter, so my face is to the danger. Did you notice, Giulia, a minute ago? I was frightened.

GIULIA. Yes, Signor. I saw it in your face.

FERRUCCIO. The terror of terrors.

GIULIA. The terror of death.

FERRUCCIO. No: death is nothing. I can face a stab just as I faced having my tooth pulled out at Faenza.

GIULIA [*shuddering with sincere sympathy*] Poor Signorino! That must have hurt horribly.

FERRUCCIO. What! You pity me for the tooth affair, and you did not pity me in that hideous agony of terror that is not the terror of death nor of anything else, but pure grim terror in itself.

GIULIA. It was the terror of the soul, Signor. And I do not pity your soul: you have a wicked soul. But you have pretty teeth.

FERRUCCIO. The toothache lasted a week; but the agony of my soul was too dreadful to last five minutes: I should have died of it if it could have kept its grip of me. But you helped me out of it.

GIULIA. I, Signor!

FERRUCCIO. Yes: you. If you had pitied me: if you had been less inexorable than death itself, I should have broken down and cried and begged for mercy. But now I have come up against something hard: something real: something that does not care for me. I see now the truth of my excellent uncle's opinion that I was a spoilt cub. When I wanted anything I threatened men or ran crying to women; and they gave it to me. I dreamed and romanced: imagining things as I wanted them, not as they really are. There is nothing like a good look into the face of death: close up: right on you: for shewing you how little you really believe and how little you really are. A priest said to me once, 'In your last hour everything will fall away from you except your religion.' But I have lived through my last hour; and my religion was the first thing that fell away from me. When I was forced at last to believe in grim death I knew at last what belief was, and that I had never believed in anything before: I had only flattered myself with pretty stories, and sheltered myself behind Mumbo Jumbo, as a soldier will shelter himself from arrows behind a clump of thistles that only hide the shooters from him. When I believe in everything that is real as I believed for that moment in death, then I shall be a man at last. I have tasted the water of life from the cup of death; and it may be now that my real life began with this [*he holds up the rosary*] and will end with the triple crown or the heretic's fire: I care not which. [*Springing to his feet*] Come out, then, dog of a bandit, and fight a man who has found his soul. [*Squarcio appears at the door, sword in hand. Ferruccio leaps at him and strikes him full in the chest with his dagger. Squarcio puts back his left foot to brace himself against the shock. The dagger snaps as if it had struck a stone wall*].

GIULIA. Quick, Sandro.

Sandro, who has come stealing round the corner of the inn with a fishing net, casts it over Ferruccio, and draws it tight.

SQUARCIO. Your Excellency will excuse my shirt of mail. A good home blow, nevertheless, Excellency.

SANDRO. Your Excellency will excuse my net: it is a little damp.

FERRUCCIO. Well, what now? Accidental drowning, I suppose.

SANDRO. Eh, Excellency, it is such a pity to throw a good fish back into the water when once you have got him safe in your net. My Giulietta: hold the net for me.

GIULIA [*taking the net and twisting it in her hands to draw it tighter round him*] I have you very fast now, Signorino, like a little bird in a cage.

FERRUCCIO. You have my body, Giulia. My soul is free.

GIULIA. Is it, Signor? I think Saint Barbara has got that in her net too. She has turned your jest into earnest.

SANDRO. It is indeed true, sir, that those who come under the special protection of God and the Saints are always a little mad; and this makes us think it very unlucky to kill a madman. And since from what Father Squarcio and I overheard, it is clear that your Excellency, though a very wise and reasonable young gentleman in a general way, is somewhat cracked on the subject of the soul and so forth, we have resolved to see that no harm comes to your Excellency.

FERRUCCIO. As you please. My life is only a drop falling from the vanishing clouds to the everlasting sea, from finite to infinite, and itself part of the infinite.

SANDRO [*impressed*] Your Excellency speaks like a crazy but very holy book. Heaven forbid that we should raise a hand against you! But your Excellency will notice that this good action will cost us thirty crowns.

FERRUCCIO. Is it not worth it?

SANDRO. Doubtless, doubtless. It will in fact save us the price of certain masses which we should otherwise have had said for the souls of certain persons who – ahem! Well, no matter. But we think it dangerous and unbecoming that a nobleman like your Excellency should travel without a retinue, and unarmed; for your dagger is unfortunately broken, Excellency. If you would therefore have the condescension to accept Father Squarcio as your man-at-arms – your servant in all but the name, to save his nobility – he will go with you to any town in which you will feel safe from His Eminence the Cardinal, and will leave it to your Excellency's graciousness as to whether his magnanimous conduct will not then deserve some trifling present: say a wedding gift for my Giulietta.

FERRUCCIO. Good: the man I tried to slay will save me from being slain. Who would have thought Saint Barbara so full of irony!

SANDRO. And if the offer your Excellency was good enough to make in respect of Giulietta still stands –

FERRUCCIO. Rascal: have you then no soul?

SANDRO. I am a poor man, Excellency: I cannot afford these luxuries of the rich.

FERRUCCIO. There is a certain painter will presently make a great picture of St Barbara; and Giulia will be his model. He will pay her well. Giulia: release the bird. It is time for it to fly.

She takes the net from his shoulders

The Dark Lady of
the Sonnets

An Interlude

WITH

Preface

Composition begun 17 June 1910; completed 20 June 1910. First published in German translation, as *Die schwarze Dame der Sonette*, in the *Neue Freie Presse* (Vienna), 25 December 1910. Published in the *English Review* and *Redbook Magazine* (New York), January 1911. First collected in *Misalliance, The Dark Lady of the Sonnets*, and *Fanny's First Play*, 1914. First presented at the Haymarket Theatre, London, on 24 November 1910, for two charity matinées on behalf of the Shakespeare Memorial National Theatre.

The Warder   *Hugh B. Tabberer*
William Shakespear   *Harley Granville Barker*
Queen Elizabeth   *Suzanne Sheldon*
Mary Fitton   *Mona Limerick*

Period – The spacious times of Great Elizabeth. Fin de siècle 15–1600

Scene – *The Terrace, Whitehall Palace. Midsummer Night*

❧ PREFACE ❧

HOW THE PLAY CAME TO BE WRITTEN

I had better explain why, in this little *pièce d'occasion*, written for a performance in aid of the funds of the project of establishing a National Theatre as a memorial to Shakespear, I have identified the Dark Lady with Mistress Mary Fitton. First, let me say that I do not contend that the Dark Lady was Mary Fitton, because when the case in Mary's favor (or against her, if you please to consider that the Dark Lady was no better than she ought to have been) was complete, a portrait of Mary came to light and turned out to be that of a fair lady, not of a dark one. That settles the question, if the portrait is authentic, which I see no reason to doubt, and the lady's hair undyed, which is perhaps less certain. Shakespear rubbed in the lady's complexion in his sonnets mercilessly; for in his day black hair was as unpopular as red hair was in the early days of Queen Victoria. Any tinge lighter than raven black must be held fatal to the strongest claim to be the Dark Lady. And so, unless it can be shewn that Shakespear's sonnets exasperated Mary Fitton into dyeing her hair and getting painted in false colors, I must give up all pretence that my play is historical. The later suggestion of Mr Acheson that the Dark Lady, far from being a maid of honor, kept a tavern in Oxford, and was the mother of Davenant the poet, is the one I should have adopted had I wished to be up to date. Why, then, did I introduce the Dark Lady as Mistress Fitton?

Well, I had two reasons. The play was not to have been written by me at all, but by Dame Edith Lyttelton; and it was she who suggested a scene of jealousy between Queen Elizabeth and the Dark Lady at the expense of the unfortunate Bard. Now this, if the Dark Lady was a maid of honor, was quite easy. If she were a tavern landlady, it would have strained all probability. So I stuck to Mary Fitton. But I had another and more personal reason. I was, in a manner, present at the birth of the Fitton theory. Its parent and I had become acquainted; and he used to consult me on obscure passages in the sonnets, on which, as far as I can remember, I never succeeded in throwing the faintest light, at a time when nobody else thought my opinion, on that or any other subject, of the slightest importance. I thought it would be friendly to immortalize him, as the silly literary saying is, much as Shakespear immortalized Mr W. H., as he said he would, simply by writing about him.

Let me tell the story formally.

THOMAS TYLER

Throughout the eighties at least, and probably for some years before, the British Museum reading room was used daily by a gentleman of such astonishing and crushing ugliness that no one who had once seen him could ever thereafter forget him. He was of fair complexion, rather golden red than sandy; aged between forty-five and sixty; and dressed in frock coat and tall hat of presentable but never new appearance. His figure was rectangular, waistless, neckless, ankleless, of middle height, looking shortish because, though he was not particularly stout, there was nothing slender about him. His ugliness was not unamiable: it was accidental, external, excrescential. Attached to his face from the left ear to the point of his chin was a monstrous goitre, which hung down to his collar bone, and was very inadequately balanced by a smaller one on his right eyelid. Nature's malice was so overdone in his case that it somehow failed to produce the effect of repulsion it seemed to have aimed at. When you first met Thomas Tyler you could think of nothing else but whether surgery could really do nothing for him. But after a very brief acquaintance you never thought of his disfigurements at all, and talked to him as you might to Romeo or Lovelace; only, so many people, especially women, would not risk the preliminary ordeal, that he remained a man apart and a bachelor all his days. I am not to be frightened or prejudiced by a tumor; and I struck up a cordial acquaintance with him, in the course of which he kept me pretty closely on the track of his work at the Museum, in which I was then, like himself, a daily reader.

He was by profession a man of letters of an uncommercial kind. He was a specialist in pessimism; had made a translation of Ecclesiastes of which eight copies a year were sold; and followed up the pessimism of Shakespear and Swift with keen interest. He delighted in a hideous conception which he called the theory of the cycles, according to which the history of mankind and the universe keeps eternally repeating itself without the slightest variation throughout all eternity; so that he had lived and died and had his goitre before and would live and die and have it again and again and again. He liked to believe that nothing that happened to him was completely novel: he was persuaded that he often had some recollection of its previous occurrence in the last cycle. He hunted out allusions to this favorite theory in his three favorite pessimists. He tried his hand occasionally at deciphering ancient inscriptions, reading them as people seem to read the stars, by discovering bears and bulls and swords and goats where, as it seems to me, no sane human being can see anything but stars higgledy-piggledy. Next to the translation of Ecclesiastes, his *magnum opus* was his work on Shakespear's Sonnets, in which he accepted a previous identification of Mr W. H., the 'onlie begetter' of the sonnets, with the Earl of Pembroke (William Herbert), and promulgated his own identification of Mistress Mary Fitton with the Dark Lady. Whether he was right or wrong about the Dark Lady did not matter urgently to me: she might have been Maria Tompkins for all I cared. But Tyler would have it that she was Mary Fitton; and he tracked Mary down from the first of her marriages in her teens to her tomb in Cheshire, whither he made a pilgrimage and whence returned in triumph with a picture of her statue, and the news that he was convinced she was a dark lady by traces of paint still discernible.

In due course he published his edition of the Sonnets, with the evidence he had collected. He lent me a copy of the book, which I never returned. But I reviewed it in the Pall Mall Gazette on the 7th of January 1886, and thereby let loose the Fitton theory in a wider circle of readers than the book could reach. Then Tyler died, sinking unnoted like a stone in the sea. I observe that Mr Acheson, Mrs Davenant's champion, calls him Reverend. It may very well be that he got his knowledge of Hebrew in reading for the Church; and there was always something of the clergyman or the school-master in his dress and air. Possibly he may actually have been ordained. But he never told me that or anything else about his affairs; and his black pessimism would have shot him violently out of any church at present established in the West. We never talked about affairs: we talked about Shakespear, and the Dark Lady, and Swift, and Koheleth, and the cycles, and the mysterious moments when a feeling came over us that this had happened to us before, and about the forgeries of the Pentateuch which were offered for sale to the British Museum, and about literature and things of the spirit generally. He always came to my desk at the Museum and spoke to me about something or other, no doubt finding that people who were keen on this sort of conversation were rather scarce. He remains a vivid spot of memory in the void of my forgetfulness, a quite considerable and dignified soul in a grotesquely disfigured body.

FRANK HARRIS

To the review in the Pall Mall Gazette I attribute, rightly or wrongly, the introduction of Mary Fitton to Mr Frank Harris. My reason for this is that Mr Harris wrote a play about Shakespear and Mary Fitton; and when I, as a pious duty to Tyler's ghost, reminded the world that it was to Tyler we owed the Fitton theory, Frank Harris, who clearly had not a notion of what had first put Mary into his head, believed, I think, that I had invented Tyler expressly for his discomfiture; for the stress I laid on Tyler's claims must have seemed unaccountable and perhaps malicious on the assumption that he was to me a mere name among the thousands of names in the British Museum catalogue. Therefore I make it clear that I had and have personal reasons for remembering Tyler, and for regarding myself as in some sort charged with the duty of reminding the world of his work. I am sorry for his sake that Mary's portrait is fair, and that Mr W. H. has veered round again from Pembroke to Southampton; but even so his work was not wasted: it is by exhausting all the hypotheses that we reach the verifiable one; and after all, the wrong road always leads somewhere.

Frank Harris's play was written long before mine. I read it in manuscript before the Shakespear Memorial National Theatre was mooted; and if there is anything except the Fitton theory (which is Tyler's property) in my play which is also in Mr Harris's it was I who annexed it from him and not he from me. It does not matter anyhow, because this play of mine is a brief trifle, and full of manifest impossibilities at that; whilst Mr Harris's play is serious both in size, intention, and quality. But there could not in the nature of things be much resemblance, because Frank conceives Shakespear to have been a broken-hearted, melancholy, enormously sentimental person, whereas I am convinced that he was very like myself: in fact, if I had been born in 1556 instead of 1856, I should have taken to blank verse and given Shakespear a harder run for his money than all the other Elizabethans put together. Yet the success of Frank Harris's book on Shakespear gave me great delight.

To those who know the literary world of London there was a sharp stroke of ironic comedy in the irresistible verdict in its favor. In critical literature there is one prize that is always open to competition, one blue ribbon that always carries the highest critical rank with it. To win, you must write the best book of your generation on Shakespear. It is felt on all sides that to do this a certain fastidious refinement, a delicacy of taste, a correctness of manner and tone, and high academic distinction in addition to the indispensable scholarship and literary reputation, are needed; and men who pretend to these qualifications are constantly looked to with a gentle expectation that presently they will achieve the great feat. Now if there is a man on earth who is the utter contrary of everything that this description implies; whose very existence is an insult to the ideal it realizes; whose eye disparages, whose resonant voice denounces, whose cold shoulder jostles every decency, every delicacy, every amenity, every dignity, every sweet usage of that quiet life of mutual admiration in which perfect Shakespearean appreciation is expected to arise, that man is Frank Harris. Here is one who is extraordinarily qualified, by a range of sympathy and understanding that extends from the ribaldry of a buccaneer to the shyest tendernesses of the most sensitive poetry, to be all things to all men, yet whose proud humor it is to be to every man, provided the man is eminent and pretentious, the champion of his enemies. To the Archbishop he is an atheist, to the atheist a Catholic mystic, to the Bismarckian Imperialist an Anacharsis Klootz, to Anacharsis Klootz a Washington, to Mrs Proudie a Don Juan, to Aspasia a John Knox: in short, to everyone his complement rather than his counterpart, his antagonist rather than his fellow-creature. Always provided, however, that the persons thus affronted are respectable persons. Sophie Perovskaia, who perished on the scaffold for blowing Alexander II to fragments, may perhaps have echoed Hamlet's

> Oh God, Horatio, what a wounded name –
> Things standing thus unknown – I leave behind!

but Frank Harris, in his Sonia, has rescued her from that injustice, and enshrined her among the saints. He has lifted the Chicago anarchists out of their infamy, and shewn that, compared with the Capitalism that killed them, they were heroes and martyrs. He has done this with the most unusual power of conviction. The story, as he tells it, inevitably and irresistibly displaces all the vulgar, mean, purblind, spiteful versions. There is a precise realism and an unsmiling, measured, determined sincerity which gives a strange dignity to the work of one whose fixed practice and ungovernable impulse it is to kick conventional dignity whenever he sees it.

HARRIS 'DURCH MITLEID WISSEND'

Frank Harris is everything except a humorist, not, apparently, from stupidity, but because scorn overcomes humor in him. Nobody ever dreamt of reproaching Milton's Lucifer for not seeing the comic side of his fall; and nobody who has read Mr Harris's stories desires to have them lightened by chapters from the hand of Artemus Ward. Yet he knows the taste and the value of humor. He was one of the few men of letters who really appreciated Oscar Wilde, though he did not rally fiercely to Wilde's side until the world deserted Oscar in his ruin. I myself was present at a curious meeting between the two, when Harris, on the eve of the Queensberry trial, prophesied to Wilde with miraculous precision exactly what immediately afterwards happened to him, and warned him to leave the country. It was the first time within my knowledge that such a forecast proved true. Wilde, though under no illusion as to the folly of the quite unselfish suit-at-law he had been persuaded to begin, nevertheless so miscalculated the force of the social vengeance he was unloosing on himself that he fancied it could be stayed by putting up the editor of The Saturday Review (as Mr Harris then was) to declare that he considered Dorian Gray a highly moral book, which it certainly is. When Harris foretold him the truth, Wilde denounced him as a fainthearted friend who was failing him in his hour of need, and left the room in anger. Harris's idiosyncratic power of pity saved him from feeling or shewing the smallest resentment; and events presently proved to Wilde how insanely he had been advised in taking the action, and how accurately Harris had gauged the situation.

The same capacity for pity governs Harris's study of Shakespear, whom, as I have said, he pities too much; but that he is not insensible to humor is shewn not only by his appreciation of Wilde, but by the fact that the group of contributors who made his editorship of The Saturday Review so remarkable, and of whom I speak none the less highly because I happened to be one of them myself, were all, in their various ways, humorists.

'SIDNEY'S SISTER: PEMBROKE'S MOTHER'

And now to return to Shakespear. Though Mr Harris followed Tyler in identifying Mary Fitton as the Dark Lady, and the Earl of Pembroke as the addressee of the other sonnets and the man who made love successfully to Shakespear's mistress, he very characteristically refuses to follow Tyler on one point, though for the life of me I cannot remember whether it was one of the surmises which Tyler published, or only one which he submitted to me to see what I would say about it, just as he used to submit difficult lines from the sonnets.

This surmise was that 'Sidney's sister: Pembroke's mother' set Shakespear on to persuade Pembroke to marry, and that this was the explanation of those earlier sonnets which so persistently and unnaturally urged matrimony on Mr W. H. I take this to be one of the brightest of Tyler's ideas, because the persuasions in the sonnets are unaccountable and out of character unless they were offered to please somebody whom Shakespear desired to please, and who took a motherly interest in Pembroke. There is a further temptation in the theory for me. The most charming of all Shakespear's old women, indeed the most charming of all his women, young or old, is the Countess of Rousillon in All's Well That Ends Well. It has a certain individuality among them which suggests a portrait. Mr Harris will have it that all Shakespear's nice old women are drawn from his beloved mother; but I see no evidence whatever that Shakespear's mother was a particularly nice woman or that he was particularly fond of her. That she was a simple incarnation of extravagant maternal pride like the mother of Coriolanus in Plutarch, as Mr Harris asserts, I cannot believe: she is quite as likely to have borne her son a grudge for becoming 'one of these harlotry players' and disgracing the Ardens. Anyhow, as a conjectural model for the Countess of Rousillon, I prefer that one of whom Jonson wrote

> Sidney's sister: Pembroke's mother:
> Death ere thou has slain another,
> Learned and fair and good as she,
> Time shall throw a dart at thee.

But Frank will not have her at any price, because his ideal Shakespear is rather like a sailor in a melodrama; and a sailor in a melodrama must adore his mother. I do not at all belittle such sailors. They are the emblems of human generosity; but Shakespear was not an emblem; he was a man and the author of Hamlet, who had no illusions about his mother. In weak moments one almost wishes he had.

SHAKESPEAR'S SOCIAL STANDING

On the vexed question of Shakespear's social standing Mr Harris says that Shakespear 'had not had the advantage of a middle-class training.' I suggest that Shakespear missed this questionable advantage, not because he was socially too low to have attained to it, but because he conceived himself as belonging to the upper class from which our public school boys are now drawn. Let Mr Harris survey for a moment the field of contemporary journalism. He will see there some men who have the very characteristics from which he infers that Shakespear was at a social disadvantage through his lack of middle-class training. They are rowdy, ill-mannered, abusive, mischievous, fond of quoting obscene schoolboy anecdotes, adepts in that sort of blackmail which consists in mercilessly libelling and insulting every writer whose opinions are sufficiently heterodox to make it almost impossible for him to risk perhaps five years of a slender income by an appeal to a prejudiced orthodox jury; and they see nothing in all this cruel blackguardism but an uproariously jolly rag, although they are by no means without genuine literary ability, a love of letters, and even some artistic conscience. But he will find not one of the models of this type (I say nothing of mere imitators of it) below the rank that looks at the middle class, not humbly and enviously from below, but insolently from above. Mr Harris himself notes Shakespear's contempt for the tradesman and mechanic, and his incorrigible addiction to smutty jokes. He does us the public service of sweeping away the familiar plea of the Bardolatrous ignoramus, that Shakespear's coarseness was part of the manners of his time, putting his pen with precision on the one name, Spenser, that is necessary to expose such a libel on Elizabethan decency. There was nothing whatever to prevent Shakespear from being as decent as More was before him, or Bunyan after him, and as self-respecting as Raleigh or Sidney, except the tradition of his class, in which education or statesmanship may no doubt be acquired by those who have a turn for them, but in which insolence, derision, profligacy, obscene jesting, debt contracting, and rowdy mischievousness, give continual scandal to the pious, serious, industrious, solvent bourgeois. No other class is infatuated enough to believe that gentlemen are born and not made by a very elaborate process of culture. Even kings are taught and coached and drilled from their earliest boyhood to play their part. But the man of family (I am convinced that Shakespear took that view of himself) will plunge into society without a lesson in table manners, into politics without a lesson in history, into the city without a lesson in business, and into the army without a lesson in honor.

It has been said, with the object of proving Shakespear a laborer, that he could hardly write his name. Why? Because he 'had not the advantage of a middle-class training.' Shakespear himself tells us, through Hamlet, that gentlemen purposely wrote badly lest they should be mistaken for scriveners; but most of them, then as now, wrote badly because they could not write any better. In short, the

whole range of Shakespear's foibles: the snobbishness, the naughti-
ness, the contempt for tradesmen and mechanics, the assumption
that witty conversation can only mean smutty conversation, the
flunkeyism towards social superiors and insolence towards social
inferiors, the easy ways with servants which is seen not only
between The Two Gentlemen of Verona and their valets, but in the
affection and respect inspired by a great servant like Adam: all
these are the characteristics of Eton and Harrow, not of the public
elementary or private adventure school. They prove, as everything
we know about Shakespear suggests, that he thought of the
Shakespears and Ardens as families of consequence, and regarded
himself as a gentleman under a cloud through his father's ill luck in
business, and never for a moment as a man of the people. This is at
once the explanation of and excuse for his snobbery. He was not a
parvenu trying to cover his humble origin with a purchased coat of
arms: he was a gentleman resuming what he conceived to be his
natural position as soon as he gained the means to keep it up.

THIS SIDE IDOLATRY

There is another matter which I think Mr Harris should ponder.
He says that Shakespear was but 'little esteemed by his own
generation.' He even describes Jonson's description of his 'little
Latin and less Greek' as a sneer, whereas it occurs in an unmistakeably sincere eulogy of Shakespear, written after his death, and is
clearly meant to heighten the impression of Shakespear's pro-
digious natural endowments by pointing out that they were not
due to scholastic acquirements. Now there is a sense in which it is
true enough that Shakespear was too little esteemed by his own
generation, or, for the matter of that, by any subsequent generation. The bargees on the Regent's Canal do not chant Shakespear's
verses as the gondoliers in Venice are said to chant the verses of
Tasso (a practice which was suspended for some reason during my
stay in Venice: at least no gondolier ever did it in my hearing).
Shakespear is no more a popular author than Rodin is a popular
sculptor or Richard Strauss a popular composer. But Shakespear
was certainly not such a fool as to expect the Toms, Dicks, and
Harrys of his time to be any more interested in dramatic poetry
than Newton, later on, expected them to be interested in fluxions.
And when we come to the question whether Shakespear missed
that assurance which all great men have had from the more

capable and susceptible members of their generation that they were great men, Ben Jonson's evidence disposes of so improbable a notion at once and for ever. 'I loved the man,' says Ben, 'this side idolatry, as well as any.' Now why in the name of common sense should he have made that qualification unless there had been, not only idolatry, but idolatry fulsome enough to irritate Jonson into an express disavowal of it? Jonson, the bricklayer, must have felt sore sometimes when Shakespear spoke and wrote of bricklayers as his inferiors. He must have felt it a little hard that being a better scholar, and perhaps a braver and tougher man physically than Shakespear, he was not so successful or so well liked. But in spite of this he praised Shakespear to the utmost stretch of his powers of eulogy: in fact, notwithstanding his disclaimer, he did not stop 'this side idolatry.' If, therefore, even Jonson felt himself forced to clear himself of extravagance and absurdity in his appreciation of Shakespear, there must have been many people about who idolized Shakespear as American ladies idolize Paderewski, and who carried Bardolatry, even in the Bard's own time, to an extent that threatened to make his reasonable admirers ridiculous.

SHAKESPEAR'S PESSIMISM

I submit to Mr Harris that by ruling out this idolatry, and its possible effect in making Shakespear think that his public would stand anything from him, he has ruled out a far more plausible explanation of the faults of such a play as Timon of Athens than his theory that Shakespear's passion for the Dark Lady 'cankered and took on proud flesh in him, and tortured him to nervous breakdown and madness.' In Timon the intellectual bankruptcy is obvious enough: Shakespear tried once too often to make a play out of the cheap pessimism which is thrown into despair by a comparison of actual human nature with theoretical morality, actual law and administration with abstract justice, and so forth. But Shakespear's perception of the fact that all men, judged by the moral standard which they apply to others and by which they justify their punishment of others, are fools and scoundrels, does not date from the Dark Lady complication: he seems to have been born with it. If in The Comedy of Errors and A Midsummer Night's Dream the persons of the drama are not quite so ready for treachery and murder as Laertes and even Hamlet himself (not to mention the procession of ruffians who pass through the latest plays) it is certainly not because they have any more regard for law or religion. There is only one place in Shakespear's plays where the sense of shame is used as a human attribute; and that is where Hamlet is ashamed, not of anything he himself has done, but of his mother's relations with his uncle. This scene is an unnatural one: the son's reproaches to his mother, even the fact of his being able to discuss the subject with her, is more repulsive than her relations with her deceased husband's brother.

Here, too, Shakespear betrays for once his religious sense by making Hamlet, in his agony of shame, declare that his mother's conduct makes 'sweet religion a rhapsody of words.' But for that passage we might almost suppose that the feeling of Sunday morning in the country which Orlando describes so perfectly in As You Like It was the beginning and end of Shakespear's notion of religion. I say almost, because Isabella in Measure for Measure has religious charm, in spite of the conventional theatrical assumption that female religion means an inhumanly ferocious chastity. But for the most part Shakespear differentiates his heroes from his villains much more by what they do than by what they are. Don Juan in Much Ado is a true villain: a man with a malicious will; but he is too dull a duffer to be of any use in a leading part; and when we come to the great villains like Macbeth, we find, as Mr Harris points out, that they are precisely identical with the heroes: Macbeth is only Hamlet incongruously committing murders and engaging in hand-to-hand combats. And Hamlet, who does not dream of apologizing for the three murders he commits, is always apologizing because he has not yet committed a fourth, and finds, to his great bewilderment, that he does not want to commit it. 'It cannot be,' he says, 'but I am pigeon-livered, and lack gall to make oppression bitter; else, ere this, I should have fatted all the region kites with this slave's offal.' Really one is tempted to suspect that when Shylock asks 'Hates any man the thing he would not kill?' he is expressing the natural and proper sentiments of the human race as Shakespear understood them, and not the vindictiveness of a stage Jew.

GAIETY OF GENIUS

In view of these facts, it is dangerous to cite Shakespear's pessimism as evidence of the despair of a heart broken by the Dark Lady. There is an irrepressible gaiety of genius which enables it to bear the whole weight of the world's misery without blenching. There is a laugh always ready to avenge its tears of discouragement. In the lines which Mr Harris quotes only to declare that he can make nothing of them, and to condemn them as out of character, Richard III, immediately after pitying himself because

> There is no creature loves me
> And if I die no soul will pity me,

adds, with a grin,

> Nay, wherefore should they, since that I myself
> Find in myself no pity for myself?

Let me again remind Mr Harris of Oscar Wilde. We all dreaded to read De Profundis: our instinct was to stop our ears, or run away from the wail of a broken, though by no means contrite, heart. But we were throwing away our pity. De Profundis was de profundis indeed: Wilde was too good a dramatist to throw away so powerful an effect; but none the less it was de profundis in excelsis. There was more laughter between the lines of that book than in a thousand farces by men of no genius. Wilde, like Richard and Shakespear, found in himself no pity for himself. There is nothing that marks the born dramatist more unmistakeably than this discovery of comedy in his own misfortunes almost in proportion to the pathos with which the ordinary man announces their tragedy. I cannot for the life of me see the broken heart in Shakespear's latest works. 'Hark, hark! the lark at heaven's gate sings' is not the lyric of a broken man; nor is Cloten's comment that if Imogen does not appreciate it, 'it is a vice in her ears which horse hairs, and cats' guts, and the voice of unpaved eunuch to boot, can never amend,' the sally of a saddened one. Is it not clear that to the last there was in Shakespear an incorrigible divine levity, an inexhaustible joy that derided sorrow? Think of the poor Dark Lady having to stand up to this unbearable power of extracting a grim fun from everything. Mr Harris writes as if Shakespear did all the suffering and the Dark Lady all the cruelty. But why does he not put himself in the Dark Lady's place for a moment as he has put himself so successfully in Shakespear's? Imagine her reading the hundred and thirtieth sonnet!

> My mistress' eyes are nothing like the sun;
> Coral is far more red than her lips' red;

If snow be white, why then her breasts are dun;
If hairs be wire, black wires grow on her head;
I have seen roses damasked, red and white,
But no such roses see I in her cheeks;
And in some perfumes is there more delight
Than in the breath that from my mistress reeks.
I love to hear her speak; yet well I know
That music hath a far more pleasing sound.
I grant I never saw a goddess go:
My mistress, when she walks, treads on the ground.
    And yet, by heaven, I think my love as rare
    As any she belied with false compare.

Take this as a sample of the sort of compliment from which she was never for a moment safe with Shakespear. Bear in mind that she was not a comedian; that the Elizabethan fashion of treating brunettes as ugly women must have made her rather sore on the subject of her complexion; that no human being, male or female, can conceivably enjoy being chaffed on that point in the fourth couplet about the perfumes; that Shakespear's revulsions, as the sonnet immediately preceding shews, were as violent as his ardors, and were expressed with the realistic power and horror that makes Hamlet say that the heavens got sick when they saw the queen's conduct; and then ask Mr Harris whether any woman could have stood it for long, or have thought the 'sugred' compliment worth the cruel wounds, the cleaving of the heart in twain, that seemed to Shakespear as natural and amusing a reaction as the burlesquing of his heroics by Pistol, his sermons by Falstaff, and his poems by Cloten and Touchstone.

JUPITER AND SEMELE

This does not mean that Shakespear was cruel: evidently he was not; but it was not cruelty that made Jupiter reduce Semele to ashes: it was the fact that he could not help being a god nor she help being a mortal. The one thing Shakespear's passion for the Dark Lady was not, was what Mr Harris in one passage calls it: idolatrous. If it had been, she might have been able to stand it. The man who dotes 'yet doubts; suspects, yet strongly loves,' is tolerable even by a spoilt and tyrannical mistress; but what woman could possibly endure a man who dotes without doubting; who *knows* and who is hugely amused at the absurdity of his infatuation for a woman of whose mortal imperfections not one escapes him: a man always exchanging grins with Yorick's skull, and inviting 'my lady' to laugh at the sepulchral humor of the fact that though she paint an inch thick (which the Dark Lady may have done), to Yorick's favor she must come at last. To the Dark Lady he must sometimes have seemed cruel beyond description: an intellectual Caliban. True, a Caliban who could say

> Be not afeard: the isle is full of noises,
> Sounds and sweet airs that give delight and hurt not.
> Sometimes a thousand twangling instruments
> Will hum about mine ears; and sometimes voices,
> That, if I then had waked after long sleep,
> Will make me sleep again; and then, in dreaming,
> The clouds, methought, would open and shew riches
> Ready to drop on me: that when I wak'd
> I cried to dream again.

which is very lovely; but the Dark Lady may have had that vice in her ears which Cloten dreaded: she may not have seen the beauty of it, whereas there can be no doubt at all that of 'My mistress' eyes are nothing like the sun,' &c., not a word was lost on her.

And is it to be supposed that Shakespear was too stupid or too modest not to see at last that it was a case of Jupiter and Semele? Shakespear was most certainly not modest in that sense. The timid cough of the minor poet was never heard from him.

> Not marble, nor the gilded monuments
> Of princes, shall outlive this powerful rhyme

is only one out of a dozen passages in which he (possibly with a keen sense of the fun of scandalizing the modest coughers) proclaimed his place and his power in 'the wide world dreaming of things to come.' The Dark Lady most likely thought this side of him insufferably conceited; for there is no reason to suppose that she liked his plays any better than Minna Wagner liked Richard's music dramas: as likely as not, she thought The Spanish Tragedy worth six Hamlets. He was not stupid either: if his class limitations and a profession that cut him off from actual participation in great affairs of State had not confined his opportunities of intellectual and political training to private conversation and to the Mermaid

Tavern, he would probably have become one of the ablest men of his time instead of being merely its ablest playwright. One might surmise that Shakespear found out that the Dark Lady's brains could no more keep pace with his than Anne Hathaway's, if there were any evidence that their friendship ceased when he stopped writing sonnets to her. As a matter of fact the consolidation of a passion into an enduring intimacy generally puts an end to sonnets.

That the Dark Lady broke Shakespear's heart, as Mr Harris will have it she did, is an extremely unShakespearean hypothesis. 'Men have died from time to time, and worms have eaten them; but not for love,' says Rosalind. Richard of Gloster, into whom Shakespear put all his own impish superiority to vulgar sentiment, exclaims

> And this word 'love,' which greybeards call divine,
> Be resident in men like one another
> And not in me: I am myself alone.

Hamlet has not a tear for Ophelia: her death moves him to fierce disgust for the sentimentality of Laertes by her grave; and when he discusses the scene with Horatio immediately after, he utterly forgets her, though he is sorry he forgot himself, and jumps at the proposal of a fencing match to finish the day with. As against this view Mr Harris pleads Romeo, Orsino, and even Antonio; and he does it so penetratingly that he convinces you that Shakespear did betray himself again and again in these characters; but self-betrayal is one thing; and self-portrayal, as in Hamlet and Mercutio, is another. Shakespear never 'saw himself,' as actors say, in Romeo or Orsino or Antonio. In Mr Harris's own play Shakespear is presented with the most pathetic tenderness. He is tragic, bitter, pitiable, wretched and broken among a robust crowd of Jonsons and Elizabeths; but to me he is not Shakespear because I miss the Shakespearean irony and the Shakespearean gaiety. Take these away and Shakespear is no longer Shakespear: all the bite, the impetus, the strength, the grim delight in his own power of looking terrible facts in the face with a chuckle, is gone; and you have nothing left but that most depressing of all things: a victim. Now who can think of Shakespear as a man with a grievance? Even in that most thoroughgoing and inspired of all Shakespear's loves: his love of music (which Mr Harris has been the first to appreciate at anything like its value), there is a dash of mockery. 'Spit in the hole, man; and tune again.' 'Divine air! Now is his soul ravished. Is it not strange that sheep's guts should hale the souls out of men's bodies?' 'An he had been a dog that should have howled thus, they would have hanged him.' There is just as much Shakespear here as in the inevitable quotation about the sweet south and the bank of violets.

I lay stress on this irony of Shakespear's, this impish rejoicing in pessimism, this exultation in what breaks the hearts of common men, not only because it is diagnostic of that immense energy of life which we call genius, but because its omission is the one glaring defect in Mr Harris's otherwise extraordinarily penetrating book. Fortunately, it is an omission that does not disable the book as (in my judgment) it disabled the hero of the play, because Mr Harris left himself out of his play, whereas he pervades his book, mordant, deep-voiced, and with an unconquerable style which is the man.

THE IDOL OF THE BARDOLATERS

There is even an advantage in having a book on Shakespear with the Shakespearean irony left out of account. I do not say that the missing chapter should not be added in the next edition: the hiatus is too great: it leaves the reader too uneasy before this touching picture of a writhing worm substituted for the invulnerable giant. But it is none the less probable that in no other way could Mr Harris have got at his man as he has. For, after all, what is the secret of the hopeless failure of the academic Bardolaters to give us a credible or even interesting Shakespear, and the easy triumph of Mr Harris in giving us both? Simply that Mr Harris has assumed that he was dealing with a man, whilst the others have assumed that they were writing about a god, and have therefore rejected every consideration of fact, tradition, or interpretation, that pointed to any human imperfection in their hero. They thus leave themselves with so little material that they are forced to begin by saying that we know very little about Shakespear. As a matter of fact, with the plays and sonnets in our hands, we know much more about Shakespear than we know about Dickens or Thackeray: the only difficulty is that we deliberately suppress it because it proves that Shakespear was not only very unlike the conception of a god current in Clapham, but was not, according to the same reckoning, even a respectable man. The academic view starts with a Shakespear who was not scurrilous; therefore the verses about 'lousy Lucy' cannot have been written by him, and the cognate passages in the plays are either strokes of character-drawing or gags interpolated by the actors. This ideal Shakespear was too well behaved to get drunk; therefore the tradition that his death was hastened by a drinking bout with Jonson and Drayton must be rejected, and the remorse of Cassio treated as a thing observed, not experienced; nay, the disgust of Hamlet at the drinking customs of Denmark is taken to establish Shakespear as the superior of Alexander in self-control, and the greatest of teetotalers.

Now this system of inventing your great man to start with, and then rejecting all the materials that do not fit him, with the ridiculous result that you have to declare that there are no materials at all (with your waste-paper basket full of them), ends in leaving Shakespear with a much worse character than he deserves. For though it does not greatly matter whether he wrote the lousy Lucy lines or not, and does not really matter at all whether he got drunk when he made a night of it with Jonson and Drayton, the sonnets raise an unpleasant question which does matter a good deal; and the refusal of the academic Bardolaters to discuss or even mention this question has had the effect of producing a silent verdict against Shakespear. Mr Harris tackles the question openly, and has no difficulty whatever in convincing us that Shakespear was a man of normal constitution sexually, and was not the victim of that most cruel and pitiable of all the freaks of nature: the freak which transposes the normal aim of the affections. Silence on this point means condemnation; and the condemnation has been general throughout the present generation, though it only needed Mr Harris's fearless handling of the matter to sweep away what is nothing but a morbid and very disagreeable modern fashion. There is always some stock accusation brought against eminent persons. When I was a boy every well-known man was accused of beating his wife. Later on, for some unexplained reason, he was accused of psychopathic derangement. And this fashion is retrospective. The cases of Shakespear and Michel Angelo are cited as proving that every genius of the first magnitude was a sufferer; and both here and in Germany there are circles in which such derangement is grotesquely reverenced as part of the stigmata of heroic powers. All of which is gross nonsense. Unfortunately, in Shakespear's case, prudery, which cannot prevent the accusation from being whispered, does prevent the refutation from being shouted. Mr Harris, the deep-voiced, refuses to be silenced. He dismisses with proper contempt the stupidity which places an outrageous construction on Shakespear's apologies in the sonnets for neglecting that 'perfect ceremony' of love which consists in returning calls and making protestations and giving presents and paying the trumpery attentions which men of genius always refuse to bother about, and to which touchy people who have no genius attach so much importance. No reader who had not been tampered with by the psychopathic monomaniacs could ever put any construction but the obvious and innocent one on these passages. But the general vocabulary of the sonnets to Pembroke (or whoever 'Mr W. H.' really was) is so overcharged according to modern ideas that a reply on the general case is necessary.

SHAKESPEAR'S ALLEGED SYCOPHANCY AND PERVERSION

That reply, which Mr Harris does not hesitate to give, is twofold: first, that Shakespear was, in his attitude towards earls, a sycophant; and, second, that the normality of Shakespear's sexual constitution is only too well attested by the excessive susceptibility to the normal impulse shewn in the whole mass of his writings. This latter is the really conclusive reply. In the case of Michel Angelo, for instance, one must admit that if his words are set beside those of Titian or Paul Veronese, it is impossible not to be struck by the absence in the Florentine of that susceptibility to feminine charm which pervades the pictures of the Venetians. But, as Mr Harris points out (though he does not use this particular illustration) Paul Veronese is an anchorite compared to Shakespear. The language of the sonnets addressed to Pembroke, extravagant as it now seems, is the language of compliment and fashion, transfigured no doubt by Shakespear's verbal magic, and hyperbolical, as Shakespear always seems to people who cannot conceive so vividly as he, but still unmistakeable for anything else than the expression of a friendship delicate enough to be wounded, and a manly loyalty deep enough to be outraged. But the language of the sonnets to the Dark Lady is the language of passion: their cruelty shews it. There is no evidence that Shakespear was capable of being unkind in cold blood. But in his revulsions from love, he was bitter, wounding, even ferocious; sparing neither himself nor the unfortunate woman whose only offence was that she had reduced the great man to the common human denominator.

In seizing on these two points Mr Harris has made so sure a stroke, and places his evidence so featly that there is nothing left for me to do but to plead that the second is sounder than the first, which is, I think, marked by the prevalent mistake as to Shakespear's social position, or, if you prefer it, the confusion between his actual social position as a penniless tradesman's son taking to the theatre for a livelihood, and his own conception of himself as a gentleman of good family. I am prepared to contend that though Shakespear was undoubtedly sentimental in his expressions of devotion to Mr W. H. even to a point which nowadays makes both ridiculous, he was not sycophantic if Mr W. H. was really attractive and promising, and Shakespear deeply attached to him. A sycophant does not tell his patron that his fame will survive, not in the renown of his own actions, but in the sonnets of his sycophant. A sycophant, when his patron cuts him out in a love affair, does not tell his patron exactly what he thinks of him. Above all, a sycophant does not write to his patron precisely as he feels on all occasions: and this rare kind of sincerity is all over the sonnets. Shakespear, we are told, was 'a very civil gentleman.' This must mean that his desire to please people and be liked by them, and his reluctance to hurt their feelings, led him into amiable flattery even when his feelings were not strongly stirred. If this be taken into account along with the fact that Shakespear conceived and expressed all his emotions with a vehemence that sometimes carried him into ludicrous extravagance, making Richard offer his kingdom for a horse and Othello declare of Cassio that

> Had all his hairs been lives, my great revenge
> Had stomach for them all,

we shall see more civility and hyperbole than sycophancy even in the earlier and more coldblooded sonnets.

SHAKESPEAR AND DEMOCRACY

Now take the general case pled against Shakespear as an enemy of democracy by Tolstoy, the late Ernest Crosbie and others, and endorsed by Mr Harris. Will it really stand fire? Mr Harris emphasizes the passages in which Shakespear spoke of mechanics and even of small master tradesmen as base persons whose clothes were greasy, whose breath was rank, and whose political imbecility and caprice moved Coriolanus to say to the Roman Radical who demanded at least 'good words' from him

> He that will give good words to thee will flatter
> Beneath abhorring.

But let us be honest. As political sentiments these lines are an abomination to every democrat. But suppose they are not political sentiments! Suppose they are merely a record of observed fact. John Stuart Mill told our British workmen that they were mostly liars. Carlyle told us all that we are mostly fools. Matthew Arnold and Ruskin were more circumstantial and more abusive. Everybody, including the workers themselves, know that they are dirty, drunken, foul-mouthed, ignorant, gluttonous, prejudiced: in short, heirs to the peculiar ills of poverty and slavery, as well as co-heirs with the plutocracy to all the failings of human nature. Even Shelley admitted, 200 years after Shakespear wrote Coriolanus, that universal suffrage was out of the question. Surely the real test, not of Democracy, which was not a live political issue in Shakespear's time, but of impartiality in judging classes, which is what one demands from a great human poet, is not that he should flatter the poor and denounce the rich, but that he should weigh them both in the same balance. Now whoever will read Lear and Measure for Measure will find stamped on his mind such an appalled sense of the danger of dressing man in a little brief authority, such a merciless stripping of the purple from the 'poor, bare, forked animal' that calls itself a king and fancies itself a god, that one wonders what was the real nature of the mysterious restraint that kept 'Eliza and our James' from teaching Shakespear to be civil to crowned heads, just as one wonders why Tolstoy was allowed to go free when so many less terrible levellers went to the galleys or Siberia. From the mature Shakespear we get no such scenes of village snobbery as that between the stage country gentleman Alexander Iden and the stage Radical Jack Cade. We get the shepherd in As You Like It, and many honest, brave, human, and loyal servants, beside the inevitable comic ones. Even in the Jingo play, Henry V, we get Bates and Williams drawn with all respect and honor as normal rank and file men. In Julius Caesar, Shakespear went to work with a will when he took his cue from Plutarch in glorifying regicide and transfiguring the republicans. Indeed hero-worshippers have never forgiven him for belittling Caesar and failing to see that side of his assassination which made Goethe denounce it as the most senseless of crimes. Put the play beside the Charles I of Wills, in which Cromwell is written down to a point at which the Jack Cade of Henry VI becomes a hero in comparison; and then believe, if you can, that Shakespear was one of them that 'crook the pregnant hinges of the knee where thrift may follow fawning.' Think of Rosencrantz, Guildenstern, Osric, the fop who annoyed Hotspur, and a dozen passages concerning such people! If such evidence can prove anything (and Mr Harris relies throughout on such evidence) Shakespear loathed courtiers.

If, on the other hand, Shakespear's characters are mostly members of the leisured classes, the same thing is true of Mr Harris's own plays and mine. Industrial slavery is not compatible with that freedom of adventure, that personal refinement and intellectual culture, that scope of action, which the higher and subtler drama demands. Even Cervantes had finally to drop Don Quixote's troubles with innkeepers demanding to be paid for his food and lodging, and make him as free of economic difficulties as Amadis de Gaul. Hamlet's experiences simply could not have happened to a plumber. A poor man is useful on the stage only as a blind man is: to excite sympathy. The poverty of the apothecary in Romeo and Juliet produces a great effect, and even points the sound moral that a poor man cannot afford to have a conscience; but if all the characters of the play had been as poor as he, it would have been nothing but a melodrama of the sort that the Sicilian players gave us here; and that was not the best that lay in Shakespear's power. When poverty is abolished, and leisure and grace of life become general, the only plays surviving from our epoch which will have any relation to life as it will be lived then will be those in which none of the persons represented are troubled with want of money or wretched drudgery. Our plays of poverty and squalor, now the only ones that are true to the life of the majority of living men, will then be classed with the records of misers and monsters, and read only by historical students of social pathology.

Then consider Shakespear's kings and lords and gentlemen! Would even John Ball or Jeremiah complain that they are flattered? Surely a more mercilessly exposed string of scoundrels never crossed the stage. The very monarch who paralyses a rebel by appealing to the divinity that hedges a king, is a drunken and sensual assassin, and is presently killed contemptuously before our eyes in spite of his hedge of divinity. I could write as convincing a chapter on Shakespear's Dickensian prejudice against the throne and the nobility and gentry in general as Mr Harris or Ernest

Crosbie on the other side. I could even go so far as to contend that one of Shakespear's defects is his lack of an intelligent comprehension of feudalism. He had of course no prevision of democratic Collectivism. He was, except in the common-places of war and patriotism, a privateer through and through. Nobody in his plays, whether king or citizen, has any civil public business or conception of such a thing, except in the method of appointing constables, to the abuses in which he called attention quite in the vein of the Fabian Society. He was concerned about drunkenness and about the idolatry and hypocrisy of our judicial system; but his implied remedy was personal sobriety and freedom from idolatrous illusion in so far as he had any remedy at all, and did not merely despair of human nature. His first and last word on parliament was 'Get thee glass eyes, and, like a scurvy politician, seem to see the thing thou dost not.' He had no notion of the feeling with which the land nationalizers of today regard the fact that he was a party to the enclosure of common lands at Wellcome. The explanation is, not a general deficiency in his mind, but the simple fact that in his day what English land needed was individual appropriation and cultivation, and what the English Constitution needed was the incorporation of Whig principles of individual liberty.

SHAKESPEAR AND THE BRITISH PUBLIC

I have rejected Mr Harris's view that Shakespear died broken-hearted of 'the pangs of love despised.' I have given my reasons for believing that Shakespear died game, and indeed in a state of levity which would have been considered unbecoming in a bishop. But Mr Harris's evidence does prove that Shakespear had a grievance and a very serious one. He might have been jilted by ten dark ladies and been none the worse for it; but his treatment by the British Public was another matter. The idolatry which exasperated Ben Jonson was by no means a popular movement; and, like all such idolatries, it was excited by the magic of Shakespear's art rather than by his views. He was launched on his career as a successful playwright by the Henry VI trilogy, a work of no originality, depth, or subtlety except the originality, depth, and subtlety of the feelings and fancies of the common people. But Shakespear was not satisfied with this. What is the use of being Shakespear if you are not allowed to express any notions but those of Autolycus? Shakespear did not see the world as Autolycus did: he saw it, if not exactly as Ibsen did (for it was not quite the same world), at least with much of Ibsen's power of penetrating its illusions and idolatries, and with all Swift's horror of its cruelty and uncleanliness.

Now it happens to some men with these powers that they are forced to impose their fullest exercise on the world because they cannot produce popular work. Take Wagner and Ibsen for instance! Their earlier works are no doubt much cheaper than their later ones; still, they were not popular when they were written. The alternative of doing popular work was never really open to them: had they stooped they would have picked up less than they snatched from above the people's heads. But Handel and Shakespear were not held to their best in this way. They could turn out anything they were asked for, and even heap up the measure. They reviled the British Public, and never forgave it for ignoring their best work and admiring their splendid commonplaces; but they produced the commonplaces all the same, and made them sound magnificent by mere brute faculty for their art. When Shakespear was forced to write popular plays to save his theatre from ruin, he did it mutinously, calling the plays As *You* Like it, and Much Ado About Nothing. All the same, he did it so well that to this day these two genial vulgarities are the main Shakespearean stock-in-trade of our theatres. Later on Burbage's power and popularity as an actor enabled Shakespear to free himself from the tyranny of the box office, and to express himself more freely in plays consisting largely of monologue to be spoken by a great actor from whom the public would stand a good deal. The history of Shakespear's tragedies has thus been the history of a long line of famous actors, from Burbage and Betterton to Forbes Robertson; and the man of whom we are told that 'when he would have said that Richard died, and cried A horse! A horse! he Burbage cried' was the father of nine generations of Shakespearean playgoers, all speaking of Garrick's Richard, and Kean's Othello, and Irving's Shylock, and Forbes Robertson's Hamlet without knowing or caring how much these had to do with Shakespear's Richard and Othello and so forth. And the plays which were written without great and predominant parts, such as Troilus and Cressida, All's Well That Ends Well, and Measure for Measure, have dropped on our stage as dead as the second part of Goethe's Faust or Ibsen's Emperor or Galilean.

Here, then, Shakespear had a real grievance; and though it is a sentimental exaggeration to describe him as a broken-hearted man in the face of the passages of reckless jollity and serenely happy poetry in his latest plays, yet the discovery that his most serious work could reach success only when carried on the back of a very fascinating actor who was enormously overcharging his part, and that the serious plays which did not contain parts big enough to hold the overcharge were left on the shelf, amply accounts for the evident fact that Shakespear did not end his life in a glow of enthusiastic satisfaction with mankind and with the theatre, which is all that Mr Harris can allege in support of his broken-heart theory. But even if Shakespear had had no failures, it was not possible for a man of his powers to observe the political and moral conduct of his contemporaries without perceiving that they were incapable of dealing with the problems raised by their own civilization, and that their attempts to carry out the codes of law and to practise the religions offered to them by great prophets and law-givers were and still are so foolish that we now call for The Superman, virtually a new species, to rescue the world from mismanagement. This is the real sorrow of great men; and in the face of it the notion that when a great man speaks bitterly or looks melancholy he must be troubled by a disappointment in love seems to me sentimental trifling.

If I have carried the reader with me thus far, he will find that trivial as this little play of mine is, its sketch of Shakespear is more complete than its levity suggests. Alas! its appeal for a National Theatre as a monument to Shakespear failed to touch the very stupid people who cannot see that a National Theatre is worth having for the sake of the National Soul. I had unfortunately represented Shakespear as treasuring and using (as I do myself) the jewels of unconsciously musical speech which common people utter and throw away every day; and this was taken as a disparagement of Shakespear's 'originality.' Why was I born with such contemporaries? Why is Shakespear made ridiculous by such a posterity?

POSTSCRIPT 1933

The recent death of Frank Harris has refreshed the interest of the sketch of him in this preface, especially as he died in the act of finishing a curious biography of me which has attracted a good deal of notice, and which is truthful as to its record of bare facts, though its critical side is badly lamed through Frank's having lost touch with me before the end of the nineteenth century, and never reconsidered his estimates in the light of my later exploits.

The appeal for a national theatre with which the play concludes, and for the sake of which it was written, elicited applause but no subscriptions. Two years ago a great Shakespear Memorial Theatre was completed at Stratford-upon-Avon through the efforts of Sir Archibald Flower, replacing the old Shakespear theatre which owed its existence to his family; but Sir Archibald had wasted no time in appealing to Shakespear's countrymen: he had turned to America and received a noble response. The attempt to establish a National Theatre in London to commemorate Shakespear's exploits in that old city, now expanded into a concentration camp much too big for any civic consciousness, was and still is a complete failure, though there is enough money (not English money, of course) available to carry out the project if the Government would provide a site, and the municipality forgo its rates, as foreign Governments and municipalities do.

❧ THE DARK LADY OF THE ❧ SONNETS

Fin de siècle 15–1600. *Midsummer night on the terrace of the Palace at Whitehall, overlooking the Thames. The Palace clock chimes four quarters and strikes eleven.*
A Beefeater on guard. A Cloaked Man approaches.

THE BEEFEATER. Stand. Who goes there? Give the word.

THE MAN. Marry! I cannot. I have clean forgotten it.

THE BEEFEATER. Then you cannot pass here. What is your business? Who are you? Are you a true man?

THE MAN. Far from it, Master Warder. I am not the same man two days together: sometimes Adam, sometimes Benvolio, and anon the Ghost.

THE BEEFEATER [*recoiling*] A ghost! Angels and ministers of grace defend us!

THE MAN. Well said, Master Warder. With your leave I will set that down in writing; for I have a very poor and unhappy brain for remembrance. [*He takes out his tablets and writes*]. Methinks this is a good scene, with you on your lonely watch, and I approaching like a ghost in the moonlight. Stare not so amazedly at me; but mark what I say. I keep tryst here tonight with a dark lady. She promised to bribe the warder. I gave her the where-withal: four tickets for the Globe Theatre.

THE BEEFEATER. Plague on her! She gave me two only.

THE MAN [*detaching a tablet*] My friend: present this tablet, and you will be welcomed at any time when the plays of Will Shakespear are in hand. Bring your wife. Bring your friends. Bring the whole garrison. There is ever plenty of room.

THE BEEFEATER. I care not for these new-fangled plays. No man can understand a word of them. They are all talk. Will you not give me a pass for The Spanish Tragedy?

THE MAN. To see The Spanish Tragedy one pays, my friend. Here are the means. [*He gives him a piece of gold*].

THE BEEFEATER [*overwhelmed*] Gold! Oh, sir, you are a better paymaster than your dark lady.

THE MAN. Women are thrifty, my friend.

THE BEEFEATER. Tis so, sir. And you have to consider that the most open handed of us must een cheapen that which we buy every day. This lady has to make a present to a warder nigh every night of her life.

THE MAN [*turning pale*] I'll not believe it.

THE BEEFEATER. Now you, sir, I dare be sworn, do not have an adventure like this twice in the year.

THE MAN. Villain: wouldst tell me that my dark lady hath ever done thus before? that she maketh occasions to meet other men?

THE BEEFEATER. Now the Lord bless your innocence, sir, do you think you are the only pretty man in the world? A merry lady, sir: a warm bit of stuff. Go to: I'll not see her pass a deceit on a gentleman that hath given me the first piece of gold I ever handled.

THE MAN. Master Warder: is it not a strange thing that we, knowing that all women are false, should be amazed to find our own particular drab no better than the rest?

THE BEEFEATER. Not all, sir. Decent bodies, many of them.

THE MAN [*intolerantly*] No. All false. All. If thou deny it, thou liest.

THE BEEFEATER. You judge too much by the Court, sir. There, indeed, you may say of frailty that its name is woman.

THE MAN [*pulling out his tablets again*] Prithee say that again: that about frailty: the strain of music.

THE BEEFEATER. What strain of music, sir? I'm no musician, God knows.

THE MAN. There is music in your soul: many of your degree have it very notably. [*Writing*] 'Frailty: thy name is woman!' [*Repeating it affectionately*] 'Thy name is woman.'

THE BEEFEATER. Well, sir, it is but four words. Are you a snapper-up of such unconsidered trifles?

THE MAN [*eagerly*] Snapper-up of – [*he gasps*] Oh! Immortal phrase! [*He writes it down*]. This man is a greater than I.

THE BEEFEATER. You have my lord Pembroke's trick, sir.

THE MAN. Like enough: he is my near friend. But what call you his trick?

THE BEEFEATER. Making sonnets by moonlight. And to the same lady too.

THE MAN. No!

THE BEEFEATER. Last night he stood here on your errand, and in your shoes.

THE MAN. Thou, too, Brutus! And I called him friend!

THE BEEFEATER. Tis ever so, sir.

THE MAN. Tis ever so. Twas ever so. [*He turns away, overcome*]. Two Gentlemen of Verona! Judas! Judas!!

THE BEEFEATER. Is he so bad as that, sir?

THE MAN [*recovering his charity and self-possession*] Bad? O no. Human, Master Warder, human. We call one another names when we are offended, as children do. That is all.

THE BEEFEATER. Ay, sir: words, words, words. Mere wind, sir. We fill our bellies with the east wind, sir, as the Scripture hath it. You cannot feed capons so.

THE MAN. A good cadence. By your leave. [*He makes a note of it*].

THE BEEFEATER. What manner of thing is a cadence, sir? I have not heard of it.

THE MAN. A thing to rule the world with, friend.

THE BEEFEATER. You speak strangely, sir: no offence. But, an't like you, you are a very civil gentleman; and a poor man feels drawn to you, you being, as twere, willing to share your thought with him.

THE MAN. Tis my trade. But alas! the world for the most part will none of my thoughts.

Lamplight streams from the palace door as it opens from within.

THE BEEFEATER. Here comes your lady, sir. I'll to t'other end of my ward. You may een take your time about your business: I shall not return too suddenly unless my sergeant comes prowling round. Tis a fell sergeant, sir: strict in his arrest. Good een, sir; and good luck! [*He goes*].

THE MAN. 'Strict in his arrest'! 'Fell sergeant'! [*As if tasting a ripe plum*] O-o-o-h! [*He makes a note of them*].

A Cloaked Lady gropes her way from the palace and wanders along the terrace, walking in her sleep.

THE LADY [*rubbing her hands as if washing them*] Out, damned spot. You will mar all with these cosmetics. God made you one face; and you make yourself another. Think of your grave, woman, not ever of being beautified. All the perfumes of Arabia will not whiten this Tudor hand.

THE MAN. 'All the perfumes of Arabia'! 'Beautified'! 'Beautified'! a poem in a single word. Can this be my Mary? [*To the Lady*] Why do you speak in a strange voice, and utter poetry for the first time? Are you ailing? You walk like the dead. Mary! Mary!

THE LADY [*echoing him*] Mary! Mary! Who would have thought that woman to have had so much blood in her! Is it my fault that my counsellors put deeds of blood on me? Fie! If you were women you would have more wit than to stain the floor so foully. Hold not up her head so: the hair is false. I tell you yet again, Mary's buried: she cannot come out of her grave. I fear her not: these cats that dare jump into thrones though they be fit only for men's laps must be put away. Whats done cannot be undone. Out, I say. Fie! a queen, and freckled!

THE MAN [*shaking her arm*] Mary, I say: art asleep?

The Lady wakes; starts; and nearly faints. He catches her on his arm.

THE LADY. Where am I? What art thou?

THE MAN. I cry your mercy. I have mistook your person all this while. Methought you were my Mary: my mistress.

THE LADY [*outraged*] Profane fellow: how do you dare?

THE MAN. Be not wroth with me, lady. My mistress is a marvellous proper woman. But she does not speak so well as you. 'All the perfumes of Arabia'! That was well said: spoken with good accent and excellent discretion.

THE LADY. Have I been in speech with you here?

THE MAN. Why, yes, fair lady. Have you forgot it?

THE LADY. I have walked in my sleep.

THE MAN. Walk ever in your sleep, fair one; for then your words drop like honey.

THE LADY [*with cold majesty*] Know you to whom you speak, sir, that you dare express yourself so saucily?

THE MAN [*unabashed*] Not I, nor care neither. You are some lady of the Court, belike. To me there are but two sorts of women: those with excellent voices, sweet and low, and cackling hens that cannot make me dream. Your voice has all manner of loveliness in it. Grudge me not a short hour of its music.

THE LADY. Sir: you are overbold. Season your admiration for a while with –

THE MAN [*holding up his hand to stop her*] 'Season your admiration for a while –'

THE LADY. Fellow: do you dare mimic me to my face?

THE MAN. Tis music. Can you not hear? When a good musician sings a song, do you not sing it and sing it again til you have caught and fixed its perfect melody? 'Season your admiration for a while': God! the history of man's heart is in that one word admiration. Admiration! [*Taking up his tablets*] What was it? 'Suspend your admiration for a space –'

THE LADY. A very vile jingle of esses. I said 'Season your –

THE MAN [*hastily*] Season; ay, season, season, season. Plague on my memory, my wretched memory! I must een write it down. [*He begins to write, but stops, his memory failing him*]. Yet tell me which was the vile jingle? You said very justly: mine own ear caught it ever as my false tongue said it.

THE LADY. You said 'for a space.' I said 'for a while.'

THE MAN. 'For a while' [*he corrects it*]. Good! [*Ardently*] And now be mine neither for a space nor a while, but for ever.

THE LADY. Odds my life! Are you by chance making love to me, knave?

THE MAN. Nay: tis you have made the love: I but pour it out at your feet. I cannot but love a lass that sets such store by an apt word. Therefore vouchsafe, divine perfection of a woman – no: I have said that before somewhere; and the wordy garment of my love for you must be fire-new –

THE LADY. You talk too much, sir. Let me warn you: I am more accustomed to be listened to than preached at.

THE MAN. The most are like that that do talk well. But though you spake with the tongues of angels, as indeed you do, yet know that I am the king of words –

THE LADY. A king, ha!

THE MAN. No less. We are poor things, we men and women –

THE LADY. Dare you call me woman?

THE MAN. What nobler name can I tender you? How else can I love you? Yet you may well shrink from the name: have I not said we are but poor things? Yet there is a power that can redeem us.

THE LADY. Gramercy for your sermon, sir. I hope I know my duty.

THE MAN. This is no sermon, but the living truth. The power I speak of is the power of immortal poesy. For know that vile as this world is, and worms as we are, you have but to invest all this vileness with a magical garment of words to transfigure us and uplift our souls til earth flowers into a million heavens.

THE LADY. You spoil your heaven with your million. You are extravagant. Observe some measure in your speech.

THE MAN. You speak now as Ben does.

THE LADY. And who, pray, is Ben?

THE MAN. A learned bricklayer who thinks that the sky is at the top of his ladder, and so takes it on him to rebuke me for flying. I tell you there is no word yet coined and no melody yet sung that is extravagant and majestical enough for the glory that lovely words can reveal. It is heresy to deny it: have you not been taught that in the beginning was the Word? that the Word was with God? nay, that the Word was God?

THE LADY. Beware, fellow, how you presume to speak of holy things. The Queen is the head of the Church.

THE MAN. You are the head of my Church when you speak as you did at first. 'All the perfumes of Arabia'! Can the Queen speak thus? They say she playeth well upon the virginals. Let her play so to me; and I'll kiss her hands. But until then, you are my Queen; and I'll kiss those lips that have dropt music on my heart. [*He puts his arms about her*].

THE LADY. Unmeasured impudence! On your life, take your hands from me.

The Dark Lady comes stooping along the terrace behind them like a running thrush. When she sees how they are employed, she rises angrily to her full height, and listens jealously.

THE MAN [*unaware of the Dark Lady*] Then cease to make my hands tremble with the streams of life you pour through them. You hold me as the lodestar holds the iron: I cannot but cling to you. We are lost, you and I: nothing can separate us now.

THE DARK LADY. We shall see that, false lying hound, you and your filthy trull. [*With two vigorous cuffs, she knocks the pair asunder, sending the man, who is unlucky enough to receive a righthanded blow, sprawling on the flags*]. Take that, both of you!

THE CLOAKED LADY [*in towering wrath, throwing off her cloak and turning in outraged majesty on her assailant*] High treason!

THE DARK LADY [*recognizing her and falling on her knees in abject terror*] Will: I am lost: I have struck the Queen.

THE MAN [*sitting up as majestically as his ignominious posture allows*] Woman: you have struck WILLIAM SHAKESPEARE!!!!!!

QUEEN ELIZABETH [*stupent*] Marry, come up!!! Struck William Shakespear quotha! And who in the name of all the sluts and jades and light-o'-loves and fly-by-nights that infest this palace of mine, may William Shakespear be?

THE DARK LADY. Madam: he is but a player. Oh, I could have my hand cut off –

QUEEN ELIZABETH. Belike you will, mistress. Have you bethought you that I am like to have your head cut off as well?

THE DARK LADY. Will: save me. Oh, save me.

ELIZABETH. Save you! A likely savior, on my royal word! I had thought this fellow at least an esquire; for I had hoped that even the vilest of my ladies would not have dishonoured my Court by wantoning with a baseborn servant.

SHAKESPEAR [*indignantly scrambling to his feet*] Baseborn! I, a Shakespear of Stratford! I, whose mother was an Arden! baseborn! You forget yourself, madam.

ELIZABETH [*furious*] S'blood! do I so? I will teach you —

THE DARK LADY [*rising from her knees and throwing herself between them*] Will: in God's name anger her no further. It is death. Madam: do not listen to him.

SHAKESPEAR. Not were it een to save your life, Mary, not to mention mine own, will I flatter a monarch who forgets what is due to my family. I deny not that my father was brought down to be a poor bankrupt; but twas his gentle blood that was ever too generous for trade. Never did he disown his debts. Tis true he paid them not; but it is an attested truth that he gave bills for them; and twas those bills, in the hands of base hucksters, that were his undoing.

ELIZABETH [*grimly*] The son of your father shall learn his place in the presence of the daughter of Harry the Eighth.

SHAKESPEAR [*swelling with intolerant importance*] Name not that inordinate man in the same breath with Stratford's worthiest alderman. John Shakespear wedded but once: Harry Tudor was married six times. You should blush to utter his name.

THE DARK LADY ⎱ *crying out* ⎰Will: for pity's sake —
ELIZABETH   ⎰ *together*   ⎱Insolent dog —

SHAKESPEAR [*cutting them short*] How know you that King Harry was indeed your father?

ELIZABETH   ⎰Zounds! Now by — [*she stops to grind her teeth with rage*].
THE DARK LADY ⎱She will have me whipped through the streets. Oh God! Oh God!

SHAKESPEAR. Learn to know yourself better, madam. I am an honest gentleman of unquestioned parentage, and have already sent in my demand for the coat-of-arms that is lawfully mine. Can you say as much for yourself?

ELIZABETH [*almost beside herself*] Another word; and I begin with mine own hands the work the hangman shall finish.

SHAKESPEAR. You are no true Tudor: this baggage here has as

good a right to your royal seat as you. What maintains you on the throne of England? Is it your renownéd wit? your wisdom that sets at nought the craftiest statesmen of the Christian world? No. Tis the mere chance that might have happened to any milkmaid, the caprice of Nature that made you the most wondrous piece of beauty the age hath seen. [*Elizabeth's raised fists, on the point of striking him, fall to her side*]. That is what hath brought all men to your feet, and founded your throne on the impregnable rock of your proud heart, a stony island in a sea of desire. There, madam, is some wholesome blunt honest speaking for you. Now do your worst.

ELIZABETH [*with dignity*] Master Shakespear: it is well for you that I am a merciful prince. I make allowance for your rustic ignorance. But remember that there are things which be true, and are yet not seemly to be said (I will not say to a queen; for you will have it that I am none) but to a virgin.

SHAKESPEAR [*bluntly*] It is no fault of mine that you are a virgin, madam, albeit tis my misfortune.

THE DARK LADY [*terrified again*] In mercy, madam, hold no further discourse with him. He hath ever some lewd jest on his tongue. You hear how he useth me! calling me baggage and the like to your Majesty's face.

ELIZABETH. As for you, mistress, I have yet to demand what your business is at this hour in this place, and how you come to be so concerned with a player that you strike blindly at your sovereign in your jealousy of him.

THE DARK LADY. Madam: as I live and hope for salvation –

SHAKESPEAR [*sardonically*] Ha!

THE DARK LADY [*angrily*] – ay, I'm as like to be saved as thou that believest naught save some black magic or words and verses – I say, madam, as I am a living woman I came here to break with him for ever. Oh, madam, if you would know what misery is, listen to this man that is more than man and less at the same time. He will tie you down to anatomize your very soul: he will wring tears of blood from your humiliation; and then he will heal the wound with flatteries that no woman can resist.

SHAKESPEAR. Flatteries! [*Kneeling*] Oh, madam, I put my case at your royal feet. I confess to much. I have a rude tongue: I am unmannerly: I blaspheme against the holiness of anointed royalty; but oh, my royal mistress, AM I a flatterer?

ELIZABETH. I absolve you as to that. You are far too plain a dealer to please me. [*He rises gratefully*].

THE DARK LADY. Madam: he is flattering you even as he speaks.

ELIZABETH [*a terrible flash in her eye*] Ha! Is it so?

SHAKESPEAR. Madam: she is jealous; and, heaven help me! not without reason. Oh, you say you are a merciful prince; but that was cruel of you, that hiding of your royal dignity when you found me here. For how can I ever be content with this black-haired, black-eyed, black-avised devil again now that I have looked upon real beauty and real majesty?

THE DARK LADY [*wounded and desperate*] He hath swore to me ten times over that the day shall come in England when black women, for all their foulness, shall be more thought on than fair ones. [*To Shakespear, scolding at him*] Deny it if thou canst. Oh, he is compact of lies and scorns. I am tired of being tossed up to heaven and dragged down to hell at every whim that takes him. I am ashamed to my very soul that I have abased myself to love one that my father would not have deemed fit to hold my stirrup – one that will talk to all the world about me – that will put my love and my shame into his plays and make me blush for myself there – that will write sonnets about me that no man of gentle strain would put his hand to. I am all disordered: I know not what I am saying to your Majesty: I am of all ladies most deject and wretched –

SHAKESPEAR. Ha! At last sorrow hath struck a note of music out of thee. 'Of all ladies most deject and wretched.' [*He makes a note of it*].

THE DARK LADY. Madam: I implore you give me leave to go. I am distracted with grief and shame. I –

ELIZABETH. Go. [*The Dark Lady tries to kiss her hand*]. No more. Go. [*The Dark Lady goes, convulsed*]. You have been cruel to that poor fond wretch, Master Shakespear.

SHAKESPEAR. I am not cruel, madam; but you know the fable of Jupiter and Semele. I could not help my lightnings scorching her.

ELIZABETH. You have an overweening conceit of yourself, sir, that displeases your Queen.

SHAKESPEAR. Oh, madam, can I go about with the modest cough of a minor poet, belittling my inspiration and making the mightiest wonder of your reign a thing of nought? I have said that 'not marble nor the gilded monuments of princes shall outlive' the words with which I make the world glorious or foolish at my will. Besides, I would have you think me great enough to grant me a boon.

ELIZABETH. I hope it is a boon that may be asked of a virgin Queen without offence, sir. I mistrust your forwardness; and I bid you remember that I do not suffer persons of your degree (if I may say so without offence to your father the alderman) to presume too far.

SHAKESPEAR. Oh, madam, I shall not forget myself again; though by my life, could I make you a serving wench, neither a queen nor a virgin should you be for so much longer as a flash of lightning might take to cross the river to the Bankside. But since you are a queen and will none of me, nor of Philip of Spain, nor of any other mortal man, I must een contain myself as best I may, and ask you only for a boon of State.

ELIZABETH. A boon of State already! You are becoming a courtier like the rest of them. You lack advancement.

SHAKESPEAR. 'Lack advancement.' By your Majesty's leave: a queenly phrase. [*He is about to write it down*].

ELIZABETH [*striking the tablets from his hand*] Your tables begin to anger me, sir. I am not here to write your plays for you.

SHAKESPEAR. You are here to inspire them, madam. For this, among the rest, were you ordained. But the boon I crave is that you do endow a great playhouse, or, if I may make bold to coin a scholarly name for it, a National Theatre, for the better instruction and gracing of your Majesty's subjects.

ELIZABETH. Why, sir, are there not theatres enow on the Bankside and in Blackfriars?

SHAKESPEAR. Madam: these are the adventures of needy and desperate men that must, to save themselves from perishing of want, give the sillier sort of people what they best like; and what they best like, God knows, is not their own betterment and instruction, as we well see by the example of the churches, which must needs compel men to frequent them, though they be open to all without charge. Only when there is a matter of a murder, or a plot, or a pretty youth in petticoats, or some naughty tale of wantonness, will your subjects pay the great cost of good players and their finery, with a little profit to boot. To prove this I will tell you that I have written two noble and excellent plays setting forth the advancement of women of high nature and fruitful industry even as your Majesty is: the one a skilful physician, the other a sister devoted to good works. I have also stole from a book of idle wanton tales two of the most damnable foolishnesses in the world, in the one of which a woman goeth in man's attire and maketh impudent love to her swain, who pleaseth the groundlings by overthrowing a wrestler; whilst, in the other, one of the same kidney sheweth her wit by saying endless naughtinesses to a gentleman as lewd as herself. I have writ these to save my friends from penury, yet shewing my scorn for such follies and for them that praise them by calling the one As You Like It, meaning that it is not as *I* like it, and the other Much Ado About Nothing, as it truly is. And now these two filthy pieces drive their nobler fellows from the stage, where indeed I cannot have my lady physician presented at all, she being too honest a woman for the taste of the town. Wherefore I humbly beg your Majesty to give order that a theatre be endowed out of the public revenue for the playing of those pieces of mine which no merchant will touch, seeing that his gain is so much greater with the worse than with the better. Thereby you shall also encourage other men to undertake the writing of plays who do now despise it and leave it wholly to those whose counsels will work little good to your realm. For this writing of plays is a great matter, forming as it does the minds and affections of men in such sort that whatsoever they see done in show on the stage, they will presently be doing in earnest in the world, which is but a larger stage. Of late, as you know, the Church taught the people by means of plays; but the people flocked only to such as were full of superstitious miracles and bloody martyrdoms; and so the Church, which also was just then brought into straits by the policy of your royal father, did abandon and discountenance the art of playing; and thus it fell into the hands of poor players and greedy merchants that had their pockets to look to and not the greatness of this your kingdom. Therefore now must your Majesty take up that good work that your Church hath abandoned, and restore the art of playing to its former use and dignity.

ELIZABETH. Master Shakespear: I will speak of this matter to the Lord Treasurer.

SHAKESPEAR. Then am I undone, madam; for there was never yet a Lord Treasurer that could find a penny for anything over and above the necessary expenses of your government, save for a war or a salary for his own nephew.

ELIZABETH. Master Shakespear: you speak sooth; yet cannot I in any wise mend it. I dare not offend my unruly Puritans by making so lewd a place as the playhouse a public charge; and there be a thousand things to be done in this London of mine before your poetry can have its penny from the general purse. I tell thee, Master Will, it will be three hundred years and more before my subjects learn that man cannot live by bread alone, but by every word that cometh from the mouth of those whom God inspires. By that time you and I will be dust beneath the feet of the horses, if indeed there be any horses then, and men be still riding instead of flying. Now it may be that by then your works will be dust also.

SHAKESPEAR. They will stand, madam: fear not for that.

ELIZABETH. It may prove so. But of this I am certain (for I know my countrymen) that until every other country in the Christian world, even to barbarian Muscovy and the hamlets of the boorish Germans, have its playhouse at the public charge, England will never adventure. And she will adventure then only because it is her desire to be ever in the fashion, and to do humbly and dutifully whatso she seeth everybody else doing. In the meantime you must content yourself as best you can by the playing of those two pieces which you give out as the most damnable ever writ, but which your countrymen, I warn you, will swear are the best you have ever done. But this I will say, that if I could speak across the ages to our descendants, I should heartily recommend them to fulfil your wish; for the Scottish minstrel hath well said that he that maketh the songs of a nation is mightier than he that maketh its laws; and the same may well be true of plays and interludes. [*The clock chimes the first quarter. The warder returns on his round*]. And now, sir, we are upon the hour when it better beseems a virgin queen to be abed than to converse alone with the naughtiest of her subjects. Ho there! Who keeps ward on the queen's lodgings tonight?

THE WARDER. I do, an't please your majesty.

ELIZABETH. See that you keep it better in future. You have let pass a most dangerous gallant even to the very door of our royal chamber. Lead him forth; and bring me word when he is safely locked out; for I shall scarce dare disrobe until the palace gates are between us.

SHAKESPEAR [*kissing her hand*] My body goes through the gate into the darkness, madam; but my thoughts follow you.

ELIZABETH. How! to my bed!

SHAKESPEAR. No, madam, to your prayers, in which I beg you to remember my theatre.

ELIZABETH. That is my prayer to posterity. Forget not your own to God; and so goodnight, Master Will.

SHAKESPEAR. Goodnight, great Elizabeth. God save the Queen!

ELIZABETH. Amen.

Exeunt severally: she to her chamber: he, in custody of the warder, to the gate nearest Blackfriars.

AYOT ST LAWRENCE
20 June 1910

Overruled

A Demonstration

WITH

Preface

Composition begun 2 July 1912; completed 23 July 1912. First published in German translation, as *Es hat nicht sollen sein*, in the *Neue Freie Presse* (Vienna), 23 March 1913. Published in the *English Review* and in *Hearst's Magazine* (New York), May 1913. First collected in *Androcles and the Lion, Overruled, Pygmalion*, 1916. First presented at the Duke of York's Theatre, London, 14 October 1912.

Gregory Lunn   *Claude King*
Mrs Juno   *Mirian Lewes*
Sibthorpe Juno   *Adolphus Vane Tempest*
Seraphita Lunn   *Geraldine Olliffe*

Period – A Summer Night

Scene – *A Corner of the Lounge of a Seaside Hotel*

❧ PREFACE ❧

Contents

THE ALLEVIATIONS OF MONOGAMY

This piece is not an argument for or against polygamy. It is a clinical study of how the thing actually occurs among quite ordinary people, innocent of all unconventional views concerning it. The enormous majority of cases in real life are those of people in that position. Those who deliberately and conscientiously profess what are oddly called advanced views by those others who believe them to be retrograde, are often, and indeed mostly, the last people in the world to engage in unconventional adventures of any kind, not only because they have neither time nor disposition for them, but because the friction set up between the individual and the community by the expression of unusual views of any sort is quite enough hindrance to the heretic without being complicated by personal scandals. Thus the theoretic libertine is usually a person of blameless family life, whilst the practical libertine is mercilessly severe on all other libertines, and excessively conventional in professions of social principle.

What is more, these professions are not hypocritical: they are for the most part quite sincere. The common libertine, like the drunkard, succumbs to a temptation which he does not defend, and against which he warns others with an earnestness proportionate to the intensity of his own remorse. He (or she) may be a liar and a humbug, pretending to be better than the detected libertines, and clamoring for their condign punishment; but this is mere self-defence. No reasonable person expects the burglar to confess his pursuits, or to refrain from joining in the cry of Stop Thief when the police get on the track of another burglar. If society chooses to penalize candor, it has itself to thank if its attack is countered by falsehood. The clamorous virtue of the libertine is therefore no more hypocritical than the plea of Not Guilty which is allowed to every criminal. But one result is that the theorists who write most sincerely and favorably about polygamy know least about it; and the practitioners who know most about it keep their knowledge very jealously to themselves. Which is hardly fair to the practice.

INACCESSIBILITY OF THE FACTS

Also, it is impossible to estimate its prevalence. A practice to which nobody confesses may be both universal and unsuspected, just as a virtue which everybody is expected, under heavy penalties, to claim, may have no existence. It is often assumed – indeed it is the official assumption of the Churches and the divorce courts – that a gentleman and a lady cannot be alone together innocently. And that is manifest blazing nonsense, though many women have been stoned to death in the east, and divorced in the west, on the strength of it. On the other hand, the innocent and conventional people who regard gallant adventures as crimes of so horrible a nature that only the most depraved and desperate characters engage in them or would listen to advances in that direction without raising an alarm with the noisiest indignation, are clearly examples of the fact that most sections of society do not know how the other sections live. Industry is the most effective check on gallantry. Women may, as Napoleon said, be the occupation of the idle man just as men are the preoccupation of the idle woman; but the mass of mankind is too busy and too poor for the long and expensive sieges which the professed libertine lays to virtue. Still, wherever there is idleness or even a reasonable supply of elegant leisure there is a good deal of coquetry and philandering. It is so much pleasanter to dance on the edge of a precipice than to go over it that leisured society is full of people who spend a great part of their lives in flirtation, and conceal nothing but the humiliating secret that they have never gone any further. For there is no pleasing people in the matter of reputation in this department: every insult is a flattery: every testimonial is a disparagement: Joseph is despised and promoted, Potiphar's wife admired and condemned: in short, you are never on solid ground until you get away from the subject altogether. There is a continual and irreconcilable conflict between the natural and conventional sides of the case, between spontaneous human relations between independent men and women on the one hand and the property relation between husband and wife on the other, not to mention the confusion under the common name of love of a generous natural attraction and interest with the murderous jealousy that fastens on and clings to its mate (especially a hated mate) as a tiger fastens on a carcase. And the confusion is natural; for these extremes are extremes of the same passion; and most cases lie somewhere on the scale between them, and are so complicated by ordinary likes and dislikes, by incidental wounds to vanity or gratifications of it, and by class feeling, that A will be jealous of B and not of C, and will tolerate infidelities on the part of D whilst being furiously angry when they are committed by E.

THE CONVENTION OF JEALOUSY

That jealousy is independent of sex is shewn by its intensity in children, and by the fact that very jealous people are jealous of everybody without regard to relationship or sex, and cannot bear to hear the person they 'love' speak favorably of anyone under any circumstances (many women, for instance, are much more jealous of their husbands' mothers and sisters than of unrelated women whom they suspect him of fancying); but it is seldom possible to disentangle the two passions in practice. Besides, jealousy is an inculcated passion, forced by society on people in whom it would not occur spontaneously. In Brieux's Bourgeois aux Champs, the benevolent hero finds himself detested by the neighboring peasants and farmers, not because he preserves game, and sets mantraps for poachers, and defends his legal rights over his land to the extremest point of unsocial savagery, but because, being an amiable and public-spirited person, he refuses to do all this, and thereby offends and disparages the sense of property in his neighbors. The same thing is true of matrimonial jealousy: the man who does not at least pretend to feel it, and behave as badly as if he really felt it, is despised and insulted; and many a man has shot or stabbed a friend or been shot or stabbed by him in a duel, or disgraced himself and ruined his own wife in a divorce scandal, against his conscience, against his instinct, and to the destruction of his home, solely because Society conspired to drive him to keep its own lower morality in countenance in this miserable and undignified manner.

Morality is confused in such matters. In an elegant plutocracy, a jealous husband is regarded as a boor. Among the tradesmen who supply that plutocracy with its meals, a husband who is not jealous, and refrains from assailing his rival with his fists, is regarded as a ridiculous, contemptible, and cowardly cuckold. And the laboring class is divided into the respectable section which takes the tradesman's view, and the disreputable section which enjoys the license of the plutocracy without its money: creeping below the law as its exemplars prance above it; cutting down all expenses of respectability and even decency; and frankly accepting squalor and disrepute as the price of anarchic self-indulgence. The conflict between Malvolio and Sir Toby, between the marquis and the bourgeois, the cavalier and the puritan, the ascetic and the voluptuary, goes on continually, and goes on not only between class and class and individual and individual, but in the selfsame breast in a series of reactions and revulsions in which the irresistible becomes the unbearable, and the unbearable the irresistible, until none of us can say what our characters really are in this respect.

THE MISSING DATA OF A SCIENTIFIC NATURAL HISTORY OF MARRIAGE

Of one thing I am persuaded: we shall never attain to a reasonably healthy public opinion on sex questions until we offer, as the data for that opinion, our actual conduct and our real thoughts instead of a moral fiction which we agree to call virtuous conduct, and which we then – and here comes in the mischief – pretend is our conduct and our thoughts. If the result were that we all believed one another to be better than we really are, there would be something to be said for it; but the actual result appears to be a monstrous exaggeration of the power and continuity of sexual passion. The whole world shares the fate of Lucrezia Borgia, who, though she seems on investigation to have been quite a suitable wife for a modern British Bishop, has been invested by the popular historical imagination with all the extravagances of a Messalina or a Cenci. Writers of belles lettres who are rash enough to admit that their whole life is not one constant preoccupation with adored members of the opposite sex, and who even countenance La Rochefoucauld's remark that very few people would ever imagine themselves in love if they had never read anything about it, are gravely declared to be abnormal or physically defective by critics of crushing unadventurousness and domestication. French authors of saintly temperament are forced to include in their retinue countesses of ardent complexion with whom they are supposed to live in sin. Sentimental controversies on the subject are endless; but they are useless, because nobody tells the truth. Rousseau did it by an extraordinary effort, aided by a superhuman faculty for human natural history; but the result was curiously disconcerting because, though the facts were so conventionally shocking that people felt that they ought to matter a great deal, they actually mattered very little. And even at that everybody pretends not to believe him.

ARTIFICIAL RETRIBUTION

The worst of this is that busybodies with perhaps rather more than a normal taste for mischief are continually trying to make negligible things matter as much in fact as they do in convention by deliberately inflicting injuries – sometimes atrocious injuries – on the parties concerned. Few people have any knowledge of the savage punishments that are legally inflicted for aberrations and absurdities to which no sanely instructed community would call any attention. We create an artificial morality, and consequently an artificial conscience, by manufacturing disastrous consequences for events which, left to themselves, would do very little harm (sometimes not any) and be forgotten in a few days.

But the artificial morality is not therefore to be condemned offhand. In many cases it may save mischief instead of making it: for example, though the hanging of a murderer is the duplication of a murder, yet it may be less murderous than leaving the matter to be settled by blood feud or vendetta. As long as human nature insists on revenge, the official organization and satisfaction of revenge by the State may be also its minimization. The mischief begins when the official revenge persists after the passion it satisfies has died out of the race. Stoning a woman to death in the east because she has ventured to marry again after being deserted by her husband may be more merciful than allowing her to be mobbed to death; but the official stoning or burning of an adulteress in the west would be an atrocity, because few of us hate an adulteress to the extent of desiring such a penalty, or of being prepared to take the law into our own hands if it were withheld. Now what applies to this extreme case applies also in due degree to the other cases. Offences in which sex is concerned are often needlessly magnified by penalties, ranging from various forms of social ostracism to long sentences of penal servitude, which would be seen to be monstrously disproportionate to the real feeling against them if the removal of both the penalties and the taboo on their discussion made it possible for us to ascertain their real prevalence and estimation. Fortunately there is one outlet for the truth. We are permitted to discuss in jest what we may not discuss in earnest. A serious comedy about sex is taboo: a farcical comedy is privileged.

THE FAVORITE SUBJECT OF FARCICAL COMEDY

The little piece which follows this preface accordingly takes the form of a farcical comedy, because it is a contribution to the very extensive dramatic literature which takes as its special department the gallantries of married people. The stage has been preoccupied by such affairs for centuries, not only in the jesting vein of Restoration Comedy and Palais Royal farce, but in the more tragically turned adulteries of the Parisian school which dominated the stage until Ibsen put them out of countenance and relegated them to their proper place as articles of commerce. Their continued vogue in that department maintains the tradition that adultery is the dramatic subject *par excellence*, and indeed that a play that is not about adultery is not a play at all. I was considered a heresiarch of the most extravagant kind when I expressed my opinion, at the outset of my career as a playwright, that adultery is the dullest of themes on the stage, and that from Francesca and Paolo down to the latest guilty couple of the school of Dumas *fils*, the romantic adulterers have all been intolerable bores.

THE PSEUDO SEX PLAY

Later on, I had occasion to point out to the defenders of sex as the proper theme of drama, that though they were right in ranking sex as an intensely interesting subject, they were wrong in assuming that sex is an indispensable motive in popular plays. The plays of Molière are, like the novels of the Victorian epoch or Don Quixote, as nearly sexless as anything not absolutely inhuman can be; and some of Shakespear's plays are sexually on a par with the census: they contain women as well as men, and that is all. This had to be admitted; but it was still assumed that the plays of the nineteenth century Paris school are, in contrast with the sexless masterpieces, saturated with sex; and this I strenuously denied. A play about the convention that a man should fight a duel or come to fisticuffs with his wife's lover if she has one, or the convention that he should strangle her like Othello, or turn her out of the house and never see her or allow her to see her children again, or the convention that she should never be spoken to again by any decent person and should finally drown herself, or the convention that persons involved in scenes of recrimination or confession by these conventions should call each other certain abusive names and describe their conduct as guilty and frail and so on: all these may provide material for very effective plays; but such plays are not dramatic studies of sex; one might as well say that Romeo and Juliet is a dramatic study of pharmacy because the catastrophe is brought about through an apothecary. Duels are not sex; divorce cases are not sex; the Trade Unionism of married women is not sex. Only the most insignificant fraction of the gallantries of married people produce any of the conventional results; and plays occupied wholly with the conventional results are therefore utterly unsatisfying as sex plays, however interesting they may be as plays of intrigue and plot puzzles.

The world is finding this out rapidly. The Sunday papers, which in the days when they appealed almost exclusively to the lower middle class were crammed with police intelligence, and more especially with divorce and murder cases, now lay no stress on them; and police papers which confined themselves entirely to such matters, and were once eagerly read, have perished through the essential dulness of their topics. And yet the interest in sex is stronger than ever: in fact, the literature that has driven out the journalism of the divorce courts is a literature occupied with sex to an extent and with an intimacy and frankness that would have seemed utterly impossible to Thackeray or Dickens if they had been told that the change would complete itself within fifty years of their own time.

ART AND MORALITY

It is ridiculous to say, as inconsiderate amateurs of the arts do, that art has nothing to do with morality. What is true is that the artist's business is not that of the policeman; and that such factitious consequences and put-up jobs as divorces and executions and the detective operations that lead up to them are no essential part of life, though, like poisons and buttered slides and red-hot pokers, they· provide material for plenty of thrilling or amusing stories suited to people who are incapable of any interest in psychology. But the fine artist must keep the policeman out of his studies of sex and studies of crime. It is by clinging nervously to the policeman that most of the pseudo sex plays convince me that the writers have either never had any serious personal experience of their ostensible subject, or else have never conceived it possible that the stage dare present the phenomena of sex as they appear in nature.

THE LIMITS OF STAGE PRESENTATION

But the stage presents much more shocking phenomena than those of sex. There is, of course, a sense in which you cannot present sex on the stage, just as you cannot present murder. Macbeth must no more really kill Duncan than he must himself be really slain by Macduff. But the feelings of a murderer can be expressed in a certain artistic convention; and a carefully prearranged sword exercise can be gone through with sufficient pretence of earnestness to be accepted by the willing imaginations of the younger spectators as a desperate combat.

The tragedy of love has been presented on the stage in the same way. In Tristan and Isolde, the curtain does not, as in Romeo and Juliet, rise with the lark: the whole night of love is played before the spectators. The lovers do not discuss marriage in an elegantly sentimental way: they utter the visions and feelings that come to lovers at the supreme moments of their love, totally forgetting that there are such things in the world as husbands and lawyers and duelling codes and theories of sin and notions of propriety and all the other irrelevancies which provide hackneyed and bloodless material for our so-called plays of passion.

PRUDERIES OF THE FRENCH STAGE

To all stage presentations there are limits. If Macduff were to stab Macbeth, the spectacle would be intolerable; and even the pretence which we allow on our stage is ridiculously destructive to the illusion of the scene. Yet pugilists and gladiators will actually fight and kill in public without shame, even as a spectacle for money. But no sober couple of lovers of any delicacy could endure to be watched. We in England, accustomed to consider the French stage much more licentious than the British, are always surprised and puzzled when we learn, as we may do any day if we come within reach of such information, that French actors are often scandalized by what they consider the indecency of the English stage, and that French actresses who desire a greater license in appealing to the sexual instincts than the French stage allows them, learn English and establish themselves on the English stage. The German and Russian stages are in the same relation to the French and, perhaps more or less, all the Latin stages. The reason is that, partly from a want of respect for the theatre, partly from a sort of respect for art in general which moves them to accord moral privileges to artists, partly from the very objectionable tradition that the realm of art is Alsatia and the contemplation of works of art a holiday from the burden of virtue, partly because French prudery does not attach itself to the same points of behavior as British prudery, and has a different code of the mentionable and the unmentionable, and for many other reasons, the French tolerate plays which are never performed in England until they have been spoiled by a process of bowdlerization; yet French taste is more fastidious than ours as to the exhibition and treatment on the stage of the physical incidents of sex. On the French stage a kiss is as obvious a convention as the thrust under the arm by which Macduff runs Macbeth through. It is even a purposely unconvincing convention: the actors rather insisting that it shall be impossible for any spectator to mistake a stage kiss for a real one. In England, on the contrary, realism is carried to the point at which nobody except the two performers can perceive that the caress is not genuine. And here the English stage is certainly in the right; for whatever question there arises as to what incidents are proper for representation on the stage or not, my experience as a playgoer leaves me in no doubt that once it is decided to represent an incident, it will be offensive, no matter whether it be a prayer or a kiss, unless it is presented with a convincing appearance of sincerity.

OUR DISILLUSIVE SCENERY

For example, the main objection to the use of illusive scenery (in most modern plays scenery is not illusive: everything visible is as real as in your drawing room at home) is that it is unconvincing; whilst the imaginary scenery with which the audience transfigures a platform or tribune like the Elizabethan stage or the Greek stage used by Sophocles, is quite convincing. In fact, the more scenery you have the less illusion you produce. The wise playwright, when he cannot get absolute reality of presentation, goes to the other extreme, and aims at atmosphere and suggestion of mood rather than at direct simulative illusion. The theatre, as I first knew it, was a place of wings and flats which destroyed both atmosphere and illusion. This was tolerated, and even intensely enjoyed, but not in the least because nothing better was possible; for all the devices employed in the productions of Mr Granville Barker or Max Reinhardt or the Moscow Art Theatre were equally available for Colley Cibber and Garrick, except the intensity of our artificial light. When Garrick played Richard III in slashed trunk hose and plumes, it was not because he believed that the Plantagenets dressed like that, or because the costumiers could not have made him a XV century dress as easily as a nondescript combination of the state robes of George III with such scraps of older fashions as seemed to playgoers for some reason to be romantic. The charm of the theatre in those days was its makebelieve. It has that charm still not only for the amateurs, who are happiest when they are most unnatural and impossible and absurd, but for audiences as well. I have seen performances of my own plays which were to me far wilder burlesques than Sheridan's Critic or Buckingham's Rehearsal; yet they have produced sincere laughter and tears such as the most finished metropolitan productions have failed to elicit. Fielding was entirely right when he represented Partridge as enjoying intensely the performance of the king in Hamlet because anybody could see that the king was an actor, and resenting Garrick's Hamlet because it might have been a real man. Yet we have only to look at the portraits of Garrick to see that his performances would nowadays seem almost as extravagantly stagey as his costumes. In our day Calvé's intensely real Carmen never pleased the mob as much as the obvious fancy ball masquerading of suburban young ladies in the same character.

HOLDING THE MIRROR UP TO NATURE

Theatrical art begins as the holding up to Nature of a distorting mirror. In this phase it pleases people who are childish enough to believe that they can see what they look like and what they are when they look at a true mirror. Naturally they think that a true mirror can teach them nothing. Only by giving them back some monstrous image can the mirror amuse them or terrify them. It is not until they grow up to the point at which they learn that they know very little about themselves, and that they do not see themselves in a true mirror as other people see them, that they become consumed with curiosity as to what they really are like, and begin to demand that the stage shall be a mirror of such accuracy and intensity of illumination that they shall be able to get glimpses of their real selves in it, and also learn a little how they appear to other people.

For audiences of this highly developed class, sex can no longer be ignored or conventionalized or distorted by the playwright who makes the mirror. The old sentimental extravagances and the old grossnesses are of no further use to him. Don Giovanni and Zerlina are not gross: Tristan and Isolde are not extravagant or sentimental. They say and do nothing that you cannot bear to hear and see; and yet they give you, the one pair briefly and slightly, and the other fully and deeply, what passes in the minds of lovers. The love depicted may be that of a philosophic adventurer tempting an ignorant country girl, or of a tragically serious poet entangled with a woman of noble capacity in a passion which has become for them the reality of the whole universe. No matter: the thing is dramatized and dramatized directly, not talked about as something that happened before the curtain rose, or that will happen after it falls.

FARCICAL COMEDY SHIRKING ITS SUBJECT

Now if all this can be done in the key of tragedy and philosophic comedy, it can, I have always contended, be done in the key of farcical comedy; and Overruled is a trifling experiment in that manner. Conventional farcical comedies are always finally tedious because the heart of them, the inevitable conjugal infidelity, is always evaded. Even its consequences are evaded. Mr Granville Barker has pointed out rightly that if the third acts of our farcical comedies dared to describe the consequences that would follow from the first and second in real life, they would end as squalid tragedies; and in my opinion they would be greatly improved thereby even as entertainments; for I have never seen a three-act farcical comedy without being bored and tired by the third act, and observing that the rest of the audience were in the same condition, though they were not vigilantly introspective enough to find that out, and were apt to blame one another, especially the husbands and wives, for their crossness. But it is happily by no means true that conjugal infidelities always produce tragic consequences, or that they need produce even the unhappiness which they often do produce. Besides, the more momentous the consequences, the more interesting become the impulses and imaginations and reasonings, if any, of the people who disregard them. If I had an opportunity of conversing with the ghost of an executed murderer, I have no doubt he would begin to tell me eagerly about his trial, with the names of the distinguished ladies and gentlemen who honored him with their presence on that occasion, and then about his execution. All of which would bore me exceedingly. I should say, 'My dear sir: such manufactured ceremonies do not interest me in the least. I know how a man is tried, and how he is hanged. I should have had you killed in a much less disgusting, hypocritical, and unfriendly manner if the matter had been in my hands. What I want to know about is the murder. How did you feel when you committed it? Why did you do it? What did you say to yourself about it? If, like most murderers, you had not been hanged, would you have committed other murders? Did you really dislike the victim, or did you want his money, or did you murder a person whom you did not dislike, and from whose death you had nothing to gain merely for the sake of murdering? If so, can you describe the charm to me? Does it come upon you periodically; or is it chronic? Has curiosity anything to do with it?' I would ply him with all manner of questions to find out what murder is really like; and I should not be satisfied until I had realized that I, too, might commit a murder, or else that there is some specific quality present in a murderer and lacking in me. And, if so, what that quality is.

In just the same way, I want the unfaithful husband or the unfaithful wife in a farcical comedy not to bother me with their divorce cases or the stratagems they employ to avoid a divorce case, but to tell me how and why married couples are unfaithful. I dont want to hear the lies they tell one another to conceal what they have done, but the truths they tell one another when they have to face what they have done without concealment or excuse. No doubt prudent and considerate people conceal such adventures, when they can, from those who are most likely to be wounded by them; but it is not to be presumed that, when found out, they necessarily disgrace themselves by irritating lies and transparent subterfuges.

My playlet, which I offer as a model to all future writers of farcical comedy, may now, I hope, be read without shock. I may just add that Mr Sibthorpe Juno's view that morality demands, not that we should behave morally (an impossibility to our sinful nature) but that we shall not attempt to defend our immoralities, is a standard view in England, and was advanced in all seriousness by an earnest and distinguished British moralist shortly after the first performance of Overruled. My objection to that aspect of the doctrine of original sin is that no necessary and inevitable operation of human nature can reasonably be regarded as sinful at all, and that a morality which assumes the contrary is an absurd morality, and can be kept in countenance only by hypocrisy. When people were ashamed of sanitary problems, and refused to face them, leaving them to solve themselves clandestinely in dirt and secrecy, the solution arrived at was the Black Death. A similar policy as to sex problems has solved itself by an even worse plague than the Black Death; and the remedy for that is not salvarsan, but sound moral hygiene, the first foundation of which·is the discontinuance of our habit of telling not only the comparatively harmless lies that we know we ought not to tell but the ruinous lies that we foolishly think we ought to tell.

❦ OVERRULED ❦

A lady and gentleman are sitting together on a chesterfield in a retired corner of the lounge of a seaside hotel. It is a summer night: the French window behind them stands open. The terrace without overlooks a moonlit harbor. The lounge is dark. The chesterfield, upholstered in silver grey, and the two figures on it in evening dress, catch the light from an arc lamp somewhere; but the walls, covered with a dark green paper, are in gloom. There are two stray chairs, one on each side. On the gentleman's right, behind him up near the window, is an unused fireplace. Opposite it on the lady's left is a door. The gentleman is on the lady's right.

The lady is very attractive, with a musical voice and soft appealing manners. She is young: that is, one feels sure that she is under thirty-five and over twenty-four. The gentleman does not look much older. He is rather handsome, and has ventured as far in the direction of poetic dandyism in the arrangement of his hair as any man who is not a professional artist can afford to in England. He is obviously very much in love with the lady, and is, in fact, yielding to an irresistible impulse to throw his arms round her.

THE LADY. Dont – oh dont be horrid. Please, Mr Lunn [*she rises from the lounge and retreats behind it*]! Promise me you wont be horrid.

GREGORY LUNN. I'm not being horrid, Mrs Juno. I'm not going to be horrid. I love you: thats all. I'm extraordinarily happy.

MRS JUNO. You will really be good?

GREGORY. I'll be whatever you wish me to be. I tell you I love you. I love loving you. I dont want to be tired and sorry, as I should be if I were to be horrid. I dont want you to be tired and sorry. Do come and sit down again.

MRS JUNO [*coming back to her seat*] Youre sure you dont want anything you oughtnt to?

GREGORY. Quite sure. I only want you [*she recoils*]. Dont be alarmed: I like wanting you. As long as I have a want, I have a reason for living. Satisfaction is death.

MRS JUNO. Yes; but the impulse to commit suicide is sometimes irresistible.

GREGORY. Not with you.

MRS JUNO. What!

GREGORY. Oh, it sounds uncomplimentary; but it isnt really. Do you know why half the couples who find themselves situated as we are now behave horridly?

MRS JUNO. Because they cant help it if they let things go too far.

GREGORY. Not a bit of it. It's because they have nothing else to do, and no other way of entertaining each other. You dont know what it is to be alone with a woman who has little beauty and less conversation. What is a man to do? She cant talk interestingly; and if he talks that way himself she doesnt understand him. He cant look at her: if he does, he only finds out that she isnt beautiful. Before the end of five minutes they are both hideously bored. Theres only one thing that can save the situation; and thats what you call being horrid. With a beautiful, witty, kind woman, theres no time for such follies. It's so delightful to look at her, to listen to her voice, to hear all she has to say, that nothing else happens. That is why the woman who is supposed to have a thousand lovers seldom has one; whilst the stupid, graceless animals of women have dozens.

MRS JUNO. I wonder! It's quite true that when one feels in danger one talks like mad to stave it off, even when one doesnt quite want to stave it off.

GREGORY. One never does quite want to stave it off. Danger is delicious. But death isnt. We court the danger; but the real delight is in escaping, after all.

MRS JUNO. I dont think we'll talk about it any more. Danger is all very well when you do escape; but sometimes one doesnt. I tell you frankly I dont feel as safe as you do – if you really do.

GREGORY. But surely you can do as you please without injuring anyone, Mrs Juno. That is the whole secret of your extraordinary charm for me.

MRS JUNO. I dont understand.

GREGORY. Well, I hardly know how to begin to explain. But the root of the matter is that I am what people call a good man.

MRS JUNO. I thought so until you began making love to me.

GREGORY. But you knew I loved you all along.

MRS JUNO. Yes, of course; but I depended on you not to tell me so;

because I thought you were good. Your blurting it out spoilt it. And it was wicked besides.

GREGORY. Not at all. You see, it's a great many years since Ive been able to allow myself to fall in love. I know lots of charming women; but the worst of it is, theyre all married. Women dont become charming, to my taste, until theyre fully developed; and by that time, if theyre really nice, theyre snapped up and married. And then, because I am a good man, I have to place a limit to my regard for them. I may be fortunate enough to gain friendship and even very warm affection from them; but my loyalty to their husbands and their hearths and their happiness obliges me to draw a line and not overstep it. Of course I value such affectionate regard very highly indeed. I am surrounded with women who are most dear to me. But every one of them has a post sticking up, if I may put it that way, with the inscription: Trespassers Will be Prosecuted. How we all loathe that notice! In every lovely garden, in every dell full of primroses, on every fair hillside, we meet that confounded board; and there is always a gamekeeper round the corner. But what is that to the horror of meeting it on every beautiful woman, and knowing that there is a husband round the corner? I have had this accursed board standing between me and every dear and desirable woman until I thought I had lost the power of letting myself fall really and wholeheartedly in love.

MRS JUNO. Wasnt there a widow?

GREGORY. No. Widows are extraordinarily scarce in modern society. Husbands live longer than they used to; and even when they do die, their widows have a string of names down for their next.

MRS JUNO. Well, what about the young girls?

GREGORY. Oh, who cares for young girls? Theyre unsympathetic. Theyre beginners. They dont attract me. I'm afraid of them.

MRS JUNO. Thats the correct thing to say to a woman of my age. But it doesnt explain why you seem to have put your scruples in your pocket when you met me.

GREGORY. Surely thats quite clear. I –

MRS JUNO. No: please dont explain. I dont want to know. I take your word for it. Besides, it doesnt matter now. Our voyage is over; and tomorrow I start for the north to my poor father's place.

GREGORY [surprised] Your poor father! I thought he was alive.

MRS JUNO. So he is. What made you think he wasnt?

GREGORY. You said your poor father.

MRS JUNO. Oh, thats a trick of mine. Rather a silly trick, I suppose; but theres something pathetic to me about men: I find myself calling them poor So-and-So when theres nothing whatever the matter with them.

GREGORY [*who has listened in growing alarm*] But – I – is? – wa – ? Oh Lord!

MRS JUNO. Whats the matter?

GREGORY. Nothing.

MRS JUNO. Nothing! [*Rising anxiously*] Nonsense: youre ill.

GREGORY. No. It was something about your late husband –

MRS JUNO. My late husband! What do you mean? [*Clutching him, horror-stricken*] Dont tell me he's dead.

GREGORY [*rising, equally appalled*] Dont tell me he's alive.

MRS JUNO. Oh, dont frighten me like this. Of course he's alive – unless youve heard anything.

GREGORY. The first day we met – on the boat – you spoke to me of your poor dear husband.

MRS JUNO [*releasing him, quite reassured*] Is that all?

GREGORY. Well, afterwards you called him poor Tops. Always poor Tops, or poor dear Tops. What could I think?

MRS JUNO [*sitting down again*] I wish you hadnt given me such a shock about him; for I havnt been treating him at all well. Neither have you.

GREGORY [*relapsing into his seat, overwhelmed*] And you mean to tell me youre not a widow!

MRS JUNO. Gracious, no! I'm not in black.

GREGORY. Then I have been behaving like a blackguard! I have broken my promise to my mother. I shall never have an easy conscience again.

MRS JUNO. I'm sorry. I thought you knew.

GREGORY. You thought I was a libertine?

MRS JUNO. No: of course I shouldnt have spoken to you if I had thought that. I thought you liked me, but that you knew, and would be good.

GREGORY [*stretching his hand towards her breast*] I thought the burden of being good had fallen from my soul at last. I saw nothing there but a bosom to rest on: the bosom of a lovely woman of whom I could dream without guilt. What do I see now?

MRS JUNO. Just what you saw before.

GREGORY [*despairingly*] No, no.

MRS JUNO. What else?

GREGORY. Trespassers Will Be Prosecuted: Trespassers Will Be Prosecuted.

MRS JUNO. They wont if they hold their tongues. Dont be such a coward. My husband wont eat you.

GREGORY. I'm not afraid of your husband. I'm afraid of my conscience.

MRS JUNO [*losing patience*] Well! I dont consider myself at all a badly behaved woman; for nothing has passed between us that was not perfectly nice and friendly; but really! to hear a grown-up man talking about promises to his mother! —

GREGORY [*interrupting her*] Yes, yes: I know all about that. It's not romantic: it's not Don Juan: it's not advanced; but we feel it all the same. It's far deeper in our blood and bones than all the romantic stuff. My father got into a scandal once: that was why my mother made me promise never to make love to a married woman. And now Ive done it I cant feel honest. Dont pretend to despise me or laugh at me. You feel it too. You said just now that your own conscience was uneasy when you thought of your husband. What must it be when you think of my wife?

MRS JUNO [*rising aghast*] Your wife!! You dont dare sit there and tell me coolly that youre a married man!

GREGORY. I never led you to believe I was unmarried.

MRS JUNO. Oh! You never gave me the faintest hint that you had a wife.

GREGORY. I did indeed. I discussed things with you that only married people really understand.

MRS JUNO. Oh!!

GREGORY. I thought it the most delicate way of letting you know.

MRS JUNO. Well, you are a daisy, I must say. I suppose thats vulgar; but really! really!! You and your goodness! However, now weve found one another out theres only one thing to be done. Will you please go?

GREGORY [*rising slowly*] I ought to go.

MRS JUNO. Well, go.

GREGORY. Yes. Er — [*he tries to go*] I — I somehow cant. [*He sits down again helplessly*]. My conscience is active: my will is paralyzed. This is really dreadful. Would you mind ringing the bell and asking them to throw me out? You ought to, you know.

MRS JUNO. What! make a scandal in the face of the whole hotel! Certainly not. Dont be a fool.

GREGORY. Yes; but I cant go.

MRS JUNO. Then I can. Goodbye.

GREGORY [clinging to her hand] Can you really?

MRS JUNO. Of course I – [she wavers] Oh dear! [They contemplate one another helplessly]. I cant. [She sinks on the lounge, hand in hand with him].

GREGORY. For heaven's sake pull yourself together. It's a question of self-control.

MRS JUNO [dragging her hand away and retreating to the end of the chesterfield] No: it's a question of distance. Self-control is all very well two or three yards off, or on a ship, with everybody looking on. Dont come any nearer.

GREGORY. This is a ghastly business. I want to go away; and I cant.

MRS JUNO. I think you ought to go [he makes an effort; and she adds quickly] but if you try to I shall grab you round the neck and disgrace myself. I implore you to sit still and be nice.

GREGORY. I implore you to run away. I believe I can trust myself to let you go for your own sake. But it will break my heart.

MRS JUNO. I dont want to break your heart. I cant bear to think of your sitting here alone. I cant bear to think of sitting alone myself somewhere else. It's so senseless – so ridiculous – when we might be so happy. I dont want to be wicked, or coarse. But I like you very much; and I do want to be affectionate and human.

GREGORY. I ought to draw a line.

MRS JUNO. So you shall, dear. Tell me: do you really like me? I dont mean love me: you might love the housemaid –

GREGORY [vehemently] No!

MRS JUNO. Oh yes you might; and what does that matter, anyhow? Are you really fond of me? Are we friends – comrades? Would you be sorry if I died?

GREGORY [shrinking] Oh dont.

MRS JUNO. Or was it the usual aimless man's lark: a mere shipboard flirtation?

GREGORY. Oh no, no: nothing half so bad, so vulgar, so wrong. I assure you I only meant to be agreeable. It grew on me before I noticed it.

MRS JUNO. And you were glad to let it grow?

GREGORY. I let it grow because the board was not up.

MRS JUNO. Bother the board! I am just as fond of Sibthorpe as —

GREGORY. Sibthorpe!

MRS JUNO. Sibthorpe is my husband's Christian name. I oughtnt to call him Tops to you now.

GREGORY [*chuckling*] It sounded like something to drink. But I have no right to laugh at him. My Christian name is Gregory, which sounds like a powder.

MRS JUNO [*chilled*] That is so like a man! I offer you my heart's warmest friendliest feeling; and you think of nothing but a silly joke. A quip that makes you forget me.

GREGORY. Forget you! Oh, if only I could!

MRS JUNO. If you could, would you?

GREGORY [*burying his shamed face in his hands*] No: I'd die first. Oh, I hate myself.

MRS JUNO. I glory in myself. It's so jolly to be reckless. Can a man be reckless, I wonder?

GREGORY [*straightening himself desperately*] No. I'm not reckless. I know what I'm doing: my conscience is awake. Oh, where is the intoxication of love? the delirium? the madness that makes a man think the world well lost for the woman he adores? I dont think anything of the sort: I see that it's not worth it: I know that it's wrong: I have never in my life been cooler, more businesslike.

MRS JUNO [*opening her arms to him*] But you cant resist me.

GREGORY. I must. I ought. [*Throwing himself into her arms*] Oh my darling, my treasure, we shall be sorry for this.

MRS JUNO. We can forgive ourselves. Could we forgive ourselves if we let this moment slip?

GREGORY. I protest to the last. I'm against this. I have been pushed over a precipice. I'm innocent. This wild joy, this exquisite tenderness, this ascent into heaven can thrill me to the uttermost fibre of my heart [*with a gesture of ecstasy she hides her face on his shoulder*]; but it cant subdue my mind or corrupt my conscience, which still shouts to the skies that I'm not a willing party to this outrageous conduct. I repudiate the bliss with which you are filling me.

MRS JUNO. Never mind your conscience. Tell me how happy you are.

GREGORY. No: I recall you to your duty. But oh, I will give you my life with both hands if you can tell me that you feel for me one millionth part of what I feel for you now.

MRS JUNO. Oh yes, yes. Be satisfied with that. Ask for no more. Let me go.

GREGORY. I cant. I have no will. Something stronger than either of us is in command here. Nothing on earth or in heaven can part us now. You know that, dont you?

MRS JUNO. Oh, dont make me say it. Of course I know. Nothing – not life nor death nor shame nor anything can part us.

A MATTER-OF-FACT MALE VOICE IN THE CORRIDOR. All right. This must be it.

The two recover with a violent start; release one another; and spring back to opposite sides of the lounge.

GREGORY. That did it.

MRS JUNO [*in a thrilling whisper*] Sh-sh-sh! That was my husband's voice.

GREGORY. Impossible: it's only our guilty fancy.

A WOMAN'S VOICE. This is the way to the lounge. I know it.

GREGORY. Great Heaven! we're both mad. Thats my wife's voice.

MRS JUNO. Ridiculous! Oh, we're dreaming it all. We – [*the door opens; and Sibthorpe Juno appears in the roseate glow of the corridor (which happens to be papered in pink) with Mrs Lunn, like Tannhäuser in the hill of Venus. He is a fussily energetic little man, who gives himself an air of gallantry by greasing the points of his moustaches and dressing very carefully. She is a tall, imposing, handsome, languid woman, with flashing dark eyes and long lashes. They make for the chesterfield, not noticing the two palpitating figures blotted against the walls in the gloom on either side. The figures flit away noiselessly through the window and disappear*].

JUNO [*officiously*] Ah: here we are. [*He leads the way to the sofa*]. Sit down: I'm sure youre tired. [*She sits*]. Thats right. [*He sits beside her on her left*]. Hullo! [*he rises*] this sofa's quite warm.

MRS LUNN [*bored*] Is it? I dont notice it. I expect the sun's been on it.

JUNO. I felt it quite distinctly: I'm more thinly clad than you. [*He sits down again, and proceeds, with a sigh of satisfaction*] What a relief to get off the ship and have a private room! Thats the worst of a ship. Youre under observation all the time.

MRS LUNN. But why not?

JUNO. Well, of course theres no reason: at least I suppose not. But, you know, part of the romance of a journey is that a man keeps imagining that something might happen; and he cant do that if there are a lot of people about and it simply cant happen.

MRS LUNN. Mr Juno: romance is all very well on board ship: but when your foot touches the soil of England theres an end of it.

JUNO. No: believe me, thats a foreigner's mistake: we are the most romantic people in the world, we English. Why, my very presence here is a romance.

MRS LUNN [*faintly ironical*] Indeed?

JUNO. Yes. Youve guessed, of course, that I'm a married man.

MRS LUNN. Oh, thats all right! I'm a married woman.

JUNO. Thank Heaven for that! To my English mind, passion is not real passion without guilt. I am a red-blooded man, Mrs Lunn: I cant help it. The tragedy of my life is that I married, when quite young, a woman whom I couldnt help being very fond of. I longed for a guilty passion – for the real thing – the wicked thing; and yet I couldnt care twopence for any other woman when my wife was about. Year after year went by: I felt my youth slipping away without ever having had a romance in my life; for marriage is all very well: but it isnt romance. Theres nothing wrong in it, you see.

MRS LUNN. Poor man! How you must have suffered!

JUNO. No: that was what was so tame about it. I wanted to suffer. You get so sick of being happily married. It's always the happy marriages that break up. At last my wife and I agreed that we ought to take a holiday.

MRS LUNN. Hadnt you holidays every year?

JUNO. Oh, the seaside and so on! Thats not what we meant. We meant a holiday from one another.

MRS LUNN. How very odd!

JUNO. She said it was an excellent idea; that domestic felicity was making us perfectly idiotic; that she wanted a holiday too. So we agreed to go round the world in opposite directions. I started for Suez on the day she sailed for New York.

MRS LUNN [*suddenly becoming attentive*] Thats precisely what Gregory and I did. Now I wonder did he want a holiday from me! What he said was that he wanted the delight of meeting me after a long absence.

JUNO. Could anything be more romantic than that? Would anyone else than an Englishman have thought of it? I daresay my temperament seems tame to your boiling southern blood –

MRS LUNN. My what!

JUNO. Your southern blood. Dont you remember how you told me, that night in the saloon when I sang 'Farewell and adieu to you dear Spanish ladies,' that you were by birth a lady of Spain? Your splendid Andalusian beauty speaks for itself.

MRS LUNN. Stuff! I was born in Gibraltar. My father was Captain Jenkins. In the artillery.

JUNO [*ardently*] It is climate and not race that determines the temperament. The fiery sun of Spain blazed on your cradle; and it rocked to the roar of British cannon.

MRS LUNN. What eloquence! It reminds me of my husband when he was in love – before we were married. Are you in love?

JUNO. Yes; and with the same woman.

MRS LUNN. Well, of course, I didnt suppose you were in love with two women.

JUNO. I dont think you quite understand. I meant that I am in love with you.

MRS LUNN [*relapsing into deepest boredom*] Oh, that! Men do fall in love with me. They all seem to think me a creature with volcanic passions: I'm sure I dont know why; for all the volcanic women I know are plain little creatures with sandy hair. I dont consider human volcanoes respectable. And I'm so tired of the subject! Our house is always full of women who are in love with my husband and men who are in love with me. We encourage it because it's pleasant to have company.

JUNO. And is your husband as insensible as yourself?

MRS LUNN. Oh, Gregory's not insensible: very far from it; but I am the only woman in the world for him.

JUNO. But you? Are you really as insensible as you say you are?

MRS LUNN. I never said anything of the kind. I'm not at all insensible by nature; but (I dont know whether youve noticed it) I am what people call rather a fine figure of a woman.

JUNO [*passionately*] Noticed it! Oh, Mrs Lunn! Have I been able to notice anything else since we met?

MRS LUNN. There you go, like all the rest of them! I ask you, how do you expect a woman to keep up what you call her sensibility when this sort of thing has happened to her about three times a week ever since she was seventeen? It used to upset me and terrify me at first. Then I got rather a taste for it. It came to a climax with Gregory: that was why I married him. Then it became a mild lark, hardly worth the trouble. After that I found it valuable once or twice as a spinal tonic when I was run down; but now it's an unmitigated bore. I dont mind your declaration: I daresay it gives you a certain pleasure to make it. I quite understand that you adore me; but (if you dont mind) I'd rather you didnt keep on saying so.

JUNO. Is there then no hope for me?

MRS LUNN. Oh, yes. Gregory has an idea that married women keep lists of the men theyll marry if they become widows. I'll put your name down, if that will satisfy you.

JUNO. Is the list a long one?

MRS LUNN. Do you mean the real list? Not the one I shew to Gregory: there are hundreds of names on that; but the little private list that he'd better not see?

JUNO. Oh, will you really put me on that? Say you will.

MRS LUNN. Well, perhaps I will. [*He kisses her hand*]. Now dont begin abusing the privilege.

JUNO. May I call you by your Christian name?

MRS LUNN. No: it's too long. You cant go about calling a woman Seraphita.

JUNO [*ecstatically*] Seraphita!

MRS LUNN. I used to be called Sally at home; but when I married a man named Lunn, of course that became ridiculous. Thats my one little pet joke. Call me Mrs Lunn for short. And change the subject, or I shall go to sleep.

JUNO. I cant change the subject. For me there is no other subject. Why else have you put me on your list?

MRS LUNN. Because youre a solicitor. Gregory's a solicitor. I'm accustomed to my husband being a solicitor and telling me things he oughtnt to tell anybody.

JUNO [*ruefully*] Is that all? Oh, I cant believe that the voice of love has ever thoroughly awakened you.

MRS LUNN. No: it sends me to sleep. [*Juno appeals against this by an amorous demonstration*]. It's no use, Mr Juno: I'm hopelessly respectable: the Jenkinses always were. Dont you realize that unless most women were like that, the world couldnt go on as it does?

JUNO [*darkly*] You think it goes on respectably; but I can tell you as a solicitor –

MRS LUNN. Stuff! of course all the disreputable people who get into trouble go to you, just as all the sick people go to the doctors; but most people never go to a solicitor.

JUNO [*rising, with a growing sense of injury*] Look here, Mrs Lunn: do you think a man's heart is a potato? or a turnip? or a ball of knitting wool? that you can throw it away like this?

MRS LUNN. I dont throw away balls of knitting wool. A man's heart seems to me much like a sponge, it sops up dirty water as well as clean.

JUNO. I have never been treated like this in my life. Here am I, a married man, with a most attractive wife: a wife I adore, and who adores me, and has never as much as looked at any other man since we were married. I come and throw all this at your feet. I! I, a solicitor! braving the risk of your husband putting me into the divorce court and making me a beggar and an outcast! I do this for your sake. And you go on as if I were making no sacrifice: as if I had told you it's a fine evening, or asked you to have a cup of tea. It's not human. It's not right. Love has its rights as well as respectability. [*He sits down again, aloof and sulky*].

MRS LUNN. Nonsense! Here! heres a flower [*she gives him one*]. Go and dream over it until you feel hungry. Nothing brings people to their senses like hunger.

JUNO [*contemplating the flower without rapture*] What good's this?

MRS LUNN [*snatching it from him*] Oh! you dont love me a bit.

JUNO. Yes I do. Or at least I did. But I'm an Englishman; and I think you ought to respect the conventions of English life.

MRS LUNN. But I am respecting them; and youre not.

JUNO. Pardon me. I may be doing wrong; but I'm doing it in a proper and customary manner. You may be doing right; but youre doing it in an unusual and questionable manner. I am not prepared to put up with that. I can stand being badly treated: I'm no baby, and can take care of myself with anybody. And of course I can stand being well treated. But the one thing I cant stand is being unexpectedly treated. It's outside my scheme of life. So come now! youve got to behave naturally and straight-forwardly with me. You can leave husband and child, home, friends, and country, for my sake, and come with me to some southern isle – or say South America – where we can be all in all to one another. Or you can tell your husband and let him jolly well punch my head if he can. But I'm damned if I'm going to stand any eccentricity. It's not respectable.

GREGORY [*coming in from the terrace and advancing with dignity to his wife's end of the chesterfield*] Will you have the goodness, sir, in addressing this lady, to keep your temper and refrain from using profane language?

MRS LUNN [*rising, delighted*] Gregory! Darling [*she enfolds him in a copious embrace*]!

JUNO [*rising*] You make love to another man to my face!

MRS LUNN. Why, he's my husband.

JUNO. That takes away the last rag of excuse for such conduct. A nice world it would be if married people were to carry on their endearments before everybody!

GREGORY. This is ridiculous. What the devil business is it of yours what passes between my wife and myself? Youre not her husband, are you?

JUNO. Not at present; but I'm on the list. I'm her prospective husband: youre only her actual one. I'm the anticipation: youre the disappointment.

MRS LUNN. Oh, my Gregory is not a disappointment. [*Fondly*] Are you, dear?

GREGORY. You just wait, my pet. I'll settle this chap for you. [*He disengages himself from her embrace, and faces Juno. She sits down placidly*]. You call me a disappointment, do you? Well, I suppose every husband's a disappointment. What about yourself? Dont try to look like an unmarried man. I happen to know the lady you disappointed. I travelled in the same ship with her; and —

JUNO. And you fell in love with her.

GREGORY [*taken aback*] Who told you that?

JUNO. Aha! you confess it. Well, if you want to know, nobody told me. Everybody falls in love with my wife.

GREGORY. And do you fall in love with everybody's wife?

JUNO. Certainly not. Only with yours.

MRS LUNN. But whats the good of saying that, Mr Juno? I'm married to him; and theres an end of it.

JUNO. Not at all. You can get a divorce.

MRS LUNN. What for?

JUNO. For his misconduct with my wife.

GREGORY [*deeply indignant*] How dare you, sir, asperse the character of that sweet lady? a lady whom I have taken under my protection.

JUNO. Protection!

MRS JUNO [*returning hastily*] Really you must be more careful what you say about me, Mr Lunn.

JUNO. My precious! [*He embraces her*]. Pardon this betrayal of feeling; but Ive not seen my wife for several weeks; and she is very dear to me.

GREGORY. I call this cheek. Who is making love to his own wife before people now, pray?

MRS LUNN. Wont you introduce me to your wife, Mr Juno?

MRS JUNO. How do you do? [*They shake hands; and Mrs Juno sits down beside Mrs Lunn, on her left*].

MRS LUNN. I'm so glad to find you do credit to Gregory's taste. I'm naturally rather particular about the women he falls in love with.

JUNO [*sternly*] This is no way to take your husband's unfaithfulness. [*To Lunn*] You ought to teach your wife better. Wheres her feelings? It's scandalous.

GREGORY. What about your own conduct, pray?

JUNO. I dont defend it; and theres an end of the matter.

GREGORY. Well, upon my soul! What difference does your not defending it make?

JUNO. A fundamental difference. To serious people I may appear wicked. I dont defend myself: I am wicked, though not bad at heart. To thoughtless people I may even appear comic. Well, laugh at me: I have given myself away. But Mrs Lunn seems to have no opinion at all about me. She doesnt seem to know whether I'm wicked or comic. She doesnt seem to care. She has no moral sense. I say it's not right. I repeat, I have sinned; and I'm prepared to suffer.

MRS JUNO. Have you really sinned, Tops?

MRS LUNN [*blandly*] I dont remember your sinning. I have a shocking bad memory for trifles; but I think I should remember that — if you mean me.

JUNO [*raging*] Trifles! I have fallen in love with a monster.

GREGORY. Dont you dare call my wife a monster.

MRS JUNO [*rising quickly and coming between them*] Please dont lose your temper, Mr Lunn: I wont have my Tops bullied.

GREGORY. Well, then, let him not brag about sinning with my wife. [*He turns impulsively to his wife; makes her rise; and takes her proudly on his arm*]. What pretension has he to any such honor?

JUNO. I sinned in intention. [*Mrs Juno abandons him and resumes her seat, chilled*]. I'm as guilty as if I had actually sinned. And I insist on being treated as a sinner, and not walked over as if I'd done nothing, by your wife or any other man.

MRS LUNN. Tush! [*She sits down again contemptuously*].

JUNO [*furious*] I wont be belittled.

MRS LUNN [*to Mrs Juno*] I hope youll come and stay with us now that you and Gregory are such friends, Mrs Juno.

JUNO. This insane magnanimity —

MRS LUNN. Dont you think youve said enough, Mr Juno? This is a matter for two women to settle. Wont you take a stroll on the beach with my Gregory while we talk it over? Gregory is a splendid listener.

JUNO. I dont think any good can come of a conversation between Mr Lunn and myself. We can hardly be expected to improve one another's morals. [*He passes behind the chesterfield to Mrs Lunn's end; seizes a chair; deliberately pushes it between Gregory and Mrs Lunn; and sits down with folded arms, resolved not to budge*].

GREGORY. Oh! Indeed! Oh, all right. If you come to that – [*He crosses to Mrs Juno; plants a chair by her side; and sits down with equal determination*].

JUNO. Now we are both equally guilty.

GREGORY. Pardon me. I'm not guilty.

JUNO. In intention. Dont quibble. You were guilty in intention, as I was.

GREGORY. No. I should rather describe myself as being guilty in fact, but not in intention.

JUNO	*rising and*	What!
MRS JUNO	*exclaiming*	No, really –
MRS LUNN	*simultaneously*	Gregory!

GREGORY. Yes: I maintain that I am responsible for my intentions only, and not for reflex actions over which I have no control. [*Mrs Juno sits down, ashamed*]. I promised my mother that I would never tell a lie, and that I would never make love to a married woman. I never have told a lie –

MRS LUNN [*remonstrating*] Gregory! [*She sits down again*].

GREGORY. I say never. On many occasions I have resorted to prevarication; but on great occasions I have always told the truth. I regard this as a great occasion; and I wont be intimidated into breaking my promise. I solemnly declare that I did not know until this evening that Mrs Juno was married. She will bear me out when I say that from that moment my intentions were strictly and resolutely honorable; though my conduct, which I could not control and am therefore not responsible for, was disgraceful – or would have been had this gentleman not walked in and begun making love to my wife under my very nose.

JUNO [*flinging himself back into his chair*] Well, I like this!

MRS LUNN. Really, darling, theres no use in the pot calling the kettle black.

GREGORY. When you say darling, may I ask which of us you are addressing?

MRS LUNN. I really dont know. I'm getting hopelessly confused.

JUNO. Why dont you let my wife say something? I dont think she ought to be thrust into the background like this.

MRS LUNN. I'm sorry, I'm sure. Please excuse me, dear.

MRS JUNO [*thoughtfully*] I dont know what to say. I must think over it. I have always been rather severe on this sort of thing; but when it came to the point I didnt behave as I thought I should behave. I didnt intend to be wicked; but somehow or other, Nature, or whatever you choose to call it, didnt take much notice of my intentions. [*Gregory instinctively seeks her hand and presses it*]. And I really did think, Tops, that I was the only woman in the world for you.

JUNO [*cheerfully*] Oh, thats all right, my precious. Mrs Lunn thought she was the only woman in the world for him.

GREGORY [*reflectively*] So she is, in a sort of way.

JUNO [*flaring up*] And so is my wife. Dont you set up to be a better husband than I am; for youre not. Ive owned I'm wrong. You havnt.

MRS LUNN. Are you sorry, Gregory?

GREGORY [*perplexed*] Sorry?

MRS LUNN. Yes, sorry. I think it's time for you to say youre sorry, and to make friends with Mr Juno before we all dine together.

GREGORY. Seraphita: I promised my mother –

MRS JUNO [*involuntarily*] Oh, bother your mother! [*Recovering herself*] I beg your pardon.

GREGORY. A promise is a promise. I cant tell a deliberate lie. I know I ought to be sorry; but the flat fact is that I'm not sorry. I find that in this business, somehow or other, there is a disastrous separation between my moral principles and my conduct.

JUNO. Theres nothing disastrous about it. It doesnt matter about your conduct if your principles are all right.

GREGORY. Bosh! It doesnt matter about your principles if your conduct is all right.

JUNO. But your conduct isnt all right; and my principles are.

GREGORY. Whats the good of your principles being right if they wont work?

JUNO. They will work, sir, if you exercise self-sacrifice.

GREGORY. Oh yes: if, if, if. You know jolly well that self-sacrifice doesnt work either when you really want a thing. How much have you sacrificed yourself, pray?

MRS LUNN. Oh, a great deal, Gregory. Dont be rude. Mr Juno is a very nice man: he has been most attentive to me on the voyage.

GREGORY. And Mrs Juno's a very nice woman. She oughtnt to be; but she is.

JUNO. Why oughtnt she to be a nice woman, pray?

GREGORY. I mean she oughtnt to be nice to me. And you oughtnt to be nice to my wife. And your wife oughtnt to like me. And my wife oughtnt to like you. And if they do, they oughtnt to go on liking us. And I oughtnt to like your wife; and you oughtnt to like mine; and if we do, we oughtnt to go on liking them. But we do, all of us. We oughtnt; but we do.

JUNO. But, my dear boy, if we admit we are in the wrong wheres the harm of it? We're not perfect; but as long as we keep the ideal before us –

GREGORY. How?

JUNO. By admitting we're wrong.

MRS LUNN [springing up, out of patience, and pacing round the lounge intolerantly] Well, really, I must have my dinner. These two men, with their morality, and their promises to their mothers, and their admissions that they were wrong, and their sinning and suffering, and their going on at one another as if it meant anything, or as if it mattered, are getting on my nerves. [Stooping over the back of the chesterfield to address Mrs Juno] If you will be so very good, my dear, as to take my sentimental husband off my hands occasionally, I shall be more than obliged to you: I'm sure you can stand more male sentimentality than I can. [Sweeping away to the fireplace] I, on my part, will do my best to amuse your excellent husband when you find him tiresome.

JUNO. I call this polyandry.

MRS LUNN. I wish you wouldnt call innocent things by offensive names, Mr Juno. What do you call your own conduct?

JUNO [rising] I tell you I have admitted –

GREGORY		Whats the good of keeping on at that?
MRS JUNO	together	Oh, not that again, please.
MRS LUNN		Tops: I'll scream if you say that again.

JUNO. Oh, well, if you wont listen to me –! [He sits down again].

MRS JUNO. What is the position now exactly? [Mrs Lunn shrugs her shoulders and gives up the conundrum. Gregory looks at Juno. Juno turns away his head huffily]. I mean, what are we going to do?

MRS LUNN. What would you advise, Mr Juno?

JUNO. I should advise you to divorce your husband.

MRS LUNN. You want me to drag your wife into court and disgrace her?

JUNO. No: I forgot that. Excuse me; but for the moment I thought I was married to you.

GREGORY. I think we had better let bygones be bygones. [*To Mrs Juno, very tenderly*] You will forgive me, wont you? Why should you let a moment's forgetfulness embitter all our future life?

MRS JUNO. But it's Mrs Lunn who has to forgive you.

GREGORY. Oh, dash it, I forgot. This is getting ridiculous.

MRS LUNN. I'm getting hungry.

MRS JUNO. Do you really mind, Mrs Lunn?

MRS LUNN. My dear Mrs Juno, Gregory is one of those terribly uxorious men who ought to have ten wives. If any really nice woman will take him off my hands for a day or two occasionally, I shall be greatly obliged to her.

GREGORY. Seraphita: you cut me to the soul [*he weeps*].

MRS LUNN. Serve you right! Youd think it quite proper if it cut me to the soul.

MRS JUNO. Am I to take Sibthorpe off your hands too, Mrs Lunn?

JUNO [*rising*] Do you suppose I'll allow this?

MRS JUNO. Youve admitted that youve done wrong, Tops. Whats the use of your allowing or not allowing after that?

JUNO. I do not admit that I have done wrong. I admit that what I did was wrong.

GREGORY. Can you explain the distinction?

JUNO. It's quite plain to anyone but an imbecile. If you tell me Ive done something wrong you insult me. But if you say that something that I did is wrong you simply raise a question of morals. I tell you flatly if you say I did anything wrong you will have to fight me. In fact I think we ought to fight anyhow. I dont particularly want to; but I feel that England expects us to.

GREGORY. I wont fight. If you beat me my wife would share my humiliation. If I beat you, she would sympathize with you and loathe me for my brutality.

MRS LUNN. Not to mention that as we are human beings and not reindeer or barndoor fowl, if two men presumed to fight for us we couldnt decently ever speak to either of them again.

GREGORY. Besides, neither of us could beat the other, as we

neither of us know how to fight. We should only blacken each other's eyes and make fools of ourselves.

JUNO. I dont admit that. Every Englishman can use his fists.

GREGORY. Youre an Englishman. Can you use yours?

JUNO. I presume so: I never tried.

MRS JUNO. You never told me you couldnt fight, Tops. I thought you were an accomplished boxer.

JUNO. My precious: I never gave you any ground for such a belief.

MRS JUNO. You always talked as if it were a matter of course. You spoke with the greatest contempt of men who didnt kick other men downstairs.

JUNO. Well, I cant kick Mr Lunn downstairs. We're on the ground floor.

MRS JUNO. You could throw him into the harbor.

GREGORY. Do you want me to be thrown into the harbor?

MRS JUNO. No: I only want to shew Tops that he's making a ghastly fool of himself.

GREGORY [rising and prowling disgustedly between the chesterfield and the windows] We're all making fools of ourselves.

JUNO [following him] Well, if we're not to fight, I must insist at least on your never speaking to my wife again.

GREGORY. Does my speaking to your wife do you any harm?

JUNO. No. But it's the proper course to take. [Emphatically] We must behave with some sort of decency.

MRS LUNN. And are you never going to speak to me again, Mr Juno?

JUNO. I'm prepared to promise never to do so. I think your husband has a right to demand that. Then if I speak to you after, it will not be his fault. It will be a breach of my promise; and I shall not attempt to defend my conduct.

GREGORY [facing him] I shall talk to your wife as often as she'll let me.

MRS JUNO. I have no objection to your speaking to me, Mr Lunn.

JUNO. Then I shall take steps.

GREGORY. What steps?

JUNO. Steps. Measures. Proceedings. Such steps as may seem advisable.

MRS LUNN [to Mrs Juno] Can your husband afford a scandal, Mrs Juno?

MRS JUNO. No.

MRS LUNN. Neither can mine.

GREGORY. Mrs Juno: I'm very sorry I let you in for all this. I dont know how it is that we contrive to make feelings like ours, which seem to me to be beautiful and sacred feelings, and which lead to such interesting and exciting adventures, end in vulgar squabbles and degrading scenes.

JUNO. I decline to admit that my conduct has been vulgar or degrading.

GREGORY. I promised –

JUNO. Look here, old chap: I dont say a word against your mother; and I'm sorry she's dead; but really, you know, most women are mothers; and they all die some time or other; yet that doesnt make them infallible authorities on morals, does it?

GREGORY. I was about to say so myself. Let me add that if you do things merely because you think some other fool expects you to do them, and he expects you to do them because he thinks you expect him to expect you to do them, it will end in everybody doing what nobody wants to do, which is in my opinion a silly state of things.

JUNO. Lunn: I love your wife; and thats all about it.

GREGORY. Juno: I love yours. What then?

JUNO. Clearly she must never see you again.

MRS JUNO. Why not?

JUNO. Why not! My love: I'm surprised at you.

MRS JUNO. Am I to speak only to men who dislike me?

JUNO. Yes: I think that is, properly speaking, a married woman's duty.

MRS JUNO. Then I wont do it: thats flat. I like to be liked. I like to be loved. I want everyone round me to love me. I dont want to meet or speak to anyone who doesnt like me.

JUNO. But, my precious, this is the most horrible immorality.

MRS LUNN. I dont intend to give up meeting you, Mr Juno. You amuse me very much. I dont like being loved: it bores me. But I do like to be amused.

JUNO. I hope we shall meet very often. But I hope also we shall not defend our conduct.

MRS JUNO [rising] This is unendurable. Weve all been flirting. Need we go on footling about it?

JUNO [huffily] I dont know what you call footling –

MRS JUNO [cutting him short] You do. Youre footling. Mr Lunn is footling. Cant we admit that we're human and have done with it?

JUNO. I have admitted it all along. I —

MRS JUNO [*almost screaming*] Then stop footling.

The dinner gong sounds.

MRS LUNN [*rising*] Thank heaven! Lets go into dinner. Gregory: take in Mrs Juno.

GREGORY. But surely I ought to take in our guest, and not my own wife.

MRS LUNN. Well, Mrs Juno is not your wife, is she?

GREGORY. Oh, of course: I beg your pardon. I'm hopelessly confused. [*He offers his arm to Mrs Juno, rather apprehensively*].

MRS JUNO. You seem quite afraid of me [*she takes his arm*].

GREGORY. I am. I simply adore you. [*They go out together; and as they pass through the door he turns and says in a ringing voice to the other couple*] I have said to Mrs Juno that I simply adore her. [*He takes her out defiantly*].

MRS LUNN [*calling after him*] Yes, dear. She's a darling. [*To Juno*] Now, Sibthorpe.

JUNO [*giving her his arm gallantly*] You have called me Sibthorpe! Thank you. I think Lunn's conduct fully justifies me in allowing you to do it.

MRS LUNN. Yes: I think you may let yourself go now.

JUNO. Seraphita: I worship you beyond expression.

MRS LUNN. Sibthorpe: you amuse me beyond description. Come. [*They go in to dinner together*].

The Music-Cure

A Piece of Utter Nonsense

Composition begun 27 April 1913; completed 21 January 1914. First published in German translation, as *Eine musikalische Kur*, in *Die Grosse Katharina: Funf Einakter*, 1919. First English publication in *Translations and Tomfooleries*, 1926. First presented at the Little Theatre, London, on 28 January 1914.

Lord Reginald Fitzambey   *William Armstrong*
Dr Dawkins   *Frank Randell*
Strega Thundridge   *Madge McIntosh*

Period – The Present

Scene – *A Room in the Fitzcarlton Hotel*

This is not a serious play: it is what is called a Variety Turn for two musicians. It is written for two pianists, but can be adapted to any instruments on which the performers happen to be proficient. At its first performance by Miss Madge McIntosh and Mr William Armstrong the difficulty arose that, though Mr Armstrong was an accomplished pianist, Miss McIntosh's virtuosity was confined to the English concertina. That did just as well.

As a last desperate resort a pianola behind the scenes can be employed; but the result will lack spontaneity.

There is, however, no pressing reason why the thing should be performed at all.

Lord Reginald Fitzambey, a fashionably dressed, rather pretty young man of 22, is prostrate on a sofa in a large hotel drawing room, crying convulsively. His doctor is trying to soothe him. The doctor is about a dozen years his senior; and his ways are the ways of a still youthful man who considers himself in smart society as well as professionally attendant on it.

The drawing room has tall central doors, at present locked. If anyone could enter under these circumstances, he would find on his left a grand piano with the keyboard end towards him, and a smaller door beyond the piano. On his right would be the window, and, further on, the sofa on which the unhappy youth is wallowing, with, close by it, the doctor's chair and a little table accommodating the doctor's hat, a plate, a medicine bottle, a half emptied glass, and a bell call.

THE DOCTOR. Come come! be a man. Now really this is silly. You mustnt give way like this. I tell you nothing's happened to you. Hang it all! it's not the end of the world if you did buy a few shares —

REGINALD [*interrupting him frantically*] I never meant any harm in buying those shares. I am ready to give them up. Oh, I never meant any harm in buying those shares. I never meant any harm in buying those shares. [*Clutching the doctor imploringly*] Wont you believe me, Doctor? I never meant any harm in buying those shares. I never —

THE DOCTOR [*extricating himself and replacing Reginald on the couch, not very gently*] Of course you didnt. I know you didnt.

REGINALD. I never —

THE DOCTOR [*desperate*] Dont go on saying that over and over again or you will drive us all as distracted as you are yourself. This is nothing but nerves. Remember that youre in a hotel. Theyll put you out if you make a row.

REGINALD [*tearfully*] But you dont understand. Oh, why wont anybody understand? I never —

THE DOCTOR [*shouting him down*] You never meant any harm in buying those shares. This is the four hundredth time youve said it.

REGINALD [*wildly*] Then why do you keep asking me the same

questions over and over again? It's not fair. Ive told you I never meant any harm in —

THE DOCTOR. Yes, yes, yes: I know, I know. You think you made a fool of yourself before that committee. Well, you didnt. You stood up to it for six days with the coolness of an iceberg and the cheerfulness of an idiot. Every member of it had a go at you; and everyone of them, including some of the cleverest cross-examiners in London, fell back baffled before your fatuous self-satisfaction, your impenetrable inability to see any reason why you shouldnt have bought those shares.

REGINALD. But why shouldnt I have bought them? I made no secret of it. When the Prime Minister ragged me about it I offered to sell him the shares for what I gave for them.

THE DOCTOR. Yes, after they had fallen six points. But never mind that. The point for you is that you are an under-secretary in the War Office. You knew that the Army was going to be put on vegetarian diet, and that the British Maccaroni Trust shares would go up with a rush when this became public. And what did you do?

REGINALD. I did what any fellow would have done. I bought all the shares I could afford.

THE DOCTOR. You bought a great many more than you could afford.

REGINALD. But why shouldnt I? Explain it to me. I'm anxious to learn. I meant no harm. I see no harm. Why am I to be badgered because the beastly Opposition papers and all the Opposition rotters on that committee try to make party capital out of it by saying that it was disgraceful? It wasnt disgraceful: it was simple common sense. I'm not a financier; but you cant persuade me that if you happen to know that certain shares are going to rise you shouldnt buy them. It would be flying in the face of Providence not to. And they wouldnt see that. They pretended not to see it. They worried me, and kept asking me the same thing over and over again, and wrote blackguardly articles about me —

THE DOCTOR. And you got the better of them all because you couldnt see their point of view. But what beats me is why you broke down afterwards.

REGINALD. Everyone was against me. I thought the committee a pack of fools; and I as good as told them so. But everyone took their part. The governor said I had disgraced the family name. My brothers said I ought to resign from my clubs. My mother said that all her hopes of marrying me to a rich woman were shattered. And I'd done nothing: absolutely nothing to what other chaps are doing every day.

THE DOCTOR. Well, the long and short of it is that officials mustnt gamble.

REGINALD. But I wasnt gambling. I know. It isnt gambling if you know that the shares will go up. It's a cert.

THE DOCTOR. Well, all I can tell you is that if you werent a son of the Duke of Dunmow, youd have to resign; and –

REGINALD [*breaking down*] Oh, stop talking to me about it. Let me alone. I cant bear it. I never meant any harm in buying those shares. I never meant any harm –

THE DOCTOR. Sh-sh-sh-sh-sh! There: I shouldnt have started the subject again. Take some of this valerian [*he puts the glass to Reginald's lips*]. Thats right. Now youre better.

REGINALD [*exhausted but calm*] Why does valerian soothe me when it excites cats? Theres a question to reflect on! You know, they ought to have made me a philosopher.

THE DOCTOR. Philosophers are born, not made.

REGINALD. Fine old chestnut, that. Everybody's born, not made.

THE DOCTOR. Youre getting almost clever. I dont like it: youre not yourself today. I wish I could take your mind off your troubles. Suppose you try a little music.

REGINALD. I cant play. My fingers wont obey me. And I cant stand the sound of the piano. I sounded a note this morning; and it made me scream.

THE DOCTOR. But why not get somebody to play to you?

REGINALD. Whom could I get, even if I could bear it? You cant play.

THE DOCTOR. Well: I'm not the only person in the world.

REGINALD. If you bring anyone else in here, I shall go mad. I'll throw myself out of the window. I cant bear the idea of music. I dread it, hate it, loathe it.

THE DOCTOR. Thats very serious, you know.

REGINALD. Why is it serious?

THE DOCTOR. Well, what would become of you without your turn for music? You have absolutely no capacity in any other direction.

REGINALD. I'm in Parliament. And I'm an under-secretary.

THE DOCTOR. Thats because your father is a Duke. If you were in a Republic you wouldnt be trusted to clean boots, unless your father was a millionaire. No, Reginald: the day you give up vamping accompaniments and playing the latest ragtimes by ear, youre a lost man socially.

REGINALD [*deprecating*] Oh, I say!

THE DOCTOR [*rising*] However, perhaps it's too soon for you to try the music-cure yet. It was your mother's idea; but I'll call and tell her to wait a day or two. I think she meant to send somebody to play. I must be off now. Look in again later. Meanwhile, sleep as much as you can. Or you might read a little.

REGINALD. What can I read?

THE DOCTOR. Try the Strand Magazine.

REGINALD. But it's so frightfully intellectual. It would overtax my brain.

THE DOCTOR. Oh, well, I suppose it would. Well, sleep. Perhaps I'd better give you something to send you off [*he produces a medicine case*].

REGINALD. Whats this? Veronal?

THE DOCTOR. Dont be alarmed. Only the old-fashioned remedy: opium. Take this [*Reginald takes a pill*]: that will do the trick, I expect. If you find after half an hour that it has only excited you, take another. I'll leave one for you [*he puts one on the plate, and pockets his medicine case*].

REGINALD. Better leave me a lot. I like pills.

THE DOCTOR. Thank you: I'm not treating you with a view to a coroner's inquest. You know, dont you, that opium is a poison?

REGINALD. Yes, opium. But not pills.

THE DOCTOR. Well, Heaven forbid that I, a doctor, should shake anybody's faith in pills. But I shant leave you enough to kill you. [*He puts on his hat*].

REGINALD. Youll tell them, wont you, not to let anyone in. Really and truly I shall throw myself out of the window if any stranger comes in. I should go out of my mind.

THE DOCTOR. None of us have very far to go to do that, my young friend. Ta ta, for the moment [*he makes for the central doors*].

REGINALD. You cant go out that way. I made my mother lock it and take away the key. I felt sure theyd let somebody in that way if she didnt. Youll have to go the way you came.

THE DOCTOR [*returning*] Right. Now let me see you settle down before I go. I want you to be asleep before I leave the room.

Reginald settles himself to sleep with his face to the back of the sofa. The doctor goes softly to the side door and goes out.

REGINALD [*sitting up wildly and staring affrightedly at the piano*]
Doctor! Doctor! Help!!!

THE DOCTOR [*returning hastily*] What is it?

REGINALD [*after another doubtful look at the piano*] Nothing. [*He composes himself to sleep again*].

THE DOCTOR. Nothing! There must have been something or you wouldnt have yelled like that. [*Pulling Reginald over so as to see his face*] Here! what was it?

REGINALD. Well, it's gone.

THE DOCTOR. Whats gone?

REGINALD. The crocodile.

THE DOCTOR. The crocodile!

REGINALD. Yes. It laughed at me, and was going to play the piano with its tail.

THE DOCTOR. Opium in small doses doesnt agree with you, my young friend. [*Taking the spare pill from the plate*] I shall have to give you a second pill.

REGINALD. But suppose two crocodiles come!

THE DOCTOR. They wont. If anything comes it will be something pretty this time. Thats how opium acts. Anyhow, youll be fast asleep in ten minutes. Here. Take it.

REGINALD [*after taking the pill*] It was awfully silly of me. But you know I really saw the thing.

THE DOCTOR. You neednt trouble about what you see with your eyes shut. [*He turns to the door*].

REGINALD. Would you mind looking under the sofa to make sure the crocodile isnt there?

THE DOCTOR. Why not look yourself? that would be more convincing.

REGINALD. I darent.

THE DOCTOR. You duffer! [*He looks*]. All serene. No crocodile. Now go bye bye. [*He goes out*].

> *Reginald again composes himself to sleep. Somebody unlocks the central doors. A lovely lady enters with a bouquet in her hand. She looks about her; takes a letter from wherever she carries letters; and starts on a voyage of discovery round the room, checking her observations by the contents of the letter. The piano seems specially satisfactory: she nods as she sees it. Reginald seems also to be quite expected. She does not speak to him. When she is quite satisfied that she is in the right room, she goes to the piano and tantalizes the expectant audience for about two minutes by putting down her flowers on the candle-stand; taking off her gloves and putting them with the*

flowers; taking off half a dozen diamond rings in the same way; sitting down to the keyboard and finding it too near to the piano, then too far, then too high, then too low: in short, exhausting all the tricks of the professional pianist before she at last strikes the keys and preludes brilliantly. At the sound, Reginald, with a scream, rolls from the sofa and writhes on the carpet in horrible contortions. She stops playing, amazed.

REGINALD. Oh! Oh! Oh! The crocodiles! Stop! Ow! Oh! Oh! [*He looks at the piano and sees the lady*] Oh I say!

THE LADY. What on earth do you mean by making that noise when I'm playing? Have you no sense? Have you no manners?

REGINALD [*sitting on the floor*] I'm awfully sorry.

THE LADY. Sorry! Why did you do it?

REGINALD. I thought you were a crocodile.

THE LADY. What a silly thing to say! Do I look like a crocodile?

REGINALD. No.

THE LADY. Do I play like a crocodile!

REGINALD [*cautiously rising and approaching her*] Well, you know, it's so hard to know how a crocodile would play.

THE LADY. Stuff! [*She resumes her playing*].

REGINALD. Please! [*He stops her by shutting the keyboard lid*]. Who let you in?

THE LADY [*rising threateningly*] What is that to you, pray?

REGINALD [*retreating timidly*] It's my room, you know.

THE LADY. It's nothing of the sort. It's the Duchess of Dunmow's room. I know it's the right one, because she gave me the key; and it was the right key.

REGINALD. But what did she do that for? Who are you, if you dont mind my asking?

THE LADY. I do mind your asking. It's no business of yours. However, youd better know to whom you are speaking. I am Strega Thundridge. [*She pronounces it Strayga*].

REGINALD. What! The female Paderewski!

STREGA. Pardon me. I believe Mr Paderewski has been called the male Thundridge; but no gentleman would dream of repeating such offensive vulgarities. Will you be good enough to return to your sofa, and hold your tongue, or else leave the room.

REGINALD. But, you know, I am ill.

STREGA. Then go to bed, and send for a doctor. [*She sits down again to the keyboard*].

REGINALD [*falling to his knees*] You mustnt play. You really mustnt. I cant stand it. I shall simply not be myself if you start playing.

STREGA [*raising the lid*] Then I shall start at once.

REGINALD [*running to her on his knees and snatching at her hands*] No, you shant. [*She rises indignantly. He holds on to her hands, but exclaims ecstatically*] Oh, I say, what lovely hands youve got!

STREGA. The idea! [*She hurls him to the carpet*].

REGINALD [*on the floor staring at her*] You are strong.

STREGA. My strength has been developed by playing left hand octave passages—like this. [*She begins playing Liszt's transcription of Schubert's Erl König*].

REGINALD [*puts his fingers in his ears, but continues to stare at her*].

STREGA [*stopping*] I really cannot play if you keep your ears stopped. It is an insult. Leave the room.

REGINALD. But I tell you it's my room.

STREGA [*rising*] Leave the room, or I will ring your bell and have you put out. [*She goes to the little table, and poises her fingers over the bell call*].

REGINALD [*rushing to her*] No no: somebody will come if you ring; and I shall go distracted if a stranger comes in. [*With a touch of her left hand she sends him reeling. He appeals to her plaintively*] Dont you see that I am ill?

STREGA. I see that you are mentally afflicted. But that doesnt matter to me. The Duchess of Dunmow has engaged me to come to this room and play for two hours. I never break an engagement, especially a two hundred and fifty guinea one. [*She turns towards the piano*].

REGINALD. But didnt she tell you anything about me?

STREGA [*turning back to him*] She said there would be a foolish young man in the room, but that I was not to mind him. She assured me you were not dangerous except to yourself. [*Collaring him and holding him bent backwards over the piano*]. But I will have no nonsense about not listening. All the world listens when I play. Listen, or go.

REGINALD [*helpless*] But I shall have to sit on the stairs. I darent go into any of the rooms: I should meet people there.

STREGA. You will meet plenty of people on the stairs, young man. They are sitting six on each stair, not counting those who are sitting astride the banisters on the chance of hearing me play.

REGINALD. How dreadful! [*Tearfully*] Youve no right to bully me like this. I'm ill: I cant bear it. I'll throw myself out of the window.

STREGA [*releasing him*] Do. What an advertisement! It will be really kind of you [*She goes back to the keyboard and sits down to play*].

REGINALD [*crossing to the window*] Youll be sorry you were so unfeeling when you see my mangled body. [*He opens the window; looks out; shuts it hastily, and retreats with a scream*]. Theres a crowd. I darent.

STREGA [*pleased*] Waiting to hear me play [*she preludes softly*].

REGINALD [*ravished*] Oh! I can stand that, you know.

STREGA [*ironically, still preluding*] Thank you.

REGINALD. The fact is, I can play a bit myself.

STREGA [*still preluding*] An amateur, I presume.

REGINALD. I have often been told I could make a living at it if I tried. But of course it wouldnt do for a man in my position to lower himself by becoming a professional.

STREGA [*abruptly ceasing to play*] Tactful, that, I dont think! And what do you play, may I ask?

REGINALD. Oh, all the very best music.

STREGA. For instance?

REGINALD. I wish you belonged to me.

STREGA [*rising outraged*] You young blackguard! How dare you?

REGINALD. You dont understand: it's the name of a tune. Let me play it for you. [*He sits down at the keyboard*] I dont think you believe I can play.

STREGA. Pardon me. I have heard a horse play the harmonium at a music hall. I can believe anything.

REGINALD. Aha! [*He plays*]. Do you like that?

STREGA. What is it? Is it intended for music?

REGINALD. Oh, you beautiful doll.

STREGA. Take that [*she knocks him sprawling over the keyboard*]! Beautiful doll indeed!

REGINALD. Oh, I say! Look here: thats the name of the tune too. You seem quite ignorant of the best music. Dont you know Rum Tum Tiddle, and Alexander's Rag Time Band, and Take me back to the Garden of Love, and Everybody likes our Mary.

STREGA. Young man: I have never even heard of these abominations. I am now going to educate you musically. I am going to play Chopin, and Brahms, and Bach, and Schumann, and –

REGINALD [*horrified*] You dont mean classical music?

STREGA. I do [*he bolts through the central doors*].

STREGA [*disgusted*] Pig! [*She sits down at the piano again*].

REGINALD [*rushing back into the room*] I forgot the people on the stairs: crowds of them. Oh, what shall I do! Oh dont, Dont,

DONT play classical music to me. Say you wont. Please.

STREGA [*looks at him enigmatically and softly plays a Liebeslieder Waltz*]!!

REGINALD. Oh, I say: thats rather pretty.

STREGA. Like it?

REGINALD. Awfully. Oh, I say, you know: I really do wish you belonged to me. [*Strega suddenly plays a violent Chopin study. He goes into convulsions*]. Oh! Stop! Mercy! Help! Oh please, please!

STREGA [*pausing with her hands raised over the keyboard, ready to pounce on the chords*] Will you ever say that again?

REGINALD. Never. I beg your pardon.

STREGA [*satisfied*] Hm! [*She drops her hands in her lap*].

REGINALD [*wiping his brow*] Oh, that was fearfully classical.

STREGA. You want your back stiffened a little, my young friend. Besides, I really cannot earn two hundred and fifty guineas by playing soothing syrup to you. Now prepare for the worst. I'm going to make a man of you.

REGINALD. How?

STREGA. With Chopin's Polonaise in A Flat. Now. Imagine yourself going into battle. [*He runs away as before*] Goose!

REGINALD [*returning as before*] The crowd is worse than ever. Have you no pity?

STREGA. Come here. Dont imagine yourself going into battle Imagine that you have just been in a battle; and that you have saved your country by deeds of splendid bravery; and that you are going to dance with beautiful women who are proud of you. Can you imagine that?

REGINALD. Rathe-e-e-errr. Thats how I always do imagine myself.

STREGA. Right. Now listen. [*She plays the first section of the Polonaise. Reginald flinches at first, but gradually braces himself; stiffens; struts; throws up his head and slaps his chest*]. Thats better. What a hero! [*After a difficult passage*]. Takes a bit of doing, that, dearest child. [*Coming to the chords which announce the middle section*] Now for it.

REGINALD [*unable to contain himself*] Oh, this is too glorious. I must have a turn or I shall forget myself.

STREGA. Can you play this? Nothing but this. [*She plays the octave passage in the bass*].

REGINALD. Just riddle tiddle, riddle tiddle, riddle tiddle, riddle tiddle? Nothing but that?

STREGA. Very softly at first. Like the ticking of a watch. Then louder and louder, as you feel my soul swelling.

REGINALD. I understand. Just give me those chords again to buck me up to it. [*She plays the chords again. He plays the octave passages; and they play the middle section as a duet. At the repeat he cries*] Again! again!

STREGA. It's meant to be played again. Now.

> *They repeat it. At the end of the section she pushes him off the bench on to the floor, and goes on with the Polonaise alone.*

REGINALD. Wonderful woman: I have a confession to make, a confidence to impart. Your playing draws it from me. Listen, Strega [*she plays a horrible discord*] I mean Miss Thundridge.

STREGA. Thats better; but I prefer Wonderful Woman.

REGINALD. You are a wonderful woman, you know. Adored one — would you mind my taking a little valerian? I'm so excited [*he takes some*]. A – a – ah! Now I feel that I can speak. Listen to me, goddess. I am not happy. I hate my present existence. I loathe parliament. I am not fit for public affairs. I am condemned to live at home with five coarse and brutal sisters who care for nothing but Alpine climbing, and looping the loop on aeroplanes, and going on deputations, and fighting the police. Do you know what they call me?

STREGA [*playing softly*] What do they call you, dear?

REGINALD. They call me a Clinger. Well, I confess it. I am a Clinger. I am not fit to be thrown unprotected upon the world. I want to be shielded. I want a strong arm to lean on, a dauntless heart to be gathered to and cherished, a breadwinner on whose income I can live without the sordid horrors of having to make money for myself. I am a poor little thing, I know, Strega; but I could make a home for you. I have great taste in carpets and pictures. I can cook like anything. I can play quite nicely after dinner. Though you mightnt think it, I can be quite stern and strongminded with servants. I get on splendidly with children: they never talk over my head as grown-up people do. I have a real genius for home life. And I shouldnt at all mind being tyrannized over a little: in fact, I like it. It saves me the trouble of having to think what to do. Oh, Strega, dont you want a dear little domesticated husband who would have no concern but to please you, no thought outside our home, who would be un-spotted and unsoiled by the rude cold world, who would never meddle in politics or annoy you by interfering with your profession? Is there any hope for me?

STREGA [*coming away from the piano*] My child: I am a hard, strong, independent, muscular woman. How can you, with your delicate soft nature, see anything to love in me? I should hurt you, shock you, perhaps – yes: let me confess it – I have a violent temper, and might even, in a transport of rage, beat you.

REGINALD. Oh do, do. Dont laugh at this ridiculous confession; but ever since I was a child I have had only one secret longing, and that was to be mercilessly beaten by a splendid, strong, beautiful woman.

STREGA [*solemnly*] Reginald – I think your mother spoke of you as Reginald? –

REGINALD. Rejjy.

STREGA. I too have a confession to make. I too need some music to speak through. Will you be so good?

REGINALD. Angel. [*He rushes to the piano and plays sympathetically whilst she speaks*].

STREGA. I, too, have had my dream. It has consoled me through the weary hours when I practised scales for eight hours a day. It has pursued me through the applause of admiring thousands in Europe and America. It is a dream of a timid little heart fluttering against mine, of a gentle voice to welcome me home, of a silky moustache to kiss my weary fingers when I return from a Titanic struggle with Tchaikovsky's Concerto in G major, of somebody utterly dependent on me, utterly devoted to me, utterly my own, living only to be cherished and worshipped by me.

REGINALD. But you would be angry sometimes: terrible, splendid, ruthless, violent. You would throw down the thing you loved and trample on it as it clung to your feet.

STREGA. Yes – oh, why do you force me to confess it? – I should beat it to a jelly, and then cast myself in transports of remorse on its quivering frame and smother it with passionate kisses.

REGINALD [*transported*] Let it be me, let it be me.

STREGA. You dare face this terrible destiny?

REGINALD. I embrace it. I adore you. I am wholly yours. Oh, let me cling, cling, cling.

STREGA [*embracing him fiercely*] Nothing shall tear you from my arms now.

REGINALD. Nothing. I am provided for. Oh how happy this will make my mother!

STREGA. Sweet: name the day.

He plays a wedding march. She plays the bass.

Great Catherine

(Whom Glory Still Adores)

WITH

The Author's Apology for Great Catherine

Composition begun 29 July 1913; completed 13 August 1913. First published in German translation, as *Die Grosse Katharina*, in the *Neue Rundschau* (Berlin), April 1914. Published in *Everybody's Magazine* (New York), February 1915. First English publication in *Heartbreak House, Great Catherine, & Playlets of the War*, 1919. First presented at the Vaudeville Theatre, London, on 18 November 1913.

Prince Patiomkin   *Norman McKinnel*
Varinka   *Miriam Lewes*
Cossack Sergeant   *J. Cooke Beresford*
Captain Charles Edstaston (Light Dragoons)   *Edmond Breon*
Naryshkin (Chamberlain)   *Eugene Mayeur*
Empress Catherine II   *Gertrude Kingston*
Princess Dashkoff   *Annie Hill*
Claire   *Dorothy Massingham*

Period – 1776

Scene 1: *Prince Patiomkin's Chancery in the Winter Palace*

Scene 2: *The Empress's Bedchamber*

Scene 3: *A Terrace Garden*

Scene 4: *A Recess in the Grand Ballroom of the Palace*

THE AUTHOR'S APOLOGY
FOR GREAT CATHERINE

Exception has been taken to the title of this seeming tomfoolery on the ground that the Catherine it represents is not Great Catherine, but the Catherine whose gallantries provide some of the lightest pages of modern history. Great Catherine, it is said, was the Catherine whose diplomacy, whose campaigns and conquests, whose plans of Liberal reform, whose correspondence with Grimm and Voltaire enabled her to cut such a magnificent figure in the XVIII century. In reply, I can only confess that Catherine's diplomacy and her conquests do not interest me. It is clear to me that neither she nor the statesmen with whom she played this mischievous kind of political chess had any notion of the real history of their own times, or of the real forces that were moulding Europe. The French Revolution, which made such short work of Catherine's Voltairean principles, surprised and scandalized her as much as it surprised and scandalized any provincial governess in the French chateaux.

The main difference between her and our modern Liberal Governments was that whereas she talked and wrote quite intelligently about Liberal principles before she was frightened into making such talking and writing a flogging matter, our Liberal ministers take the name of Liberalism in vain without knowing or caring enough about its meaning even to talk and scribble about it, and pass their flogging Bills, and institute their prosecutions for sedition and blasphemy and so forth, without the faintest suspicion that such proceedings need any apology from the Liberal point of view.

It was quite easy for Patiomkin to humbug Catherine as to the condition of Russia by conducting her through sham cities run up for the occasion by scenic artists; but in the little world of European court intrigue and dynastic diplomacy which was the only world she knew she was more than a match for him and for all the rest of her contemporaries. In such intrigue and diplomacy, however, there was no romance, no scientific political interest, nothing that a sane mind can now retain even if it can be persuaded to waste time in reading it up. But Catherine as a woman, with plenty of character and (as we should say) no morals, still fascinates and amuses us as she fascinated and amused her contemporaries. They were great sentimental comedians, these Peters, Elizabeths, and Catherines who played their Tsarships as eccentric character parts, and produced scene after scene of furious harlequinade with the monarch as clown, and of tragic relief in the torture chamber with the monarch as pantomime demon committing real atrocities, not forgetting the indispensable love interest on an enormous and utterly indecorous scale. Catherine kept this vast Guignol Theatre open for nearly half a century, not as a Russian, but as a highly domesticated German lady whose household routine was not at all so unlike that of Queen Victoria as might be expected from the difference in their notions of propriety in sexual relations.

In short, if Byron leaves you with an impression that he said very little about Catherine, and that little not what was best worth saying, I beg to correct your impression by assuring you that what Byron said was all there really is to say that is worth saying. His Catherine is my Catherine and everybody's Catherine. The young man who gains her favor is a Spanish nobleman in his version. I have made him an English country gentleman, who gets out of his rather dangerous scrape by simplicity, sincerity, and the courage of these qualities. By this I have given some offence to the many Britons who see themselves as heroes: what they mean by heroes being theatrical snobs of superhuman pretensions which, though quite groundless, are admitted with awe by the rest of the human race. They say I think an Englishman a fool. When I do, they have themselves to thank.

I must not, however, pretend that historical portraiture was the motive of a play that will leave the reader as ignorant of Russian history as he may be now before he has turned the page. Nor is the sketch of Catherine complete even idiosyncratically, leaving her politics out of the question. For example, she wrote bushels of plays. I confess I have not yet read any of them. The truth is, this play grew out of the relations which inevitably exist in the theatre between authors and actors. If the actors have sometimes to use their skill as the author's puppets rather than in full self-expression, the author has sometimes to use his skill as the actors' tailor, fitting them with parts written to display the virtuosity of the performer rather than to solve problems of life, character, or history. Feats of this kind may tickle an author's technical vanity; but he is bound on such occasions to admit that the performer for whom he writes is 'the onlie begetter' of his work, which must be regarded critically as an addition to the debt dramatic literature owes to the art of acting and its exponents. Those who have seen Miss Gertrude Kingston play the part of Catherine will have no difficulty in believing that it was her talent rather than mine that brought the play into existence. I once recommended Miss Kingston professionally to play queens. Now in the modern drama there were no queens for her to play; and as to the older literature of our stage, did it not provoke the veteran actress in Sir Arthur Pinero's Trelawny of the Wells to declare that, as parts, queens are not worth a tinker's oath? Miss Kingston's comment on my suggestion, though more elegantly worded, was to the same effect; and it ended in my having to make good my advice by writing Great Catherine. History provided no other queen capable of standing up to our joint talents.

In composing such bravura pieces, the author limits himself only by the range of the virtuoso, which by definition far transcends the modesty of nature. If my Russians seem more Muscovite than any Russian, and my English people more insular than any Briton, I will not plead, as I honestly might, that the fiction has yet to be written that can exaggerate the reality of such subjects; that the apparently outrageous Patiomkin is but a timidly bowdlerized ghost of the original; and that Captain Edstaston is no more than a miniature that might hang appropriately on the walls of nineteen out of twenty English country houses to this day. An artistic presentment must not condescend to justify itself by a comparison with crude nature; and I prefer to admit that in this kind my *dramatis personæ* are, as they should be, of the stage stagey, challenging the actor to act up to them or beyond them, if he can. The more heroic the overcharging, the better for the performance.

In dragging the reader thus for a moment behind the scenes, I am departing from a rule which I have hitherto imposed on myself so rigidly that I never permit myself, even in a stage direction, to let slip a word that could bludgeon the imagination of the reader by reminding him of the boards and the footlights and the sky borders and the rest of the theatrical scaffolding, for which nevertheless I have to plan as carefully as if I were the head carpenter as well as the author. But even at the risk of talking shop, an honest playwright should take at least one opportunity of acknowledging that his art is not only limited by the art of the actor, but often stimulated and developed by it. No sane and skilled author writes plays that present impossibilities to the actor or to the stage engineer. If, as occasionally happens, he asks them to do things that they have never done before and cannot conceive as presentable or possible (as Wagner and Thomas Hardy have done, for example), it is always found that the difficulties are not really insuperable, the author having foreseen unsuspected possibilities both in the actor and in the audience, whose will-tó-make-believe can perform the quaintest miracles. Thus may authors advance the arts of acting and of staging plays. But the actor also may enlarge the scope of the drama by displaying powers not previously discovered by the author. If the best available actors are only Horatios, the authors will have to leave Hamlet out, and be content with Horatios for heroes. Some of the difference between Shakespear's Orlandos and Bassanios and Bertrams and his Hamlets and Macbeths must have been due not only to his development as a dramatic poet, but to the development of Burbage as an actor. Playwrights do not write for ideal actors when their livelihood is at stake: if they did, they would write parts for heroes with twenty arms like an Indian god. Indeed the actor often influences the author too much; for I can remember a time (I am not implying that it is yet wholly past) when the art of writing a fashionable play had become very largely the art of writing it 'round' the personalities of a group of fashionable performers of whom Burbage would certainly have said that their parts needed no acting. Everything has its abuse as well as its use.

It is also to be considered that great plays live longer than great actors, though little plays do not live nearly as long as the worst of their exponents. The consequence is that the great actor, instead of putting pressure on contemporary authors to supply him with heroic parts, falls back on the Shakespearean repertory, and takes what he needs from a dead hand. In the nineteenth century, the careers of Kean, Macready, Barry Sullivan, and Irving ought to have produced a group of heroic plays comparable in intensity to those of Æschylus, Sophocles, and Euripides; but nothing of the kind happened: these actors played the words of dead authors, or, very occasionally, of live poets who were hardly regular professional playwrights. Sheridan Knowles, Bulwer Lytton, Wills and Tennyson produced a few glaringly artificial high horses for the great actors of their time; but the playwrights proper, who really kept the theatre going, and were kept going by the theatre, did not cater for the great actors: they could not afford to compete with a bard who was not of an age but for all time, and who had, moreover, the overwhelming attraction for the actor-managers of not charging authors' fees. The result was that the playwrights and the great actors ceased to think of themselves as having any concern with one another: Tom Robertson, Ibsen, Pinero, and Barrie might as well have belonged to a different solar system as far as Irving was concerned; and the same was true of their respective predecessors.

Thus was established an evil tradition; but I at least can plead that it does not always hold good. If Forbes Robertson had not been there to play Caesar, I should not have written Caesar and Cleopatra. If Ellen Terry had never been born, Captain Brass-bound's conversion would never have been effected. The Devil's Disciple, with which I won my *cordon bleu* in America as a potboiler, would have had a different sort of hero if Richard Mansfield had been a different sort of actor, though the actual commission to write it came from an English actor, William Terriss, who was assassinated before he recovered from the dismay into which the result of his rash proposal threw him. For it must be said that the actor or actress who inspires or commissions a play as often as not regards it as a Frankenstein's monster, and will none of it. That does not make him or her any the less parental in the fecundity of the playwright.

To an author who has any feeling of his business there is a keen and whimsical joy in divining and revealing a side of an actor's genius overlooked before, and unsuspected even by the actor himself. When I snatched Mr Louis Calvert from Shakespear, and made him wear a frock coat and silk hat on the stage for perhaps the first time in his life, I do not think he expected in the least that his performance would enable me to boast of his Tom Broadbent as a genuine stage classic. Mrs Patrick Campbell was famous before I wrote for her, but not for playing illiterate cockney flowermaidens. And in the case which is provoking me to all these impertinences, I am quite sure that Miss Gertrude Kingston, who first made her reputation as an impersonator of the most delightfully feather-headed and inconsequent ingenues, thought me more than usually mad when I persuaded her to play the Helen of Euripides, and then launched her on a queenly career as Catherine of Russia.

It is not the whole truth that if we take care of the actors the plays will take care of themselves; nor is it any truer that if we take care of the plays the actors will take care of themselves. There is both give and take in the business. I have seen plays written for actors that made me exclaim, 'How oft the sight of means to do ill deeds makes deeds ill done!' But Burbage may have flourished the prompt copy of Hamlet under Shakespear's nose at the tenth rehearsal and cried 'How oft the sight of means to do great deeds makes playwrights great!' I say the tenth because I am convinced that at the first he denounced his part as a rotten one; thought the ghost's speech ridiculously long; and wanted to play the king. Anyhow, whether he had the wit to utter it or not, the boast would have been a valid one. The best conclusion is that every actor should say, 'If I create the hero in myself, God will send an author to write his part.' For in the long run the actors will get the authors, and the authors the actors, they deserve.

❧ GREAT CATHERINE ❧

THE FIRST SCENE

1776. Patiomkin in his bureau in the Winter Palace, St Petersburg. Huge palatial apartment: style, Russia in the XVIII century imitating the Versailles du Roi Soleil. Extravagant luxury. Also dirt and disorder.

Patiomkin, gigantic in stature and build, his face marred by the loss of one eye and a marked squint in the other, sits at the end of a table littered with papers and the remains of three or four successive breakfasts. He has supplies of coffee and brandy at hand sufficient for a party of ten. His coat, encrusted with diamonds, is on the floor. It has fallen off a chair placed near the other end of the table for the convenience of visitors. His court sword, with its attachments, is on the chair. His three-cornered hat, also bejewelled, is on the table. He himself is half dressed in an unfastened shirt and an immense dressing-gown, once gorgeous, now food-splashed and dirty, as it serves him for towel, handkerchief, duster, and every other use to which a textile fabric can be put by a slovenly man. It does not conceal his huge hairy chest, nor his half-buttoned knee breeches, nor his legs. These are partly clad in silk stockings, which he occasionally hitches up to his knees, and presently shakes down to his shins, by his restless movements. His feet are thrust into enormous slippers, worth, with their crust of jewels, several thousand roubles apiece.

Superficially Patiomkin is a violent, brutal barbarian, an upstart despot of the most intolerable and dangerous type, ugly, lazy, and disgusting in his personal habits. Yet ambassadors report him the ablest man in Russia, and the one who can do most with the still abler Empress Catherine II, who is not a Russian but a German, by no means barbarous or intemperate in her personal habits. She not only disputes with Frederick the Great the reputation of being the cleverest monarch in Europe, but may even put in a very plausible claim to be the cleverest and most attractive individual alive. Now she not only tolerates Patiomkin long after she has got over her first romantic attachment to him, but esteems him highly as a counsellor and a good friend. His love letters are among the best on record. He has a wild sense of humor, which enables him to laugh at himself as well as at everybody else. In the eyes of the English visitor now about to be admitted to his presence he may be an outrageous ruffian. In fact he actually is an outrageous ruffian, in no matter whose eyes; but the visitor will find out, as everyone else sooner or later finds out, that he is a man to be reckoned with even by those who are not intimidated by his temper, bodily strength, and exalted rank.

A pretty young lady, Varinka, his favorite niece, is lounging on an ottoman between his end of the table and the door, very sulky and dissatisfied, perhaps because he is preoccupied with his papers and his brandy bottle, and she can see nothing of him but his broad back.

There is a screen behind the ottoman.

An old soldier, a Cossack sergeant, enters.

THE SERGEANT [*softly to the lady, holding the door handle*] Little darling honey: is his Highness the prince very busy?

VARINKA. His Highness the prince is very busy. He is singing out of tune; he is biting his nails; he is scratching his head; he is hitching up his untidy stockings; he is making himself disgusting and odious to everybody; and he is pretending to read state papers that he does not understand because he is too lazy and selfish to talk and be companionable.

PATIOMKIN [*growls; then wipes his nose with his dressing-gown*]!!

VARINKA. Pig. Ugh! [*She curls herself up with a shiver of disgust and retires from the conversation*].

THE SERGEANT [*stealing across to the coat, and picking it up to replace it on the back of the chair*] Little Father: the English captain, so highly recommended to you by old Fritz of Prussia, by the English ambassador, and by Monsieur Voltaire (whom [*crossing himself*] may God in his infinite mercy damn eternally!), is in the antechamber and desires audience.

PATIOMKIN [*deliberately*] To hell with the English captain; and to hell with old Fritz of Prussia; and to hell with the English ambassador; and to hell with Monsieur Voltaire; and to hell with you too!

THE SERGEANT. Have mercy on me, Little Father. Your head is bad this morning. You drink too much French brandy and too little good Russian kvass.

PATIOMKIN [*with sudden fury*] Why are visitors of consequence announced by a sergeant? [*Springing at him and seizing him by the throat*] What do you mean by this, you hound? Do you want five thousand blows of the stick? Where is General Volkonsky?

THE SERGEANT [*on his knees*] Little Father: you kicked his Highness downstairs.

PATIOMKIN [*flinging him down and kicking him*] You lie, you dog. You lie.

THE SERGEANT. Little Father: life is hard for the poor. If you say it is a lie, it is a lie. He fell downstairs. I picked him up; and he kicked me. They all kick me when you kick them. God knows that is not just, Little Father!

PATIOMKIN [*laughs ogreishly; then returns to his place at the table, chuckling*]!!!

VARINKA. Savage! Boor! It is a disgrace. No wonder the French sneer at us as barbarians.

THE SERGEANT [*who has crept round the table to the screen, and insinuated himself between Patiomkin's back and Varinka*] Do you think the Prince will see the Captain, little darling?

PATIOMKIN. He will not see any captain. Go to the devil!

THE SERGEANT. Be merciful, Little Father. God knows it is your duty to see him! [*To Varinka*] Intercede for him and for me, beautiful little darling. He has given me a rouble.

PATIOMKIN. Oh, send him in, send him in; and stop pestering me. Am I never to have a moment's peace?

The Sergeant salutes joyfully and hurries out, divining that Patiomkin has intended to see the English captain all along, and has played this comedy of fury and exhausted impatience to conceal his interest in the visitor.

VARINKA. Have you no shame? You refuse to see the most exalted persons. You kick princes and generals downstairs. And then you see an English captain merely because he has given a rouble to that common soldier. It is scandalous.

PATIOMKIN. Darling beloved, I am drunk; but I know what I am doing. I wish to stand well with the English.

VARINKA. And you think you will impress an Englishman by receiving him as you are now, half drunk?

PATIOMKIN [*gravely*] It is true: the English despise men who cannot drink. I must make myself wholly drunk [*he takes a huge draught of brandy*].

VARINKA. Sot!

The Sergeant returns ushering a handsome strongly built young English officer in the uniform of a Light Dragoon. He is evidently on fairly good terms with himself, and very sure of his social position. He crosses the room to the end of the table opposite Patiomkin's, and awaits the civilities of that statesman with confidence. The Sergeant remains prudently at the door.

THE SERGEANT [*paternally*] Little Father: this is the English captain, so well recommended to her sacred Majesty the Empress. God knows, he needs your countenance and protec – [*he vanishes precipitately, seeing that Patiomkin is about to throw a bottle at him. The Captain contemplates these preliminaries with astonishment, and with some displeasure, which is not allayed when Patiomkin, hardly condescending to look at his visitor, of whom he nevertheless takes stock with the corner of his one eye, says gruffly*] Well?

EDSTASTON. My name is Edstaston: Captain Edstaston of the Light Dragoons. I have the honor to present to your Highness this letter from the British ambassador, which will give you all necessary particulars. [*He hands Patiomkin the letter*].

PATIOMKIN [*tearing it open and glancing at it for about a second*] What do you want?

EDSTASTON. The letter will explain to your Highness who I am.

PATIOMKIN. I dont want to know who you are. What do you want?

EDSTASTON. An audience of the Empress. [*Patiomkin contemptuously throws the letter aside. Edstaston adds hotly*] Also some civility, if you please.

PATIOMKIN [*with derision*] Ho!

VARINKA. My uncle is receiving you with unusual civility, Captain. He has just kicked a general downstairs.

EDSTASTON. A Russian general, madam?

VARINKA. Of course.

EDSTASTON. I must allow myself to say, madam, that your uncle had better not attempt to kick an English officer downstairs.

PATIOMKIN. You want me to kick you upstairs: eh? You want an audience of the Empress.

EDSTASTON. I have said nothing about kicking, sir. If it comes to that, my boots shall speak for me. Her Majesty has signified a desire to have news of the rebellion in America. I have served against the rebels; and I am instructed to place myself at the disposal of her Majesty, and to describe the events of the war to her, as an eye-witness, in a discreet and agreeable manner.

PATIOMKIN. Psha! I know. You think if she once sets eyes on your face and your uniform your fortune is made. You think that if she could stand a man like me, with only one eye, and a cross eye at that, she must fall down at your feet at first sight, eh?

EDSTASTON [*shocked and indignant*] I think nothing of the sort; and I'll trouble you not to repeat it. If I were a Russian subject and you made such a boast about my queen, I'd strike you across the face with my sword. [*Patiomkin, with a yell of fury, rushes at him*]. Hands off, you swine! [*As Patiomkin, towering over him, attempts to seize him by the throat, Edstaston, who is a bit of a wrestler, adroitly backheels him. He falls, amazed, on his back*].

VARINKA [*rushing out*] Help! Call the guard! The Englishman is murdering my uncle! Help! Help!

The guard and the Sergeant rush in. Edstaston draws a pair of small pistols from his boots, and points one at the Sergeant and the other at Patiomkin, who is sitting on the floor, somewhat sobered. The soldiers stand irresolute.

EDSTASTON. Stand off. [*To Patiomkin*] Order them off, if you dont want a bullet through your silly head.

THE SERGEANT. Little Father: tell us what to do. Our lives are yours; but God knows you are not fit to die.

PATIOMKIN [*absurdly self-possessed*] Get out.

THE SERGEANT. Little Father —

PATIOMKIN [*roaring*] Get out. Get out, all of you. [*They withdraw, much relieved at their escape from the pistol. Patiomkin attempts to rise, and rolls over*]. Here! help me up, will you? Dont you see that I'm drunk and cant get up?

EDSTASTON [*suspiciously*] You want to get hold of me.

PATIOMKIN [*squatting resignedly against the chair on which his clothes hang*] Very well, then: I shall stay where I am, because I'm drunk and youre afraid of me.

EDSTASTON. I'm not afraid of you, damn you!

PATIOMKIN [*ecstatically*] Darling: your lips are the gates of truth. Now listen to me. [*He marks off the items of his statement with ridiculous stiff gestures of his head and arms, imitating a puppet*] You are Captain Whathisname; and your uncle is the Earl of What-dyecallum; and your father is Bishop of Thingummybob; and you are a young man of the highest spr-promise (I told you I was drunk), educated at Cambridge, and got your step as captain in the field at the GLORIOUS battle of Bunker's Hill. Invalided home from America at the request of Aunt Fanny, Lady-in-Waiting to the Queen. All right, eh?

EDSTASTON. How do you know all this?

PATIOMKIN [*crowing fantastically*] In er lerrer, darling, darling, darling, darling. Lerrer you shewed me.

EDSTASTON. But you didnt read it.

PATIOMKIN [*flapping his fingers at him grotesquely*] Only one eye, darling. Cross eye. Sees everything. Read lerrer ince-inceistastaneously. Kindly give me vinegar borle. Green borle. On'y to sober me. Too drunk to speak proply. If you would be so kind, darling. Green borle. [*Edstaston, still suspicious, shakes his head and keep his pistols ready*]. Reach it myself [*He reaches behind him up to the table and snatches at the green bottle, from which he takes a copious draught. Its effect is appalling. His wry faces and agonized belchings are so heartrending that they almost upset Edstaston. When the victim at last staggers to his feet, he is a pale fragile nobleman, aged and quite sober, extremely dignified in manner and address, though shaken by his recent convulsions*]. Young man: it is not better to be drunk than sober; but it is happier. Goodness is not happiness. That is an epigram. But I have overdone this. I am too sober to be good company. Let me redress the balance [*He takes a generous draught of brandy, and recovers his geniality*]. Aha! Thats better. And now listen, darling. You must not come to Court with pistols in your boots.

EDSTASTON. I have found them useful.

PATIOMKIN. Nonsense. I'm your friend. You mistook my intention because I was drunk. Now that I am sober – in moderation – I will prove that I am your friend. Have some diamonds. [*Roaring*] Hullo there! Dogs, pigs: hullo!

The Sergeant comes in.

THE SERGEANT. God be praised, Little Father: you are still spared to us.

PATIOMKIN. Tell them to bring some diamonds. Plenty of diamonds. And rubies. Get out. [*He aims a kick at the Sergeant, who flees*]. Put up your pistols, darling. I'll give you a pair with gold handgrips. I am your friend.

EDSTASTON [*replacing the pistols in his boots rather unwillingly*] Your Highness understands that if I am missing, or if anything happens to me, there will be trouble.

PATIOMKIN [*enthusiastically*] Call me darling.

EDSTASTON. It is not the English custom.

PATIOMKIN. You have no hearts, you English! [*Slapping his right breast*] Heart! Heart!

EDSTASTON. Pardon, your Highness: your heart is on the other side.

PATIOMKIN [*surprised and impressed*] Is it? You are learned! You are a doctor! You English are wonderful! We are barbarians, drunken pigs. Catherine does not know it; but we are. Catherine's a German. But I have given her a Russian heart [*he is about to slap himself again*].

EDSTASTON [*delicately*] The other side, your Highness.

PATIOMKIN [*maudlin*] Darling: a true Russian has a heart on both sides.

The Sergeant enters carrying a goblet filled with precious stones.

PATIOMKIN. Get out. [*He snatches the goblet and kicks the Sergeant out, not maliciously but from habit, indeed not noticing that he does it*]. Darling: have some diamonds. Have a fistful. [*He takes up a handful and lets them slip back through his fingers into the goblet, which he then offers to Edstaston*].

EDSTASTON. Thank you: I dont take presents.

PATIOMKIN [*amazed*] You refuse!

EDSTASTON. I thank your Highness; but it is not the custom for English gentlemen to take presents of that kind.

PATIOMKIN. Are you really an Englishman?

EDSTASTON [*bows*]!

PATIOMKIN. You are the first Englishman I ever saw refuse anything he could get. [*He puts the goblet on the table; then turns again to Edstaston*]. Listen, darling. You are a wrestler: a splendid wrestler. You threw me on my back like magic, though I could lift you with one hand. Darling: you are a giant, a paladin.

EDSTASTON [*complacently*] We wrestle rather well in my part of England.

PATIOMKIN. I have a Turk who is a wrestler: a prisoner of war. You shall wrestle with him for me. I'll stake a million roubles on you.

EDSTASTON [*incensed*] Damn you! do you take me for a prize-fighter? How dare you make me such a proposal?

PATIOMKIN [*with wounded feeling*] Darling: there is no pleasing you. Dont you like me?

EDSTASTON [*mollified*]Well, in a sort of way I do; though I dont know why I should. But my instructions are that I am to see the Empress; and –

PATIOMKIN. Darling: you shall see the Empress. A glorious woman, the greatest woman in the world. But lemme give you piece 'vice – pah! still drunk. They water my vinegar. [*He shakes himself; clears his throat; and resumes soberly*] If Catherine takes a fancy to you, you may ask for roubles, diamonds, palaces, titles, orders, anything! and you may aspire to everything: field-marshal, admiral, minister, what you please – except Tsar.

EDSTASTON. I tell you I dont want to ask for anything. Do you suppose I am an adventurer and a beggar?

PATIOMKIN [*plaintively*] Why not, darling? *I* was an adventurer. *I* was a beggar.

EDSTASTON. Oh, you!

PATIOMKIN. Well: whats wrong with me?

EDSTASTON. You are a Russian. Thats different.

PATIOMKIN [*effusively*] Darling: I am a man, and you are a man; and Catherine is a woman. Woman reduces us all to the common denominator. [*Chuckling*]. Again an epigram! [*Gravely*] You understand it, I hope. Have you had a college education, darling? *I* have.

EDSTASTON. Certainly. I am a Bachelor of Arts.

PATIOMKIN. It is enough that you are a bachelor, darling: Catherine will supply the arts. Aha! Another epigram! I am in the vein today.

EDSTASTON [*embarrassed and a little offended*] I must ask your Highness to change the subject. As a visitor in Russia, I am the guest of the Empress; and I must tell you plainly that I have neither the right nor the disposition to speak lightly of her Majesty.

PATIOMKIN. You have conscientious scruples?

EDSTASTON. I have the scruples of a gentleman.

PATIOMKIN. In Russia a gentleman has no scruples. In Russia we face facts.

EDSTASTON. In England, sir, a gentleman never faces any facts if they are unpleasant facts.

PATIOMKIN. In real life, darling, all facts are unpleasant. [*Greatly pleased with himself*] Another epigram! Where is my accursed chancellor? these gems should be written down and recorded for posterity. [*He rushes to the table; sits down; and snatches up a pen. Then, recollecting himself,*] But I have not asked you to sit down. [*He rises and goes to the other chair*]. I am a savage: a barbarian. [*He throws the shirt and coat over the table on to the floor and puts his sword on the table*]. Be seated, Captain.

EDSTASTON. Thank you.

They bow to one another ceremoniously. Patiomkin's tendency to grotesque exaggeration costs him his balance: he nearly falls over Edstaston, who rescues him and takes the proffered chair.

PATIOMKIN [*resuming his seat*] By the way, what was the piece of advice I was going to give you?

EDSTASTON. As you did not give it, I dont know. Allow me to add that I have not asked for your advice.

PATIOMKIN. I give it to you unasked, delightful Englishman. I remember it now. It was this. Dont try to become Tsar of Russia.

EDSTASTON [*in astonishment*] I havnt the slightest intention –

PATIOMKIN. Not now; but you will have: take my word for it. It will strike you as a splendid idea to have conscientious scruples – to desire the blessing of the Church on your union with Catherine.

EDSTASTON [*rising in utter amazement*] My union with Catherine! Youre mad.

PATIOMKIN [*unmoved*] The day you hint at such a thing will be the day of your downfall. Besides, it is not lucky to be Catherine's husband. You know what happened to Peter?

EDSTASTON [*shortly: sitting down again*] I do not wish to discuss it.

PATIOMKIN. You think she murdered him?

EDSTASTON. I know that people have said so.

PATIOMKIN [*thunderously: springing to his feet*] It is a lie: Orloff murdered him. [*Subsiding a little*] He also knocked my eye out; but [*sitting down placidly*] I succeeded him for all that. And [*patting Edstaston's hand very affectionately*] I'm sorry to say, darling, that if you become Tsar, *I* shall murder you.

EDSTASTON [*ironically returning the caress*] Thank you. The occasion will not arise. [*Rising*] I have the honor to wish your Highness good morning.

PATIOMKIN [*jumping up and stopping him on his way to the door*] Tut tut! I'm going to take you to the Empress now, this very instant.

EDSTASTON. In these boots? Impossible! I must change.

PATIOMKIN. Nonsense! You shall come just as you are. You shall shew her your calves later on.

EDSTASTON. But it will take me only half an hour to –

PATIOMKIN. In half an hour it will be too late for the *petit lever*. Come along. Damn it, man, I must oblige the British ambassador, and the French ambassador, and old Fritz, and Monsieur Voltaire and the rest of them. [*He shouts rudely to the door*] Varinka! [*To Edstaston, with tears in his voice*] Varinka shall persuade you: nobody can refuse Varinka anything. My niece. A treasure, I assure you. Beautiful! devoted! fascinating! [*Shouting again*] Varinka: where the devil are you?

VARINKA [*returning*] I'll not be shouted for. You have the voice of a bear, and the manners of a tinker.

PATIOMKIN. Tsh-sh-sh. Little angel Mother: you must behave yourself before the English captain. [*He takes off his dressing gown and throws it over the papers and the breakfasts; picks up his coat; and disappears behind the screen to complete his toilette*].

EDSTASTON. Madam! [*He bows*].

VARINKA [*curtseying*] Monsieur le Capitaine!

EDSTASTON. I must apologize for the disturbance I made, madam.

PATIOMKIN [*behind the screen*] You must not call her madam. You must call her Little Mother, and beautiful darling.

EDSTASTON. My respect for the lady will not permit it.

VARINKA. Respect! How can you respect the niece of a savage?

EDSTASTON [*deprecating*] Oh, madam!

VARINKA. Heaven is my witness, Little English Father, we need someone who is not afraid of him. He is so strong! I hope you will throw him down on the floor many, many, many times.

PATIOMKIN [*behind the screen*] Varinka!

VARINKA. Yes?

PATIOMKIN. Go and look through the keyhole of the Imperial bed-chamber; and bring me word whether the Empress is awake yet.

VARINKA. Fi donc! I do not look through keyholes.

PATIOMKIN [*emerging, having arranged his shirt and put on his diamonded coat*] You have been badly brought up, little darling. Would any lady or gentleman walk unannounced into a room without first looking through the keyhole? [*Taking his sword from the table and putting it on*] The great thing in life is to be simple; and the perfectly simple thing is to look through keyholes. Another epigram: the fifth this morning! Where is my fool of a chancellor? Where is Popof?

EDSTASTON [*choking with suppressed laughter*] !!!!

PATIOMKIN [*gratified*] Darling: you appreciate my epigram.

EDSTASTON. Excuse me. Pop off! Ha! ha! I cant help laughing. Whats his real name, by the way, in case I meet him?

VARINKA [*surprised*] His real name? Popof, of course. Why do you laugh, Little Father?

EDSTASTON. How can anyone with a sense of humor help laughing? Pop off! [*He is convulsed*].

VARINKA [*looking at her uncle, taps her forehead significantly*] !!

PATIOMKIN [*aside to Varinka*] No: only English. He will amuse Catherine. [*To Edstaston*] Come! you shall tell the joke to the Empress: she is by way of being a humorist [*he takes him by the arm, and leads him towards the door*].

EDSTASTON [*resisting*] No, really. I am not fit —

PATIOMKIN. Persuade him, Little angel Mother.

VARINKA [*taking his other arm*] Yes, yes, yes, Little English Father: God knows it is your duty to be brave and wait on the Empress. Come.

EDSTASTON. No. I had rather –

PATIOMKIN [*hauling him along*] Come.

VARINKA [*pulling him and coaxing him*] Come, little love: you cant refuse me.

EDSTASTON. But how can I?

PATIOMKIN. Why not? She wont eat you.

VARINKA. She will; but you must come.

EDSTASTON. I assure you – it is quite out of the question – my clothes.

VARINKA. You look perfect.

PATIOMKIN. Come along, darling.

EDSTASTON [*struggling*] Impossible –

VARINKA. Come, come, come.

EDSTASTON. No. Believe me – I dont wish – I –

VARINKA. Carry him, uncle.

PATIOMKIN [*lifting him in his arms like a father carrying a little boy*] Yes: I'll carry you.

EDSTASTON. Dash it all, this is ridiculous!

VARINKA [*seizing his ankles and dancing as he is carried out*] You must come. If you kick you will blacken my eyes.

PATIOMKIN. Come, baby, come.

By this time they have made their way through the door and are out of hearing.

THE SECOND SCENE

The Empress's petit lever. The central doors are closed. Those who enter through them find on their left, on a dais of two broad steps, a magnificent curtained bed. Beyond it a door in the panelling leads to the Empress's cabinet. Near the foot of the bed, in the middle of the room, stands a gilt chair, with the Imperial arms carved and the Imperial monogram embroidered.

The Court is in attendance, standing in two melancholy rows down the side of the room opposite to the bed, solemn, bored, waiting for the Empress to awaken. The Princess Dashkoff, with two ladies, stands a little in front of the line of courtiers, by the Imperial chair. Silence, broken only by the yawns and whispers of the courtiers. Naryshkin, the Chamberlain, stands by the head of the bed.

A loud yawn is heard from behind the curtains.

NARYSHKIN [*holding up a warning hand*] Ssh!
> *The courtiers hastily cease whispering; dress up their lines; and stiffen. Dead silence. A bell tinkles within the curtains. Naryshkin and the Princess solemnly draw them and reveal the Empress.*
> *Catherine turns over on her back, and stretches herself.*

CATHERINE [*yawning*] Heigho – ah – yah – ah – ow – what o'clock is it? [*Her accent is German*].

NARYSHKIN [*formally*] Her Imperial Majesty is awake. [*The Court falls on its knees*].

ALL. Good morning to your Majesty.

NARYSHKIN. Half-past ten, Little Mother.

CATHERINE [*sitting up abruptly*] Potztausend! [*Contemplating the kneeling courtiers*] Oh, get up, get up. [*All rise*]. Your etiquette bores me. I am hardly awake in the morning before it begins. [*Yawning again, and relapsing sleepily against her pillows*] Why do they do it, Naryshkin?

NARYSHKIN. God knows it is not for your sake, Little Mother. But you see if you were not a great queen they would all be nobodies.

CATHERINE [*sitting up*] They make me do it to keep up their own little dignities? So?

NARYSHKIN. Exactly. Also because if they didnt you might have them flogged, dear Little Mother.

CATHERINE [*springing energetically out of bed and seating herself on the edge of it*] Flogged! I! A Liberal Empress! A philosopher! You are a barbarian, Naryshkin. [*She rises and turns to the courtiers*] And then, as if I cared! [*She turns again to Naryshkin*] You should know by this time that I am frank and original in character, like an Englishman. [*She walks about restlessly*]. No: what maddens me about all this ceremony is that I am the only person in Russia who gets no fun out of being Empress. You all glory in me: you bask in my smiles: you get titles and honors and favors from me: you are dazzled by my crown and my robes: you feel splendid when you have been admitted to my presence; and when I say a gracious word to you, you talk about it to everyone you meet for a week afterwards. But what do *I* get out of it? Nothing. [*She throws herself into the chair. Naryshkin deprecates with a gesture: she hurls an emphatic repetition at him*] Nothing!! I wear a crown until my neck aches: I stand looking majestic until I am ready to drop: I have to smile at ugly old ambassadors and frown and turn my back on young and handsome ones. Nobody gives me anything. When I was only an Archduchess, the English ambassador used to give me money whenever I wanted it – or rather whenever he wanted to get anything out of my sacred predecessor Elizabeth [*the Court bows to the ground*]; but now that I am Empress he never gives me a kopek. When I have headaches and colics I envy the scullerymaids. And you are not a bit grateful to me for all my care of you, my work, my thought, my fatigue, my sufferings.

THE PRINCESS DASHKOFF. God knows, Little Mother, we all implore you to give your wonderful brain a rest. That is why you get headaches. Monsieur Voltaire also has headaches. His brain is just like yours.

CATHERINE. Dashkoff: what a liar you are! [*Dashkoff curtsies with impressive dignity*]. And you think you are flattering me! Let me tell you I would not give a rouble to have the brains of all the philosophers in France. What is our business for today?

NARYSHKIN. The new museum, Little Mother. But the model will not be ready until tonight.

CATHERINE [*rising eagerly*] Yes: the museum. An enlightened capital should have a museum. [*She paces the chamber with a deep sense of the importance of the museum*]. It shall be one of the wonders of the world. I must have specimens: specimens, specimens, specimens.

NARYSHKIN. You are in high spirits this morning, Little Mother.

CATHERINE [*with sudden levity*] I am always in high spirits, even when people do not bring me my slippers. [*She runs to the chair and sits down, thrusting her feet out*].

The two ladies rush to her feet, each carrying a slipper. Catherine, about to put her feet into them, is checked by a disturbance in the antechamber.

PATIOMKIN [*carrying Edstaston through the antechamber*] Useless to struggle. Come along, beautiful baby darling. Come to Little Mother. [*He sings*]

> March him baby,
> Baby, baby,
> Lit-tle ba-by bumpkins.

VARINKA [*joining in to the same doggerel in canon, a third above*] March him, baby, etc., etc.

EDSTASTON [*trying to make himself heard*] No, no. This is carrying a joke too far. I must insist. Let me down! Hang it, will you let me down! Confound it! No, no. Stop playing the fool, will you? We dont understand this sort of thing in England. I shall be disgraced. Let me down.

CATHERINE [*meanwhile*] What a horrible noise! Naryshkin: see what it is.

Naryshkin goes to the door.

CATHERINE [*listening*] That is Prince Patiomkin.

NARYSHKIN [*calling from the door*] Little Mother: a stranger.

Catherine plunges into bed again and covers herself up. Patiomkin, followed by Varinka, carries Edstaston in; dumps him down on the foot of the bed; and staggers past it to the cabinet door. Varinka joins the courtiers at the opposite side of the room. Catherine, blazing with wrath, pushes Edstaston off her bed on to the floor; gets out of bed; and turns on Patiomkin with so terrible an expression that all kneel down hastily except Edstaston, who is sprawling on the carpet in angry confusion.

CATHERINE. Patiomkin: how dare you? [*Looking at Edstaston*] What is this?

PATIOMKIN [*on his knees: tearfully*] I dont know. I am drunk. What is this, Varinka?

EDSTASTON [*scrambling to his feet*] Madam: this drunken ruffian —

PATIOMKIN. Thas true. Drungn ruffian. Took dvantage of my being drunk. Said: take me to Lil angel Mother. Take me to beaufl Empress. Take me to the grea'st woman on earth. Thas whas he said. I took him. I was wrong. I am not sober.

CATHERINE. Men have grown sober in Siberia for less, Prince.

PATIOMKIN. Serve em right! Sgusting habit. Ask Varinka.

Catherine turns her face from him to the Court. The courtiers see that she is trying not to laugh, and know by experience that she will not succeed. They rise, relieved and grinning.

VARINKA. It is true. He drinks like a pig.

PATIOMKIN [*plaintively*] No: not like a pig. Like prince. Lil Mother made poor Patiomkin prince. What use being prince if I maynt drink?

CATHERINE [*biting her lips*] Go. I am offended.

PATIOMKIN. Dont scold, Lil Mother.

CATHERINE [*imperiously*] Go.

PATIOMKIN [*rising unsteadily*] Yes: go. Go bye bye. Very sleepy. Berr go bye bye than go Siberia. Go bye bye in Lil Mother's bed [*he pretends to make an attempt to get into the bed*].

CATHERINE [*energetically pulling him back*] No, no! Patiomkin! What are you thinking of? [*He falls like a log on the floor, apparently dead drunk*].

THE PRINCESS DASHKOFF. Scandalous! An insult to your Imperial Majesty!

CATHERINE. Dashkoff: you have no sense of humor. [*She steps down to the floor level and looks indulgently at Patiomkin. He gurgles brutishly. She has an impulse of disgust*]. Hog. [*She kicks him as hard as she can*]. Oh! You have broken my toe. Brute. Beast. Dashkoff is quite right. Do you hear?

PATIOMKIN. If you ask my pi-pinion of Dashkoff, my pipinion is that Dashkoff is drunk. Scanlous. Poor Patiomkin go bye bye. [*He relapses into drunken slumbers*].

Some of the courtiers move to carry him away.

CATHERINE [*stopping them*] Let him lie. Let him sleep it off. If he goes out it will be to a tavern and low company for the rest of the day. [*Indulgently*] There! [*She takes a pillow from the bed and puts it under his head; then turns to Edstaston; surveys him with perfect dignity; and asks, in her queenliest manner*] Varinka: who is this gentleman?

VARINKA. A foreign captain: I cannot pronounce his name. I think he is mad. He came to the Prince and said he must see your Majesty. He can talk of nothing else. We could not prevent him.

EDSTASTON [*overwhelmed by this apparent betrayal*] Oh! Madam: I am perfectly sane: I am actually an Englishman. I should never have dreamt of approaching your Majesty without the fullest credentials. I have letters from the English ambassador, from the Prussian ambassador. [*Naïvely*] But everybody assured me that Prince Patiomkin is all-powerful with your Majesty; so I naturally applied to him.

PATIOMKIN [*interrupts the conversation by an agonized wheezing groan, as of a donkey beginning to bray*] !!!

CATHERINE [*like a fishfag*] Schweig, du Hund. [*Resuming her impressive Royal manner*] Have you never been taught, sir, how a gentleman should enter the presence of a sovereign?

EDSTASTON. Yes, Madam; but I did not enter your presence: I was carried.

CATHERINE. But you say you asked the Prince to carry you.

EDSTASTON. Certainly not, Madam. I protested against it with all my might. I appeal to this lady to confirm me.

VARINKA [*pretending to be indignant*] Yes: you protested. But, all the same, you were very very very anxious to see her Imperial Majesty. You blushed when the Prince spoke of her. You threatened to strike him across the face with your sword because you thought he did not speak enthusiastically enough of her. [*To Catherine*] Trust me: he has seen your Imperial Majesty before.

CATHERINE [*to Edstaston*] You have seen us before?

EDSTASTON. At the review, Madam.

VARINKA [*triumphantly*] Aha! I knew it. Your Majesty wore the hussar uniform. He saw how radiant! how splendid! your Majesty looked. Oh! he has dared to admire your Majesty. Such insolence is not to be endured.

EDSTASTON. All Europe is a party to that insolence, Madam.

THE PRINCESS DASHKOFF. All Europe is content to do so at a respectful distance. It is possible to admire her Majesty's policy and her eminence in literature and philosophy without performing acrobatic feats in the Imperial bed.

EDSTASTON. I know nothing about her Majesty's eminence in policy or philosophy: I dont pretend to understand such things. I speak as a practical man. And I never knew that foreigners had any policy: I always thought that policy was Mr Pitt's business.

CATHERINE [*lifting her eyebrows*] So?

VARINKA. What else did you presume to admire her Majesty for, pray?

EDSTASTON [*addled*] Well, I – I – I – that is, I – [*He stammers himself dumb*].

CATHERINE [*after a pitiless silence*] We are waiting for your answer.

EDSTASTON. But I never said I admired your Majesty. The lady has twisted my words.

VARINKA. You dont admire her, then?

EDSTASTON. Well, I — naturally — of course, I cant deny that the uniform was very becoming — perhaps a little unfeminine — still —
  Dead silence. Catherine and the court watch him stonily. He is wretchedly embarrassed.

CATHERINE [*with cold majesty*] Well, sir: is that all you have to say?

EDSTASTON. Surely there is no harm in noticing that er — that er — [*He stops again*].

CATHERINE. Noticing that er — ? [*He gazes at her, speechless, like a fascinated rabbit. She repeats fiercely*] That er — ?

EDSTASTON [*Startled into speech*] Well, that your Majesty was — was — [*Soothingly*] Well, let me put it this way: that it was rather natural for a man to admire your Majesty without being a philosopher.

CATHERINE [*suddenly smiling and extending her hand to him to be kissed*] Courtier!

EDSTASTON [*kissing it*] Not at all. Your Majesty is very good. I have been very awkward; but I did not intend it. I am rather stupid, I am afraid.

CATHERINE. Stupid! By no means. Courage, Captain: we are pleased. [*He falls on his knee. She takes his cheeks in her hands; turns up his face; and adds*] We are greatly pleased. [*She slaps his cheek coquettishly: he bows almost to his knee*]. The *petit lever* is over. [*She turns to go into the cabinet, and stumbles against the supine Patiomkin*]. Ach! [*Edstaston springs to her assistance, seizing Patiomkin's heels and shifting him out of the Empress's path*]. We thank you, Captain.
  He bows gallantly, and is rewarded by a very gracious smile. Then Catherine goes into her cabinet, followed by the Princess Dashkoff, who turns at the door to make a deep curtsey to Edstaston.

VARINKA. Happy Little Father! Remember: *I* did this for you. [*She runs out after the Empress*].
  Edstaston, somewhat dazed, crosses the room to the courtiers, and is received with marked deference, each courtier making him a profound bow or curtsey before withdrawing through the central doors. He returns each obeisance with a nervous jerk, and turns away from it, only to find another courtier bowing at the other side. The process finally reduces him to distraction, as he bumps into one in the act of bowing to another and then has to bow his apologies. But at last they are all gone except Naryshkin.

EDSTASTON. Ouf!

PATIOMKIN [*jumping up vigorously*] You have done it, darling. Superbly! Beautifully!

EDSTASTON [*astonished*] Do you mean to say you are not drunk?

PATIOMKIN. Not dead drunk, darling. Only diplomatically drunk. As a drunken hog, I have done for you in five minutes what I could not have done in five months as a sober man. Your fortune is made. She likes you.

EDSTASTON. The devil she does!

PATIOMKIN. Why? Arnt you delighted?

EDSTASTON. Delighted! Gracious heavens, man, I am engaged to be married.

PATIOMKIN. What matter? She is in England, isnt she?

EDSTASTON. No. She has just arrived in St Petersburg.

THE PRINCESS DASHKOFF [*returning*] Captain Edstaston: the Empress is robed, and commands your presence.

EDSTASTON. Say I was gone before you arrived with the message. [*He hurries out. The other three, too taken aback to stop him, stare after him in the utmost astonishment*].

NARYSHKIN [*turning from the door*] She will have him knouted. He is a dead man.

THE PRINCESS DASHKOFF. But what am *I* to do? I cannot take such an answer to the Empress.

PATIOMKIN. P-P-P-P-P-P-W-W-W-W-W-rrrrrr [*a long puff, turning into a growl*]! [*He spits*]. I must kick somebody.

NARYSHKIN [*flying precipitately through the central doors*] No, no. Please.

THE PRINCESS DASHKOFF [*throwing herself recklessly in front of Patiomkin as he starts in pursuit of the Chamberlain*] Kick me. Disable me. It will be an excuse for not going back to her. Kick me hard.

PATIOMKIN. Yah! [*He flings her on the bed and dashes after Naryshkin*].

THE THIRD SCENE

In a terrace garden overlooking the Neva. Claire, a robust young English lady, is leaning on the river wall. She turns expectantly on hearing the garden gate opened and closed. Edstaston hurries in. With a cry of delight she throws her arms round his neck.

CLAIRE. Darling.

EDSTASTON [*making a wry face*] Dont call me darling.

CLAIRE [*amazed and chilled*] Why?

EDSTASTON. I have been called darling all the morning.

CLAIRE [*with a flash of jealousy*] By whom?

EDSTASTON. By everybody. By the most unutterable swine. And if we do not leave this abominable city now: do you hear? now: I shall be called darling by the Empress.

CLAIRE [*with magnificent snobbery*] She would not dare. Did you tell her you were engaged to me?

EDSTASTON. Of course not.

CLAIRE. Why?

EDSTASTON. Because I didnt particularly want to have you knouted, and to be hanged or sent to Siberia myself.

CLAIRE. What on earth do you mean.

EDSTASTON. Well, the long and short of it is – dont think me a coxcomb, Claire: it is too serious to mince matters – I have seen the Empress; and –

CLAIRE. Well: you wanted to see her.

EDSTASTON. Yes; but the Empress has seen me.

CLAIRE. She has fallen in love with you!

EDSTASTON. How did you know?

CLAIRE. Dearest: as if anyone could help it.

EDSTASTON. Oh, dont make me feel like a fool. But, though it does sound conceited to say, I flatter myself I'm better looking than Patiomkin and the other hogs she is accustomed to. Anyhow, I darent risk staying.

CLAIRE. What a nuisance! Mamma will be furious at having to pack, and at missing the Court ball this evening.

EDSTASTON. I cant help that. We havnt a moment to lose.

CLAIRE. May I tell her she will be knouted if we stay?

EDSTASTON. Do, dearest.

He kisses her and lets her go, expecting her to run into the house.

CLAIRE [*pausing thoughtfully*] Is she – is she good-looking when you see her close?

EDSTASTON. Not a patch on you, dearest.

CLAIRE [*jealous*] Then you did see her close?

EDSTASTON. Fairly close.

CLAIRE. Indeed! How close? No: thats silly of me: I will tell mamma. [*She is going out when Naryshkin enters with the Sergeant and a squad of soldiers*]. What do you want here?

The Sergeant goes to Edstaston; plumps down on his knees; and takes out a magnificent pair of pistols with gold grips. He proffers them to Edstaston, holding them by the barrels.

NARYSHKIN. Captain Edstaston: his Highness Prince Patiomkin sends you the pistols he promised you.

THE SERGEANT. Take them, Little Father; and do not forget us poor soldiers who have brought them to you; for God knows we get but little to drink.

EDSTASTON [*irresolutely*] But I cant take these valuable things. By Jiminy, though, theyre beautiful! Look at them, Claire.

As he is taking the pistols the kneeling Sergeant suddenly drops them; flings himself forward; and embraces Edstaston's hips to prevent him from drawing his own pistols from his boots.

THE SERGEANT. Lay hold of him there. Pin his arms. I have his pistols. [*The soldiers seize Edstaston*].

EDSTASTON. Ah, would you, damn you! [*He drives his knee into the Sergeant's epigastrium, and struggles furiously with his captors*].

THE SERGEANT [*rolling on the ground, gasping and groaning*] Owgh! Murder! Holy Nicholas! Owwwgh!

CLAIRE. Help! help! They are killing Charles. Help!

NARYSHKIN [*seizing her and clapping his hand over her mouth*] Tie him neck and crop. Ten thousand blows of the stick if you let him go. [*Claire twists herself loose; turns on him; and cuffs him furiously*] Yow – ow! Have mercy, Little Mother.

CLAIRE. You wretch! Help! Help! Police! We are being murdered. Help!

The Sergeant, who has risen, comes to Naryshkin's rescue, and grasps Claire's hands, enabling Naryshkin to gag her again. By this time Edstaston and his captors are all rolling on the ground together. They get

Edstaston on his back and fasten his wrists together behind his knees. Next they put a broad strap round his ribs. Finally they pass a pole through this breast strap and through the wrist strap and lift him by it, helplessly trussed up, to carry him off. Meanwhile he is by no means suffering in silence.

EDSTASTON [*gasping*] You shall hear more of this. Damn you, will you untie me? I will complain to the ambassador. I will write to the Gazette. England will blow your trumpery little fleet out of the water and sweep your tinpot army into Siberia for this. Will you let me go? Damn you! Curse you! What the devil do you mean by it? I'll – I'll – I'll – [*he is carried out of hearing*].

NARYSHKIN [*snatching his hands from Claire's face with a scream, and shaking his finger frantically*] Agh! [*The Sergeant amazed, lets go her hands*]. She has bitten me, the little vixen.

CLAIRE [*spitting and wiping her mouth disgustedly*] How dare you put your dirty paws on my mouth? Ugh! Psha!

THE SERGEANT. Be merciful, Little angel Mother.

CLAIRE. Do not presume to call me your little angel mother. Where are the police?

NARYSHKIN. We are the police in St Petersburg, little spitfire.

THE SERGEANT. God knows we have no orders to harm you, Little Mother. Our duty is done. You are well and strong; but I shall never be the same man again. He is a mighty and terrible fighter, as stout as a bear. He has broken my sweetbread with his strong knees. God knows poor folk should not be set upon by such dangerous adversaries!

CLAIRE. Serve you right! Where have they taken Captain Edstaston to?

NARYSHKIN [*spitefully*] To the Empress, little beauty. He has insulted the Empress. He will receive a hundred and one blows of the knout. [*He laughs and goes out, nursing his bitten finger*].

THE SERGEANT. He will feel only the first twenty; and he will be mercifully dead long before the end, little darling.

CLAIRE [*sustained by an invincible snobbery*] They dare not touch an English officer. I will go to the Empress myself: she cannot know who Captain Edstaston is – who we are.

THE SERGEANT. Do so in the name of the Holy Nicholas, little beauty.

CLAIRE. Dont be impertinent. How can I get admission to the palace?

THE SERGEANT. Everybody goes in and out of the palace, little love.

CLAIRE. But I must get into the Empress's presence. I must speak to her.

THE SERGEANT. You shall, dear Little Mother. You shall give the poor old Sergeant a rouble; and the blessed Nicholas will make your salvation his charge.

CLAIRE [*impetuously*] I will give you [*she is about to say fifty roubles, but checks herself cautiously*] – Well: I dont mind giving you two roubles if I can speak to the Empress.

THE SERGEANT [*joyfully*] I praise Heaven for you, Little Mother. Come. [*He leads the way out*]. It was the temptation of the devil that led your man to bruise my vitals and deprive me of breath. We must be merciful to one another's faults.

THE FOURTH SCENE

A triangular recess communicating by a heavily curtained arch with the huge ballroom of the palace. The light is subdued by red shades on the candles. In the wall adjoining that pierced by the arch is a door. The only piece of furniture is a very handsome chair on the arch side. In the ballroom they are dancing a polonaise to the music of a brass band.

Naryshkin enters through the door, followed by the soldiers carrying Edstaston, still trussed to the pole. Exhausted and dogged, he makes no sound.

NARYSHKIN. Halt. Get that pole clear of the prisoner. [*They dump Edstaston on the floor, and detach the pole. Naryshkin stoops over him and addresses him insultingly*]. Well! are you ready to be tortured? This is the Empress's private torture chamber. Can I do anything to make you quite comfortable? You have only to mention it.

EDSTASTON. Have you any back teeth?

NARYSHKIN [*surprised*] Why?

EDSTASTON. His Majesty King George the Third will send for six of them when the news of this reaches London; so look out, damn your eyes!

NARYSHKIN [*frightened*] Oh, I assure you I am only obeying my orders. Personally I abhor torture, and would save you if I could. But the Empress is proud; and what woman would forgive the slight you put upon her?

EDSTASTON. As I said before: Damn your eyes!

NARYSHKIN [*almost in tears*] Well, it isnt my fault. [*To the soldiers, insolently*] You know your orders? You remember what you have to do when the Empress gives you the word? [*The soldiers salute in assent*].

Naryshkin passes through the curtains, admitting a blare of music and a strip of the brilliant white candle-light from the chandeliers in the ballroom as he does so. The white light vanishes and the music is muffled as the curtains fall together behind him. Presently the band stops abruptly; and Naryshkin comes back through the curtains. He makes a warning gesture to the soldiers, who stand at attention. Then he moves the curtains to allow Catherine to enter. She is in full Imperial regalia, and stops sternly just where she has entered. The soldiers fall on their knees.

CATHERINE. Obey your orders.

The soldiers seize Edstaston, and throw him roughly at the feet of the Empress.

CATHERINE [*looking down coldly on him*] Also [*the German word*], you have put me to the trouble of sending for you twice. You had better have come the first time.

EDSTASTON [*exsufflicate, and pettishly angry*] I havnt come either time. Ive been carried. I call it infernal impudence.

CATHERINE. Take care what you say.

EDSTASTON. No use. I daresay you look very majestic and very handsome; but I cant see you; and I am not intimidated. I am an Englishman; and you can kidnap me; but you cant bully me.

NARYSHKIN. Remember to whom you are speaking.

CATHERINE [*violently, furious at his intrusion*] Remember that dogs should be dumb. [*He shrivels*]. And do you, Captain, remember that famous as I am for my clemency, there are limits to the patience even of an Empress.

EDSTASTON. How is a man to remember anything when he is trussed up in this ridiculous fashion? I can hardly breathe. [*He makes a futile struggle to free himself*]. Here: dont be unkind, your Majesty: tell these fellows to unstrap me. You know you really owe me an apology.

CATHERINE. You think you can escape by appealing, like Prince Patiomkin, to my sense of humor?

EDSTASTON. Sense of humor! Ho! Ha, ha! I like that. Would anybody with a sense of humor make a guy of a man like this, and then expect him to take it seriously? I say: do tell them to loosen these straps.

CATHERINE [*seating herself*] Why should I, pray?

EDSTASTON. Why! Why!! Why, because theyre hurting me.

CATHERINE. People sometimes learn through suffering. Manners, for instance.

EDSTASTON. Oh, well, of course, if youre an ill-natured woman, hurting me on purpose, I have nothing more to say.

CATHERINE. A monarch, sir, has sometimes to employ a necessary and salutary severity —

EDSTASTON [*interrupting her petulantly*] Quack! quack! quack!

CATHERINE. Donnerwetter!

EDSTASTON [*continuing recklessly*] This isnt severity: it's tomfoolery. And if you think it's reforming my character or teaching me anything, youre mistaken. It may be a satisfaction to you; but if it is, all I can say is that it's not an amiable satisfaction.

CATHERINE [*turning suddenly and balefully on Naryshkin*] What are you grinning at?

NARYSHKIN [*falling on his knees in terror*] Be merciful, Little Mother. My heart is in my mouth.

CATHERINE. Your heart and your mouth will be in two separate parts of your body if you again forget in whose presence you stand. Go. And take your men with you. [*Naryshkin crawls to the door. The soldiers rise*]. Stop. Roll that [*indicating Edstaston*] nearer. [*The soldiers obey*]. Not so close. Did I ask you for a footstool? [*She pushes Edstaston away with her foot*].

EDSTASTON [*with a sudden squeal*] Agh!!! I must really ask your Majesty not to put the point of your Imperial toe between my ribs. I am ticklesome.

CATHERINE. Indeed? All the more reason for you to treat me with respect, Captain. [*To the others*] Begone. How many times must I give an order before it is obeyed?

NARYSHKIN. Little Mother: they have brought some instruments of torture. Will they be needed?

CATHERINE [*indignantly*] How dare you name such abominations to a Liberal Empress? You will always be a savage and a fool, Naryshkin. These relics of barbarism are buried, thank God, in the grave of Peter the Great. My methods are more civilized. [*She extends her toe towards Edstaston's ribs*].

EDSTASTON [*shrieking hysterically*] Yagh! Ah! [*Furiously*] If your Majesty does that again I will write to the London Gazette.

CATHERINE [*to the soldiers*] Leave us. Quick! do you hear? Five thousand blows of the stick for the soldier who is in the room when I speak next. [*The soldiers rush out*]. Naryshkin: are you waiting to be knouted? [*Naryshkin backs out hastily*].

Catherine and Edstaston are now alone. Catherine has in her hand a sceptre or baton of gold. Wrapped round it is a new pamphlet, in French, entitled L'Homme aux Quarante Écus. She calmly unrolls this and begins to read it at her ease as if she were quite alone. Several seconds elapse in dead silence. She becomes more and more absorbed in the pamphlet, and more and more amused by it.

CATHERINE [*greatly pleased by a passage, and turning over the leaf*] Ausgezeichnet!

EDSTASTON. Ahem!

Silence. Catherine reads on.

CATHERINE. Wie komisch!

EDSTASTON. Ahem! ahem!

Silence.

CATHERINE [*soliloquizing enthusiastically*] What a wonderful author is Monsieur Voltaire! How lucidly he exposes the folly of this crazy plan for raising the entire revenue of the country from a single tax on land! how he withers it with his irony! how he makes you laugh whilst he is convincing you! how sure one feels that the proposal is killed by his wit and economic penetration: killed never to be mentioned again among educated people!

EDSTASTON. For Heaven's sake, Madam, do you intend to leave me tied up like this while you discuss the blasphemies of that abominable infidel? Agh!!! [*She has again applied her toe*]. Oh! Oo!

CATHERINE [*calmly*] Do I understand you to say that Monsieur Voltaire is a great philanthropist and a great philosopher as well as the wittiest man in Europe?

EDSTASTON. Certainly not. I say that his books ought to be burnt by the common hangman [*her toe touches his ribs*]. Yagh! Oh dont. I shall faint. I cant bear it.

CATHERINE. Have you changed your opinion of Monsieur Voltaire?

EDSTASTON. But you cant expect me as a member of the Church of England [*she tickles him*] – Agh! Ow! Oh Lord! he is anything you like. He is a philanthropist, a philosopher, a beauty: he ought to have a statue, damn him! [*she tickles him*] No! bless him! save him victorious, happy and glorious! Oh, let eternal honors crown his name: Voltaire thrice worthy on the rolls of fame! [*Exhausted*]. Now will you let me up? And look here! I can see your ankles when you tickle me: it's not ladylike.

CATHERINE. [*sticking out her toe and admiring it critically*] Is the spectacle so disagreeable?

EDSTASTON. It's agreeable enough; only [*with intense expression*] for heaven's sake dont touch me in the ribs.

CATHERINE [*putting aside the pamphlet*] Captain Edstaston: why did you refuse to come when I sent for you?

EDSTASTON. Madam: I cannot talk tied up like this.

CATHERINE. Do you still admire me as much as you did this morning?

EDSTASTON. How can I possibly tell when I cant see you? Let me get up and look. I cant see anything now except my toes and yours.

CATHERINE. Do you still intend to write to the London Gazette about me?

EDSTASTON. Not if you will loosen these straps. Quick: loosen me. I'm fainting.

CATHERINE. I dont think you are [*tickling him*].

EDSTASTON. Agh! Cat!

CATHERINE. What [*she tickles him again*]!

EDSTASTON [*with a shriek*] No: angel, angel!

CATHERINE [*tenderly*] Geliebter!

EDSTASTON. I dont know a word of German; but that sounded kind. [*Becoming hysterical*] Little Mother, beautiful little darling angel mother: dont be cruel: untie me. Oh, I beg and implore you. Dont be unkind. I shall go mad.

CATHERINE. You are expected to go mad with love when an Empress deigns to interest herself in you. When an Empress allows you to see her foot you should kiss it. Captain Edstaston: you are a booby.

EDSTASTON [*indignantly*] I am nothing of the kind. I have been mentioned in dispatches as a highly intelligent officer. And let me warn your Majesty that I am not so helpless as you think. The English Ambassador is in that ballroom. A shout from me will bring him to my side; and then where will your Majesty be?

CATHERINE. I should like to see the English Ambassador or anyone else pass through that curtain against my orders. It might be a stone wall ten feet thick. Shout your loudest. Sob. Curse. Scream. Yell [*she tickles him unmercifully*].

EDSTASTON [*frantically*] Ahowyow!!!! Agh! Ooh! Stop! Oh Lord! Ya-a-a-ah! [*A tumult in the ballroom responds to his cries*].

VOICES FROM THE BALLROOM. Stand back. You cannot pass. Hold her back there. The Empress's orders. It is out of the question. No, little darling, not in there. Nobody is allowed in there. You will be sent to Siberia. Dont let her through there, on your life. Drag her back. You will be knouted. It is hopeless, Mademoiselle: you must obey orders. Guard there! Send some men to hold her.

CLAIRE'S VOICE. Let me go. They are torturing Charles in there. I will go. How can you all dance as if nothing was happening? Let me go, I tell you. Let – me – go. [*She dashes through the curtain. No one dares follow her*].

CATHERINE [*rising in wrath*] How dare you?

CLAIRE [*recklessly*] Oh, dare your grandmother! Where is my Charles? What are they doing to him?

EDSTASTON [*shouting*] Claire: loosen these straps, in Heaven's name. Quick.

CLAIRE [*seeing him and throwing herself on her knees at his side*] Oh, how dare they tie you up like that! [*To Catherine*] You wicked wretch! You Russian savage! [*She pounces on the straps, and begins unbuckling them*].

CATHERINE [*conquering herself with a mighty effort*] Now self-control. Self-control, Catherine. Philosophy. Europe is looking on. [*She forces herself to sit down*].

EDSTASTON. Steady, dearest: it is the Empress. Call her your Imperial Majesty. Call her Star of the North, Little Mother, Little Darling: thats what she likes; but get the straps off.

CLAIRE. Keep quiet, dear: I cannot get them off if you move.

CATHERINE [*calmly*] Keep quite still, Captain [*she tickles him*].

EDSTASTON. Ow! Agh! Ahowyow!

CLAIRE [*stopping dead in the act of unbuckling the straps and turning sick with jealousy as she grasps the situation*] Was that what I thought was your being tortured?

CATHERINE [*urbanely*] That is the favourite torture of Catherine the Second, Mademoiselle. I think the Captain enjoys it very much.

CLAIRE. Then he can have as much more of it as he wants. I am sorry I intruded. [*She rises to go*].

EDSTASTON [*catching her train in his teeth and holding on like a bull-dog*] Dont go. Dont leave me in this horrible state. Loosen me. [*This is what he is saying; but as he says it with the train in his mouth it is not very intelligible*].

CLAIRE. Let go. You are undignified and ridiculous enough yourself without making me ridiculous. [*She snatches her train away*].

EDSTASTON. Ow! Youve nearly pulled my teeth out: youre worse than the Star of the North. [*To Catherine*] Darling Little Mother: you have a kind heart, the kindest in Europe. Have pity. Have mercy. I love you. [*Claire bursts into tears*]. Release me.

CATHERINE. Well, just to shew you how much kinder a Russian savage can be than an English one (though I am sorry to say I am a German) here goes! [*She stoops to loosen the straps*].

CLAIRE [*jealously*] You neednt trouble, thank you. [*She pounces on the straps; and the two set Edstaston free between them*]. Now get up, please; and conduct yourself with some dignity if you are not utterly demoralized.

EDSTASTON. Dignity! Ow! I cant. I'm stiff all over. I shall never be able to stand up again. Oh Lord! how it hurts! [*They seize him by the shoulders and drag him up*]. Yah! Agh! Wow! Oh! Mmmmmm! Oh, Little Angel Mother, dont ever do this to a man again. Knout him; kill him; roast him; baste him; head, hang, and quarter him; but dont tie him up like that and tickle him.

CATHERINE. Your young lady seems still to think that you enjoyed it.

CLAIRE. I know what I think. I will never speak to him again. Your Majesty can keep him, as far as I am concerned.

CATHERINE. I would not deprive you of him for worlds; though really I think he's rather a darling [*she pats his cheek*].

CLAIRE [*snorting*] So I see, indeed.

EDSTASTON. Dont be angry, dearest: in this country everybody's a darling. I'll prove it to you. [*To Catherine*] Will your Majesty be good enough to call Prince Patiomkin?

CATHERINE [*surprised into haughtiness*] Why?

EDSTASTON. To oblige me.

Catherine laughs good-humoredly and goes to the curtains and opens them. The band strikes up a Redowa.

CATHERINE [*calling imperiously*] Patiomkin! [*The music stops suddenly*]. Here! To me! Go on with your music there, you fools. [*The Redowa is resumed*].

The sergeant rushes from the ballroom to relieve the Empress of the curtain. Patiomkin comes in dancing with Varinka.

CATHERINE [*to Patiomkin*] The English captain wants you, little darling.

Catherine resumes her seat as Patiomkin intimates by a grotesque bow that he is at Edstaston's service. Varinka passes behind Edstaston and Claire, and posts herself on Claire's right.

EDSTASTON. Precisely. [*To Claire*] You observe, my love: 'little darling.' Well, if her Majesty calls him a darling, is it my fault that she calls me one too?

CLAIRE. I dont care: I dont think you ought to have done it. I am very angry and offended.

EDSTASTON. They tied me up, dear. I couldnt help it. I fought for all I was worth.

THE SERGEANT [*at the curtains*] He fought with the strength of lions and bears. God knows I shall carry a broken sweetbread to my grave.

EDSTASTON. You cant mean to throw me over, Claire. [*Urgently*] Claire. Claire.

VARINKA [*in a transport of sympathetic emotion, pleading with clasped hands to Claire*] Oh, sweet little angel lamb, he loves you: it shines in his darling eyes. Pardon him, pardon him.

PATIOMKIN [*rushing from the Empress's side to Claire and falling on his knees to her*] Pardon him, pardon him, little cherub! little wild duck! little star! little glory! little jewel in the crown of heaven!

CLAIRE. This is perfectly ridiculous.

VARINKA [*kneeling to her*] Pardon him, pardon him, little delight, little sleeper in a rosy cradle.

CLAIRE. I'll do anything if youll only let me alone.

THE SERGEANT [*kneeling to her*] Pardon him, pardon him, lest the mighty man bring his whip to you. God knows we all need pardon!

CLAIRE [*at the top of her voice*] I pardon him! I pardon him!

PATIOMKIN [*springing up joyfully and going behind Claire, whom he raises in his arms*] Embrace her, victor of Bunker's Hill. Kiss her till she swoons.

THE SERGEANT. Receive her in the name of the holy Nicholas.

VARINKA. She begs you for a thousand dear little kisses all over her body.

CLAIRE [*vehemently*] I do not. [*Patiomkin throws her into Edstaston's arms*]. Oh! [*The pair, awkward and shamefaced, recoil from one another, and remain utterly inexpressive*].

CATHERINE [*pushing Edstaston towards Claire*] There is no help for it, Captain. This is Russia, not England.

EDSTASTON [*plucking up some geniality, and kissing Claire ceremoniously on the brow*] I have no objection.

VARINKA [*disgusted*] Only one kiss! and on the forehead! Fish. See how I kiss, though it is only my horribly ugly old uncle [*she throws her arms round Patiomkin's neck and covers his face with kisses*].

THE SERGEANT [*moved to tears*] Sainted Nicholas: bless your lambs!

CATHERINE. Do you wonder now that I love Russia as I love no other place on earth?

NARYSHKIN [*appearing at the door*] Majesty: the model for the new museum has arrived.

CATHERINE [*rising eagerly and making for the curtains*] Let us go. I can think of nothing but my museum. [*In the archway she stops and turns to Edstaston, who has hurried to lift the curtain for her*]. Captain: I wish you every happiness that your little angel can bring you. [*For his ear alone*] I could have brought you more; but you did not think so. Farewell.

EDSTASTON [*kissing her hand, which, instead of releasing, he holds caressingly and rather patronizingly in his own*] I feel your Majesty's kindness so much that I really cannot leave you without a word of plain wholesome English advice.

CATHERINE [*snatching her hand away and bounding forward as if he had touched her with a spur*] Advice!!!

PATIOMKIN. Madman: take care!

NARYSHKIN. Advise the Empress!!

THE SERGEANT. Sainted Nicholas!

VARINKA. Hoo hoo! [*a stifled splutter of laughter*].

[*exclaiming simultaneously*].

EDSTASTON [*following the Empress and resuming kindly but judicially*] After all, though your Majesty is of course a great queen, yet when all is said, I am a man; and your Majesty is only a woman.

CATHERINE. Only a wo– [*she chokes*].

EDSTASTON [*continuing*] Believe me, this Russian extravagance will not do. I appreciate as much as any man the warmth of heart that prompts it; but it is overdone: it is hardly in the best taste: it is – really I must say it – it is not proper.

CATHERINE [*ironically, in German*] So!

EDSTASTON. Not that I cannot make allowances. Your Majesty has, I know, been unfortunate in your experience as a married woman –

CATHERINE [*furious*] Alle Wetter!!!

EDSTASTON [*sentimentally*] Dont say that. Dont think of him in that way. After all, he was your husband; and whatever his faults may have been, it is not for you to think unkindly of him.

CATHERINE [*almost bursting*] I shall forget myself.

EDSTASTON. Come! I am sure he really loved you; and you truly loved him.

CATHERINE [*controlling herself with a supreme effort*] No, Catherine. What would Voltaire say?

EDSTASTON. Oh, never mind that vile scoffer. Set an example to Europe, Madam, by doing what I am going to do. Marry again. Marry some good man who will be a strength and a support to your old age.

CATHERINE. My old – [*she again becomes speechless*].

EDSTASTON. Yes: we must all grow old, even the handsomest of us.

CATHERINE [*sinking into her chair with a gasp*] Thank you.

EDSTASTON. You will thank me more when you see your little ones round your knee, and your man there by the fireside in the winter evenings – by the way, I forgot that you have no firesides here in spite of the coldness of the climate; so shall I say by the stove?

CATHERINE. Certainly, if you wish. The stove, by all means.

EDSTASTON [*impulsively*] Ah, Madam, abolish the stove: believe me, there is nothing like the good old open grate. Home! duty! happiness! they all mean the same thing; and they all flourish best on the drawingroom hearthrug. [*Turning to Claire*] And now, my love, we must not detain the Queen: she is anxious to inspect the model of her museum, to which I am sure we wish every success.

CLAIRE [*coldly*] *I* am not detaining her.

EDSTASTON. Well, goodbye [*wringing Patiomkin's hand*], goooo-oodbye, Prince: come and see us if ever you visit England. Spire View, Deepdene, Little Mugford, Devon, will always find me. [*To Varinka, kissing her hand*] Goodbye, Mademoiselle: goodbye, Little Mother, if I may call you that just once. [*Varinka puts up her face to be kissed*]. Eh? No, no, no, no: you dont mean that, you know. Naughty! [*To the Sergeant*] Goodbye, my friend. You will drink our healths with this [*tipping him*].

THE SERGEANT. The blessed Nicholas will multiply your fruits, Little Father.

EDSTASTON. Goodbye, goodbye, goodbye, goodbye, goodbye, goodbye.

> *He goes out backwards bowing, with Claire curtseying, having been listened to in utter dumbfoundedness by Patiomkin and Naryshkin, in childlike awe by Varinka, and with quite inexpressible feelings by Catherine. When he is out of sight she rises with clenched fists and raises her arms and her closed eyes to Heaven. Patiomkin, rousing himself from his stupor of amazement, springs to her like a tiger, and throws himself at her feet.*

PATIOMKIN. What shall I do to him for you? Skin him alive? Cut off his eyelids and stand him in the sun? Tear his tongue out? What shall it be?

CATHERINE [*opening her eyes*] Nothing. But oh, if I could only have had him for my — for my — for my —

PATIOMKIN [*in a growl of jealousy*] For your lover?

CATHERINE [*with an ineffable smile*] No: for my museum.

The Inca of Perusalem

An Almost Historical Comedietta

Composition begun August 1915; completed before 9 August 1915. Published in *Heartbreak House, Great Catherine, & Playlets of the War*, 1919. First presented at the Repertory Theatre, Birmingham, 7 October 1916.

The Archdeacon   *Joseph A. Dodd*
Ermyntrude Roosenhonkers-Pipstein   *Gertrude Kingston*
Hotel Manager   *Noel Shammon*
The Princess   *Cathleen Orford*
Waiter   *William Armstrong*
The Inca of Perusalem   *Felix Aylmer*

Period – 1916

Prologue: *Before the Curtain*

The Play: *A Hotel Sitting Room*

I must remind the reader that this playlet was written when its principal character, far from being a fallen foe and virtually a prisoner in our victorious hands, was still the Caesar whose legions we were resisting with our hearts in our mouths. Many were so horribly afraid of him that they could not forgive me for not being afraid of him: I seemed to be trifling heartlessly with a deadly peril. I knew better; and I have represented Caesar as knowing better himself. But it was one of the quaintnesses of popular feeling during the war that anyone who breathed the slightest doubt of the absolute perfection of German organization, the Machiavellian depth of German diplomacy, the omniscience of German science, the equipment of every German with a complete philosophy of history, and the consequent hopelessness of overcoming so magnificently accomplished an enemy except by the sacrifice of every recreative activity to incessant and vehement war work, including a heartbreaking mass of fussing and cadging and bluffing that did nothing but waste our energies and tire our resolution, was called a pro-German.

Now that this is all over, and the upshot of the fighting has shewn that we could quite well have afforded to laugh at the doomed Inca, I am in another difficulty. I may be supposed to be hitting Caesar when he is down. That is why I preface the play with this reminder that when it was written he was not down. To make quite sure, I have gone through the proof sheets very carefully, and deleted everything that could possibly be mistaken for a foul blow. I have of course maintained the ancient privilege of comedy to chasten Caesar's foibles by laughing at them, whilst introducing enough obvious and outrageous fiction to relieve both myself and my model from the obligations and responsibilities of sober history and biography. But I should certainly put the play in the fire instead of publishing it if it contained a word against our defeated enemy that I would not have written in 1913.

PROLOGUE

The tableau curtains are closed. An English archdeacon comes through them in a condition of extreme irritation. He speaks through the curtains to someone behind them.

THE ARCHDEACON. Once for all, Ermyntrude, I cannot afford to maintain you in your present extravagance. [*He goes to a flight of steps leading to the stalls and sits down disconsolately on the top step. A fashionably dressed lady comes through the curtains and contemplates him with patient obstinacy. He continues, grumbling*] An English clergyman's daughter should be able to live quite respectably and comfortably on an allowance of £150 a year, wrung with great difficulty from the domestic budget.

ERMYNTRUDE. You are not a common clergyman: you are an archdeacon.

THE ARCHDEACON [*angrily*] That does not affect my emoluments to the extent of enabling me to support a daughter whose extravagance would disgrace a royal personage. [*Scrambling to his feet and scolding at her*] What do you mean by it, Miss?

ERMYNTRUDE. Oh really, father! Miss! Is that the way to talk to a widow? `

THE ARCHDEACON. Is that the way to talk to a father? Your marriage was a most disastrous imprudence. It gave you habits that are absolutely beyond your means – I mean beyond my means: you have no means. Why did you not marry Matthews: the best curate I ever had?

ERMYNTRUDE. I wanted to; and you wouldnt let me. You insisted on my marrying Roosenhonkers-Pipstein.

THE ARCHDEACON. I had to do the best for you, my child. Roosenhonkers-Pipstein was a millionaire.

ERMYNTRUDE. How did you know he was a millionaire?

THE ARCHDEACON. He came from America. Of course he was a millionaire. Besides, he proved to my solicitors that he had fifteen million dollars when you married him.

ERMYNTRUDE. His solicitors proved to me that he had sixteen millions when he died. He was a millionaire to the last.

THE ARCHDEACON. O Mammon, Mammon! I am punished now for bowing the knee to him. Is there nothing left of your settlement? Fifty thousand dollars a year it secured to you, as we all thought. Only half the securities could be called speculative. The other half were gilt-edged. What has become of it all?

ERMYNTRUDE. The speculative ones were not paid up; and the gilt-edged ones just paid the calls on them until the whole show burst up.

THE ARCHDEACON. Ermyntrude: what expressions!

ERMYNTRUDE. Oh bother! If you had lost ten thousand a year what expressions would you use, do you think? The long and the short of it is that I cant live in the squalid way you are accustomed to.

THE ARCHDEACON. Squalid!

ERMYNTRUDE. I have formed habits of comfort.

THE ARCHDEACON. Comfort!!

ERMYNTRUDE. Well, elegance if you like. Luxury, if you insist. Call it what you please. A house that costs less than a hundred thousand dollars a year to run is intolerable to me.

THE ARCHDEACON. Then, my dear, you had better become lady's maid to a princess until you can find another millionaire to marry you.

ERMYNTRUDE. Thats an idea. I will [*She vanishes through the curtains*].

THE ARCHDEACON. What! Come back, Miss. Come back this instant. [*The lights are lowered*]. Oh, very well: I have nothing more to say. [*He descends the steps into the auditorium and makes for the door, grumbling all the time*]. Insane, senseless extravagance! [*Barking*] Worthlessness!! [*Muttering*] I will not bear it any longer. Dresses, hats, furs, gloves, motor rides: one bill after another: money going like water. No restraint, no self-control, no decency. [*Shrieking*] I say, no decency! [*Muttering again*] Nice state of things we are coming to! A pretty world! But I simply will not bear it. She can do as she likes. I wash my hands of her: I am not going to die in the workhouse for any good-for-nothing, undutiful, spendthrift daughter; and the sooner that is understood by everybody the better for all par – [*He is by this time out of hearing in the corridor*].

THE PLAY

A hotel sitting room. A table in the centre. On it a telephone. Two chairs at it, opposite one another. Behind it, the door. The fireplace has a mirror in the mantelpiece.

A spinster Princess, hatted and gloved, is ushered in by the Hotel Manager, spruce and artificially bland by professional habit, but treating his customer with a condescending affability which sails very close to the east wind of insolence.

THE MANAGER. I am sorry I am unable to accommodate Your Highness on the first floor.

THE PRINCESS [*very shy and nervous*] Oh please dont mention it. This is quite nice. Very nice. Thank you very much.

THE MANAGER. We could prepare a room in the annexe —

THE PRINCESS. Oh no. This will do very well.

She takes off her gloves and hat; puts them on the table; and sits down.

THE MANAGER. The rooms are quite as good up here. There is less noise; and there is the lift. If Your Highness desires anything, there is the telephone —

THE PRINCESS. Oh, thank you, I dont want anything. The telephone is so difficult: I am not accustomed to it.

THE MANAGER. Can I take any order? Some tea?

THE PRINCESS. Oh, thank you. Yes: I should like some tea, if I might — if it would not be too much trouble.

He goes out. The telephone rings. The Princess starts out of her chair, terrified, and recoils as far as possible from the instrument.

THE PRINCESS. Oh dear! [*It rings again. She looks scared. It rings again. She approaches it timidly. It rings again. She retreats hastily. It rings repeatedly. She runs to it in desperation and puts the receiver to her ear*]. Who is there? What do I do? I am not used to the telephone: I dont know how — What! Oh, I can hear you speaking quite distinctly. [*She sits down, delighted, and settles herself for a conversation*]. How wonderful! What! A lady? Oh! a person. Oh yes: I know. Yes, please, send her up. Have my servants finished their lunch yet? Oh no: please dont disturb them: I'd rather not. It doesnt matter. Thank you. What? Oh yes, it's quite easy. I had no idea – am I to hang it up just as it was? Thank you. [*She hangs it up*].

Ermyntrude enters, presenting a plain and staid appearance in a long straight waterproof with a hood over her head gear. She comes to the end of the table opposite to that at which the Princess is seated.

THE PRINCESS. Excuse me. I have been talking through the telephone; and I heard quite well, though I have never ventured before. Wont you sit down?

ERMYNTRUDE. No, thank you, Your Highness. I am only a lady's maid. I understood you wanted one.

THE PRINCESS. Oh no: you mustnt think I want one. It's so unpatriotic to want anything now, on account of the war, you know. I sent my maid away as a public duty; and now she has married a soldier and is expecting a war baby. But I dont know how to do without her. Ive tried my very best; but somehow it doesnt answer: everybody cheats me; and in the end it isnt any saving. So Ive made up my mind to sell my piano and have a maid. That will be a real saving, because I really dont care a bit for music, though of course one has to pretend to. Dont you think so?

ERMYNTRUDE. Certainly I do, Your Highness. Nothing could be more correct. Saving and self-denial both at once; and an act of kindness to me, as I am out of place.

THE PRINCESS. I'm so glad you see it in that way. Er – you wont mind my asking, will you? – how did you lose your place?

ERMYNTRUDE. The war, Your Highness, the war.

THE PRINCESS. Oh yes, of course. But how –

ERMYNTRUDE [*taking out her handkerchief and shewing signs of grief*] My poor mistress –

THE PRINCESS. Oh please say no more. Dont think about it. So tactless of me to mention it.

ERMYNTRUDE [*mastering her emotion and smiling through her tears*] Your Highness is too good.

THE PRINCESS. Do you think you could be happy with me? I attach such importance to that.

ERMYNTRUDE [*gushing*] Oh, I know I shall.

THE PRINCESS. You must not expect too much. There is my uncle. He is very severe and hasty; and he is my guardian. I once had a maid I liked very much; but he sent her away the very first time.

ERMYNTRUDE. The first time of what, Your Highness?

THE PRINCESS. Oh, something she did. I am sure she had never done it before; and I know she would never have done it again, she was so truly contrite and nice about it.

ERMYNTRUDE. About what, Your Highness?

THE PRINCESS. Well, she wore my jewels and one of my dresses at a rather improper ball with her young man; and my uncle saw her.

ERMYNTRUDE. Then he was at the ball too, Your Highness?

THE PRINCESS [*struck by the inference*] I suppose he must have been. I wonder! You know, it's very sharp of you to find that out. I hope you are not too sharp.

ERMYNTRUDE. A lady's maid has to be, Your Highness. [*She produces some letters*]. Your Highness wishes to see my testimonials, no doubt. I have one from an Archdeacon. [*She proffers the letters*].

THE PRINCESS [*taking them*] Do archdeacons have maids? How curious!

ERMYNTRUDE. No, Your Highness. They have daughters. I have first-rate testimonials from the Archdeacon and from his daughter.

THE PRINCESS [*reading them*] The daughter says you are in every respect a treasure. The Archdeacon says he would have kept you if he could possibly have afforded it. Most satisfactory, I'm sure.

ERMYNTRUDE. May I regard myself as engaged then, Your Highness?

THE PRINCESS [*alarmed*] Oh, I'm sure I dont know. If you like, of course; but do you think I ought to?

ERMYNTRUDE. Naturally I think Your Highness ought to, most decidedly.

THE PRINCESS. Oh well, if you think that, I daresay youre quite right. Youll excuse my mentioning it, I hope; but what wages – er – ?

ERMYNTRUDE. The same as the maid who went to the ball. Your Highness need not make any change.

THE PRINCESS. M'yes. Of course she began with less. But she had such a number of relatives to keep! It was quite heartbreaking: I had to raise her wages again and again.

ERMYNTRUDE. I shall be quite content with what she began on;

and I have no relatives dependent on me. And I am willing to wear my own dresses at balls.

THE PRINCESS. I am sure nothing could be fairer than that. My uncle cant object to that: can he?

ERMYNTRUDE. If he does, Your Highness, ask him to speak to me about it. I shall regard it as part of my duties to speak to your uncle about matters of business.

THE PRINCESS. Would you? You must be frightfully courageous.

ERMYNTRUDE. May I regard myself as engaged, Your Highness? I should like to set about my duties immediately.

THE PRINCESS. Oh yes, I think so. Oh certainly. I –

A waiter comes in with the tea. He places the tray on the table.

THE PRINCESS. Oh, thank you.

ERMYNTRUDE [*raising the cover from the tea cake and looking at it*] How long has that been standing at the top of the stairs?

THE PRINCESS [*terrified*] Oh please! It doesnt matter.

THE WAITER. It has not been waiting. Straight from the kitchen, madam, believe me.

ERMYNTRUDE. Send the manager here.

THE WAITER. The manager! What do you want with the manager?

ERMYNTRUDE. He will tell you when I have done with him. How dare you treat Her Highness in this disgraceful manner? What sort of pothouse is this? Where did you learn to speak to persons of quality? Take away your cold tea and cold cake instantly. Give them to the chambermaid you were flirting with whilst Her Highness was waiting. Order some fresh tea at once; and do not presume to bring it yourself: have it brought by a civil waiter who is accustomed to wait on ladies, and not, like you, on commercial travellers.

THE WAITER. Alas, madam, I am not accustomed to wait on anybody. Two years ago I was an eminent medical man. My waiting-room was crowded with the flower of the aristocracy and the higher bourgeoisie from nine to six every day. But the war came; and my patients were ordered to give up their luxuries. They gave up their doctors, but kept their week-end hotels, closing every career to me except the career of a waiter. [*He puts his fingers on the teapot to test its temperature, and automatically takes out his watch with the other hand as if to count the teapot's pulse*]. You are right: the tea is cold: it was made by the wife of a once fashionable architect. The cake is only half toasted: what can you expect from a ruined west-end tailor whose attempt to

establish a second-hand business failed last Tuesday week?
Have you the heart to complain to the manager? Have we not
suffered enough? Are our miseries nev – [*the manager enters*] Oh
Lord! here he is. [*The waiter withdraws abjectly, taking the tea tray
with him*].

THE MANAGER. Pardon, Your Highness; but I have received an
urgent inquiry for rooms from an English family of importance;
and I venture to ask you to let me know how long you intend to
honor us with your presence.

THE PRINCESS [*rising anxiously*] Oh! am I in the way?

ERMYNTRUDE [*sternly*] Sit down, madam [*The Princess sits down
forlornly. Ermyntrude turns imperiously to the Manager*]. Her Highness
will require this room for twenty minutes.

THE MANAGER. Twenty minutes!

ERMYNTRUDE. Yes: it will take fully that time to find a proper
apartment in a respectable hotel.

THE MANAGER. I do not understand.

ERMYNTRUDE. You understand perfectly. How dare you offer Her
Highness a room on the second floor?

THE MANAGER. But I have explained. The first floor is occupied.
At least –

ERMYNTRUDE. Well? At least?

THE MANAGER. It is occupied.

ERMYNTRUDE. Dont you dare tell Her Highness a falsehood.
It is not occupied. You are saving it up for the arrival of the
five fifteen express, from which you hope to pick up some
fat armaments contractor who will drink all the bad champagne in your cellar at 25 francs a bottle, and pay twice over
for everything because he is in the same hotel with Her
Highness, and can boast of having turned her out of the best
rooms.

THE MANAGER. But Her Highness was so gracious. I did not know
that her Highness was at all particular.

ERMYNTRUDE. And you take advantage of Her Highness's
graciousness. You impose on her with your stories. You give her
a room not fit for a dog. You send cold tea to her by a decayed
professional person disguised as a waiter. But dont think you can
trifle with me. I am a lady's maid; and I know the ladies' maids
and valets of all the aristocracies of Europe and all the
millionaires of America. When I expose your hotel as the
second-rate little hole it is, not a soul above the rank of a curate

with a large family will be seen entering it. I shake its dust off my feet. Order the luggage to be taken down at once.

THE MANAGER [*appealing to the Princess*] Can Your Highness believe this of me? Have I had the misfortune to offend Your Highness?

THE PRINCESS. Oh no. I am quite satisfied. Please —

ERMYNTRUDE. Is Your Highness dissatisfied with me?

THE PRINCESS [*intimidated*] Oh no: please dont think that. I only meant —

ERMYNTRUDE [*to the Manager*] You hear. Perhaps you think Her Highness is going to do the work of teaching you your place herself, instead of leaving it to her maid.

THE MANAGER. Oh please, mademoiselle. Believe me: our only wish is to make you perfectly comfortable. But in consequence of the war, all royal personages now practise a rigid economy, and desire us to treat them like their poorest subjects.

THE PRINCESS. Oh yes. You are quite right —

ERMYNTRUDE [*interrupting*] There! Her Highness forgives you; but dont do it again. Now go downstairs, my good man, and get that suite on the first floor ready for us. And send some proper tea. And turn on the heating apparatus until the temperature in the rooms is comfortably warm. And have hot water put in all the bedrooms —

THE MANAGER. There are basins with hot and cold taps.

ERMYNTRUDE [*scornfully*] Yes: there would be. I suppose we must put up with that: sinks in our rooms, and pipes that rattle and bang and guggle all over the house whenever anyone washes his hands. *I* know.

THE MANAGER [*gallant*] You are hard to please, mademoiselle.

ERMYNTRUDE. No harder than other people. But when I'm not pleased I'm not too ladylike to say so. Thats all the difference. There is nothing more, thank you.

The Manager shrugs his shoulders resignedly; makes a deep bow to the Princess; goes to the door; wafts a kiss surreptitiously to Ermyntrude; and goes out.

THE PRINCESS. It's wonderful! How have you the courage?

ERMYNTRUDE. In Your Highness's service I know no fear. Your Highness can leave all unpleasant people to me.

THE PRINCESS. How I wish I could! The most dreadful thing of all I have to go through myself.

ERMYNTRUDE. Dare I ask what it is, Your Highness?

THE PRINCESS. I'm going to be married. I'm to be met here and married to a man I never saw. A boy! A boy who never saw me! One of the sons of the Inca of Perusalem.

ERMYNTRUDE. Indeed? Which son?

THE PRINCESS. I dont know. They havnt settled which. It's a dreadful thing to be a princess: they just marry you to anyone they like. The Inca is to come and look at me, and pick out whichever of his sons he thinks will suit. And then I shall be an alien enemy everywhere except in Perusalem, because the Inca has made war on everybody. And I shall have to pretend that everybody has made war on him. It's too bad.

ERMYNTRUDE. Still, a husband is a husband. I wish I had one.

THE PRINCESS. Oh, how can you say that! I'm afraid youre not a nice woman.

ERMYNTRUDE. Your Highness is provided for. I'm not.

THE PRINCESS. Even if you could bear to let a man touch you, you shouldnt say so.

ERMYNTRUDE. I shall not say so again, Your Highness, except perhaps to the man.

THE PRINCESS. It's too dreadful to think of. I wonder you can be so coarse. I really dont think youll suit. I feel sure now that you know more about men than you should.

ERMYNTRUDE. I am a widow, Your Highness.

THE PRINCESS [*overwhelmed*] Oh, I BEG your pardon. Of course I ought to have known you would not have spoken like that if you were not married. That makes it all right, doesnt it? I'm so sorry.

The Manager returns, white, scared, hardly able to speak

THE MANAGER. Your Highness: an officer asks to see you on behalf of the Inca of Perusalem.

THE PRINCESS [*rising distractedly*] Oh, I cant, really. Oh, what shall I do?

THE MANAGER. On important business, he says, Your Highness. Captain Duval.

ERMYNTRUDE. Duval! Nonsense! The usual thing. It is the Inca himself, incognito.

THE PRINCESS. Oh, send him away. Oh, I'm so afraid of the Inca. I'm not properly dressed to receive him; and he is so particular: he would order me to stay in my room for a week. Tell him to call tomorrow: say I'm ill in bed. I cant: I wont: I darent: you must get rid of him somehow.

ERMYNTRUDE. Leave him to me, Your Highness.

THE PRINCESS. Youd never dare!

ERMYNTRUDE. I am an Englishwoman, Your Highness, and perfectly capable of tackling ten Incas if necessary. I will arrange the matter. [*To the Manager*] Shew Her Highness to her bedroom; and then shew Captain Duval in here.

THE PRINCESS. Oh, thank you so much. [*She goes to the door. Ermyntrude, noticing that she has left her hat and gloves on the table, runs after her with them*]. Oh, thank you. And oh, please, if I must have one of his sons, I should like a fair one that doesnt shave, with soft hair and a beard. I couldnt bear being kissed by a bristly person. [*She runs out, the Manager bowing as she passes. He follows her*].

Ermyntrude whips off her waterproof; hides it; and gets herself swiftly into perfect trim at the mirror, before the Manager, with a large jewel case in his hand, returns, ushering in the Inca.

THE MANAGER. Captain Duval.

The Inca, in military uniform, advances with a marked and imposing stage walk; stops; orders the trembling Manager by a gesture to place the jewel case on the table; dismisses him with a frown; touches his helmet graciously to Ermyntrude; and takes off his cloak.

THE INCA. I beg you, madam, to be quite at your ease, and to speak to me without ceremony.

ERMYNTRUDE [*moving haughtily and carelessly to the table*] I hadnt the slightest intention of treating you with ceremony. [*She sits down: a liberty which gives him a perceptible shock*]. I am quite at a loss to imagine why I should treat a perfect stranger named Duval: a captain! almost a subaltern! with the smallest ceremony.

THE INCA. That is true. I had for the moment forgotten my position.

ERMYNTRUDE. It doesnt matter. You may sit down.

THE INCA [*frowning*] What!

ERMYNTRUDE. I said, you . . . may . . . sit . . . down.

THE INCA. Oh [*His moustache droops. He sits down*].

ERMYNTRUDE. What is your business?

THE INCA. I come on behalf of the Inca of Perusalem.

ERMYNTRUDE. The Allerhöchst?

THE INCA. Precisely.

ERMYNTRUDE. I wonder does he feel ridiculous when people call him the Allerhöchst.

THE INCA [*surprised*] Why should he? He is the Allerhöchst.

ERMYNTRUDE. Is he nice looking?

THE INCA. I – er. Er – I. I – er. I am not a good judge.

ERMYNTRUDE. They say he takes himself very seriously.

THE INCA. Why should he not, madam? Providence has entrusted to his family the care of a mighty empire. He is in a position of half divine, half paternal responsibility towards sixty millions of people, whose duty it is to die for him at the word of command. To take himself otherwise than seriously would be blasphemous. It is a punishable offence – severely punishable – in Perusalem. It is called Incadisparagement.

ERMYNTRUDE. How cheerful! Can he laugh?

THE INCA. Certainly, madam. [*He laughs, harshly and mirthlessly*]. Ha ha! Ha ha ha!

ERMYNTRUDE [*frigidly*] I asked could the Inca laugh. I did not ask could you laugh.

THE INCA. That is true, madam. [*Chuckling*] Devilish amusing, that! [*He laughs, genially and sincerely, and becomes a much more agreeable person*]. Pardon me: I am now laughing because I cannot help it. I am amused. The other was merely an imitation: a failure, I admit.

ERMYNTRUDE. You intimated that you had some business?

THE INCA [*producing a very large jewel case, and relapsing into solemnity*] I am instructed by the Allerhöchst to take a careful note of your features and figure, and, if I consider them satisfactory, to present you with this trifling token of His Imperial Majesty's regard. I do consider them satisfactory. Allow me [*he opens the jewel case and presents it*]!

ERMYNTRUDE [*staring at the contents*] What awful taste he must have! I cant wear that.

THE INCA [*reddening*] Take care, madam! This brooch was designed by the Inca himself. Allow me to explain the design. In the centre, the shield of Arminius. The ten surrounding medallions represent the ten castles of His Majesty. The rim is a piece of the telephone cable laid by His Majesty across the Shipskeel canal. The pin is a model in miniature of the sword of Henry the Bird-catcher.

ERMYNTRUDE. Miniature! It must be bigger than the original. My good man, you dont expect me to wear this round my neck: it's as big as a turtle. [*He shuts the case with an angry snap*]. How much did it cost?

THE INCA. For materials and manufacture alone, half a million Perusalem dollars, madam. The Inca's design constitutes it a work of art. As such, it is now worth probably ten million dollars.

ERMYNTRUDE. Give it to me [*she snatches it*]. I'll pawn it and buy something nice with the money.

THE INCA. Impossible, madam. A design by the Inca must not be exhibited for sale in the shop window of a pawnbroker. [*He flings*] *himself into his chair, fuming*].

ERMYNTRUDE. So much the better. The Inca will have to redeem it to save himself from that disgrace; and the poor pawnbroker will get his money back. Nobody would buy it, you know.

THE INCA. May I ask why?

ERMYNTRUDE. Well, look at it! Just look at it! I ask you!

THE INCA [*his moustache drooping ominously*] I am sorry to have to report to the Inca that you have no soul for fine art. [*He rises sulkily*]. The position of daughter-in-law to the Inca is not compatible with the tastes of a pig. [*He attempts to take back the brooch*].

ERMYNTRUDE [*rising and retreating behind her chair with the brooch*] Here! you let that brooch alone. You presented it to me on behalf of the Inca. It is mine. You said my appearance was satisfactory.

THE INCA. Your appearance is not satisfactory. The Inca would not allow his son to marry you if the boy were on a desert island and you were the only other human being on it [*he strides up the room*].

ERMYNTRUDE [*calmly sitting down and replacing the case on the table*] How could he? There would be no clergyman to marry us. It would have to be quite morganatic.

THE INCA [*returning*] Such an expression is out of place in the mouth of a princess aspiring to the highest destiny on earth. You have the morals of a dragoon. [*She receives this with a shriek of laughter. He struggles with his sense of humor*]. At the same time [*he sits down*] there is a certain coarse fun in the idea which compels me to smile [*he turns up his moustache and smiles*].

ERMYNTRUDE. When I marry the Inca's son, Captain, I shall make the Inca order you to cut off that moustache. It is too irresistible. Doesnt it fascinate everyone in Perusalem?

THE INCA [*leaning forward to her energetically*] By all the thunders of Thor, madam, it fascinates the whole world.

ERMYNTRUDE. What I like about you, Captain Duval, is your modesty.

THE INCA [*straightening up suddenly*] Woman: do not be a fool.

ERMYNTRUDE [*indignant*] Well!

THE INCA. You must look facts in the face. This moustache is an exact copy of the Inca's moustache. Well, does the world occupy itself with the Inca's moustache or does it not? Does it ever occupy itself with anything else? If that is the truth, does its recognition constitute the Inca a coxcomb? Other potentates have moustaches: even beards and moustaches. Does the world occupy itself with those beards and moustaches? Do the hawkers in the streets of every capital on the civilized globe sell ingenious cardboard representations of their faces on which, at the pulling of a simple string, the moustaches turn up and down, so – [*he makes his moustache turn up and down several times*]? No! I say No. The Inca's moustache is so watched and studied that it has made his face the political barometer of the whole continent. When that moustache goes up, culture rises with it. Not what you call culture; but Kultur, a word so much more significant that I hardly understand it myself except when I am in specially good form. When it goes down, millions of men perish.

ERMYNTRUDE. You know, if I had a moustache like that, it would turn my head. I should go mad. Are you quite sure the Inca isnt mad?

THE INCA. How can he be mad, madam? What is sanity? The condition of the Inca's mind. What is madness? The condition of the people who disagree with the Inca.

ERMYNTRUDE. Then I am a lunatic because I dont like that ridiculous brooch.

THE INCA. No, madam: you are only an idiot.

ERMYNTRUDE. Thank you.

THE INCA. Mark you: it is not to be expected that you should see eye to eye with the Inca. That would be presumption. It is for you to accept without question or demur the assurance of your Inca that the brooch is a masterpiece.

ERMYNTRUDE. My Inca! Oh, come! I like that. He is not my Inca yet.

THE INCA. He is everybody's Inca, madam. His realm will yet extend to the confines of the habitable earth. It is his divine right; and let those who dispute it look to themselves. Properly speaking, all those who are now trying to shake his world predominance are not at war with him, but in rebellion against him.

ERMYNTRUDE. Well, he started it, you know.

THE INCA. Madam, be just. When the hunters surround the lion, the lion will spring. The Inca had kept the peace for years. Those who attacked him were steeped in blood, black blood, white blood, brown blood, yellow blood, blue blood. The Inca had never shed a drop.

ERMYNTRUDE. He had only talked.

THE INCA. Only talked! Only talked! What is more glorious than talk? Can anyone in the world talk like him? Madam: when he signed the declaration of war, he said to his foolish generals and admirals, 'Gentlemen: you will all be sorry for this.' And they are. They know now that they had better have relied on the sword of the spirit: in other words, on their Inca's talk, than on their murderous cannons. The world will one day do justice to the Inca as the man who kept the peace with nothing but his tongue and his moustache. While he talked: talked just as I am talking now to you, simply, quietly, sensibly, but GREATLY, there was peace; there was prosperity; Perusalem went from success to success. He has been silenced for a year by the roar of trinitrotoluene and the bluster of fools; and the world is in ruins. What a tragedy! [*He is convulsed with grief*].

ERMYNTRUDE. Captain Duval: I dont want to be unsympathetic; but suppose we get back to business.

THE INCA. Business! What business?

ERMYNTRUDE. Well, my business. You want me to marry one of the Inca's sons: I forget which.

THE INCA. As far as I can recollect the name, it is His Imperial Highness Prince Eitel William Frederick George Franz Josef Alexander Nicholas Victor Emmanuel Albert Theodore Wilson –

ERMYNTRUDE [*interrupting*] Oh, please, please, maynt I have one with a shorter name? What is he called at home?

THE INCA. He is usually called Sonny, madam. [*With great charm of manner*] But you will please understand that the Inca has no desire to pin you to any particular son. There is Chips and Spots and Lulu and Pongo and the Corsair and the Piffler and Jack Johnson the Second, all unmarried. At least not seriously married: nothing, in short, that cannot be arranged. They are all at your service.

ERMYNTRUDE. Are they all as clever and charming as their father?

THE INCA [*lifts his eyebrows pityingly; shrugs his shoulders; then, with indulgent paternal contempt*] Excellent lads, madam. Very honest affectionate creatures. I have nothing against them. Pongo imitates farmyard sounds – cock-crowing and that sort of thing – extremely well. Lulu plays Strauss's Sinfonia Domestica on the mouth organ really screamingly. Chips keeps owls and rabbits. Spots motor bicycles. The Corsair commands canal barges and steers them himself. The Piffler writes plays, and paints most abominably. Jack Johnson trims ladies' hats, and boxes with professionals hired for that purpose. He is invariably victorious. Yes: they all have their different little talents. And also, of course, their family resemblances. For example, they all smoke; they all quarrel with one another; and they none of them appreciate their father, who, by the way, is no mean painter, though the Piffler pretends to ridicule his efforts.

ERMYNTRUDE. Quite a large choice, eh?

THE INCA. But very little to choose, believe me. I should not recommend Pongo, because he snores so frightfully that it has been necessary to build him a sound-proof bedroom: otherwise the royal family would get no sleep. But any of the others would suit equally well – if you are really bent on marrying one of them.

ERMYNTRUDE. If! What is this? I never wanted to marry one of them. I thought you wanted me to.

THE INCA. I did, madam; but [*confidentially, flattering her*] you are not quite the sort of person I expected you to be; and I doubt whether any of these young degenerates would make you happy. I trust I am not shewing any want of natural feeling when I say that from the point of view of a lively, accomplished, and beautiful woman [*Ermyntrude bows*] they might pall after a time. I suggest that you might prefer the Inca himself.

ERMYNTRUDE. Oh, Captain, how could a humble person like myself be of any interest to a prince who is surrounded with the ablest and most far-reaching intellects in the world?

THE INCA [*explosively*] What on earth are you talking about, madam? Can you name a single man in the entourage of the Inca who is not a born fool?

ERMYNTRUDE. Oh, how can you say that! There is Admiral von Cockpits –

THE INCA [*rising intolerantly and striding about the room*] Von Cockpits! Madam: if Von Cockpits ever goes to heaven, before three weeks are over, the Angel Gabriel will be at war with the man in the moon.

ERMYNTRUDE. But General Von Schinkenburg –

THE INCA. Schinkenburg! I grant you, Schinkenburg has a genius for defending market gardens. Among market gardens he is invincible. But what is the good of that? The world does not consist of market gardens. Turn him loose in pasture and he is lost. The Inca has defeated all these generals again and again at manœuvres; and yet he has to give place to them in the field because he would be blamed for every disaster – accused of sacrificing the country to his vanity. Vanity! Why do they call him vain? Just because he is one of the few men who are not afraid to live. Why do they call themselves brave? Because they have not sense enough to be afraid to die. Within the last year the world has produced millions of heroes. Has it produced more than one Inca? [*He resumes his seat*].

ERMYNTRUDE. Fortunately not, Captain. I'd rather marry Chips.

THE INCA [*making a wry face*] Chips! Oh no: I wouldnt marry Chips.

ERMYNTRUDE. Why?

THE INCA [*whispering the secret*] Chips talks too much about himself.

ERMYNTRUDE. Well, what about Snooks?

THE INCA. Snooks? Who is he? Have I a son named Snooks? There are so many – [*wearily*] so many – that I often forget. [*Casually*] But I wouldnt marry him, anyhow, if I were you.

ERMYNTRUDE. But hasnt any of them inherited the family genius? Surely, if Providence has entrusted them with the care of Perusalem – if they are all descended from Bedrock the Great –

THE INCA [*interrupting her impatiently*] Madam: if you ask me, I consider Bedrock a grossly overrated monarch.

ERMYNTRUDE [*shocked*] Oh, Captain! Take care! Incadisparagement.

THE INCA. I repeat, grossly overrated. Strictly between ourselves, I do not believe all this about Providence entrusting the care of sixty million human beings to the abilities of Chips and the Piffler and Jack Johnson. I believe in individual genius. That is the Inca's secret. It must be. Why, hang it all, madam, if it were a mere family matter, the Inca's uncle would have been as great a man as the Inca. And – well, everybody knows what the Inca's uncle was.

ERMYNTRUDE. My experience is that the relatives of men of genius are always the greatest duffers imaginable.

THE INCA. Precisely. That is what proves that the Inca is a man of genius. His relatives are duffers.

ERMYNTRUDE. But bless my soul, Captain, if all the Inca's

generals are incapables, and all his relatives duffers, Perusalem will be beaten in the war; and then it will become a republic, like France after 1871, and the Inca will be sent to St Helena.

THE INCA [*triumphantly*] That is just what the Inca is playing for, madam. It is why he consented to the war.

ERMYNTRUDE. What!

THE INCA. Aha! The fools talk of crushing the Inca; but they little know their man. Tell me this. Why did St Helena extinguish Napoleon?

ERMYNTRUDE. I give it up.

THE INCA. Because, madam, with certain rather remarkable qualities, which I should be the last to deny, Napoleon lacked versatility. After all, any fool can be a soldier: we know that only too well in Perusalem, where every fool is a soldier. But the Inca has a thousand other resources. He is an architect. Well, St Helena presents an unlimited field to the architect. He is a painter: need I remind you that St Helena is still without a National Gallery? He is a composer: Napoleon left no symphonies in St Helena. Send the Inca to St Helena, madam, and the world will crowd thither to see his works as they crowd now to Athens to see the Acropolis, to Madrid to see the pictures of Velasquez, to Bayreuth to see the music dramas of that egotistical old rebel Richard Wagner, who ought to have been shot before he was forty, as indeed he very nearly was. Take this from me: hereditary monarchs are played out: the age for men of genius has come: the career is open to the talents: before ten years have elapsed every civilized country from the Carpathians to the Rocky Mountains will be a Republic.

ERMYNTRUDE. Then goodbye to the Inca.

THE INCA. On the contrary, madam, the Inca will then have his first real chance. He will be unanimously invited by those Republics to return from his exile and act as Superpresident of all the republics.

ERMYNTRUDE. But wont that be a come down for him? Think of it! after being Inca, to be a mere President!

THE INCA. Well, why not! An Inca can do nothing. He is tied hand and foot. A constitutional monarch is openly called an india-rubber stamp. An emperor is a puppet. The Inca is not allowed to make a speech: he is compelled to take up a screed of flatulent twaddle written by some noodle of a minister and read it aloud. But look at the American President! He is the Allerhöchst, if you like. No, madam, believe me, there is nothing like Democracy, American Democracy. Give the people voting papers: good long voting papers, American fashion; and while the people are reading the voting papers the Government does what it likes.

ERMYNTRUDE. What! You too worship before the statue of Liberty, like the Americans?

THE INCA. Not at all, madam. The Americans do not worship the statue of Liberty. They have erected it in the proper place for a statue of Liberty: on its tomb [*he turns down his moustaches*].

ERMYNTRUDE [*laughing*] Oh! Youd better not let them hear you say that, Captain.

THE INCA. Quite safe, madam: they would take it as a joke [*He rises*]. And now, prepare yourself for a surprise. [*She rises*]. A shock. Brace yourself. Steel yourself. And do not be afraid.

ERMYNTRUDE. Whatever on earth can you be going to tell me, Captain?

THE INCA. Madam: I am no captain. I –

ERMYNTRUDE. You are the Inca in disguise.

THE INCA. Good heavens! how do you know that? Who has betrayed me?

ERMYNTRUDE. How could I help divining it, Sir? Who is there in the world like you? Your magnetism –

THE INCA. True: I had forgotten my magnetism. But you know now that beneath the trappings of Imperial Majesty there is a Man: simple, frank, modest, unaffected, colloquial: a sincere friend, a natural human being, a genial comrade, one eminently calculated to make a woman happy. You, on the other hand, are the most charming woman I have ever met. Your conversation is wonderful. I have sat here almost in silence, listening to your shrewd and penetrating account of my character, my motives, if I may say so, my talents. Never has such justice been done me: never have I experienced such perfect sympathy. Will you – I hardly know how to put this – will you be mine?

ERMYNTRUDE. Oh, Sir, you are married.

THE INCA. I am prepared to embrace the Mahometan faith, which allows a man four wives, if you will consent. It will please the Turks. But I had rather you did not mention it to the Inca-ess, if you dont mind.

ERMYNTRUDE. This is really charming of you. But the time has come for me to make a revelation. It is your Imperial Majesty's turn now to brace yourself. To steel yourself. I am not the princess. I am –

THE INCA. The daughter of my old friend Archdeacon Daffodil Donkin, whose sermons are read to me every evening after dinner. I never forget a face.

ERMYNTRUDE. You knew all along!

THE INCA [*bitterly, throwing himself into his chair*] And you supposed that I, who have been condemned to the society of princesses all my wretched life, believed for a moment that any princess that ever walked could have your intelligence!

ERMYNTRUDE. How clever of you, Sir! But you cannot afford to marry me.

THE INCA [*springing up*] Why not?

ERMYNTRUDE. You are too poor. You have to eat war bread. Kings nowadays belong to the poorer classes. The King of England does not even allow himself wine at dinner.

THE INCA [*delighted*] Haw! Ha ha! Haw! haw! [*he is convulsed with laughter, and finally has to relieve his feelings by waltzing half round the room*].

ERMYNTRUDE. You may laugh, Sir; but I really could not live in that style. I am the widow of a millionaire, ruined by your little war.

THE INCA. A millionaire! What are millionaires now, with the world crumbling?

ERMYNTRUDE. Excuse me: mine was a hyphenated millionaire.

THE INCA. A highfalutin millionaire, you mean. [*Chuckling*] Haw! ha ha! really very nearly a pun, that. [*He sits down in her chair*].

ERMYNTRUDE [*revolted, sinking into his chair*] I think it quite the worst pun I ever heard.

THE INCA. The best puns have all been made years ago: nothing remained but to achieve the worst. However, madam [*he rises majestically; and she is about to rise also*] No: I prefer a seated audience [*she falls back into her seat at the imperious wave of his hand*] So [*he clicks his heels*]. Madam: I recognize my presumption in having sought the honor of your hand. As you say, I cannot afford it. Victorious as I am, I am hopelessly bankrupt; and the worst of it is, I am intelligent enough to know it. And I shall be beaten in consequence, because my most implacable enemy, though only a few months further away from bankruptcy than myself, has not a ray of intelligence, and will go on fighting until civilization is destroyed, unless I, out of sheer pity for the world, condescend to capitulate.

ERMYNTRUDE. The sooner the better, Sir. Many fine young men are dying while you wait.

THE INCA [*flinching painfully*] Why? Why do they do it?

ERMYNTRUDE. Because you make them.

THE INCA. Stuff! How can I? I am only one man; and they are millions. Do you suppose they would really kill each other if they didnt want to, merely for the sake of my beautiful eyes? Do not be deceived by newspaper claptrap, madam. I was swept away by a passion not my own, which imposed itself on me. By myself I am nothing. I dare not walk down the principal street of my own capital in a coat two years old, though the sweeper of that street can wear one ten years old. You talk of death as an unpopular thing. You are wrong: for years I gave them art, literature, science, prosperity, that they might live more abundantly; and they hated me, ridiculed me, caricatured me. Now that I give them death in its frightfullest forms, they are devoted to me. If you doubt me, ask those who for years have begged our tax-payers in vain for a few paltry thousands to spend on Life: on the bodies and minds of the nation's children, on the beauty and healthfulness of its cities, on the honor and comfort of its worn-out workers. They refused; and because they refused, death is let loose on them. They grudged a few hundreds a year for their salvation: they now pay millions a day for their own destruction and damnation. And this they call my doing! Let them say it, if they dare, before the judgment-seat at which they and I shall answer at last for what we have left undone no less than for what we have done. [*Pulling himself together suddenly*] Madam: I have the honor to be your most obedient [*he clicks his heels and bows*].

ERMYNTRUDE. Sir! [*she curtsies*].

THE INCA [*turning at the door*] Oh, by the way, there is a princess, isnt there, somewhere on the premises?

ERMYNTRUDE. There is. Shall I fetch her?

THE INCA [*dubious*] Pretty awful, I suppose, eh?

ERMYNTRUDE. About the usual thing.

THE INCA [*sighing*] Ah well! What can one expect? I dont think I need trouble her personally. Will you explain to her about the boys?

ERMYNTRUDE. I am afraid the explanation will fall rather flat without your magnetism.

THE INCA [*returning to her and speaking very humanly*] You are making fun of me. Why does everybody make fun of me? Is it fair?

ERMYNTRUDE [*seriously*] Yes: it is fair. What other defence have we poor common people against your shining armor, your mailed fist, your pomp and parade, your terrible power over us? Are these things fair?

THE INCA. Ah, well, perhaps, perhaps. [*He looks at his watch*]. By the way, there is time for a drive round the town and a cup of tea at the Zoo. Quite a bearable band there: it does not play any patriotic airs. I am sorry you will not listen to any more permanent arrangement; but if you would care to come —

ERMYNTRUDE [*eagerly*] Ratherrrrr. I shall be delighted.

THE INCA [*cautiously*] In the strictest honor, you understand.

ERMYNTRUDE. Dont be afraid. I promise to refuse any incorrect proposals.

THE INCA [*enchanted*] Oh! Charming woman: how well you understand men!

He offers her his arm: they go out together.

O'Flaherty V.C.

A Recruiting Pamphlet

Composition begun 23 July 1915, but immediately abandoned; re-begun 3 September 1915; completed 14 September 1915. Published in *Hearst's Magazine* (New York), August 1917. First English publication in *Heartbreak House, Great Catherine,* & *Playlets of the War,* 1919. First presented by Officers of the 40th Squadron, R.F.C., on the Western Front at Treizennes, Belgium, on 17 February 1917, with Robert Loraine as O'Flaherty, supported by a cast of amateurs. First professional performance at the 39th Street Theatre, New York, 21 June 1920, by the Deborah Bierne Irish Players. First presented in England by the Stage Society at the Lyric Theatre, Hammersmith, on 19 December 1920; repeated on 20 December.

Private Dennis O'Flaherty V.C.   *Arthur Sinclair*
General Sir Pearce Madigan   *Roy Byford*
Mrs O'Flaherty   *Sara Allgood*
Teresa Driscoll   *Nan Fitzgerald*

Period – Summer 1915

Scene – *Outside Sir Pearce Madigan's Country House in Ireland*

It may surprise some people to learn that in 1915 this little play was a recruiting poster in disguise. The British officer seldom likes Irish soldiers; but he always tries to have a certain proportion of them in his battalion, because, partly from a want of common sense which leads them to value their lives less than Englishmen do (lives are really less worth living in a poor country), and partly because even the most cowardly Irishman feels obliged to outdo an Englishman in bravery if possible, and at least to set a perilous pace for him, Irish soldiers give impetus to those military operations which require for their spirited execution more devilment than prudence.

Unfortunately, Irish recruiting was badly bungled in 1915. The Irish were for the most part Roman Catholics and loyal Irishmen, which means that from the English point of view they were heretics and rebels. But they were willing enough to go soldiering on the side of France and see the world outside Ireland, which is a dull place to live in. It was quite easy to enlist them by approaching them from their own point of view. But the War Office insisted on approaching them from the point of view of Dublin Castle. They were discouraged and repulsed by refusals to give commissions to Roman Catholic officers, or to allow distinct Irish units to be formed. To attract them, the walls were covered with placards headed REMEMBER BELGIUM. The folly of asking an Irishman to remember anything when you want him to fight for England was apparent to everyone outside the Castle: FORGET AND FORGIVE would have been more to the point. Remembering Belgium and its broken treaty led Irishmen to remember Limerick and its broken treaty; and the recruiting ended in a rebellion, in suppressing which the British artillery quite unnecessarily reduced the centre of Dublin to ruins, and the British commanders killed their leading prisoners of war in cold blood morning after morning with an effect of long drawn out ferocity. Really it was only the usual childish petulance in which John Bull does things in a week that disgrace him for a century, though he soon recovers his good humor, and cannot understand why the survivors of his wrath do not feel as jolly with him as he does with them. On the smouldering ruins of Dublin the appeals to remember Louvain were presently supplemented by a fresh appeal. IRISHMEN: DO YOU WISH TO HAVE THE HORRORS OF WAR BROUGHT TO YOUR OWN HEARTHS AND HOMES? Dublin laughed sourly.

As for me, I addressed myself quite simply to the business of obtaining recruits. I knew by personal experience and observation what anyone might have inferred from the records of Irish emigration, that all an Irishman's hopes and ambitions turn on his opportunities of getting out of Ireland. Stimulate his loyalty, and he will stay in Ireland and die for her; for, incomprehensible as it seems to an Englishman, Irish patriotism does not take the form of devotion to England and England's king. Appeal to his discontent, his deadly boredom, his thwarted curiosity and desire for change and adventure, and, to escape from Ireland, he will go abroad to risk his life for France, for the Papal States, for secession in America, and even, if no better may be, for England. Knowing that the ignorance and insularity of the Irishman is a danger to himself and to his neighbors, I had no scruple in making that appeal when there was something for him to fight which the whole world had to fight unless it meant to come under the jack boot of the German version of Dublin Castle.

There was another consideration unmentionable by the recruiting sergeants and war orators, which must nevertheless have helped them powerfully in procuring soldiers by voluntary enlistment. The happy home of the idealist may become common under millennial conditions. It is not common at present. No one will ever know how many men joined the army in 1914 and 1915 to escape from tyrants and taskmasters, termagants and shrews, none of whom are any the less irksome when they happen by ill-luck to be also our fathers, our mothers, our wives, and our children. Even at their amiablest, a holiday from them may be a tempting change for all parties. That is why I did not endow O'Flaherty v.c. with an ideal Irish colleen for his sweetheart, and gave him for his mother a Volumnia of the potato patch rather than an affectionate parent from whom he could not so easily have torn himself away.

I need hardly say that a play thus carefully adapted to its purpose was voted utterly inadmissible; and in due course the British Government, frightened out of its wits for the moment by the rout of the Fifth Army, ordained Irish Conscription, and then did not dare to go through with it. I still think my own line was the more businesslike. But during the war everyone except the soldiers at the front imagined that nothing but an extreme assertion of our most passionate prejudices, without the smallest regard to their effect on others, could win the war. Finally the British blockade won the war; but the wonder is that the British blockhead did not lose it. I suppose the enemy was no wiser. War is not a sharpener of wits; and I am afraid I gave great offence by keeping my head in this matter of Irish recruiting. What can I do but apologize, and publish the play now that it can no longer do any good?

At the door of an Irish country house in a park. Fine summer weather: the summer of 1915. The porch, painted white, projects into the drive; but the door is at the side and the front has a window. The porch faces east; and the door is in the north side of it. On the south side is a tree in which a thrush is singing. Under the window is a garden seat with an iron chair at each end of it.

The last four bars of God Save the King are heard in the distance, followed by three cheers. Then the band strikes up It's a Long Way to Tipperary and recedes until it is out of hearing.

Private O'Flaherty v.c. comes wearily southward along the drive, and falls exhausted into the garden seat. The thrush utters a note of alarm and flies away. The tramp of a horse is heard.

A GENTLEMAN'S VOICE. Tim! Hi! Tim! [*He is heard dismounting*].

A LABORER'S VOICE. Yes, your honor.

THE GENTLEMAN'S VOICE. Take this horse to the stables, will you?

A LABORER'S VOICE. Right, your honor. Yup there. Gwan now. Gwan. [*The horse is led away*].

General Sir Pearce Madigan, an elderly baronet in khaki, beaming with enthusiasm, arrives. O'Flaherty rises and stands at attention.

SIR PEARCE. No, no, O'Flaherty: none of that now. Youre off duty. Remember that though I am a general of forty years service, that little Cross of yours gives you a higher rank in the roll of glory than I can pretend to.

O'FLAHERTY [*relaxing*] I'm thankful to you, Sir Pearce; but I wouldnt have anyone think that the baronet of my native place would let a common soldier like me sit down in his presence without leave.

SIR PEARCE. Well, youre not a common soldier, O'Flaherty: youre a very uncommon one; and I'm proud to have you for my guest here today.

O'FLAHERTY. Sure I know, sir. You have to put up with a lot from the like of me for the sake of recruiting. All the quality shakes hands with me and says theyre proud to know me, just the way the king said when he pinned the Cross on me. And it's as true as

I'm standing here, sir, the queen said to me 'I hear you were born on the estate of General Madigan,' she says; 'and the General himself tells me you were always a fine young fellow.' 'Bedad, Mam,' I says to her, 'if the General knew all the rabbits I snared on him, and all the salmon I snatched on him, and all the cows I milked on him, he'd think me the finest ornament for the county jail he ever sent there for poaching.'

SIR PEARCE [*laughing*] Youre welcome to them all, my lad. Come [*he makes him sit down again on the garden seat*]! sit down and enjoy your holiday [*he sits down on one of the iron chairs: the one at the doorless side of the porch*].

O'FLAHERTY. Holiday, is it? I'd give five shillings to be back in the trenches for the sake of a little rest and quiet. I never knew what hard work was til I took to recruiting. What with the standing on my legs all day, and the shaking hands, and the making speeches, and – whats worse – the listening to them, and the calling for cheers for king and country, and the saluting the flag til I'm stiff with it, and the listening to them playing God Save the King and Tipperary, and the trying to make my eyes look moist like a man in a picture book, I'm that bet that I hardly get a wink of sleep. I give you my word, Sir Pearce, that I never heard the tune of Tipperary in my life til I came back from Flanders; and already it's drove me to the pitch of tiredness of it that when a poor little innocent slip of a boy in the street the other night drew himself up and saluted and began whistling it at me, I clouted his head for him, God forgive me.

SIR PEARCE [*soothingly*] Yes, yes: I know. *I* know. One does get fed up with it: Ive been dog tired myself on parade many a time. But still, you know, theres a gratifying side to it, too. After all, he is our king; and it's our own country, isnt it?

O'FLAHERTY. Well, sir, to you that have an estate in it, it would feel like your country. But the divil a perch of it ever I owned. And as to the king, God help him, my mother would have taken the skin off my back if I'd ever let on to have any other king than Parnell.

SIR PEARCE [*rising, painfully shocked*] Your mother! What are you dreaming about O'Flaherty? A most loyal woman. Always most loyal. Whenever there is an illness in the Royal Family, she asks me every time we meet about the health of the patient as anxiously as if it were yourself, her only son.

O'FLAHERTY. Well, she's my mother; and I wont utter a word

agen her. But I'm not saying a word of lie when I tell you that that old woman is the biggest kanatt from here to the cross of Monasterboice. Sure she's the wildest Fenian and rebel, and always has been, that ever taught a poor innocent lad like myself to pray night and morning to St Patrick to clear the English out of Ireland the same as he cleared the snakes. Youll be surprised at my telling you that now, maybe, Sir Pearce?

SIR PEARCE [*unable to keep still, walking away from O'Flaherty*] Surprised! I'm more than surprised, O'Flaherty. I'm overwhelmed. [*Turning and facing him*] Are you – are you joking?

O'FLAHERTY. If youd been brought up by my mother, sir, youd know better than to joke about her. What I'm telling you is the truth; and I wouldnt tell it to you if I could see my way to get out of the fix I'll be in when my mother comes here this day to see her boy in his glory, and she after thinking all the time it was against the English I was fighting.

SIR PEARCE. Do you mean to say you told her such a monstrous falsehood as that you were fighting in the German army?

O'FLAHERTY. I never told her one word that wasnt the truth and nothing but the truth. I told her I was going to fight for the French and for the Russians; and sure who ever heard of the French or the Russians doing anything to the English but fighting them? That was how it was, sir. And sure the poor woman kissed me and went about the house singing in her old cracky voice that the French was on the sea, and theyd be here without delay, and the Orange will decay, says the Shan Van Vocht.

SIR PEARCE [*sitting down again, exhausted by his feelings*] Well, I never could have believed this. Never. What do you suppose will happen when she finds out?

O'FLAHERTY. She mustnt find out. It's not that she'd half kill me, as big as I am and as brave as I am. It's that I'm fond of her, and cant bring myself to break the heart in her. You may think it queer that a man should be fond of his mother, sir, and she having bet him from the time he could feel to the time she was too slow to ketch him; but I'm fond of her; and I'm not ashamed of it. Besides, didnt she win the Cross for me?

SIR PEARCE. Your mother! How?

O'FLAHERTY. By bringing me up to be more afraid of running away than of fighting. I was timid by nature; and when the other boys hurted me, I'd want to run away and cry. But she whaled me for disgracing the blood of the O'Flahertys until I'd have fought the divil himself sooner than face her after funking a fight. That was how I got to know that fighting was easier than it looked, and that the others was as much afeard of me as I was of them, and that if I only held out long enough theyd lose heart and give up. Thats the way I came to be so courageous. I tell you, Sir Pearce, if the German army had been brought up by my mother, the Kaiser would be dining in the banqueting hall at Buckingham Palace this day, and King George polishing his jack boots for him in the scullery.

SIR PEARCE. But I dont like this, O'Flaherty. You cant go on deceiving your mother, you know. It's not right.

O'FLAHERTY. Cant go on deceiving her, cant I? It's little you know what a son's love can do, sir. Did you ever notice what a ready liar I am?

SIR PEARCE. Well, in recruiting a man gets carried away. I stretch it a bit occasionally myself. After all, it's for king and country. But if you wont mind my saying it, O'Flaherty, I think that story about your fighting the Kaiser and the twelve giants of the Prussian guard singlehanded would be the better for a little toning down. I dont ask you to drop it, you know; for it's popular, undoubtedly; but still, the truth is the truth. Dont you think it would fetch in almost as many recruits if you reduced the number of guardsmen to six?

O'FLAHERTY. Youre not used to telling lies like I am, sir. I got great practice at home with my mother. What with saving my skin when I was young and thoughtless, and sparing her feelings when I was old enough to understand them, Ive hardly told my mother the truth twice a year since I was born; and would you have me turn round on her and tell it now, when she's looking to have some peace and quiet in her old age?

SIR PEARCE [troubled in his conscience] Well, it's not my affair, of course, O'Flaherty. But hadnt you better talk to Father Quinlan about it?

O'FLAHERTY. Talk to Father Quinlan, is it! Do you know what Father Quinlan says to me this very morning?

SIR PEARCE. Oh, youve seen him already, have you? What did he say?

O'FLAHERTY. He says 'You know, dont you' he says 'that it's your duty, as a Christian and a good son of the Holy Church to love your enemies?' he says. 'I know it's my juty as a soldier to kill

them' I says. 'Thats right, Dinny,' he says: 'quite right. But' says
he 'you can kill them and do them a good turn afterwards to
shew your love for them' he says; 'and it's your duty to have a
mass said for the souls of the hundreds of Germans you say you
killed' says he; 'for many and many of them were Bavarians and
good Catholics' he says. 'Is it me that must pay for masses for the
souls of the Boshes?' I says. 'Let the King of England pay for
them' I says; 'for it was his quarrel and not mine.'

SIR PEARCE [*warmly*] It is the quarrel of every honest man and true
patriot, O'Flaherty. Your mother must see that as clearly as I
do. After all, she is a reasonable, well disposed woman, quite
capable of understanding the right and the wrong of the war.
Why cant you explain to her what the war is about?

O'FLAHERTY. Arra, sir, how the divil do I know what the war is
about?

SIR PEARCE [*rising again and standing over him*] What! O'Flaherty:
do you know what you are saying? You sit there wearing the
Victoria Cross for having killed God knows how many Germans;
and you tell me you dont know why you did it! ·

O'FLAHERTY. Asking your pardon, Sir Pearce, I tell you no such
thing. I know quite well why I kilt them. I kilt them because I
was afeard that, if I didnt, theyd kill me.

SIR PEARCE [*giving it up, and sitting down again*] Yes, yes, of course;
but have you no knowledge of the causes of the war? of the
interests at stake? of the importance — I may almost say — in fact I
will say — the sacred rights for which we are fighting? Dont you
read the papers?

O'FLAHERTY. I do when I can get them. Theres not many
newsboys crying the evening paper in the trenches. They do say,
Sir Pearce, that we shall never beat the Boshes until we make
Horatio Bottomley Lord Leftnant of England. Do you think
thats true sir?

SIR PEARCE. Rubbish, man! theres no Lord Lieutenant in England: the king is Lord Lieutenant. It's a simple question of
patriotism. Does patriotism mean nothing to you?

O'FLAHERTY. It means different to me than what it would to you,
sir. It means England and England's king to you. To me and the
like of me, it means talking about the English just the way the
English papers talk about the Boshes. And what good has it ever
done here in Ireland? It's kept me ignorant because it filled up
my mother's mind, and she thought it ought to fill up mine too.

It's kept Ireland poor, because instead of trying to better ourselves we thought we was the fine fellows of patriots when we were speaking evil of Englishmen that was as poor as ourselves and maybe as good as ourselves. The Boshes I kilt was more knowledgable men than me: and what better am I now that Ive kilt them? What better is anybody?

SIR PEARCE [*huffed, turning a cold shoulder to him*] I am sorry the terrible experience of this war — the greatest war ever fought — has taught you no better, O'Flaherty.

O'FLAHERTY [*preserving his dignity*] I dont know about its being a great war, sir. It's a big war; but thats not the same thing. Father Quinlan's new church is a big church: you might take the little old chapel out of the middle of it and not miss it. But my mother says there was more true religion in the old chapel. And the war has taught me that may be she was right.

SIR PEARCE [*grunts sulkily*] !!

O'FLAHERTY [*respectfully but doggedly*] And theres another thing it's taught me too, sir, that concerns you and me, if I may make bold to tell it to you.

SIR PEARCE [*still sulkily*] I hope it's nothing you oughtnt to say to me, O'Flaherty.

O'FLAHERTY. It's this, sir: that I'm able to sit here now and talk to you without humbugging you; and thats what not one of your tenants or your tenants' childer ever did to you before in all your long life. It's a true respect I'm shewing you at last, sir. Maybe youd rather have me humbug you and tell you lies as I used, just as the boys here, God help them, would rather have me tell them how I fought the Kaiser, that all the world knows I never saw in my life, than tell them the truth. But I cant take advantage of you the way I used, not even if I seem to be wanting in respect to you and cocked up by winning the Cross.

SIR PEARCE [*touched*] Not at all, O'Flaherty. Not at all.

O'FLAHERTY. Sure whats the Cross to me, barring the little pension it carries? Do you think I dont know that theres hundreds of men as brave as me that never had the luck to get anything for their bravery but a curse from the sergeant, and the blame for the faults of them that ought to have been their betters? Ive learnt more than youd think, sir; for how would a gentleman like you know what a poor ignorant conceited creature I was when I went from here into the wide world as a soldier? What use is all the lying, and pretending, and humbugging, and letting on, when the day comes to you that your comrade is killed in the trench beside you, and you dont as much as look round at him until you trip over his poor body, and then all you say is to ask why the hell the stretcher-bearers dont take it out of the way. Why should I read the papers to be humbugged and lied to by them that had the cunning to stay at home and send me to fight for them? Dont talk to me or to any soldier of the war being right. No war is right; and all the holy water that Father Quinlan ever blessed couldnt make one right. There, sir! Now you know what O'Flaherty v.c. thinks; and youre wiser so than the others that only knows what he done.

SIR PEARCE [*making the best of it, and turning good-humoredly to him again*] Well, what you did was brave and manly, anyhow.

O'FLAHERTY. God knows whether it was or not, better than you nor me, General. I hope He wont be too hard on me for it, anyhow.

SIR PEARCE [*sympathetically*] Oh yes: we all have to think seriously sometimes, especially when we're a little run down. I'm afraid weve been overworking you a bit over these recruiting meetings. However, we can knock off for the rest of the day; and tomorrow's Sunday. Ive had about as much as I can stand myself. [*He looks at his watch*]. It's teatime. I wonder whats keeping your mother.

O'FLAHERTY. It's nicely cocked up the old woman will be, having tea at the same table as you, sir, instead of in the kitchen. She'll be after dressing in the heighth of grandeur; and stop she will at every house on the way to shew herself off and tell them where she's going, and fill the whole parish with spite and envy. But sure, she shouldnt keep you waiting, sir.

SIR PEARCE. Oh, thats all right: she must be indulged on an occasion like this. I'm sorry my wife is in London: she'd have been glad to welcome your mother.

O'FLAHERTY. Sure, I know she would, sir. She was always a kind friend to the poor. Little her ladyship knew, God help her, the depth of divilment that was in us: we were like a play to her. You see, sir, she was English: that was how it was. We was to her what the Pathans and Senegalese was to me when I first seen them: I couldnt think, somehow, that they were liars, and thieves, and backbiters, and drunkards, just like ourselves or any other Christians. Oh, her ladyship never knew all that was going on behind her back: how would she? When I was a weeshy child, she gave me the first penny I ever had in my hand; and I wanted to pray for her conversion that night the same as my mother made me pray for yours; and –

SIR PEARCE [scandalized] Do you mean to say that your mother made you pray for my conversion?

O'FLAHERTY. Sure and she wouldnt want to see a gentleman like you going to hell after she nursing your own son and bringing up my sister Annie on the bottle. That was how it was, sir. She'd rob you; and she'd lie to you; and she'd call down all the blessings of God on your head when she was selling you your own three geese that you thought had been ate by the fox the day after youd finished fattening them, sir; and all the time you were like a bit of her own flesh and blood to her. Often has she said she'd live to see you a good Catholic yet, leading victorious armies against the English and wearing the collar of gold that Malachi won from the proud invader. Oh, she's the romantic woman is my mother, and no mistake.

SIR PEARCE [in great perturbation] I really cant believe this, O'Flaherty. I could have sworn your mother was as honest a woman as ever breathed.

O'FLAHERTY. And so she is, sir. She's as honest as the day.

SIR PEARCE. Do you call it honest to steal my geese?

O'FLAHERTY. She didnt steal them, sir. It was me that stole them.

SIR PEARCE. Oh! And why the devil did you steal them?

O'FLAHERTY. Sure we needed them, sir. Often and often we had to sell our own geese to pay you the rent to satisfy your needs; and why shouldnt we sell your geese to satisfy ours?

SIR PEARCE. Well, damn me!

O'FLAHERTY [sweetly] Sure you had to get what you could out of us; and we had to get what we could out of you. God forgive us both!

SIR PEARCE. Really, O'Flaherty, the war seems to have upset you a little.

O'FLAHERTY. It's set me thinking, sir; and I'm not used to it. It's like the patriotism of the English. They never thought of being patriotic until the war broke out; and now the patriotism has took them so sudden and come so strange to them that they run about like frightened chickens, uttering all manner of nonsense. But please God theyll forget all about it when the war's over. Theyre getting tired of it already.

SIR PEARCE. No, no: it has uplifted us all in a wonderful way. The

world will never be the same again, O'Flaherty. Not after a war
like this.

O'FLAHERTY. So they all say, sir. I see no great differ myself. It's
all the fright and the excitement; and when that quiets down
theyll go back to their natural divilment and be the same as ever.
It's like the vermin: itll wash off after a while.

SIR PEARCE [*rising and planting himself firmly behind the garden seat*]
Well, the long and the short of it is, O'Flaherty, I must decline to
be a party to any attempt to deceive your mother. I thoroughly
disapprove of this feeling against the English, especially at a
moment like the present. Even if your mother's political sym-
pathies are really what you represent them to be, I should think
that her gratitude to Gladstone ought to cure her of such disloyal
prejudices.

O'FLAHERTY [*over his shoulder*] She says Gladstone was an Irishman, sir. What call would he have to meddle with Ireland as he
did if he wasnt?

SIR PEARCE. What nonsense! Does she suppose Mr Asquith is an
Irishman?

O'FLAHERTY. She wont give him any credit for Home Rule,
sir. She says Redmond made him do it. She says you told her
so.

SIR PEARCE [*convicted out of his own mouth*] Well, I never meant her
to take it up in that ridiculous way. [*He moves to the end of the garden
seat on O'Flaherty's left*] I'll give her a good talking to when she
comes. I'm not going to stand any of her nonsense.

O'FLAHERTY. It's not a bit of use, sir. She says all the English
generals is Irish. She says all the English poets and great men
was Irish. She says the English never knew how to read their
own books until we taught them. She says we're the lost tribes of
the house of Israel and the chosen people of God. She says that
the goddess Venus, that was born out of the foam of the sea,
came up out of the water in Killiney Bay off Bray Head. She says
that Moses built the seven churches, and that Lazarus was
buried in Glasnevin.

SIR PEARCE. Bosh! How does she know he was? Did you ever ask
her?

O'FLAHERTY. I did, sir, often.

SIR PEARCE. And what did she say?

O'FLAHERTY. She asked me how did I know he wasnt, and fetched
me a clout on the side of my head.

SIR PEARCE. But have you never mentioned any famous English-man to her, and asked her what she had to say about him?

O'FLAHERTY. The only one I could think of was Shakespear, sir; and she says he was born in Cork.

SIR PEARCE [*exhausted*] Well, I give it up [*he throws himself into the nearest chair*]. The woman is – Oh, well! No matter.

O'FLAHERTY [*sympathetically*] Yes, sir: she's pigheaded and ob-stinate: theres no doubt about it. She's like the English: they think theres no one like themselves. It's the same with the Germans, though theyre educated and ought to know better. Youll never have a quiet world til you knock the patriotism out of the human race.

SIR PEARCE. Still, we –

O'FLAHERTY. Whisht, sir, for God's sake: here she is.

The General jumps up. Mrs O'Flaherty arrives, and comes between the two men. She is very clean, and carefully dressed in the old fashioned peasant costume: black silk sunbonnet with a tiara of trimmings, and black cloak.

O'FLAHERTY [*rising shyly*] Good evening, mother.

MRS O'FLAHERTY [*severely*] You hold your whisht, and learn behavior while I pay my juty to his honor. [*To Sir Pearce, heartily*] And how is your honor's good self? And how is her ladyship and all the young ladies? Oh, it's right glad we are to see your honor back again and looking the picture of health.

SIR PEARCE [*forcing a note of extreme geniality*] Thank you, Mrs O'Flaherty. Well, you see weve brought you back your son safe and sound. I hope youre proud of him.

MRS O'FLAHERTY. And indeed and I am, your honor. It's the brave boy he is; and why wouldnt he be, brought up on your honor's estate and with you before his eyes for a pattern of the finest soldier in Ireland. Come and kiss your old mother, Dinny darlint. [*O'Flaherty does so sheepishly*]. Thats my own darling boy. And look at your fine new uniform stained already with the eggs youve been eating and the porter youve been drinking. [*She takes out her handkerchief; spits on it; and scrubs his lapel with it*]. Oh, it's the untidy slovenly one you always were. There! It wont be seen on the khaki: it's not like the old red coat that would shew up everything that dribbled down on it. [*To Sir Pearce*] And they tell me down at the lodge that her ladyship is staying in London, and that Miss Agnes is to be married to a fine young nobleman. Oh, it's your honor that is the lucky and happy father! It will be bad news for many of the young gentlemen of the quality round here, sir. Theres lots thought she was going to marry young Master Lawless —

SIR PEARCE. What! That — that — that bosthoon!

MRS O'FLAHERTY [*hilariously*] Let your honor alone for finding the right word! A big bosthoon he is indeed, your honor. Oh, to think of the times and times I have said that Miss Agnes would be my lady as her mother was before her! Didnt I, Dinny?

SIR PEARCE. And now, Mrs O'Flaherty, I daresay you have a great deal to say to Dennis that doesnt concern me. I'll just go in and order tea.

MRS O'FLAHERTY. Oh, why would your honor disturb yourself? Sure I can take the boy into the yard.

SIR PEARCE. Not at all. It wont disturb me in the least. And he's too big a boy to be taken into the yard now. He has made a front seat for himself. Eh? [*He goes into the house*].

MRS O'FLAHERTY. Sure he has that, your honor. God bless your honor! [*The General being now out of hearing, she turns threateningly to her son with one of those sudden Irish changes of manner which amaze and scandalize less flexible nations, and exclaims*] And what do you mean, you lying young scald, by telling me you were going to fight agen the English? Did you take me for a fool that couldnt find out, and the papers all full of you shaking hands with the English king at Buckingham Palace?

O'FLAHERTY. I didnt shake hands with him: he shook hands with me. Could I turn on the man in his own house, before his own wife, with his money in my pocket and in yours, and throw his civility back in his face?

MRS O'FLAHERTY. You would take the hand of a tyrant red with the blood of Ireland —

O'FLAHERTY. Arra hold your nonsense, mother: he's not half the tyrant you are, God help him. His hand was cleaner than mine that had the blood of his own relations on it, may be.

MRS O'FLAHERTY [*threateningly*] Is that a way to speak to your mother, you young spalpeen?

O'FLAHERTY [*stoutly*] It is so, if you wont talk sense to me. It's a nice thing for a poor boy to be made much of by kings and queens, and shook hands with by the heighth of his country's nobility in the capital cities of the world, and then to come home and be scolded and insulted by his own mother. I'll fight for who I like; and I'll shake hands with what kings I like; and if your own son is not good enough for you, you can go and look for another. Do you mind me now?

MRS O'FLAHERTY. And was it the Belgians learned you such brazen impudence?

O'FLAHERTY. The Belgians is good men; and the French ought to be more civil to them, let alone their being half murdered by the Boshes.

MRS O'FLAHERTY. Good men is it! Good men! to come over here when they were wounded because it was a Catholic country, and then to go to the Protestant Church because it didnt cost them anything, and some of them to never go near a church at all. Thats what you call good men!

O'FLAHERTY. Oh, youre the mighty fine politician, arnt you? Much you know about Belgians or foreign parts or the world youre living in, God help you!

MRS O'FLAHERTY. Why wouldnt I know better than you? Amment I your mother?

O'FLAHERTY. And if you are itself, how can you know what you never seen as well as me that was dug into the continent of Europe for six months, and was buried in the earth of it three times with the shells bursting on the top of me? I tell you I know what I'm about. I have my own reasons for taking part in this great conflict. I'd be ashamed to stay at home and not fight when everybody else is fighting.

MRS O'FLAHERTY. If you wanted to fight, why couldnt you fight in the German army?

O'FLAHERTY. Because they only get a penny a day.

MRS O'FLAHERTY. Well, and if they do itself, isnt there the French army?

O'FLAHERTY. They only get a hapenny a day.

MRS O'FLAHERTY [much dashed] Oh murder! They must be a mean lot, Dinny.

O'FLAHERTY [sarcastic] Maybe youd have me join the Turkish army, and worship the heathen Mahomet that put a corn in his ear and pretended it was a message from the heavens when the pigeon come to pick it out and eat it. I went where I could get the biggest allowance for you; and little thanks I get for it!

MRS O'FLAHERTY. Allowance, is it! Do you know what the thieving blackguards did on me? They came to me and they says, 'Was your son a big eater?' they says. 'Oh, he was that' says I: 'ten shillings a week wouldnt keep him.' Sure I thought the more

I said the more theyd give me. 'Then' says they, 'thats ten shillings a week off your allowance' they says, 'because you save that by the king feeding him.' 'Indeed!' says I: 'I suppose if I'd six sons youd stop three pound a week from me, and make out that I ought to pay you money instead of you paying me.' 'Theres a fallacy in your argument' they says.

O'FLAHERTY. A what?

MRS O'FLAHERTY. A fallacy: thats the word he said. I says to him, 'It's a Pharisee I'm thinking you mean, sir; but you can keep your dirty money that your king grudges a poor old widow; and please God the English will be bet yet for the deadly sin of oppressing the poor'; and with that I shut the door in his face.

O'FLAHERTY [furious] Do you tell me they knocked ten shillings off you for my keep?

MRS O'FLAHERTY [soothing him] No, darlint: they only knocked off half a crown. I put up with it because Ive got the old age pension; and they know very well I'm only sixty-two; so Ive the better of them by half a crown a week anyhow.

O'FLAHERTY. It's a queer way of doing business. If theyd tell you straight out what they was going to give you, you wouldnt mind; but if there was twenty ways of telling the truth and only one way of telling a lie, the Government would find it out. It's in the nature of governments to tell lies.

Teresa Driscoll, a parlor maid, comes from the house.

TERESA. Youre to come up to the drawing room to have your tea, Mrs O'Flaherty.

MRS O'FLAHERTY. Mind you have a sup of good black tea for me in the kitchen afterwards, acushla. That washy drawing room tea will give me the wind if I leave it on my stomach. [She goes into the house, leaving the two young people alone together].

O'FLAHERTY. Is that yourself, Tessie? And how are you?

TERESA. Nicely, thank you. And hows yourself?

O'FLAHERTY. Finely, thank God. [He produces a gold chain]. Look what Ive brought you, Tessie.

TERESA [shrinking] Sure I dont like to touch it, Denny. Did you take it off a dead man?

O'FLAHERTY. No: I took it off a live one; and thankful he was to me to be alive and kept a prisoner in ease and comfort, and me left fighting in peril of my life.

TERESA [taking it] Do you think it's real gold, Denny?

O'FLAHERTY. It's real German gold, anyhow.

TERESA. But German silver isnt real, Denny.

O'FLAHERTY [*his face darkening*] Well, it's the best the Bosh could do for me, anyhow.

TERESA. Do you think I might take it to the jeweller next market day and ask him?

O'FLAHERTY [*sulkily*] You may take it to the divil if you like.

TERESA. You neednt lose your temper about it. I only thought I'd like to know. The nice fool I'd look if I went about shewing off a chain that turned out to be only brass!

O'FLAHERTY. I think you might say Thank you.

TERESA. Do you? I think you might have said something more to me than 'Is that yourself?' You couldnt say less to the postman.

O'FLAHERTY [*his brow clearing*] Oh, is that whats the matter? Here! come and take the taste of the brass out of my mouth. [*He seizes her and kisses her*].

> *Teresa, without losing her Irish dignity, takes the kiss as appreciatively as a connoisseur might take a glass of wine, and sits down with him on the garden seat.*

TERESA [*as he squeezes her waist*] Thank God the priest cant see us here!

O'FLAHERTY. It's little they care for priests in France, alanna.

TERESA. And what had the queen on her, Denny, when she spoke to you in the palace?

O'FLAHERTY. She had a bonnet on without any strings to it. And she had a plakeen of embroidery down her bosom. And she had her waist where it used to be, and not where the other ladies had it. And she had little brooches in her ears, though she hadnt half the jewelry of Mrs Sullivan that keeps the popshop in Drumpogue. And she dresses her hair down over her forehead, in a fringe like. And she has an Irish look about her eyebrows. And she didnt know what to say to me, poor woman! and I didnt know what to say to her, God help me!

TERESA. Youll have a pension now with the Cross, wont you, Denny?

O'FLAHERTY. Sixpence three farthings a day.

TERESA. That isnt much.

O'FLAHERTY. I take out the rest in glory.

TERESA. And if youre wounded, youll have a wound pension, wont you?

O'FLAHERTY. I will, please God.

TERESA. Youre going out again, arnt you, Denny?

O'FLAHERTY. I cant help myself. I'd be shot for a deserter if I didnt go; and may be I'll be shot by the Boshes if I do go; so between the two of them I'm nicely fixed up.

MRS O'FLAHERTY [*calling from within the house*] Tessie! Tessie darlint!

TERESA [*disengaging herself from his arm and rising*] I'm wanted for the tea table. Youll have a pension anyhow, Denny, wont you, whether youre wounded or not?

MRS O'FLAHERTY. Come, child, come.

TERESA [*impatiently*] Oh, sure I'm coming. [*She tries to smile at Denny, not very convincingly, and hurries into the house*].

O'FLAHERTY [*alone*] And if I do get a pension itself, the divil a penny of it youll ever have the spending of.

MRS O'FLAHERTY [*as she comes from the porch*] Oh, it's a shame for you to keep the girl from her juties, Dinny. You might get her into trouble.

O'FLAHERTY. Much I care whether she gets into trouble or not! I pity the man that gets her into trouble. He'll get himself into worse.

MRS O'FLAHERTY. Whats that you tell me? Have you been falling out with her, and she a girl with a fortune of ten pounds?

O'FLAHERTY. Let her keep her fortune. I wouldnt touch her with the tongs if she had thousands and millions.

MRS O'FLAHERTY. Oh fie for shame, Dinny! why would you say the like of that of a decent honest girl, and one of the Driscolls too?

O'FLAHERTY. Why wouldnt I say it? She's thinking of nothing but to get me out there again to be wounded so that she may spend my pension, bad scran to her!

MRS O'FLAHERTY. Why, whats come over you, child, at all at all?

O'FLAHERTY. Knowledge and wisdom has come over me with pain and fear and trouble. Ive been made a fool of and imposed upon all my life. I thought that covetious sthreal in there was a walking angel; and now if ever I marry at all I'll marry a Frenchwoman.

MRS O'FLAHERTY [*fiercely*] Youll not, so; and dont you dar repeat such a thing to me.

O'FLAHERTY. Wont I, faith! Ive been as good as married to a couple of them already.

MRS O'FLAHERTY. The Lord be praised, what wickedness have you been up to, you young blackguard?

O'FLAHERTY. One of them Frenchwomen would cook you a meal twice in the day and all days and every day that Sir Pearce himself might go begging through Ireland for, and never see the like of. I'll have a French wife, I tell you; and when I settle down to be a farmer I'll have a French farm, with a field as big as the continent of Europe that ten of your dirty little fields here wouldnt so much as fill the ditch of.

MRS O'FLAHERTY [*furious*] Then it's a French mother you may go look for; for I'm done with you.

O'FLAHERTY. And it's no great loss youd be if it wasnt for my natural feelings for you; for it's only a silly ignorant old country-woman you are with all your fine talk about Ireland: you that never stepped beyond the few acres of it you were born on!

MRS O'FLAHERTY [*tottering to the garden seat and shewing signs of breaking down*] Dinny darlint, why are you like this to me? Whats happened to you?

O'FLAHERTY [*gloomily*] Whats happened to everybody? thats what I want to know. Whats happened to you that I thought all the world of and was afeard of? Whats happened to Sir Pearce, that I thought was a great general, and that I now see to be no more fit to command an army than an old hen? Whats happened to Tessie, that I was mad to marry a year ago, and that I wouldnt take now with all Ireland for her fortune? I tell you the world's creation is crumbling in ruins about me; and then you come and ask whats happened to me?

MRS O'FLAHERTY [*giving way to wild grief*] Ochone! ochone! my son's turned agen me. Oh, whatll I do at all at all? Oh! oh! oh! oh!

SIR PEARCE [*running out of the house*] Whats this infernal noise? What on earth is the matter?

O'FLAHERTY. Arra hold your whisht, mother. Dont you see his honor?

MRS O'FLAHERTY. Oh, sir, I'm ruined and destroyed. Oh, wont you speak to Dinny, sir: I'm heart scalded with him. He wants to marry a Frenchwoman on me, and to go away and be a foreigner and desert his mother and betray his country. It's mad he is with the roaring of the cannons and he killing the Germans and the Germans killing him, bad cess to them! My boy is taken from me and turned agen me; and who is to take care of me in my old age after all Ive done for him, ochone! ochone!

O'FLAHERTY. Hold your noise, I tell you. Who's going to leave you? I'm going to take you with me. There now: does that satisfy you?

MRS O'FLAHERTY. Is it take me into a strange land among heathens and pagans and savages, and me not knowing a word of their language nor them of mine?

O'FLAHERTY. A good job they dont: may be theyll think youre talking sense.

MRS O'FLAHERTY. Ask me to die out of Ireland, is it? and the angels not to find me when they come for me!

O'FLAHERTY. And would you ask me to live in Ireland where Ive been imposed on and kept in ignorance, and to die where the divil himself wouldnt take me as a gift, let alone the blessed angels? You can come or stay. You can take your old way or take my young way. But stick in this place I will not among a lot of good-for-nothing divils thatll not do a hand's turn but watch the grass growing and build up the stone wall where the cow walked through it. And Sir Horace Plunkett breaking his heart all the time telling them how they might put the land into decent tillage like the French and Belgians.

SIR PEARCE. Yes: he's quite right, you know, Mrs O'Flaherty: quite right there.

MRS O'FLAHERTY. Well, sir, please God the war will last a long time yet: and may be I'll die before it's over and the separation allowance stops.

O'FLAHERTY. Thats all you care about. It's nothing but milch cows we men are for the women, with their separation allowances, ever since the war began, bad luck to them that made it!

TERESA [coming from the porch between the General and Mrs O'Flaherty] Hannah sent me out for to tell you, sir, that the tea will be black and the cake not fit to eat with the cold if yous all dont come at wanst.

MRS O'FLAHERTY [breaking out again] Oh, Tessie darlint, what have you been saying to Dinny at all at all? Oh! oh –

SIR PEARCE [out of patience] You cant discuss that here. We shall have Tessie beginning now.

O'FLAHERTY. Thats right, sir: drive them in.

TERESA. I havnt said a word to him. He –

SIR PEARCE. Hold your tongue; and go in and attend to your business at the tea table.

TERESA. But amment I telling your honor that I never said a word to him? He gave me a beautiful gold chain. Here it is to shew your honor thats it's no lie I'm telling you.

SIR PEARCE. Whats this, O'Flaherty? Youve been looting some unfortunate officer.

O'FLAHERTY. No sir: I stole it from him of his own accord.

MRS O'FLAHERTY. Wouldnt your honor tell him that his mother has the first call on it? What would a slip of a girl like that be doing with a gold chain round her neck?

TERESA [*venomously*] Anyhow, I have a neck to put it round and not a hank of wrinkles.

At this unfortunate remark, Mrs O'Flaherty bounds from her seat; and an appalling tempest of wordy wrath breaks out. The remonstrances and commands of the General, and the protests and menaces of O'Flaherty, only increase the hubbub. They are soon all speaking at once at the top of their voices.

MRS O'FLAHERTY [*solo*] You impudent young heifer, how dar you say such a thing to me? [*Teresa retorts furiously; the men interfere; and the solo becomes a quartet, fortissimo*]. Ive a good mind to clout your ears for you to teach you manners. Be ashamed of yourself, do; and learn to know who youre speaking to. That I maytnt sin! but I dont know what the good God was thinking about when he made the like of you. Let me not see you casting sheep's eyes at my son again. There never was an O'Flaherty yet that would demean himself by keeping company with a dirty Driscoll; and if I see you next or nigh my house I'll put you in the ditch with a flea in your ear: mind that now.

TERESA. Is it me you offer such a name to, you foul-mouthed, dirty minded, lying, sloothering old sow, you? I wouldnt soil my tongue by calling you in your right name and telling Sir Pearce whats the common talk of the town about you. You and your O'Flahertys! setting yourself up agen the Driscolls that would never lower themselves to be seen in conversation with you at the fair. You can keep your ugly stingy lump of a son; for what is he but a common soldier? and God help the girl that gets him, say I! So the back of my hand to you, Mrs O'Flaherty; and that the cat may tear your ugly old face!

SIR PEARCE. Silence. Tessie: did you hear me ordering you to go into the house? Mrs O'Flaherty! [*Louder*] Mrs O'Flaherty!! Will you just listen to me one moment? Please. [*Furiously*] Do you hear me speaking to you, woman? Are you human beings or are you wild beasts? Stop that noise immediately: do you hear?

[*Yelling*] Are you going to do what I order you, or are you not? Scandalous! Disgraceful! This comes of being too familiar with you, O'Flaherty: shove them into the house. Out with the whole damned pack of you.

O'FLAHERTY [*to the women*] Here now: none of that, none of that. Go easy, I tell you. Hold your whisht, mother, will you, or youll be sorry for it after. [*To Teresa*] Is that the way for a decent young girl to speak? [*Despairingly*] Oh, for the Lord's sake, shut up, will yous? Have yous no respect for yourselves or your betters? [*Peremptorily*] Let me have no more of it, I tell you. Och! the divil's in the whole crew of you. In with you into the house this very minute and tear one another's eyes out in the kitchen if you like. In with you.

The two men seize the two women, and push them, still violently abusing one another, into the house. Sir Pearce slams the door upon them savagely. Immediately a heavenly silence falls on the summer afternoon. The two sit down out of breath; and for a long time nothing is said. Sir Pearce sits on an iron chair. O'Flaherty sits on the garden seat. The thrush begins to sing melodiously. O'Flaherty cocks his ears, and looks up at it. A smile spreads over his troubled features. Sir Pearce, with a long sigh, takes out his pipe, and begins to fill it.

O'FLAHERTY [*idyllically*] What a discontented sort of an animal a man is, sir! Only a month ago, I was in the quiet of the country out at the front, with not a sound except the birds and the bellow of a cow in the distance as it might be, and the shrapnel making little clouds in the heavens, and the shells whistling, and may be a yell or two when one of us was hit; and would you believe it, sir, I complained of the noise and wanted to have a peaceful hour at home. Well: them two has taught me a lesson. This morning, sir, when I was telling the boys here how I was longing to be back taking my part for king and country with the others, I was lying, as you well knew, sir. Now I can go and say it with a clear conscience. Some likes war's alarums; and some likes home life. Ive tried both, sir; and I'm all for war's alarums now. I always was a quiet lad by natural disposition.

SIR PEARCE. Strictly between ourselves, O'Flaherty, and as one soldier to another [*O'Flaherty salutes, but without stiffening*], do you think we should have got an army without conscription if domestic life had been as happy as people say it is?

O'FLAHERTY. Well, between you and me and the wall, Sir Pearce,

I think the less we say about that until the war's over, the better.

He winks at the General. The General strikes a match. The thrush sings. A jay laughs. The conversation drops.

Augustus Does His Bit

A True-to-Life Farce

Composition begun 12 August 1916; completed 23 August 1916. Published in *Heartbreak House, Great Catherine, & Playlets of the War*, 1919. First presented by the Stage Society at the Royal Court Theatre, London, on 21 January 1917; repeated on 22 January.

Lord Augustus Highcastle   *F. B. J. Sharp*
Horatio Floyd Beamish   *Charles Rock*
A Lady   *Lalla Vandervelde*

Period – 1916

Scene – *The Mayor's Parlor in the Town Hall of Little Pifflington*

I wish to express my gratitude for certain good offices which Augustus secured for me in January 1917. I had been invited to visit the theatre of war in Flanders by the Commander-in-Chief: an invitation which was, under the circumstances, a summons to duty. Thus I had occasion to spend some days in procuring the necessary passports and other official facilities for my journey. It happened just then that the Stage Society gave a performance of this little play. It opened the heart of every official to me. I have always been treated with distinguished consideration in my contacts with bureaucracy during the war; but on this occasion I found myself *persona grata* in the highest degree. There was only one word when the formalities were disposed of; and that was 'We are up against Augustus all day.' The shewing-up of Augustus scandalized one or two innocent and patriotic critics who regarded the prowess of the British army as inextricably bound up with High-castle prestige. But our Government departments knew better: their problem was how to win the war with Augustus on their backs, well-meaning, brave, patriotic, but obstructively fussy, self-important, imbecile, and disastrous.

Save for the satisfaction of being able to laugh at Augustus in the theatre, nothing, as far as I know, came of my dramatic reduction of him to absurdity. Generals, admirals, Prime Ministers and Controllers, not to mention Emperors, Kaisers and Tsars, were scrapped remorselessly at home and abroad, for their sins or services, as the case might be. But Augustus stood like the Eddystone in a storm, and stands so to this day. He gave us his word that he was indispensable; and we took it.

The Mayor's parlor in the Town Hall of Little Pifflington. Lord Augustus Highcastle, a distinguished member of the governing class, in the uniform of a colonel, and very well preserved at forty-five, is comfortably seated at a writing table with his heels on it, reading The Morning Post. The door faces him, a little to his left, at the other side of the room. The window is behind him. In the fireplace, a gas stove. On the table a bell button and a telephone. Portraits of past Mayors, in robes and gold chains, adorn the walls. An elderly clerk with a short white beard and whiskers, and a very red nose, shuffles in.

AUGUSTUS [*hastily putting aside his paper and replacing his feet on the floor*] Hullo! Who are you?

THE CLERK. The staff [*a slight impediment in his speech adds to the impression of incompetence produced by his age and appearance*].

AUGUSTUS. You the staff! What do you mean, man?

THE CLERK. What I say. There aint anybody else.

AUGUSTUS. Tush! Where are the others?

THE CLERK. At the front.

AUGUSTUS. Quite right. Most proper. Why arnt you at the front?

THE CLERK. Over age. Fiftyseven.

AUGUSTUS. But you can still do your bit. Many an older man is in the G.R.'s, or volunteering for home defence.

THE CLERK. I have volunteered.

AUGUSTUS. Then why are you not in uniform?

THE CLERK. They said they wouldnt have me if I was given away with a pound of tea. Told me to go home and not be an old silly. [*A sense of unbearable wrong, til now only smouldering in him, bursts into flame*]. Young Bill Knight, that I took with me, got two and sevenpence. I got nothing. Is it justice? This country is going to the dogs, if you ask me.

AUGUSTUS [*rising indignantly*] I do not ask you, sir; I will not allow you to say such things in my presence. Our statesmen are the greatest known to history. Our generals are invincible. Our army is the admiration of the world. [*Furiously*] How dare you tell me that the country is going to the dogs!

THE CLERK. Why did they give young Bill Knight two and

sevenpence, and not give me even my tram fare? Do you call that
being great statesmen? As good as robbing me, I call it.

AUGUSTUS. Thats enough. Leave the room. [*He sits down and takes
up his pen, settling himself to work. The clerk shuffles to the door. Augustus
adds, with cold politeness*] Send me the Secretary.

THE CLERK. I'm the Secretary. I cant leave the room and send
myself to you at the same time, can I?

AUGUSTUS. Dont be insolent. Where is the gentleman I have been
corresponding with: Mr Horatio Floyd Beamish?

THE CLERK [*returning and bowing*] Here. Me.

AUGUSTUS. You! Ridiculous. What right have you to call yourself
by a pretentious name of that sort?

THE CLERK. You may drop the Horatio Floyd. Beamish is good
enough for me.

AUGUSTUS. Is there nobody else to take my instructions?

THE CLERK. It's me or nobody. And for two pins I'd chuck it. Dont
you drive me too far. Old uns like me is up in the world now.

AUGUSTUS. If we were not at war, I should discharge you on the
spot for disrespectful behavior. But England is in danger; and I
cannot think of my personal dignity at such a moment. [*Shouting
at him*] Dont you think of yours, either, worm that you are; or I'll
have you arrested under the Defence of the Realm Act, double
quick.

THE CLERK. What do I care about the realm? They done me out of
two and seven –

AUGUSTUS. Oh, damn your two and seven! Did you receive my
letters?

THE CLERK. Yes.

AUGUSTUS. I addressed a meeting here last night – went straight to
the platform from the train. I wrote to you that I should expect
you to be present and report yourself. Why did you not do so?

THE CLERK. The police wouldnt let me on the platform.

AUGUSTUS. Did you tell them who you were?

THE CLERK. They knew who I was. Thats why they wouldnt let me
up.

AUGUSTUS. This is too silly for anything. This town wants waking
up. I made the best recruiting speech I ever made in my life; and
not a man joined.

THE CLERK. What did you expect? You told them our gallant
fellows is falling at the rate of a thousand a day in the big push.
Dying for Little Pifflington, you says. Come and take their

places, you says. That aint the way to recruit.

AUGUSTUS. But I expressly told them their widows would have pensions.

THE CLERK. I heard you. Would have been all right if it had been the widows you wanted to get round.

AUGUSTUS [*rising angrily*] This town is inhabited by dastards. I say it with a full sense of responsibility, dastards! They call themselves Englishmen; and they are afraid to fight.

THE CLERK. Afraid to fight! You should see them on a Saturday night.

AUGUSTUS. Yes: they fight one another; but they wont fight the Germans.

THE CLERK. They got grudges again one another: how can they have grudges again the Huns that they never saw? Theyve no imagination: thats what it is. Bring the Huns here; and theyll quarrel with them fast enough.

AUGUSTUS [*returning to his seat with a grunt of disgust*] Mf! Theyll have them here if theyre not careful. [*Seated*] Have you carried out my order about the war saving?

THE CLERK. Yes.

AUGUSTUS. The allowance of petrol has been reduced by three quarters?

THE CLERK. It has.

AUGUSTUS. And you have told the motor-car people to come here and arrange to start munition work now that their motor business is stopped?

THE CLERK. It aint stopped. Theyre busier than ever.

AUGUSTUS. Busy at what?

THE CLERK. Making small cars.

AUGUSTUS. New cars!

THE CLERK. The old cars only do twelve miles to the gallon. Everybody has to have a car that will do thirtyfive now.

AUGUSTUS. Cant they take the train?

THE CLERK. There aint no trains now. Theyve tore up the rails and sent them to the front.

AUGUSTUS. Psha!

THE CLERK. Well, we have to get about somehow.

AUGUSTUS. This is perfectly monstrous. Not in the least what I intended.

THE CLERK. Hell —

AUGUSTUS. Sir!

THE CLERK [*explaining*] Hell, they says, is paved with good intentions.

AUGUSTUS [*springing to his feet*] Do you mean to insinuate that hell is paved with my good intentions – with the good intentions of His Majesty's Government?

THE CLERK. I dont mean to insinuate anything until the Defence of the Realm Act is repealed. It aint safe.

AUGUSTUS. They told me that this town had set an example to all England in the matter of economy. I came down here to promise the Mayor a knighthood for his exertions.

THE CLERK. The Mayor! Where do *I* come in?

AUGUSTUS. You dont come in. You go out. This is a fool of a place. I'm greatly disappointed. Deeply disappointed. [*Flinging himself back into his chair*] Disgusted.

THE CLERK. What more can we do? Weve shut up everything. The picture gallery is shut. The museum is shut. The theatres and picture shows is shut: I havnt seen a movy picture for six months.

AUGUSTUS. Man, man: do you want to see picture shows when the Hun is at the gate?

THE CLERK [*mournfully*] I dont now, though it drove me melancholy mad at first. I was on the point of taking a pennorth of rat poison –

AUGUSTUS. Why didnt you?

THE CLERK. Because a friend advised me to take a drink instead. That saved my life, though it makes me very poor company in the mornings, as [*hiccuping*] perhaps youve noticed.

AUGUSTUS. Well, upon my soul! You are not ashamed to stand there and confess yourself a disgusting drunkard.

THE CLERK. Well, what of it? We're at war now; and everything's changed. Besides, I should lose my job here if I stood drinking at the bar. I'm a respectable man and must buy my drink and take it home with me. And they wont serve me with less than a quart. If youd told me before the war that I could get through a quart of whisky in a day, I shouldnt have believed you. Thats the good of war: it brings out powers in a man that he never suspected himself capable of. You said so yourself in your speech last night.

AUGUSTUS. I did not know that I was talking to an imbecile. You ought to be ashamed of yourself. There must be an end of this drunken slacking. I'm going to establish a new order of things here. I shall come down every morning before breakfast until things are properly in train. Have a cup of coffee and two rolls for me here every morning at half-past ten.

THE CLERK. You cant have no rolls. The only baker that baked rolls was a Hun; and he's been interned.

AUGUSTUS. Quite right, too. And was there no Englishman to take his place?

THE CLERK. There was. But he was caught spying; and they took him up to London and shot him.

AUGUSTUS. Shot an Englishman!

THE CLERK. Well, it stands to reason if the Germans wanted a spy they wouldnt employ a German that everybody would suspect, dont it?

AUGUSTUS [*rising again*] Do you mean to say, you scoundrel, that an Englishman is capable of selling his country to the enemy for gold?

THE CLERK. Not as a general thing I wouldnt say it; but theres men here would sell their own mothers for two coppers if they got the chance.

AUGUSTUS. Beamish: it's an ill bird that fouls its own nest.

THE CLERK. It wasnt me that let Little Pifflington get foul. *I* dont belong to the governing classes. I only tell you why you cant have no rolls.

AUGUSTUS [*intensely irritated*] Can you tell me where I can find an intelligent being to take my orders?

THE CLERK. One of the street sweepers used to teach in the school until it was shut up for the sake of economy. Will he do?

AUGUSTUS. What! You mean to tell me that when the lives of the gallant fellows in our trenches, and the fate of the British Empire, depend on our keeping up the supply of shells, you are wasting money on sweeping the streets?

THE CLERK. We have to. We dropped it for a while; but the infant death rate went up something frightful.

AUGUSTUS. What matters the death rate of Little Pifflington in a moment like this? Think of our gallant soldiers, not of your squalling infants.

THE CLERK. If you want soldiers you must have children. You cant buy em in boxes, like toy soldiers.

AUGUSTUS. Beamish: the long and the short of it is, you are no patriot. Go downstairs to your office; and have that gas stove taken away and replaced by an ordinary grate. The Board of Trade has urged on me the necessity for economizing gas.

THE CLERK. Our orders from the Minister of Munitions is to use gas instead of coal, because it saves material. Which is it to be?

AUGUSTUS [*bawling furiously at him*] Both! Dont criticize your orders: obey them. Yours not to reason why: yours but to do and die. Thats war. [*Cooling down*] Have you anything else to say?

THE CLERK. Yes: I want a rise.

AUGUSTUS [*reeling against the table in his horror*] A rise! Horatio Floyd Beamish: do you know that we are at war?

THE CLERK [*feebly ironical*] I have noticed something about it in the papers. Heard you mention it once or twice, now I come to think of it.

AUGUSTUS. Our gallant fellows are dying in the trenches; and you want a rise!

THE CLERK. What are they dying for? To keep me alive, aint it? Well, whats the good of that if I'm dead of hunger by the time they come back?

AUGUSTUS. Everybody else is making sacrifices without a thought of self; and you —

THE CLERK. Not half, they aint. Wheres the baker's sacrifice? Wheres the coal merchant's? Wheres the butcher's? Charging me double: thats how they sacrifice themselves. Well, I want to sacrifice myself that way too. Just double next Saturday: double and not a penny less; or no secretary for you [*he stiffens himself shakily, and makes resolutely for the door*].

AUGUSTUS [*looking after him contemptuously*] Go: miserable pro-German.

THE CLERK [*rushing back and facing him*] Who are you calling a pro-German?

AUGUSTUS. Another word, and I charge you under the Act with discouraging me. Go.

The clerk blenches and goes out, cowed.

The telephone rings.

AUGUSTUS [*taking up the telephone receiver*] Hallo . . . Yes: who are you? . . . oh, Blueloo, is it? . . . Yes: theres nobody in the room: fire away . . . What? . . . A spy! . . . A woman! . . . Yes: I brought it down with me. Do you suppose I'm such a fool as to let it out of my hands? Why, it gives a list of all our anti-aircraft emplacements from Ramsgate to Skegness. The Germans would give a million for it — what? . . . But how could she possibly know about it? I havnt mentioned it to a soul, except, of course, dear

Lucy. . . . . Oh, Toto and Lady Popham and that lot: they dont count: theyre all right. I mean that I havnt mentioned it to any Germans. . . . Pooh! Dont you be nervous, old chap. I know you think me a fool: but I'm not such a fool as all that. If she tries to get it out of me I'll have her in the Tower before you ring up again. [*The clerk returns*]. Sh-sh! Somebody's just come in: ring off. Goodbye. [*He hangs up the receiver*].

THE CLERK. Are you engaged? [*His manner is strangely softened*].

AUGUSTUS. What business is that of yours? However, if you will take the trouble to read the society papers for this week, you will see that I am engaged to the Honorable Lucy Popham, youngest daughter of —

THE CLERK. That aint what I mean. Can you see a female?

AUGUSTUS. Of course I can see a female as easily as a male. Do you suppose I'm blind?

THE CLERK. You dont seem to follow me, somehow. Theres a female downstairs: what you might call a lady. She wants to know can you see her if I let her up.

AUGUSTUS. Oh, you mean am I disengaged. Tell the lady I have just received news of the greatest importance which will occupy my entire attention for the rest of the day, and that she must write for an appointment.

THE CLERK. I'll ask her to explain her business to me. *I* aint above talking to a handsome young female when I get the chance [*going*].

AUGUSTUS. Stop. Does she seem to be a person of consequence?

THE CLERK. A regular marchioness, if you ask me.

AUGUSTUS. Hm! Beautiful, did you say?

THE CLERK. A human chrysanthemum, sir, believe me.

AUGUSTUS. It will be extremely inconvenient for me to see her; but the country is in danger; and we must not consider our own comfort. Think how our gallant fellows are suffering in the trenches! Shew her up. [*The clerk makes for the door, whistling the latest popular love ballad*]. Stop whistling instantly, sir. This is not a casino.

THE CLERK. Aint it? You just wait til you see her. [*He goes out*].

Augustus produces a mirror, a comb, and a pot of moustache pomade
from the drawer of the writing-table, and sits down before the mirror to put
some touches to his toilet.

The clerk returns, devotedly ushering a very attractive lady, brilliantly
dressed. She has a dainty wallet hanging from her wrist. Augustus hastily

covers up his toilet apparatus with The Morning Post, and rises in an attitude of pompous condescension.

THE CLERK [*to Augustus*] Here she is. [*To the lady*] May I offer you a chair, lady? [*He places a chair at the writing-table opposite Augustus, and steals out on tiptoe*].

AUGUSTUS. Be seated, madam.

THE LADY [*sitting down*] Are you Lord Augustus Highcastle?

AUGUSTUS [*sitting also*] Madam: I am.

THE LADY [*with awe*] The great Lord Augustus?

AUGUSTUS. I should not dream of describing myself so, madam; but no doubt I have impressed my countrymen – and [*bowing gallantly*] may I say my countrywomen – as having some exceptional claims to their consideration.

THE LADY [*emotionally*] What a beautiful voice you have!

AUGUSTUS. What you hear, madam, is the voice of my country, which now takes a sweet and noble tone even in the harsh mouth of high officialism.

THE LADY. Please go on. You express yourself so wonderfully.

AUGUSTUS. It would be strange indeed if, after sitting on thirty-seven Royal Commissions, mostly as chairman, I had not mastered the art of public expression. Even the Radical papers have paid me the high compliment of declaring that I am never more impressive than when I have nothing to say.

THE LADY. I never read the Radical papers. All I can tell you is that what we women admire in you is not the politician, but the man of action, the heroic warrior, the *beau sabreur*.

AUGUSTUS [*gloomily*] Madam, I beg! Please! My military exploits are not a pleasant subject, unhappily.

THE LADY. Oh, I know, I know. How shamefully you have been treated! What ingratitude! But the country is with you. The women are with you. Oh, do you think all our hearts did not throb and all our nerves thrill when we heard how, when you were ordered to occupy that terrible quarry in Hulluch, and you swept into it at the head of your men like a sea-god riding on a tidal wave, you suddenly sprang over the top shouting 'To Berlin! Forward!'; dashed at the German army single-handed; and were cut off and made prisoner by the Huns?

AUGUSTUS. Yes, madam; and what was my reward? They said I had disobeyed orders, and sent me home. Have they forgotten Nelson in the Baltic? Has any British battle ever been won except by a bold individual initiative? I say nothing of professional jealousy: it exists in the army as elsewhere; but it is a bitter thought to me that the recognition denied me by my own country – or rather by the Radical cabal in the Cabinet which pursues my family with rancorous class hatred – that this recognition, I say, came to me at the hands of an enemy – of a rank Prussian.

THE LADY. You dont say so!

AUGUSTUS. How else should I be here instead of starving to death in Ruhleben? Yes, madam: the Colonel of the Pomeranian regiment which captured me, after learning what I had done, and conversing for an hour with me on European politics and military strategy, declared that nothing would induce him to deprive my country of my services, and set me free. I offered, of course, to procure the release in exchange of a German officer of equal quality; but he would not hear of it. He was kind enough to say he could not believe that a German officer answering to that description existed. [*With emotion*] I had my first taste of the ingratitude of my own country as I made my way back to our lines. A shot from our front trench struck me in the head. I still carry the flattened projectile as a trophy [*he throws it on the table: the noise it makes testifies to its weight*]. Had it penetrated to the brain I might never have sat on another Royal Commission. Fortunately we have strong heads, we Highcastles. Nothing has ever penetrated to our brains.

THE LADY. How thrilling! How simple! And how tragic! But you will forgive England? Remember: England! England! Forgive her.

AUGUSTUS [*with gloomy magnanimity*] It will make no difference whatever to my services to my country. Though she slay me, yet will I, if not exactly trust in her, at least take my part in her government. I am ever at my country's call. Whether it be the embassy in a leading European capital, a governor-generalship in the tropics, or my humble mission here to make Little Pifflington do its bit, I am always ready for the sacrifice. Whilst England remains England, wherever there is a public job to be done you will find a Highcastle sticking to it. And now, madam, enough of my tragic personal history. You have called on business. What can I do for you?

THE LADY. You have relatives at the Foreign Office, have you not?

AUGUSTUS [*haughtily*] Madam: the Foreign Office is staffed by my relatives exclusively.

THE LADY. Has the Foreign Office warned you that you are being pursued by a female spy who is determined to obtain possession of a certain list of gun emplacements —

AUGUSTUS [*interrupting her somewhat loftily*] All that is perfectly well known to this department, madam.

THE LADY [*surprised and rather indignant*] Is it? Who told you? Was it one of your German brothers-in-law?

AUGUSTUS [*injured, remonstrating*] I have only three German brothers-in-law, madam. Really, from your tone, one would suppose that I had several. Pardon my sensitiveness on that subject; but reports are continually being circulated that I have been shot as a traitor in the courtyard of the Ritz Hotel simply because I have German brothers-in-law. [*With feeling*] If you had a German brother-in-law, madam, you would know that nothing else in the world produces so strong an anti-German feeling. Life affords no keener pleasure than finding a brother-in-law's name in the German casualty list.

THE LADY. Nobody knows that better than I. Wait until you hear what I have come to tell you: you will understand me as no one else could. Listen. This spy, this woman —

AUGUSTUS [*all attention*] Yes?

THE LADY. She is a German. A Hun.

AUGUSTUS. Yes, yes. She would be. Continue.

THE LADY. She is my sister-in-law.

AUGUSTUS [*deferentially*] I see you are well connected, madam. Proceed.

THE LADY. Need I add that she is my bitterest enemy?

AUGUSTUS. May I — [*he proffers his hand. They shake, fervently. From this moment onward Augustus becomes more and more confidential, gallant and charming*].

THE LADY. Quite so. Well, she is an intimate friend of your brother at the War Office, Hungerford Highcastle: Blueloo as you call him: I dont know why.

AUGUSTUS [*explaining*] He was originally called The Singing Oyster, because he sang drawing-room ballads with such an extraordinary absence of expression. He was then called the Blue Point for a season or two. Finally he became Blueloo.

THE LADY. Oh, indeed: I didnt know. Well, Blueloo is simply infatuated with my sister-in-law; and he has rashly let out to her that this list is in your possession. He forgot himself because he was in a towering rage at its being entrusted to you: his language was terrible. He ordered all the guns to be shifted at once.

AUGUSTUS. What on earth did he do that for?

THE LADY. I cant imagine. But this I know. She made a bet with him that she would come down here and obtain possession of that list and get clean away into the street with it. He took the bet on condition that she brought it straight back to him at the War Office.

AUGUSTUS. Good heavens! And you mean to tell me that Blueloo was such a dolt as to believe that she could succeed? Does he take me for a fool!

THE LADY. Oh, impossible! He is jealous of your intellect. The bet is an insult to you: dont you feel that? After what you have done for our country –

AUGUSTUS. Oh, never mind that. It is the idiocy of the thing I look at. He'll lose his bet; and serve him right!

THE LADY. You feel sure you will be able to resist the siren? I warn you, she is very fascinating.

AUGUSTUS. You need have no fear, madam. I hope she will come and try it on. Fascination is a game that two can play at. For centuries the younger sons of the Highcastles have had nothing to do but fascinate attractive females when they were not sitting on Royal Commissions or on duty at Knightsbridge barracks. By Gad, madam, if the siren comes here she will meet her match.

THE LADY. I feel that. But if she fails to seduce you –

AUGUSTUS [blushing] Madam!

THE LADY [continuing] – from your allegiance –

AUGUSTUS. Oh, that!

THE LADY.– she will resort to fraud, to force, to anything. She will burgle your office: she will have you attacked and garotted at night in the street.

AUGUSTUS. Pooh! I'm not afraid.

THE LADY. Oh, your courage will only tempt you into danger. She may get the list after all. It is true that the guns are moved. But she would win her bet.

AUGUSTUS [cautiously] You did not say that the guns were moved. You said that Blueloo had ordered them to be moved.

THE LADY. Well, that is the same thing, isnt it?

AUGUSTUS. Not quite – at the War Office. No doubt those guns will be moved: possibly even before the end of the war.

THE LADY. Then you think they are there still! But if the German War Office gets the list – and she will copy it before she gives it back to Blueloo, you may depend on it – all is lost.

AUGUSTUS [*lazily*] Well, I should not go as far as that. [*Lowering his voice*] Will you swear to me not to repeat what I am going to say to you; for if the British public knew that I had said it, I should be at once hounded down as a pro-German.

THE LADY. I will be silent as the grave. I swear it.

AUGUSTUS [*again taking it easily*] Well, our people have for some reason made up their minds that the German War Office is everything that our War Office is not – that it carries promptitude, efficiency, and organization to a pitch of completeness and perfection that must be, in my opinion, destructive to the happiness of the staff. My own view – which you are pledged, remember, not to betray – is that the German War Office is no better than any other War Office. I found that opinion on my observation of the characters of my brothers-in-law: one of whom, by the way, is on the German general staff. I am not at all sure that this list of gun emplacements would receive the smallest attention. You see, there are always so many more important things to be attended to. Family matters, and so on, you understand.

THE LADY. Still, if a question were asked in the House of Commons –

AUGUSTUS. The great advantage of being at war, madam, is that nobody takes the slightest notice of the House of Commons. No doubt it is sometimes necessary for a Minister to soothe the more seditious members of that assembly by giving a pledge or two; but the War Office takes no notice of such things.

THE LADY [*staring at him*] Then you think this list of gun emplacements doesnt matter!!

AUGUSTUS. By no means, madam. It matters very much indeed. If this spy were to obtain possession of the list, Blueloo would tell the story at every dinner-table in London; and –

THE LADY. And you might lose your post. Of course.

AUGUSTUS [*amazed and indignant*] *I* lose my post! What are you dreaming about, madam? How could I possibly be spared? There are hardly Highcastles enough at present to fill half the posts created by this war. No: Blueloo would not go that far. He is at least a gentleman. But I should be chaffed; and, frankly, I dont like being chaffed.

THE LADY. Of course not. Who does? It would never do. Oh never, never.

AUGUSTUS. I'm glad you see it in that light. And now, as a measure of security, I shall put that list in my pocket. [*He begins searching vainly from drawer to drawer in the writing-table*]. Where on earth –? What the dickens did I –? Thats very odd: I – Where the deuce –? I thought I had put it in the – Oh, here it is! No: this is Lucy's last letter.

THE LADY [*elegiacally*] Lucy's Last Letter! What a title for a picture play!

AUGUSTUS [*delighted*] Yes: it is, isnt it? Lucy appeals to the imagination like no other woman. By the way [*handing over the letter*] I wonder could you read it for me? Lucy is a darling girl; but I really cant read her writing. In London I get the office typist to decipher it and make me a typed copy; but here there is nobody.

THE LADY [*puzzling over it*] It is really almost illegible. I think the beginning is meant for 'Dearest Gus'.

AUGUSTUS [*eagerly*] Yes: that is what she usually calls me. Please go on.

THE LADY [*trying to decipher it*] 'What a' – 'what a' – oh yes: 'what a forgetful old' – something – 'you are!' I cant make out the word.

AUGUSTUS [*greatly interested*] Is it blighter? That is a favorite expression of hers.

THE LADY. I think so. At all events it begins with a B. [*Reading*] 'What a forgetful old' – [*she is interrupted by a knock at the door*].

AUGUSTUS [*impatiently*] Come in. [*The clerk enters, clean shaven and in khaki, with an official paper and an envelope in his hand*]. What is this ridiculous mummery, sir?

THE CLERK [*coming to the table and exhibiting his uniform to both*] Theyve passed me. The recruiting officer come for me. Ive had my two and seven.

AUGUSTUS [*rising wrathfully*] I shall not permit it. What do they mean by taking my office staff? Good God! they will be taking our hunt servants next. [*Confronting the clerk*] What did the man mean? What did he say?

THE CLERK. He said that now you was on the job we'd want another million men, and he was going to take the old-age pensioners or anyone he could get.

AUGUSTUS. And did you dare knock at my door and interrupt my business with this lady to repeat this man's ineptitudes?

THE CLERK. No. I come because the waiter from the hotel brought this paper. You left it on the coffee-room breakfast-table this morning.

THE LADY [*intercepting it*] It is the list. Good heavens!

THE CLERK [*proffering the envelope*] He says he thinks this is the envelope belonging to it.

THE LADY [*snatching the envelope also*] Yes! Addressed to you. Lord Augustus! [*Augustus comes back to the table to look at it*] Oh, how imprudent! Everybody would guess its importance with your name on it. Fortunately I have some letters of my own here [*opening her wallet*]. Why not hide it in one of my envelopes? then no one will dream that the enclosure is of any political value. [*Taking out a letter, she crosses the room towards the window, whispering to Augustus as she passes him*] Get rid of that man.

AUGUSTUS [*haughtily approaching the clerk, who humorously makes a paralytic attempt to stand at attention*] Have you any further business here, pray?

THE CLERK. Am I to give the waiter anything; or will you do it yourself?

AUGUSTUS. Which waiter is it? The English one?

THE CLERK. No: the one that calls hisself a Swiss. Shouldnt wonder if he'd made a copy of that paper.

AUGUSTUS. Keep your impertinent surmises to yourself, sir. Remember that you are in the army now; and let me have no more of your civilian insubordination. Attention! Left turn! Quick march!

THE CLERK [*stolidly*] I dunno what you mean.

AUGUSTUS. Go to the guard-room and report yourself for disobeying orders. Now do you know what I mean?

THE CLERK. Now look here. I aint going to argue with you —

AUGUSTUS. Nor I with you. Out with you.

He seizes the clerk, and rushes him through the door. The moment the lady is left alone, she snatches a sheet of official paper from the stationery rack; folds it so that it resembles the list; compares the two to see that they look exactly alike; whips the list into her wallet; and substitutes the fascimile for it. Then she listens for the return of Augustus. A crash is heard, as of the clerk falling downstairs.

Augustus returns and is about to close the door when the voice of the clerk is heard from below:

THE CLERK. I'll have the law of you for this, I will.

AUGUSTUS [*shouting down to him*] Theres no more law for you, you scoundrel. Youre a soldier now. [*He shuts the door and comes to the lady*]. Thank heaven, the war has given us the upper hand of these fellows at last. Excuse my violence; but discipline is absolutely necessary in dealing with the lower middle classes.

THE LADY. Serve the insolent creature right! Look! I have found you a beautiful envelope for the list, an unmistakeable lady's envelope. [*She puts the sham list into her envelope and hands it to him*].

AUGUSTUS. Excellent. Really very clever of you. [*Slyly*] Come: would you like to have a peep at the list [*beginning to take the blank paper from the envelope*]?

THE LADY [*on the brink of detection*] No no. Oh, please, no.

AUGUSTUS. Why? It wont bite you [*drawing it out further*].

THE LADY [*snatching at his hand*] Stop. Remember: if there should be an inquiry, you must be able to swear that you never shewed that list to a mortal soul.

AUGUSTUS. Oh, that is a mere form. If you are really curious —

THE LADY. I am not. I couldnt bear to look at it. One of my dearest friends was blown to pieces by an aircraft gun; and since then I have never been able to think of one without horror.

AUGUSTUS. You mean it was a real gun, and actually went off. How sad! how sad! [*He pushes the sham list back into the envelope, and pockets it*].

THE LADY. Ah! [*great sigh of relief*]. And now, Lord Augustus, I have taken up too much of your valuable time. Goodbye.

AUGUSTUS. What! Must you go?

THE LADY. You are so busy.

AUGUSTUS. Yes; but not before lunch, you know. I never can do much before lunch. And I'm no good at all in the afternoon. From five to six is my real working time. Must you really go?

THE LADY. I must, really. I have done my business very satisfactorily. Thank you ever so much [*she proffers her hand*].

AUGUSTUS [*shaking it affectionately as he leads her to the door, but first pressing the bell button with his left hand*] Goodbye. Goodbye. So sorry to lose you. Kind of you to come; but there was no real danger. You see, my dear little lady, all this talk about war saving, and secrecy, and keeping the blinds down at night, and so forth, is all very well; but unless it's carried out with intelligence, believe me, you may waste a pound to save a penny; you may let out all sorts of secrets to the enemy; you may guide the Zeppelins right on to your own chimneys. Thats where the ability of the governing class comes in. Shall the fellow call a taxi for you?

THE LADY. No, thanks: I prefer walking. Goodbye. Again, many, many thanks.

She goes out. Augustus returns to the writing-table smiling, and takes

*another look at himself in the mirror. The clerk returns with his head
bandaged, carrying a poker.*

THE CLERK. What did you ring for? [*Augustus hastily drops the
mirror*]. Dont you come nigh me or I'll split your head with this
poker thick as it is.

AUGUSTUS. It does not seem to me an exceptionally thick poker. I
rang for you to shew the lady out.

THE CLERK. She's gone. She run out like a rabbit. I ask myself,
why was she in such a hurry?

THE LADY'S VOICE [*from the street*] Lord Augustus. Lord
Augustus.

THE CLERK. She's calling you.

AUGUSTUS [*running to the window and throwing it up*] What is it? Wont
you come up?

THE LADY. Is the clerk there?

AUGUSTUS. Yes. Do you want him?

THE LADY. Yes.

AUGUSTUS. The lady wants you at the window.

THE CLERK [*rushing to the window and putting down the poker*] Yes,
maam? Here I am, maam. What is it, maam?

THE LADY. I want you to witness that I got clean away into the
street. I am coming up now.

    The two men stare at one another.

THE CLERK. Wants me to witness that she got clean away into the
street!

AUGUSTUS. What on earth does she mean?

    The lady returns.

THE LADY. May I use your telephone?

AUGUSTUS. Certainly. Certainly. [*Taking the receiver down*] What
number shall I get you?

THE LADY. The War Office, please.

AUGUSTUS. The.War Office!?

THE LADY. If you will be so good.

AUGUSTUS. But – Oh, very well. [*Into the receiver*] Hallo. This is the
Town Hall Recruiting Office. Give me Colonel Bogey, sharp.

    A pause.

THE CLERK [*breaking the painful silence*] I dont think I'm awake.
This is a dream of a movy picture, this is.

AUGUSTUS [*his ear at the receiver*] Shut up, will you? [*Into the telephone*]
What? . . . [*To the lady*] Whom do you want to get on to?

THE LADY. Blueloo.

AUGUSTUS [*into the telephone*] Put me through to Lord Hungerford Highcastle. . . . I'm his brother, idiot . . . That you, Blueloo? Lady here at Little Pifflington wants to speak to you. Hold the line. [*To the lady*] Now, madam [*he hands her the receiver*].

THE LADY [*sitting down in Augustus's chair to speak into the telephone*] Is that Blueloo? . . . Do you recognize my voice? . . . Ive won our bet. . . .

AUGUSTUS. Your bet!

THE LADY [*into the telephone*] Yes: I have the list in my wallet. . . .

AUGUSTUS. Nothing of the kind, madam. I have it here in my pocket. [*He takes the envelope from his pocket; draws out the paper; and unfolds it*].

THE LADY [*continuing*] Yes: I got clean into the street with it. I have a witness. I could have got to London with it. Augustus wont deny it. . . .

AUGUSTUS [*contemplating the blank paper*] Theres nothing written on this. Where is the list of guns?

THE LADY [*continuing*] Oh, it was quite easy. I said I was my sister-in-law and that I was a Hun. He lapped it up like a kitten. . . .

AUGUSTUS. You dont mean to say that –

THE LADY [*continuing*] I got hold of the list for a moment and changed it for a piece of paper out of his stationery rack: it was quite easy [*she laughs, and it is clear that Blueloo is laughing too*].

AUGUSTUS. What!

THE CLERK [*laughing slowly and laboriously, with intense enjoyment*] Ha ha! Ha ha ha! Ha! [*Augustus rushes at him: he snatches up the poker and stands on guard*]. No you dont.

THE LADY [*still at the telephone, waving her disengaged hand behind her impatiently at them to stop making a noise*] Sh-sh-sh-sh-sh!!! [*Augustus, with a shrug, goes up the middle of the room. The lady resumes her conversation with the telephone*] What? . . . Oh yes: I'm coming up by the 12.35: why not have tea with me at Rumpelmeister's . . . Rum-pelmeister's. You know: they call it Robinson's now . . . Right. Ta ta. [*She hangs up the receiver, and is passing round the table on her way towards the door when she is confronted by Augustus*].

AUGUSTUS. Madam: I consider your conduct most unpatriotic. You make bets and abuse the confidence of the hardworked officials who are doing their bit for their country whilst our gallant fellows are perishing in the trenches –

THE LADY. Oh, the gallant fellows are not all in the trenches,

Augustus. Some of them have come home for a few days hard earned leave; and I am sure you wont grudge them a little fun at your expense.

THE CLERK. Hear! Hear!

AUGUSTUS [*amiably*] Ah, well! For my country's sake –!

Annajanska, The Bolshevik Empress

A Revolutionary Romancelet

Composition begun 4 December 1917; completed 7 December 1917. Published in *Heartbreak House, Great Catherine,* & *Playlets of the War,* 1919. First presented, under the title *Annajanska, The Wild Grand Duchess,* at the Coliseum, London, in a variety bill on 21 January 1918.

General Strammfest   *Randle Ayrton*
Lieutenant Schneidekind   *Henry Miller*
Grand Duchess Annajanska   *Lillah McCarthy*
First Soldier   *Drelincourt Odlum*
Second Soldier   *(Not named)*

Period – 1917

Scene – *The General's Office in a Military Station on the East Front of Beotia*

Annajanska is frankly a bravura piece. The modern variety theatre demands for its 'turns' little plays called sketches, to last twenty minutes or so, and to enable some favorite performer to make a brief but dazzling appearance on some barely passable dramatic pretext. Miss Lillah McCarthy and I, as author and actress, have helped to make one another famous on many serious occasions, from Man and Superman to Androcles; and Mr Charles Ricketts has not disdained to snatch moments from his painting and sculpture to design some wonderful dresses for us. We three unbent as Mrs Siddons, Sir Joshua Reynolds, and Dr Johnson might have unbent, to devise a 'turn' for the Coliseum variety theatre. Not that we would set down the art of the variety theatre as something to be condescended to, or our own art as elephantine. We should rather crave indulgence as three novices fresh from the awful legitimacy of the highbrow theatre.

Well, Miss McCarthy and Mr Ricketts justified themselves easily in the glamor of the footlights, to the strains of Tchaikovsky's 1812. I fear I did not. I have received only one compliment on my share; and that was from a friend who said 'it is the only one of your works that is not too long.' So I have made it a page or two longer, according to my own precept: EMBRACE YOUR REPROACHES: THEY ARE OFTEN GLORIES IN DISGUISE.

The General's office in a military station on the east front in Beotia. An office table with a telephone, writing materials, official papers, etc., is set across the room. At the end of the table, a comfortable chair for the General. Behind the chair, a window. Facing it at the other end of the table, a plain wooden bench. At the side of the table, with its back to the door, a common chair, with a typewriter before it. Beside the door, which is opposite the end of the bench, a rack for caps and coats. There is nobody in the room.

General Strammfest enters, followed by Lieutenant Schneidekind. They hang up their cloaks and caps. Schneidekind takes a little longer than Strammfest, who comes to the table.

STRAMMFEST. Schneidekind.

SCHNEIDEKIND. Yes, sir.

STRAMMFEST. Have you sent my report yet to the government [*he sits down*]?

SCHNEIDEKIND [*coming to the table*] Not yet, sir. Which government do you wish it sent to? [*He sits down*].

STRAMMFEST. That depends. Whats the latest? Which of them do you think is most likely to be in power tomorrow morning?

SCHNEIDEKIND. Well, the provisional government was going strong yesterday. But today they say that the prime minister has shot himself, and that the extreme left fellow has shot all the others.

STRAMMFEST. Yes: thats all very well; but these fellows always shoot themselves with blank cartridge.

SCHNEIDEKIND. Still, even the blank cartridge means backing down. I should send the report to the Maximilianists.

STRAMMFEST. Theyre no stronger than the Oppidoshavians; and in my own opinion the Moderate Red Revolutionaries are as likely to come out on top as either of them.

SCHNEIDEKIND. I can easily put a few carbon sheets in the typewriter and send a copy each to the lot.

STRAMMFEST. Waste of paper. You might as well send reports to an infant school. [*He throws his head on the table with a groan*].

SCHNEIDEKIND. Tired out, sir?

STRAMMFEST. O Schneidekind, Schneidekind, how can you bear to live?

SCHNEIDEKIND. At my age, sir, I ask myself how can I bear to die?

STRAMMFEST. You are young, young and heartless. You are excited by the revolution: you are attached to abstract things like liberty. But my family has served the Panjandrums of Beotia faithfully for seven centuries. The Panjandrums have kept our place for us at their courts, honored us, promoted us, shed their glory on us, made us what we are. When I hear you young men declaring that you are fighting for civilization, for democracy, for the overthrow of militarism, I ask myself how can a man shed his blood for empty words used by vulgar tradesmen and common laborers: mere wind and stink. [*He rises, exalted by his theme*]. A king is a splendid reality, a man raised above us like a god. You can see him; you can kiss his hand; you can be cheered by his smile and terrified by his frown. I would have died for my Panjandrum as my father died for his father. Your toiling millions were only too honored to receive the toes of our boots in the proper spot for them when they displeased their betters. And now what is left in life for me? [*He relapses into his chair discouraged*]. My Panjandrum is deposed and transported to herd with convicts. The army, his pride and glory, is paraded to hear seditious speeches from penniless rebels, with the colonel actually forced to take the chair and introduce the speaker. I myself am made Commander-in-Chief by my own solicitor: a Jew, Schneidekind! a Hebrew Jew! It seems only yesterday that these things would have been the ravings of a madman: today they are the commonplaces of the gutter press. I live now for three objects only: to defeat the enemy, to restore the Panjandrum, and to hang my solicitor.

SCHNEIDEKIND. Be careful, sir: these are dangerous views to utter nowadays. What if I were to betray you?

STRAMMFEST. What!

SCHNEIDEKIND. I wont, of course: my own father goes on just like that; but suppose I did?

STRAMMFEST [*chuckling*] I should accuse you of treason to the Revolution, my lad; and they would immediately shoot you, unless you cried and asked to see your mother before you died, when they would probably change their minds and make you a brigadier. Enough. [*He rises and expands his chest*]. I feel the better for letting myself go. To business. [*He takes up a telegram; opens it;*

and is thunderstruck by its contents]. Great heaven! [*He collapses into his chair*]. This is the worst blow of all.

SCHNEIDEKIND. What has happened? Are we beaten?

STRAMMFEST. Man: do you think that a mere defeat could strike me down as this news does: I, who have been defeated thirteen times since the war began? O, my master, my master, my Panjandrum! [*he is convulsed with sobs*].

SCHNEIDEKIND. They have killed him?

STRAMMFEST. A dagger has been struck through his heart —

SCHNEIDEKIND. Good God!

STRAMMFEST. — and through mine, through mine.

SCHNEIDEKIND [*relieved*] Oh: a metaphorical dagger. I thought you meant a real one. What has happened?

STRAMMFEST. His daughter, the Grand Duchess Annajanska, she whom the Panjandrina loved beyond all her other children, has — has — [*he cannot finish*].

SCHNEIDEKIND. Committed suicide?

STRAMMFEST. No. Better if she had. Oh, far far better.

SCHNEIDEKIND [*in hushed tones*] Left the Church?

STRAMMFEST [*shocked*] Certainly not. Do not blaspheme, young man.

SCHNEIDEKIND. Asked for the vote?

STRAMMFEST. I would have given it to her with both hands to save her from this.

SCHNEIDEKIND. Save her from what? Dash it, sir, out with it.

STRAMMFEST. She has joined the Revolution.

SCHNEIDEKIND. But so have you, sir. Weve all joined the Revolution. She doesnt mean it any more than we do.

STRAMMFEST. Heaven grant you may be right! But that is not the worst. She has eloped with a young officer. Eloped, Schneidekind, eloped!

SCHNEIDEKIND [*not particularly impressed*] Yes, sir.

STRAMMFEST. Annajanska, the beautiful, the innocent, my master's daughter! [*He buries his face in his hands*].

The telephone rings.

SCHNEIDEKIND [*taking the receiver*] Yes: G.H.Q. Yes. . . . Dont bawl: I'm not a general. Who is it speaking? . . . Why didnt you say so? dont you know your duty? Next time you will lose your stripe. . . . Oh, theyve made you a colonel, have they? Well, theyve made me a field-marshal: now what have you to say? . . . Look here: what did you ring up for? I cant spend the day here

listening to your cheek. . . . What! the Grand Duchess!
[*Strammfest starts*]. Where did you catch her?

STRAMMFEST [*snatching the telephone and listening for the answer*]
Speak louder, will you: I am a General . . . I know that, you dolt.
Have you captured the officer that was with her? . . . Damnation! You shall answer for this: you let him go: he bribed you. . . .
You must have seen him: the fellow is in the full dress court
uniform of the Panderobajensky Hussars. I give you twelve
hours to catch him or . . . whats that you say about the devil? Are
you swearing at me, you . . . Thousand thunders! [*To
Schneidekind*] The swine says that the Grand Duchess is a devil
incarnate. [*Into the telephone*] Filthy traitor: is that the way
you dare speak of the daughter of our anointed Panjandrum?
I'll –

SCHNEIDEKIND [*pulling the telephone from his lips*] Take care, sir.

STRAMMFEST. I wont take care: I'll have him shot. Let go that
telephone.

SCHNEIDEKIND. But for her own sake, sir –

STRAMMFEST. Eh?

SCHNEIDEKIND. For her own sake they had better send her here.
She will be safe in your hands.

STRAMMFEST [*yielding the receiver*] You are right. Be civil to him. I
should choke [*he sits down*].

SCHNEIDEKIND [*into the telephone*] Hullo. Never mind all that: it's
only a fellow here who has been fooling with the telephone. I had
to leave the room for a moment. Wash out; and send the girl
along. We'll jolly soon teach her to behave herself here. . . . Oh,
youve sent her already. Then why the devil didnt you say so, you
– [*he hangs up the telephone angrily*]. Just fancy: they started her off
this morning: and all this is because the fellow likes to get on the
telephone and hear himself talk now that he is a colonel. [*The
telephone rings again. He snatches the receiver furiously*] Whats the
matter now? . . . [*To the General*] It's our own people downstairs.
[*Into the receiver*] Here! do you suppose Ive nothing else to do than
to hang on to the telephone all day? . . . Whats that? Not men
enough to hold her! What do you mean? [*To the General*] She is
there, sir.

STRAMMFEST. Tell them to send her up. I shall have to receive her
without even rising, without kissing her hand, to keep up
appearances before the escort. It will break my heart.

SCHNEIDEKIND [*into the receiver*] Send her up. . . . Tcha! [*He hangs up the receiver*]. He says she is half way up already: they couldnt hold her.

The Grand Duchess bursts into the room, dragging with her two exhausted soldiers hanging on desperately to her arms. She is enveloped from head to foot by a fur-lined cloak, and wears a fur cap.

SCHNEIDEKIND [*pointing to the bench*] At the word Go, place your prisoner on the bench in a sitting posture; and take your seats right and left of her. Go.

The two soldiers make a supreme effort to force her to sit down. She flings them back so that they are forced to sit on the bench to save themselves from falling backwards over it, and is herself dragged into sitting between them. The second soldier, holding on tight to the Grand Duchess with one hand, produces papers with the other, and waves them towards Schneidekind, who takes them from him and passes them on to the General. He opens them and reads them with a grave expression.

SCHNEIDEKIND. Be good enough to wait, prisoner, until the General has read the papers on your case.

THE GRAND DUCHESS [*to the soldiers*] Let go. [*To Strammfest*] Tell them to let go, or I'll upset the bench backwards and bash our three heads on the floor.

FIRST SOLDIER. No, little mother. Have mercy on the poor.

STRAMMFEST [*growling over the edge of the paper he is reading*] Hold your tongue.

THE GRAND DUCHESS [*blazing*] Me, or the soldier?

STRAMMFEST [*horrified*] The soldier, madam.

THE GRAND DUCHESS. Tell him to let go.

STRAMMFEST. Release the lady.

The soldiers take their hands off her. One of them wipes his fevered brow. The other sucks his wrist.

SCHNEIDEKIND [*fiercely*] 'ttention!

The two soldiers sit up stiffly.

THE GRAND DUCHESS. Oh, let the poor man suck his wrist. It may be poisoned. I bit it.

STRAMMFEST [*shocked*] You bit a common soldier!

THE GRAND DUCHESS. Well, I offered to cauterize it with the poker in the office stove. But he was afraid. What more could I do?

SCHNEIDEKIND. Why did you bite him, prisoner?

THE GRAND DUCHESS. He would not let go.

STRAMMFEST. Did he let go when you bit him?

THE GRAND DUCHESS. No. [*Patting the soldier on the back*] You should give the man a cross for his devotion. I could not go on eating him; so I brought him along with me.

STRAMMFEST. Prisoner —

THE GRAND DUCHESS. Dont call me prisoner, General Strammfest. My grandmother dandled you on her knee.

STRAMMFEST [*bursting into tears*] O God, yes. Believe me, my heart is what it was then.

THE GRAND DUCHESS. Your brain also is what it was then. I will not be addressed by you as prisoner.

STRAMMFEST. I may not, for your own sake, call you by your rightful and most sacred titles. What am I to call you?

THE GRAND DUCHESS. The Revolution has made us comrades. Call me comrade.

STRAMMFEST. I had rather die.

THE GRAND DUCHESS. Then call me Annajanska; and I will call you Peter Piper, as grandmamma did.

STRAMMFEST [*painfully agitated*] Schneidekind: you must speak to her: I cannot — [*he breaks down*].

SCHNEIDEKIND [*officially*] The Republic of Beotia has been compelled to confine the Panjandrum and his family, for their own safety, within certain bounds. You have broken those bounds.

STRAMMFEST [*taking the word from him*] You are — I must say it — a prisoner. What am I to do with you?

THE GRAND DUCHESS. You should have thought of that before you arrested me.

STRAMMFEST. Come, come, prisoner! do you know what will happen to you if you compel me to take a sterner tone with you?

THE GRAND DUCHESS. No. But I know what will happen to you.

STRAMMFEST. Pray what, prisoner?

THE GRAND DUCHESS. Clergyman's sore throat.

 Schneidekind splutters: drops a paper; and conceals his laughter under the table.

STRAMMFEST [*thunderously*] Lieutenant Schneidekind.

SCHNEIDEKIND [*in a stifled voice*] Yes, sir. [*The table vibrates visibly*].

STRAMMFEST. Come out of it, you fool: youre upsetting the ink.

 Schneidekind emerges, red in the face with suppressed mirth.

STRAMMFEST. Why dont you laugh? Dont you appreciate Her Imperial Highness's joke?

SCHNEIDEKIND [*suddenly becoming solemn*] I dont want to, sir.

STRAMMFEST. Laugh at once, sir. I order you to laugh.

SCHNEIDEKIND [*with a touch of temper*] I really cant, sir. [*He sits down decisively*].

STRAMMFEST [*growling at him*] Yah! [*He turns impressively to the Grand Duchess*] Your Imperial Highness desires me to address you as comrade?

THE GRAND DUCHESS [*rising and waving a red handkerchief*] Long live the Revolution, comrade!

STRAMMFEST [*rising and saluting*] Proletarians of all lands, unite. Lieutenant Schneidekind: you will rise and sing the Marseillaise.

SCHNEIDEKIND [*rising*] But I cannot, sir. I have no voice, no ear.

STRAMMFEST. Then sit down; and bury your shame in your typewriter [*Schneidekind sits down*]. Comrade Annajanska: you have eloped with a young officer.

THE GRAND DUCHESS [*astounded*] General Strammfest: you lie.

STRAMMFEST. Denial, comrade, is useless. It is through that officer that your movements have been traced. [*The Grand Duchess is suddenly enlightened, and seems amused. Strammfest continues in a forensic manner*] He joined you at the Golden Anchor in Hakonsburg. You gave us the slip there; but the officer was traced to Potterdam, where you rejoined him and went alone to Premsylople. What have you done with that unhappy young man? Where is he?

THE GRAND DUCHESS [*pretending to whisper an important secret*] Where he has always been.

STRAMMFEST [*eagerly*] Where is that?

THE GRAND DUCHESS [*impetuously*] In your imagination. I came alone. I am alone. Hundreds of officers travel every day from Hakonsburg to Potterdam. What do I know about them?

STRAMMFEST. They travel in khaki. They do not travel in full dress court uniform as this man did.

SCHNEIDEKIND. Only officers who are eloping with grand duchesses wear court uniform: otherwise the grand duchesses could not be seen with them.

STRAMMFEST. Hold your tongue [*Schneidekind, in high dudgeon, folds his arms and retires from the conversation. The General returns to his paper and to his examination of the Grand Duchess*] This officer travelled with your passport. What have you to say to that?

THE GRAND DUCHESS. Bosh! How could a man travel with a woman's passport?

STRAMMFEST. It is quite simple, as you very well know. A dozen travellers arrive at the boundary. The official collects their passports. He counts twelve persons; then counts the passports. If there are twelve, he is satisfied.

THE GRAND DUCHESS. Then how do you know that one of the passports was mine?

STRAMMFEST. A waiter at the Potterdam Hotel looked at the officer's passport when he was in his bath. It was your passport.

THE GRAND DUCHESS. Stuff! Why did he not have me arrested?

STRAMMFEST. When the waiter returned to the hotel with the police the officer had vanished; and you were there with your own passport. They knouted him.

THE GRAND DUCHESS. Oh! Strammfest: send these men away. I must speak to you alone.

STRAMMFEST [*rising in horror*] No: this is the last straw: I cannot consent. It is impossible, utterly, eternally impossible, that a daughter of the Imperial House should speak to anyone alone, were it even her own husband.

THE GRAND DUCHESS. You forget that there is an exception. She may speak to a child alone. [*She rises*] Strammfest: you have been dandled on my grandmother's knee. By that gracious action the dowager Panjandrina made you a child forever. So did Nature, by the way. I order you to speak to me alone. Do you hear? I order you. For seven hundred years no member of your family has ever disobeyed an order from a member of mine. Will you disobey me?

STRAMMFEST. There is an alternative to obedience. The dead cannot disobey. [*He takes out his pistol and places the muzzle against his temple*].

SCHNEIDEKIND [*snatching the pistol from him*] For God's sake, General —

STRAMMFEST [*attacking him furiously to recover the weapon*] Dog of a subaltern, restore that pistol, and my honor.

SCHNEIDEKIND [*reaching out with the pistol to the Grand Duchess*] Take it: quick: he is as strong as a bull.

THE GRAND DUCHESS [*snatching it*] Aha! Leave the room, all of you except the General. At the double! lightning! electricity! [*she fires shot after shot, spattering bullets about the ankles of the soldiers. They fly precipitately. She turns to Schneidekind, who has by this time been flung on the floor by the General*] You too. [*He scrambles up*]. March [*He flies to the door*].

SCHNEIDEKIND [*turning at the door*] For your own sake, comrade —

THE GRAND DUCHESS [*indignantly*] Comrade! You!!! Go. [*She fires two more shots. He vanishes*].

STRAMMFEST [*making an impulsive movement towards her*] My Imperial Mistress —

THE GRAND DUCHESS. Stop. I have one bullet left, if you attempt to take this from me [*putting the pistol to her temple*].

STRAMMFEST [*recoiling, and covering his eyes with his hands*] No no: put it down: put it down. I promise everything: I swear anything; put it down, I implore you.

THE GRAND DUCHESS [*throwing it on the table*] There!

STRAMMFEST [*uncovering his eyes*] Thank God!

THE GRAND DUCHESS [*gently*] Strammfest: I am your comrade. Am I nothing more to you?

STRAMMFEST [*falling on his knee*] You are, God help me, all that is left to me of the only power I recognize on earth [*he kisses her hand*].

THE GRAND DUCHESS [*indulgently*] Idolater! When will you learn that our strength has never been in ourselves, but in your illusions about us? [*She shakes off her kindliness, and sits down in his chair*] Now tell me, what are your orders? And do you mean to obey them?

STRAMMFEST [*starting like a goaded ox, and blundering fretfully about the room*] How can I obey six different dictators, and not one gentleman among the lot of them? One of them orders me to make peace with the foreign enemy. Another orders me to offer all the neutral countries 48 hours to choose between adopting his views on·the single tax and being instantly invaded and annihilated. A third orders me to go to a damned Socialist Conference and explain that Beotia will allow no annexations and no indemnities, and merely wishes to establish the Kingdom of Heaven on Earth throughout the universe. [*He finishes behind Schneidekind's chair*].

THE GRAND DUCHESS. Damn their trifling!

STRAMMFEST. I thank Your Imperial Highness from the bottom of my heart for that expression. Europe thanks you.

THE GRAND DUCHESS. M'yes; but — [*rising*] Strammfest: you know that your cause — the cause of the dynasty — is lost.

STRAMMFEST. You must not say so. It is treason, even from you. [*He sinks, discouraged, into the chair, and covers his face with his hand*].

THE GRAND DUCHESS. Do not deceive yourself, General: never again will a Panjandrum reign in Beotia. [*She walks slowly across *the room, brooding bitterly, and thinking aloud*]. We are so decayed, so out of date, so feeble, so wicked in our own despite, that we have come at last to will our own destruction.

STRAMMFEST. You are uttering blasphemy.

THE GRAND DUCHESS. All great truths begin as blasphemies. All the king's horses and all the king's men cannot set up my father's throne again. If they could, you would have done it, would you not?

STRAMMFEST. God knows I would!

THE GRAND DUCHESS. You really mean that? You would keep the people in their hopeless squalid misery? you would fill those infamous prisons again with the noblest spirits in the land? you would thrust the rising sun of liberty back into the sea of blood from which it has risen? And all because there was in the middle of the dirt and ugliness and horror a little patch of court splendor in which you could stand with a few orders on your uniform, and yawn day after day and night after night in unspeakable boredom until your grave yawned wider still, and you fell into it because you had nothing better to do. How can you be so stupid, so heartless?

STRAMMFEST. You must be mad to think of royalty in such a way. I never yawned at court. The dogs yawned; but that was because they were dogs: they had no imagination, no ideals, no sense of honor and dignity to sustain them.

THE GRAND DUCHESS. My poor Strammfest: you were not often enough at court to tire of it. You were mostly soldiering; and when you came home to have a new order pinned on your breast, your happiness came through looking at my father and mother and at me, and adoring us. Was that not so?

STRAMMFEST. Do you reproach me with it? I am not ashamed of it.

THE GRAND DUCHESS. Oh, it was all very well for you, Strammfest. But think of me, of me! standing there for you to gape at, and knowing that I was no goddess, but only a girl like any other girl! It was cruelty to animals: you could have stuck up a wax doll or a golden calf to worship; it would not have been bored.

STRAMMFEST. Stop; or I shall renounce my allegiance to you. I have had women flogged for such seditious chatter as this.

THE GRAND DUCHESS. Do not provoke me to send a bullet through your head for reminding me of it.

STRAMMFEST. You always had low tastes. You are no true daughter of the Panjandrums: you are a changeling, thrust into the

Panjandrina's bed by some profligate nurse. I have heard stories of your childhood: of how –

THE GRAND DUCHESS. Ha, ha! Yes: they took me to the circus when I was a child. It was my first moment of happiness, my first glimpse of heaven. I ran away and joined the troupe. They caught me and dragged me back to my gilded cage; but I had tasted freedom; and they never could make me forget it.

STRAMMFEST. Freedom! To be the slave of an acrobat! to be exhibited to the public! to –

THE GRAND DUCHESS. Oh, I was trained to that. I had learnt that part of the business at court.

STRAMMFEST. You had not been taught to strip yourself half naked and turn head over heels –

THE GRAND DUCHESS. Man: I wanted to get rid of my swaddling clothes and turn head over heels. I wanted to, I wanted to, I wanted to. I can do it still. Shall I do it now?

STRAMMFEST. If you do, I swear I will throw myself from the window so that I may meet your parents in heaven without having my medals torn from my breast by them.

THE GRAND DUCHESS. Oh, you are incorrigible. You are mad, infatuated. You will not believe that we royal divinities are mere common flesh and blood even when we step down from our pedestals and tell you ourselves what a fool you are. I will argue no more with you: I will use my power. At a word from me your men will turn against you: already half of them do not salute you; and you dare not punish them: you have to pretend not to notice it.

STRAMMFEST. It is not for you to taunt me with that if it is so.

THE GRAND DUCHESS [haughtily] Taunt! I condescend to taunt! To taunt a common General! You forget yourself, sir.

STRAMMFEST [dropping on his knee submissively] Now at last you speak like your royal self.

THE GRAND DUCHESS. Oh, Strammfest, Strammfest, they have driven your slavery into your very bones. Why did you not spit in my face?

STRAMMFEST [rising with a shudder] God forbid!

THE GRAND DUCHESS. Well, since you will be my slave, take your orders from me. I have not come here to save our wretched family and our bloodstained crown. I am come to save the Revolution.

STRAMMFEST. Stupid as I am, I have come to think that I had

better save that than save nothing. But what will the Revolution do for the people? Do not be deceived by the fine speeches of the revolutionary leaders and the pamphlets of the revolutionary writers. How much liberty is there where they have gained the upper hand? Are they not hanging, shooting, imprisoning as much as ever we did? Do they ever tell the people the truth? No: if the truth does not suit them they spread lies instead, and make it a crime to tell the truth.

THE GRAND DUCHESS. Of course they do. Why should they not?

STRAMMFEST [*hardly able to believe his ears*] Why should they not!

THE GRAND DUCHESS. Yes: why should they not? We did it. You did it, whip in hand: you flogged women for teaching children to read.

STRAMMFEST. To read sedition. To read Karl Marx.

THE GRAND DUCHESS. Pshaw! How could they learn to read the Bible without learning to read Karl Marx? Why do you not stand to your guns and justify what you did, instead of making silly excuses. Do you suppose *I* think flogging a woman worse than flogging a man? I, who am a woman myself!

STRAMMFEST. I am at a loss to understand your Imperial Highness. You seem to me to contradict yourself.

THE GRAND DUCHESS. Nonsense! I say that if the people cannot govern themselves, they must be governed by somebody. If they will not do their duty without being half forced and half humbugged, somebody must force them and humbug them. Some energetic and capable minority must always be in power. Well, I am on the side of the energetic minority whose principles I agree with. The Revolution is as cruel as we were; but its aims are my aims. Therefore I stand for the Revolution.

STRAMMFEST. You do not know what you are saying. This is pure Bolshevism. Are you, the daughter of a Panjandrum, a Bolshevist?

THE GRAND DUCHESS. I am anything that will make the world less like a prison and more like a circus.

STRAMMFEST. Ah! You still want to be a circus star.

THE GRAND DUCHESS. Yes, and be billed as the Bolshevik Empress. Nothing shall stop me. You have your orders, General Strammfest: save the Revolution.

STRAMMFEST. What Revolution? Which Revolution? No two of your rabble of revolutionists mean the same thing by the

Revolution. What can save a mob in which every man is rushing in a different direction?

THE GRAND DUCHESS. I will tell you. The war can save it.

STRAMMFEST. The war?

THE GRAND DUCHESS. Yes, the war. Only a great common danger and a great common duty can unite us and weld these wrangling factions into a solid commonweath.

STRAMMFEST. Bravo! War sets everything right: I have always said so. But what is a united people without a united army? And what can *I* do? I am only a soldier. I cannot make speeches: I have won no victories: they will not rally to my call [*again he sinks into his chair with his former gesture of discouragement*].

THE GRAND DUCHESS. Are you sure they will not rally to mine?

STRAMMFEST. Oh, if only you were a man and a soldier!

THE GRAND DUCHESS. Suppose I find you a man and a soldier?

STRAMMFEST [*rising in a fury*] Ah! the scoundrel you eloped with! You think you will shove this fellow into an army command, over my head. Never.

THE GRAND DUCHESS. You promised everything. You swore anything. [*She marches as if in front of a régiment*] I know that this man alone can rouse the army to enthusiasm.

STRAMMFEST. Delusion! Folly! He is some circus acrobat; and you are in love with him.

THE GRAND DUCHESS. I swear I am not in love with him. I swear I will never marry him.

STRAMMFEST. Then who is he?

THE GRAND DUCHESS. Anybody in the world but you would have guessed long ago. He is under your very eyes.

STRAMMFEST [*staring past her right and left*] Where?

THE GRAND DUCHESS. Look out of the window.

He rushes to the window, looking for the officer. The Grand Duchess takes off her cloak and appears in the uniform of the Panderobajensky Hussars.

STRAMMFEST [*peering through the window*] Where is he? I can see no one.

THE GRAND DUCHESS. Here, silly.

STRAMMFEST [*turning*] You! Great Heavens! The Bolshevik Empress!

Village Wooing

A Comediettina for Two Voices

Composition begun 2 January 1933; completed 27 July 1933. First published in German translation, as *Ländliche Werbung*, in the *Neue Freie Presse* (Vienna), 24 December 1933. First published in English in *Too True to be Good, Village Wooing & On the Rocks*, 1934. First presented at the Little Theatre, Dallas, on 17 April 1934.

A Passenger, 'Z' *Keith Woolley*
An Author, 'A' *Charles Meredith*
Deck Steward (Not Named)

Period – The Present
First Conversation: *The Lounge Deck of the* Empress of Patagonia, *a Pleasure Ship*
Second Conversation: *In a Village Shop and Post Office on the Wiltshire Downs*
Third Conversation: *In the Same*

FIRST CONVERSATION

The lounge deck of the Empress of Patagonia, a pleasure ship. Two of the deck chairs are occupied by A, *a literary looking pale gentleman under forty in green spectacles, a limp black beard, and a tropical suit of white silk, who is writing and does not wish to be disturbed, and* Z, *a young woman, presentable but not aristocratic, who is bored with her book. She is undressed for bathing, but is very modestly covered up with a not too flamboyant wrap.*

Z. Excuse me. Could you tell me the time?

A. [*curtly*] Eleven.

Z. My watch makes it half past ten.

A. The clocks were put on half an hour last night. We are going east.

Z. I always think it adds to the interest of a voyage having to put on your watch.

A. I am glad you are so easily interested [*he resumes his writing pointedly*].

Z. The steward will be round with the soup in half an hour. I thought we should have to wait an hour.

A. I never take it. It interrupts my work.

Z. Why do you work all the time? It's not what one comes on a pleasure cruise for, is it?

A. Work is my only pleasure.

Z. Oh, thats not good sense, is it? It gives me the pip to see you always sitting there over your writing, and never enjoying yourself, nor even taking a drop of soup. You should get up and have a game of deck quoits: you will feel ever so much better after it.

A. I feel perfectly well, thank you. And I loathe deck games, especially deck quoits. The slapping of those silly things on the deck destroys the quiet of the ship.

Z. Oh, I see. That is why you select this end of the deck. I often wondered why.

A. Within the last fortnight you have inspected the priceless antiquities of Naples, Athens, Egypt, and the Holy Land. Please occupy your mind with them until the soup comes.

z. I never cared much for geography. Where are we now?

a. We are on the Red Sea.

z. But it's blue.

a. What did you expect it to be?

z. Well, I didnt know what color the sea might be in these parts. I always thought the Red Sea would be red.

a. Well, it isnt.

z. And isnt the Black Sea black?

a. It is precisely the color of the sea at Margate.

z. [*eagerly*] Oh, I am so glad you know Margate. Theres no place like it in the season, is there?

a. I dont know: I have never been there.

z. [*disappointed*] Oh, you ought to go. You could write a book about it.

a. [*shudders, sighs, and pretends to write very hard*]!
     A pause.

z. I wonder why they call it the Red Sea.

a. Because their fathers did. Why do you call America America?

z. Well, because it is America. What else would you call it?

a. Oh, call it what you like, dear lady; but I have five hundred words to write before lunch; and I cannot do that if I talk to you.

z. [*sympathetically*] Yes: it is awful to have to talk to people, isnt it? Oh, that reminds me: I have something really interesting to tell you. I believe the man in the cabin next mine beats his wife.

a. I feel a little like him myself. Some women would provoke any men to beat them.

z. I will say this for him, that she always begins it.

a. No doubt.

z. I hate a nagger: dont you?

a. It is your privilege as a woman to have the last word. Please take it and dont end all your remarks with a question.

z. You are funny.

a. Am I? I never felt less funny in my life.

z. I cant make you out at all. I am rather good at making out people as a rule; but I cant make head or tail of you.

a. I am not here to be made out. You are not here to make people out, but to revel in the enjoyments you have paid for. Deck tennis, deck quoits, shuffleboard, golf, squash rackets, the swimming pool, the gymnasium all invite you.

z. I am no good at games: besides, theyre silly. I'd rather sit and talk.

A. Then for heaven's sake talk to somebody else. I have no time for talk. I have to work my passage.

z. What do you mean: work your passage? You are not a sailor.

A. No. I make a precarious living on board ship by writing the Marco Polo Series of Chatty Guide Books. Unless I complete two thousand words a day I am bankrupt. I cannot complete them if you persist in talking to me.

z. Do you mean you are writing a book about this cruise?

A. I am trying to – under great difficulties.

z. Will I be in it?

A. [*grimly*] You will.

z. How thrilling! I have never been put in a book before. You will read me what you have written about me, wont you?

A. When the book is published you can read it to your heart's content.

z. But I should like you to get me right. After all, what do you know about me? I will tell you the whole of my life if you like.

A. Great heavens, NO. Please dont.

z. Oh, I dont care who knows it.

A. Evidently. You would hardly offer to tell it to a perfect stranger if you cared, or if it was of the smallest interest.

z. Oh, I'd never think of you as a stranger. Here we are on the same ship, arnt we? And most people would think my life quite a romance. Wouldnt you really like to hear it?

A. No, I tell you. When I want romances I invent them for myself.

z. Oh, well, perhaps you wouldnt think it very wonderful. But it was a regular treat for me. You may think because I am well dressed and travelling de lucks and all that, that I am an educated lady. But I'm not.

A. I never supposed for a moment that you were.

z. But how could you know? How did you find out?

A. I didnt find out. I knew.

z. Who told you?

A. Nobody told me.

z. Then how did you know?

A. [*exasperated*] How do I know that a parrot isnt a bird of paradise?

z. Theyre different.

A. Precisely.

z. There you are, you see. But what would you take me for if you met me in a third class carriage?

a. I should not notice you.

z. I bet you would. I maynt be a beauty; but when I get into a railway carriage every man in it has a look at me.

a. I am not Everyman. Everyman thinks that every woman that steps into a railway carriage may be the right woman. But she is always a disappointment.

z. Same with the women, isnt it? If you were a woman youd know.

a. I am a woman; and you are a man, with a slight difference that doesnt matter except on special occasions.

z. Oh, what a thing to say! I never could bring myself to believe that. I know, of course, that men have their weaknesses and their tempers; but all the same there is something wonderful you can get from a man that you never could get from a woman. Dont you think so?

a. Inexperienced men think there is something wonderful you can get from a woman that you never could get from a man. Hence many unhappy marriages.

z. Are you married?

a. Widower. Are you?

z. Oh, thats the first time youve asked me a question. We're getting on, arnt we?

a. No. I am not getting on with my work.

z. Youre an intellectual, arnt you?

a. What do you think you mean by an intellectual?

z. Only that you consider me no better than an idiot, and that you were a bad husband, most likely.

a. You are quite right on both points.

z. I thought so.

a. And now, please, may I go on with my work?

z. Please yourself. I'm not hindering you.

a. Thank you. [*He resumes his writing*].
    A pause.

z. What books would you recommend me to read to improve my mind?

a. [*shouting furiously*] Steward.

z. Oh, you shouldnt trouble the steward now. He's busy getting the soup.

a. I want him to remove my chair to the very furthest extremity of this ship.

z. I always say it's fresher under the awning at the end. You dont mind if I move too, do you?

a. If you persecute me any more I shall go overboard. Dont you see that I want to be left alone to work, and that your chatter is preventing me from working?

z. [*sympathetically*] It is annoying to have somebody talking to you all the time when you dont want to. But it's just as bad when you want to talk, and the other person wont, isnt it?

a. There are three or four hundred persons on this ship. Cannot you find one of them with the same insatiable thirst for conversation as yourself?

z. Well, but we all have to make ourselves agreeable, havnt we?

a. Not at oneanother's expense. You are not making yourself agreeable to me at present: you are driving me mad.

z. My father used to say that men and women are always driving oneanother mad.

a. That sounds literary. Was your father a man of letters?

z. Yes: I should think he was. A postman.

a. A what?

z. A postman. A village postman.

a. Ha ha! Ha ha ha!

z. What is there funny in that?

a. I dont know. Ha ha! the postman's daughter hath ripe red lips: butter and eggs and a pound of cheese! Ha ha ha!

z. Well, I'm glad Ive amused you. But I dont think it's very polite of you to laugh at my father.

a. [*punctiliously – recovering himself*] You are right. I was rude. But a good laugh is worth a hundred pounds to me. I feel a different man. Forgive me. You see, you quoted a remark of your father's – almost an epigram – which suggested that he must have been a man of genius.

z. Well, so he was. He had a genius for walking.

a. For what?

z. For walking. When he was a child, he won a prize as The Infant Pedestrian. And would you believe it, my mother was that indoory that she grudged having to go out and do her marketing. After we had a telephone put in she never went out at all.

a. Thats strange. As she was never out and he was never in, the household should have been a quiet one; but that remark of his about men and women driving oneanother mad rather suggests the opposite.

z. So it was the opposite. She was always complaining of being lonely; and he was always at her to take more exercise. When they were not quarrelling about that, they were quarrelling about me. You see, they had great ambitions for me. She wanted me to be a parlormaid in a great house. He wanted me to be a telephone operator. He said there is no future for the great houses and a great future for telephones.

a. And you? Had you no ambition for yourself?

z. Oh, I wanted to be something romantic, like an acrobat in a circus.

a. And what actually happened?

z. I became shop assistant and telephone operator in the village shop.

a. Do village shop assistants and telephone girls —

z. Operators.

a. Pardon: operators. Do they earn enough to take cruises round the world in pleasure ships?

z. Not they. I won the first prize in a newspaper competition. My mother wanted me to save it: she said it would help me to get a thrifty husband. My father told me to blue it all in a lump while I had the chance. 'You will be poor all your life,' he said; 'but now you have the chance of living at the rate of five thousand a year for four months. Dont miss it,' he said: 'see what it's like. Have your fling,' he said; 'for they never can take that away from you once youve had it.' His idea was a walking tour, spending the nights in the best hotels; but I chose the ship because it's more dressy and more people to look at. Besides, I can get all the walking I want round the deck. At the end of the cruise back I go to the village shop without a penny.

a. Have they found out here that you are not a lady?

z. The Americans dont know the difference: they think my telephone talk is aristocratic; and the English wont speak to anyone anyhow. And lots of them are just like me.

a. Well, how do you like living at the rate of five thousand a year? Is it worth it?

z. It is while the novelty lasts. You see, when youre at home you get tired of doing the same thing every day: the same places! the same faces! the same old round. When you get a holiday you go off in a crowded hot excursion train to the seaside and make yourself tired and miserable just because it's a change; and youd do anything for a change. But here it's change all the time until you begin to realize what it is to have a settled home and belong somewhere. I shant be sorry to get home to the shop and the telephone. I get such a dreadful lost dog feeling sometimes. Other times it seems such a foolish waste of money. And I hate wasting money.

A. Thats an extremely attractive point in your character. My wife used to waste my money. Stick to that and you will get married in no time.

z. Oh, I have had plenty of offers. But you know it's a terrible thing to be a poor man's wife when you have been accustomed to a clean decent job. I have seen so many bright jolly girls turn into dirty old drudges through getting married.

A. Dont be afraid of dirt. Mine is a clean job; but I often wish I had a dirty one to exercise me and keep me in health. Women are so set on clean collars that they make their sons clerks when they would be stronger and earn more money as navvies. I wish I was a navvy instead of writing guide books.

z. Well, whats to prevent you?

A. I am not trained to manual work. Half an hour of it would make me wish myself dead. And five minutes of my work would produce a strike among the navvies. I am only a writing machine, just as a navvy is a digging machine.

z. I dont think the world is rightly arranged: do you?

A. We must take the world as we find it. It's we that are not rightly arranged.

z. Thats what I mean. Well, I suppose I mustnt interrupt your work.

A. You mean that the steward is coming round with the soup at last.

z. Well, it's half past eleven, isnt it?

The steward appears with the soup and offers it to z, who seizes it eagerly; then to A.

A. No, thank you. No soup.

He buries himself in his work, unmolested.
She buries herself in the soup.

SECOND CONVERSATION

In a village shop and post office on the Wiltshire Downs on a fine summer morning. The counter is for general shopping for most of its length; but one end is reserved and railed in for postal business. A couple of chairs are available for customers. The goods for sale include ginger beer in stone bottles, tablets of milk chocolate, glass jars of sweets containing (inter alia) sugared almonds, all on the counter; cheese, butter, and Hovis bread handy to the scales; and, in front of the counter, a sack of apples on the floor and some string bags hanging from the rafters.

---

z. [*invisible*] Th-reee ni-nnn. Sorry: no such number. Whoo-mmm do you want? Doctor Byles? One fi-fff. You are through.

> *A comes in. He is in hiking costume, with stick and rucksack, but wears well cut breeches (not plus fours) instead of shorts. Seeing nobody to attend to him he raps loudly on the counter with his stick. z emerges.*

A. I want a packet of milk chocolate —

z. Thanks very much.

A. [*continuing*] — a couple of hard apples —

z. Thanks very much [*She comes out through the counter to get them from the sack*].

A. [*continuing*] — quarter of a pound of Cheddar cheese —

z. Thanks very much.

A. Dont interrupt me. You can express your gratitude for the order when I have finished. Quarter of a pound of your best butter, a small loaf of Hovis, and twopenny-worth of sugared almonds.

z. Anything else?

A. No, thank you.

z. Thanks very much [*she goes back through the counter to cut and weigh the butter and cheese*].

> *He sits down watching her deft but leisurely proceedings.*

A. Do you sell baskets?

z. We sell everything. Hadnt you better have a string bag? It's handier; and it packs away almost to nothing when it's empty.

A. What is a string bag? Shew me one.

z. [*coming out and taking one down*] This is the cheapest. Or would you like a better quality with a Zip fastening?

a. Certainly not. I should have the trouble of opening and shutting it, and the worry of wondering whether it would open or shut, with no compensatory advantage whatever.

z. Thats just like you. Youre not a bit changed.

a. What do you mean? I have been in this shop for less than two minutes. Why should I have changed in that time?

z. Excuse me: I shouldnt have mentioned it. Will you take a string bag?

a. Yes.

z. Thanks very much. Shall I put the rest of the order into it?

a. Of course. What else do you suppose I am buying it for? Have you any buttermilk?

z. Sorry. We dont stock it.

a. Any ginger beer?

z. Yes. We have a very good local brew.

a. Shove a bottle into the string bag.

z. Thanks very much.

a. How many times a day do you say thanks very much?

z. Depends on the number of orders.

a. Dont say it to me again, if you dont mind. It gets on my nerves.

z. It used to get on mine, at first. But I am used to it.

a. Have you a guide book of this village?

z. Sorry. Theres a leaflet in the church, written by the vicar. You are expected to put tuppence in the box for it. Excuse me; but the chocolates are tuppence, sixpence, and a shilling. Which size would you run to?

a. It is a poor heart that never rejoices. I will have a shilling one.

z. Thanks very much.

a. Dont.

z. Excuse me: I cant help it. I say it without thinking: same as if you touched a button.

The telephone rings.

a. Someone has touched the button.

z. [*vanishing into the post office section*] What number please? Whitehall on-n-ne two on-n-n-e two. I will ring you. Whitehall one two one two. Yes. [*She reappears*] Thats a police call.

a. You need not point the information at me. I am not the criminal.

z. Oh, it isnt a criminal. Somebody thats been broadcasted on the wireless as lost. You know the sort of thing. Missing from his home since January the first. Last seen in a deck chair on the Empress of Patagonia talking to a female. Suffering from loss of memory.

A. How extraor – [*the telephone rings again*].

Z. Excuse me. [*She vanishes*]. You are through to Whitehall. [*She reappears*].

A. You have hit on an extraordinary coincidence. I wonder whether you will believe me when I tell you that in January last I was sitting on the deck of a ship named the Empress of Patagonia, and that I was talking to a female – or rather she was talking to me. How that woman did talk!

Z. And are you suffering from loss of memory?

A. Certainly not. I never forget anything.

Z. Oh, then it cant be you, can it?

A. There! Can it? That woman always finished up with can it? wont it? isnt it? so that you had to answer her out of common politeness. Take care never to pick up that trick or you will be murdered some day.

Z. Some people are like that. It often goes with orange colored eyes [*or whatever color her eyes happen to be*]. Did you notice the color of her eyes?

A. No: I never notice things like that. I am not a detective. It is people's characters that impress me; I cant tell you the color of her hair or the shape of her nose; but I can tell you that she was a most fearful nuisance. How much does all that come to?

Z. The string bag sixpence, chocolates a shilling: one and sixpence. The ginger beer is –

A. Spare me the details. Will ten shillings cover it?

Z. Oh yes, of course. You shouldnt be so careless about money.

A. [*presenting a Treasury note*] Cease preaching. Take it; and give me the change.

Z. Let me see. Eighteenpence, and fourpence for the ginger beer is one and tenpence, isnt it?

A. Have I denied it?

Z. Cheese threepence; two and a penny; butter sixpence: two and sevenpence; apples we sell by the pound. Hadnt you better have a pound?

A. How many to the pound?

Z. Three.

A. I cannot eat more than two apples at a time. Charge me for a pound; and eat the odd one yourself.

z. Oh well, say threepence for two: thats two and tenpence, isnt it?

a. I dont know.

z. Hovis, tuppence halfpenny. Three shillings and a halfpenny. Do you happen to have a halfpenny to save having to take fippence halfpenny in coppers?

a. I hate halfpennies: I always throw them away. Stop. I have one. Here.

z. Thanks very much. [*Handing him his change coin by coin*]. Three, four, five, seven and six, ten. Thanks very much.

a. [*pocketing his change, but remaining comfortably seated*] Dont you find it rather dull in this village shop saying thanks very much all day?

z. Well, no matter where you are you are doing the same thing all day and every day, arnt you? The only way to get it off your mind is to live in the same place and stick at the same job. Then you never have to think about it. Thats the way the people live here; and they live for ever so long; eighty's no age here. Grandfather will be a hundred and two in August. Thats because he's never had to worry about what he'll do or where he'll go. He just imagines and imagines. It's the only way to be happy and longlived.

a. But if your imagination has only one village in it it must be pretty bare. How would you like to live in a room with only one chair in it.

z. Well, if you have only one seat what more do you want than one chair? Up at the castle there are thirtysix chairs of one sort or another in the big drawing room; but Lady Flopping cant flop on more than one, can she?

a. [*pointing to the vacant chair*] May I suggest that you flop on that one while we talk?

z. [*sitting down*] Thanks very much.

a. I am not interrupting your work, I hope. There is nothing so maddening as to be talked to when you want to work.

z. Talking is part of the work in a village shop.

a. Tell me: do you ever read?

z. I used to read travels and guide books. We used to stock the Marco Polo series. I was mad about travelling. I had daydreams about the glory that was Greece, the grandeur that was Rome, and all that flapdoodle.

a. Flapdoodle!

z. Well, I suppose I shouldnt call it that; but it ended in my going to Rome and Athens. They were all right; but the old parts were half knocked down; and I couldnt see any glory or grandeur different to Cheltenham. I was glad to be home again. And I had so wanted to meet the Marco Polo man and walk about with him in the ruins by moonlight and hear him go on about them!

A. The Marco Polo man! The milkman! the postman! the muffin man! the Marco Polo man! Some frustrated poet, earning his crust by quoting scraps of verse to bring the Call of the East to dreaming telephone girls.

z. Operators.

A. Operators dont dream. Girls! girls of the golden west. Did that poor devil never bring you the Call of the East?

z. I'd read about it in novels and seen it on the films. They were all about moony drunkards and sheeks and the sort of girls that go dotty about them. I went right round the world to see the reality. Pretty places, of course; but the heat! and the mosquitoes! and the smells!! Travelling just destroyed the world for me as I imagined it. Give me this village all the time.

A. Had you no thrill when you stood somewhere where a poet had said 'Stop; for thy tread is on an empire's dust'?

z. A guide, you mean. Theyd take the poetry out of anything; and all the time youre thinking what you ought to give them. If you fancy empires' dusts and all that sort of thing you should meet our vicar and start him talking about our standing stones, and the barrows on the downs, and the Mound. Every grain of our dust, he says, is full of history. Same everywhere, I expect.

A. Are you married?

z. No. Why? Have you any intentions?

A. Dont be in a hurry. Weve known each other less than ten minutes.

z. How much better do you think you will know me when we have talked for twenty years?

A. That is profoundly true. Still, I must think it over.

z. Nobody would ever marry if they thought it over. Youve got to take your chance, no matter how long you think.

A. You are in a hurry.

z. Well, I am past the age at which girls marry here, though I'm the pick of this village. Thats because I thought all my offers over. So I have made up my mind to take the next man that asks me, provided he's reasonably suitable.

A. Do I strike you as being reasonably suitable?

z. Well, I think I have the sort of commonsense you need to keep you straight. And you being a widower know what to expect from a woman. An inexperienced man expects the earth.

A. How do you know that I am a widower?

z. You told me.

A. Did I? When did I tell you?

z. Never mind. You did. I have noticed you have a bad memory; but I have a very good one; so it wont matter.

A. Steady. Steady. I have not yet made myself liable to an action for breach of promise.

z. Dont be afraid. I'm not that sort. We dont consider it respectable here.

A. Should I get any money with you? Do you own the shop?

z. No. All the money I ever had I blued on a trip round the world. But Mrs Ward is getting too old for the business: she couldnt run it now without me. If you could afford to buy her an annuity she'd sell it.

A. I dont know how much annuities cost.

z. You will find it in Whitaker's almanac.

A. This is rather upsetting. Somehow I have always taken it for granted that when I married again I'd marry a woman with money.

z. Oh, that wouldnt suit you at all. She'd want to spend it going into society and travelling about. How could you bear that sort of life? you that never spoke to anyone on the ship and wouldnt take any part in their games and dances! When it got about that you were the Marco Polo man – the man of all our dreams as you might say – I made a bet that I'd get you to talk to me; and I had all the trouble in the world to win it.

A. Do you mean to say that we have met before? That you were on that trip round the world?

z. Of course I do. But you never notice anything. Youre always reading or writing. The world doesnt exist for you. You never looked at me really. Youre shy with strangers, arnt you?

A. I am absolutely certain I never spoke to any woman on that ship. If I talk to women they always want to marry me.

z. Well, there you are, you see! The moment I set eyes on you I said to myself, 'Now thats the sort of man that would suit me as a husband.' I'd have said it even if you hadnt been the Marco Polo man.

A. Love at first sight: what?

z. Oh no. You know, if I fell in love with a man I'd never marry him: he could make me so miserable. But there was something about you: I dont exactly know what; but it made me feel that I could do with you in the house; and then I could fall in love with anyone I liked without any fear of making a fool of myself. I suppose it was because you are one of the quiet sort and dont run after women.

A. How do you know I dont run after women?

z. Well, if you want to know, it's because you didnt run after me. You mightnt believe it; but men do run after me.

A. Why?

z. Oh, how do I know? They dont know, themselves. But the lot of money they spend on things they dont want merely to come in and have a look at me and a word with me, you wouldnt believe. It's worth at least twenty pounds a year to the business.

A. [*putting on his glasses and looking at her attentively for the first time*] I shouldnt call you a pretty woman.

z. Oh, I'm not pretty. But what you might call desirable, dont you think?

A. [*alarmed*] No I dont think. May I explain? I am a man of letters and a gentleman. I am accustomed to associate with ladies. That means that I am accustomed to speak under certain well understood reserves which act as a necessary protection to both parties. You are not a lady: you are a villager; but somebody has educated you – probably the Church or the local authority – to a point at which you can impose on unobservant and unwary travellers. You have had finishing lessons on the telephone which give you a distinguished articulation: you can say Th-reee fiv-v-v-e ni-n-n-n instead of theree fauv nawn. But you have not acquired any of the reserves. You say what you think. You announce all the plans that wellbred women conceal. You play with your cards on the table instead of keeping them where a lady should keep them: up your sleeve.

z. Well, wheres the harm?

A. Oh, no harm. Quite the contrary. But I feel rushed.

z. What do you mean? rushed?

A. Rushed. Precipitated. Carried to lengths I had no intention of going to.

z. Well, it gets you somewhere: doesnt it?

A. Yes; but where?

z. Here. Theres no mystery about it. Here, in a good business in a village shop in a quiet place, with me to keep it straight and look after you.

A. May I ask how much that expression 'looking after me' includes? Let me be clear on the point. As a matter of fact I possess a small property which I could sell for enough to purchase an annuity for old Mrs Williams –

Z. Ward.

A. I believe I have enough to purchase annuities for both Mrs Ward and Mrs Williams, as they are presumably both centenarians. But why on earth should I complicate the transaction by marrying you? I could pay you your present wages –

Z. Salary.

A. I beg your pardon: salary. You will retain your present position as my shopgirl.

Z. Shop assistant.

A. I beg your pardon: shop assistant. You can then make your own matrimonial arrangements, and leave me to make mine.

Z. Oh, I'll make my own matrimonial arrangements all right enough. You may depend on that.

A. Excuse me: I added 'and leave me to make mine.' Can I depend on you for that also?

Z. Well, we'll see.

A. [angrily firm] No: you will not see.

Z. Well, what?

A. I dont know what. I will not commit myself. We'll see.

Z. Just so: we'll see. It's a bargain then?

A. No: it most certainly is not a bargain. When I entered this shop half an hour ago I had not the faintest notion of buying a village shop or marrying a village maiden or any of the things you have put into my head. Have you ever read the fable of the spider and the fly?

Z. No; but I used to sing a song called the honeysuckle and the bee.

A. [resolutely] Good morning. [He makes for the door].

Z. [following him with the string bag] You are forgetting your things.

A. [taking it] Thank you.

Z. Thanks very much.

She tempts him to kiss her.

A. No!!! [he strides out].

THIRD CONVERSATION

A is now the proprietor of the shop with z as his hired assistant. The counter has been fitted with a desk at the opposite end to the post office section. At this A sits writing. He wears pepper-and-salt trousers of country cut, with an apron. He is in his shirtsleeves, and looks every inch a shopkeeper. z comes in through the post office, very fresh and matutinal.

z. Morning, boss.

A. Good morning, slave.

z. I havnt begun slaving yet. You have been at it for half an hour. Whatever on earth are you working at so hard?

A. I am making out my balance sheet.

z. Oh, you neednt do that. The accountant's clerk from Salisbury does all that when he makes out the income tax return. Youre not expected to do figures in this village. Fancy old Mrs Ward doing such a thing!

A. When I bought this shop from Mrs Ward for an annuity I found she was much cleverer at figures than I was. She should have been a moneylender.

z. She was. She lent a shilling for a penny a week.

A. That must have been between four and five hundred per cent per annum. Shylock would have blushed.

z. Whats the good of it when you have to give credit at the shop, and then lend the customers the money to pay you?

A. Mrs Ward should have gone to Geneva. International finance would have come naturally to her.

z. Thats too clever for me. Anyhow, you neednt worry over a balance sheet. The accountant will do all that for you.

A. [*rising and waving the balance sheet proudly as he comes through the counter into the public part of the shop*] This is not an accountant's balance sheet. It is a Robinson Crusoe balance sheet.

z. [*following him*] Whatever's that?

A. Crusoe drew up a balance sheet of the advantages and disadvantages of being cast away on a desert island. I am cast away in a village on the Wiltshire Downs. I am drawing up a similar balance sheet. I propose to read it to you as far as I have got. [*He takes one of the customer's chairs*]. You can remind me of anything I have forgotten.

z. Lets have it. [*She takes the other chair*].

a. I begin with the credit entries.

z. Things to your own credit, you mean?

a. No, to the credit of village shopkeeping as a way of life.

z. Oh, you are silly, boss.

a. That is a disrespectful remark. As such, it should not be made to a boss by his slave. The understanding on which I raised your salary when I engaged you as my assistant was that our relations should be completely conventional and businesslike on your side, however I might occasionally forget myself.

z. [*rising*] Very well: you can keep your balance sheet to yourself. I will go on with the telephone call book.

a. You will do nothing of the sort. You will do what I tell you to do. That is what I pay you for. Sit down again [*She does so*]. Now listen. [*He takes up his manuscript and reads*]. Item: I have sharpened my faculties, and greatly improved in observation and mathematics.

z. Couldnt you put it into shorter words? What does it mean?

a. It means that formerly I always took what money was given me without condescending to count it or attempting to calculate it. I can now both calculate and count quite rapidly. Formerly I made no distinction between grades of butter and eggs. To me an egg was an egg: butter was butter. I now make critical distinctions of the greatest subtlety, and value them in terms of money. I am forced to admit that the shopkeeper is enormously superior to the Marco Polo man, and than I have learnt more in three months in this shop that I learnt in three years in Oxford.

z. I cant believe that about the learning. But see how your manners have improved!

a. My manners!!

z. Yes. Why, on that ship you hadnt a word to throw to a dog; and if anyone came near you you shrank up into yourself like a hedgehog, afraid that they didnt belong to your class and wanted to speak to you without an introduction. Now it's a pleasure to hear you say 'Good morning; and what can I do for you today, Mrs Burrell?' and 'Have you noticed the cauliflowers today, maam? Not a touch of frost on them!' and 'Sparrowgrass very good today, my lady, if you would be wanting some.'

A. I positively deny that I have ever in my life called asparagus sparrowgrass to an educated customer. Of course, when people are too ignorant to know the names of what they eat, that is another matter.

z. Well, anyhow, your manners have improved, havnt they?

A. I dont know. I know that they are no longer disinterested and sincere.

z. No more they never used to be. Never easy with anybody. Now you are hail fellow well met, as you might say, with everybody.

A. The world has become a world of customers. Let me write that down. [*He pencils on the back of his balance sheet*] 'Manners will never be universally good until every person is every other person's customer.'

z. Youre not a real shopkeeper yet, boss. All you want is to find something clever to write.

A. Well, why not? Find enough clever things to say, and you are a Prime Minister. Write them down, and you are a Shakespear.

z. Yes; but who wants to be a Prime Minister or a Shakespear? Youve got to make a living.

A. Well, am I not making a living? I am no poorer than when I bought the shop.

z. But if the money goes as fast as it comes you cant save anything.

A. I loathe saving. It turns human nature sour. 'Cast your bread upon the waters; and it will return to you after many days.'

z. And how are you to live for the many days with nothing to eat?

A. I dont know. One does, somehow. Stop asking questions; and let us get on with the balance sheet.

z. I speak for your good.

A. [*rising wrathfully*] The most offensive liberty one human being can possibly take with another. What business is it of yours?

z. [*rising and facing him*] If you wont think for yourself somebody else must think for you. It's my business as much as yours.

A. Oh, indeed! Who does this shop belong to? I mean to whom does this shop belong?

z. I get my living out of it, dont I. If it shuts up what becomes of me?

A. Well, if you come to that, what becomes of me? You can get another job. I very greatly doubt whether anyone would give me one. [*Calming down*] Can you not be content with the fact that the shop is making enough to support two people? [*He resumes his seat*].

z. Aye; but suppose it had to support three people!

a. Why suppose? It hasnt: thats all.

z. It's not all. If you marry a stranger there will be three. And what about the children?

a. The remedy is simple. I shall not marry.

z. You dont know.

a. Neither do you.

z. Yes I do. You have married once; and you will marry twice. Somebody will snap you up. You are that sort of man.

a. If a woman snaps me up she must take the consequences. She must assist in the shop. And you will get the sack.

z. Oh, you are tiresome. [*She sits down, discouraged*]. But you see my point, at all events.

a. No. What point?

z. Well, that it's really cheaper to keep a wife than to pay an assistant. Let alone that you dont have to live a single life.

a. You can get rid of an assistant if she doesnt suit. You cant get rid of a wife.

z. If people thought that way, theyd never get married.

a. Precisely.

z. In this life you have to take chances.

a. I have taken them, and escaped.

z. You wont escape here. We dont hold with bachelors here.

a. You cant do without a general shop here, nor a post office. While I command both I am in an impregnable strategic position.

z. Well, I dont like to say it; but people are beginning to talk.

a. Beginning! When did they ever stop?

z. Oh, theres no use talking to you.

a. Not the slightest.

z. Oh well then, take a month's notice. [*She rises*].

a. A month's notice!

z. Yes: a month's notice.

a. A month's notice because I refuse to marry some ridiculous village maiden or illiterate widow with whom I could not hold a moment's conversation!

z. Wives are not for conversation: thats for visitors. Youve had plenty of conversation with me.

a. Leave yourself out of this conversation, please.

z. Oh, very well. A month's notice.

a. Dont say that again. Utter nonsense. What have you to complain of? You are quite well off here. I purposely pay

you ten pounds a year more than you could get anywhere
else.

z. Why?

a. What do you mean, why?

z. Why do you pay me ten pounds more than you could get another
assistant for?

a. Heaven only knows!

z. [*in a fury*] I'll go this very day. I'll go this very minute. You can
keep my month. You dont know when youre well off. Youre
selfish. I dont wonder your wife died. Did she die mad?

a. [*gravely*] As a matter of fact, she did. I am one of those unlucky
men who draw the black chances in the lottery of marriage.

z. [*remorsefully*] Oh, I didnt know: I didnt indeed. I was only
joking. [*She sits again*] I wouldnt have said it for the world if I'd
known.

a. Never mind: I know you didnt mean it. By the way, I made an
inconsiderate remark which hurt you. I did not intend that. I
should have told you seriously that I pay you ten pounds more
than the market rate because I value your services in the
shop, and wish to offer you every inducement to stay here
permanently.

z. Ten pounds extra, to stay all my life here as a single woman!

a. Not necessarily. You can get married if you wish.

z. Who to?

a. To whom? Oh, anyone.

z. Anyone in the village is good enough for me; but nobody in the
village is good enough for you: is that it?

a. Dont lose your temper again.

z. I will if I like. And if you knew how near I was to putting a couple
of extra words in, youd perhaps realize that a woman wants
something more in life than a job and a salary.

a. I know that perfectly well. There is one thing we are all out for
when we are young.

z. And what is that, pray?

a. Trouble, adventure, hardship, care, disappointment, doubt,
misery, danger, and death.

z. Not me, thank you. All I want is a husband and the usual
consequences.

a. The same thing. Marriage is the village form of all these
adventures.

z. Oh, why dont you take a more cheerful view of life?

A. I have learnt not to expect too much from life. That is the secret of real cheerfulness, because I am always getting agreeable surprises instead of desolating disappointments.

z. Well, your second marriage may be an agreeable surprise, maynt it?

A. What, exactly, do you mean by my second marriage? I have only been married once. I mean I have been married only once.

z. Well, look here? Straight, now? Is there any man in this village that would be suitable to me now that I have got used to you?

A. My dear: men are all alike.

z. You mean it will make no difference to me who I marry.

A. Very little, I am afraid.

z. And women are all alike too, arnt they?

A. [suspicious] What are you getting at?

z. If it doesnt matter who anybody marries, then it doesnt matter who I marry and it doesnt who you marry.

A. Whom, not who.

z. Oh, speak English: youre not on the telephone now. What I mean is that if it doesnt matter to me it doesnt matter to you either.

A. You admit, then, that it doesnt matter?

z. No I dont. It's a lie.

A. Oh!

z. Dont 'oh' me. All men are not alike to me. There are men – and good nice men, too – that I wouldnt let touch me. But when I saw you on the ship I said to myself 'I could put up with him.'

A. Not at all. You told me just now that you said something quite different. I believe you really said something much more rapturous. Being rather a futile sort of person I attract vigorous women like you.

z. When you looked at me out of the corner of your eye – you looked at all the women out of the corner of your eye in spite of your keeping yourself so much to yourself – did you never say 'I could put up with her'?

A. No. I said 'Damn that woman: she wont stop talking to me and interrupting my work.'

z. Well, I tell you we were made for oneanother. It maynt be as plain to you as to me yet; but if it's plain to me there must be something in it; for I'm never wrong when I see a thing quite plain. I dont believe youd ever have bought this shop and given up being a gentleman if I hadnt been here.

A. Now that you mention it I believe that is true. You were one of the amenities of the estate.

z. Well, I might be one of the amenities of the estate of holy matrimony, mightnt I?

A. Take care. You may find what you are trying to do easier than you think. About five per cent of the human race consists of positive masterful acquisitive people like you, obsessed with some passion which they must gratify at all hazards. The rest let them have their own way because they have neither the strength nor the courage to resist, or because the things the masterful ones want seem trifling beside the starry heavens and the destiny of Man. I am not one of the masterful ones. I am not worth marrying. Any woman could marry me if she took trouble enough.

z. Thats just what I'm afraid of. If I let you out of my sight for a month I might find you married to someone else at the end of it. Well, I'm taking no chances. I dont set up to be masterful: I dont like selfish uppish domineering people any more than you do; but I must and will have you; and thats all about it.

A. Well, you already have me – as an employer. And you are independent of me, and can leave me if you are not satisfied.

z. How can I be satisfied when I cant lay my hands on you? I work for you like a slave for a month on end; and I would have to work harder as your wife than I do now; but there come times when I want to get hold of you in my arms, every bit of you; and when I do I'll give you something better to think about than the starry heavens, as you call them. Youll find that you have senses to gratify as well as fine things to say.

A. Senses! You dont know what youre talking about. Look around you. Here in this shop I have everything that can gratify the senses: apples, onions, and acid drops; pepper and mustard; cosy comforters and hot water bottles. Through the window I delight my eyes with the old church and market place, built in the days when beauty came naturally from the hands of mediæval craftsmen. My ears are filled with delightful sounds, from the cooing of doves and the humming of bees to the wireless echoes of Beethoven and Elgar. My nose can gloat over our sack of fresh lavender or our special sixpenny Eau de Cologne when the smell of rain on dry earth is denied me. My senses are saturated with satisfactions of all sorts. But when I am full to the neck with onions and acid drops; when I am so fed up with mediæval architecture that I had rather die than look at another cathedral; when all I desire is rest from sensation, not more of it, what use will my senses be to me if the starry heavens still seem no more than a senseless avalanche of lumps of stone and wisps of gas – if the destiny of Man holds out no higher hope to him than the final extinction and annihilation of so mischievous and miserable a creature?

z. We dont bother about all that in the village.

A. Yes you do. Our best seller here is Old Moore's Almanack; and next to it comes Napoleon's Book of Fate. Old Mrs Ward would never have sold the shop to me if she had not become persuaded that the Day of Judgment is fixed for the seventh of August next.

z. I dont believe such nonsense. Whats it all got to do with you and me?

A. You are inexperienced. You dont know. You are the dupe of thoughtless words like sensuality, sensuousness, and all the rest of the twaddle of the Materialists. I am not a Materialist: I am a poet: and I know that to be in your arms will not gratify my senses at all. As a matter of mere physical sensation you will find the bodily contacts to which you are looking forward neither convenient nor decorous.

z. Oh, dont talk like that. You mustnt let yourself think about it like that.

A. You must always let yourself think about everything. And you must think about everything as it is, not as it is talked about. Your secondhand gabble about gratifying my senses is only your virgin innocence. We shall get quite away from the world of sense. We shall light up for oneanother a lamp in the holy of holies in the temple of life; and the lamp will make its veil transparent. Aimless lumps of stone blundering through space will become stars singing in their spheres. Our dull purposeless village existence will become one irresistible purpose and nothing else. An extraordinary delight and an intense love will seize us. It will last hardly longer than the lightning flash which turns the black night into infinite radiance. It will be dark again before you can clear the light out of your eyes; but you will have seen; and for ever after you will think about what you have seen and not gabble catchwords invented by the wasted virgins that walk in darkness. It is to give ourselves this magic moment that we feel that we must and shall hold oneanother in our arms; and when the moment comes, the world of the senses will vanish; and for us there will be nothing ridiculous, nothing uncomfortable, nothing unclean, nothing but pure paradise.

z. Well, I am glad you take a nice view of it; for now I come to think of it I never could bear to be nothing more to a man than a lollipop. But you mustnt expect too much.

A. I shall expect more than you have ever dreamt of giving, in spite of the boundless audacity of women. What great men would ever have been married if the female nobodies who snapped them up had known the enormity of their own presumption? I believe they all thought they were going to refine, to educate, to make real gentlemen of their husbands. What do you intend to make of me, I wonder?

z. Well, I have made a decent shopkeeper of you already, havnt I? But you neednt be afraid of my not appreciating you. I want a fancy sort of husband, not a common villager that any woman could pick up. I shall be proud of you. And now Ive nailed you, I wonder at my own nerve.

A. So do I.

z. I'm not a bit like that, you know, really. Something above me and beyond me drove me on. Thats why I know it will be all right. Dont be afraid. I cant make a fine speech about it like you; but it will be all right. I promise you that.

A. Very well. Go round to the rectory; and put up the banns. And tell the rector's wife that we got in some prime artichokes this morning. She's fond of artichokes.

z. You are sure you feel happy about it?

A. I dont know what I feel about it. Go and do as you are told; and dont ask ridiculous questions.

The telephone rings. She hastens to answer it.

z. Number, please? . . . Oh, an order. Thanks very much. . . . Yes: we have some very fine artichokes just in this morning. . . . Thanks very much: they shall be sent round directly. Oh; and theres something else – are you there? . . . Sorry to detain you: could I speak to the rector? . . . Yes: it's rather particular. It's about banns . . . banns . . . BANNS: b for beauty, a for audacity, two enns for nonsense, and s for singing. . . . Yes, banns: thats right. . . . Who are the what? . . . Oh, the parties! Of course. Well, it's –

The Six of Calais

A Medieval War Story

Composition begun 13 May 1934; completed 16 May 1934. First published in German translation, as *Die Sechs von Calais*, in the *Neue Freie Presse* (Vienna), 25 December 1934. First published in English in *The Simpleton, The Six, and The Millionairess*, 1936. First presented at the Open Air Theatre, Regent's Park, London, on 17 July 1934.

The Black Prince   *Hubert Gregg*
John of Gaunt   *Leonard Thorne*
Edward III   *Charles Carson*
A Court Lady   *Greer Garson*
Queen Philippa of Hainault   *Phyllis Neilson-Terry*

Eustache de St Pierre }   { *Vincent Sternroyd*
Piers de Rosty   { *Leonard Shepherd*
Piers de Wissant }   The { *Clement Hamelin*
Jean d'Aire   Six { *Frank Tickle*
Gilles d'Oudebolle }   { *Derek Prentice*
Jacques de Wissant }   { *E. S. Kenney*

Also Sir Walter Manny, Lord Derby, Lord Northampton, Lord Arundel, and other noblemen, courtiers, three men-at-arms, soldiers, etc.

Period – A.D. 4th August 1347
Scene – *Before the Walls of Calais on the Last Day of the Siege. Camp of King Edward III*

✸ PREFATORY TO ✸
THE SIX OF CALAIS

The most amusing thing about the first performance of this little play was the exposure it elicited of the quaint illiteracy of our modern London journalists. Their only notion of a king was a pleasant and highly respectable gentleman in a bowler hat and Victorian beard, shaking hands affably with a blushing football team. To them a queen was a dignified lady, also Victorian as to her coiffure, graciously receiving bouquets from excessively washed children in beautiful new clothes. Such were their mental pictures of Great Edward's grandson and his queen Philippa. They were hurt, shocked, scandalized at the spectacle of a medieval soldier-monarch publicly raging and cursing, crying and laughing, asserting his authority with thrasonic ferocity and the next moment blubbering like a child in his wife's lap or snarling like a savage dog at a dauntless and defiant tradesman: in short, behaving himself like an unrestrained human being in a very trying situation instead of like a modern constitutional monarch on parade keeping up an elaborate fiction of living in a political vacuum and moving only when his ministers pull his strings. Edward Plantagenet the Third had to pull everybody else's strings and pull them pretty hard, his father having been miserably killed for taking his job too lightly. But the journalist critics knew nothing of this. A King Edward who did not behave like the son of King Edward the Seventh seemed unnatural and indecent to them, and they rent their garments accordingly.

They were perhaps puzzled by the fact that the play has no moral whatever. Every year or so I hurl at them a long play full of insidious propaganda, with a moral in every line. They never discover what I am driving at: it is always too plainly and domestically stated to be grasped by their subtle and far flung minds; but they feel that I am driving at something: probably something they had better not agree with if they value their livelihoods. A play of mine in which I am not driving at anything more than a playwright's direct business is as inconceivable by them as a medieval king.

Now a playwright's direct business is simply to provide the theatre with a play. When I write one with the additional attraction of providing the twentieth century with an up-to-date religion or the like, that luxury is thrown in gratuitously; and the play, simply as a play, is not necessarily either the better or the worse for it. What, then, is a play simply as a play?

Well, it is a lot of things. Life as we see it is so haphazard that it is only by picking out its key situations and arranging them in their significant order (which is never how they actually occur) that it can be made intelligible. The high-browed dramatic poet wants to make it intelligible and sublime. The farce writer wants to make it funny. The melodrama merchant wants to make it as exciting as some people find the police news. The pornographer wants to make it salacious. All interpreters of life in action, noble or ignoble, find their instrument in the theatre; and all the academic definitions of a play are variations of this basic function.

Yet there is one function hardly ever alluded to now, though it was made much too much of from Shakespear's time to the middle of the nineteenth century. As I write my plays it is continually in my mind and very much to my taste. The function is to provide an exhibition of the art of acting. A good play with bad parts is not an impossibility; but it is a monstrosity. A bad play with good parts will hold the stage and be kept alive by the actors for centuries after the obsolescence of its mentality would have condemned it to death without them. A great deal of the British Drama, from Shakespear to Bulwer Lytton, is as dead as mutton, and quite unbearable except when heroically acted; yet Othello and Richelieu can still draw hard money into the pay boxes; and The School For Scandal revives again and again with unabated vigor. Rosalind can always pull As You Like It through in spite of the sententious futility of the melancholy Jaques; and Millamant, impossible as she is, still produces the usual compliments to the wit and style of Congreve, who thought that syphilis and cuckoldry and concupiscent old women are things to be laughed at.

The Six of Calais is an acting piece and nothing else. As it happened, it was so well acted that in the eighteenth century all the talk would have been about Siddons as Philippa. But the company got no thanks except from the audience: the critics were prostrated with shock, damn their eyes!

I have had to improve considerably on the story as told by that absurd old snob Froissart, who believed that 'to rob and pill was a good life' if the robber was at least a baron. He made a very poor job of it in my opinion.

ON THE HIGH SEAS,
28 May 1935

A.D. 4th August 1347. Before the walls of Calais on the last day of the siege. The pavilion of Edward III, King of England, is on your left as you face the walls. The pavilion of his consort Philippa of Hainault is on your right. Between them, near the King's Pavilion, is a two-seated chair of state for public audiences. Crowds of tents cover the background; but there is a clear way in the middle through the camp to the great gate of the city with its drawbridge still up and its flag still flying.

The Black Prince, aged 17, arrives impetuously past the Queen's tent, a groom running after him.

THE PRINCE. Here is the King's pavilion without a single attendant to announce me. What can the matter be?

A child's scream is heard from the royal pavilion; and John of Gaunt, aged 7, dashes out and is making for his mother's tent when the Prince seizes him.

THE PRINCE. How now, Johnny? Whats the matter?

JOHN [*struggling*] Let me go. Father is in a frightful wax.

THE PRINCE. I shall be in a wax myself presently. [*Releasing him*] Off with you to mother. [*The child takes refuge in the Queen's pavilion*].

THE KING'S VOICE. Grrr! Yah! Why was I not told? Gogswoons, why was I not told? [*Edward III, aged 35, dashes from his pavilion, foaming*]. Out! [*The groom flies for his life*]. How long have you been here? They never tell me anything. I might be a dog instead of a king.

THE PRINCE [*about to kneel*] Majesty —

THE KING. No no: enough of that. Your news. Anything from Scotland? Anything from Wales?

THE PRINCE. I —

THE KING [*not waiting for the answers*] The state of things here is past words. The wrath of God and all his saints is upon this expedition.

THE PRINCE. I hope not, sir. I —

THE KING [*raging on*] May God wither and blast this accursed town! You would have thought that these dogs would have come out of their kennels and grovelled for mercy at my summons. Am I not their lawful king, ha?

THE PRINCE. Undoubtedly, sir. They —

THE KING. They have held me up for twelve months! A whole year!! My business ruined! My plans upset! My money exhausted! Death, disease, mutiny, a dog's life here in the field winter and summer. The bitch's bastard who is in command of their walls came to demand terms from me! to demand terms!!! looked me straight in the eyes with his head up as if I — I, his king! were dirt beneath his feet. By God, I will have that head: I will kick it to my dogs to eat. I will chop his insolent herald into four quarters —

THE PRINCE [shocked] Oh no, sir: not a herald; you cannot do that.

THE KING. They have driven me to such extremity that I am capable of cutting all the heralds in Christendom into their quarterings. [He sits down in his chair of state and suddenly becomes ridiculously sentimental]. I have not told you the worst. Your mother, the Queen, my Philippa, is here: here! Edward, in her delicate state of health. Even that did not move them. They want her to die: they are trying to murder her and our innocent unborn child. Think of that, boy: oh, think of that [he almost weeps].

THE PRINCE. Softly, father: that is not their fault: it is yours.

THE KING. Would you make a jest of this? If it is not their fault it shall be their misfortune; for I will have every man, woman, and child torn to pieces with red hot pincers for it.

THE PRINCE. Truly, dear Sir, you have great cause to be annoyed; but in sober earnest how does the matter stand? They must be suffering the last extremity of famine. Their walls may hold out; but their stomachs cannot. Cannot you offer them some sort of terms to end the business? Money is running short. Time is running short. You only make them more desperate by threatening them. Remember: it is good policy to build a bridge of silver for a flying foe.

THE KING. Do I not know it? Have I not been kind, magnanimous? Have I not done all that Christian chivalry could require of me? And they abuse my kindness: it only encourages them: they despise me for it.

THE PRINCE. What terms have you offered them?

THE KING. I have not threatened the life of a single knight. I have said that no man of gentle condition and noble blood shall be denied quarter and ransom. It was their knightly duty to make a show of arms against me. But [*rising wrathfully*] these base rascals of burgesses: these huckstering hounds of merchants who have made this port of Calais a nest of pirates: these usurers and tradesmen: these rebel curs who have dared to take up arms against their betters: am I to pardon their presumption? I should be false to our order, to Christendom, if I did not make a signal example.

THE PRINCE. By all means, sir. But what have you demanded?

THE KING. Six of the most purseproud of their burgesses, as they call themselves – by God, they begin to give themselves the airs of barons – six of them are to come in their shirts with halters round their necks for me to hang in the sight of all their people. [*Raising his voice again and storming*] They shall die the dog's death they deserve. They shall –

A court lady comes in.

THE COURT LADY. Sir: the Queen. Sssh!

THE KING [*subsiding to a whisper*] The Queen! Boy: not a word here. Her condition: she must not be upset: she takes these things so amiss: be discreet, for heaven's sake.

Queen Philippa, aged 33, comes from her pavilion, attended.

THE QUEEN. Dear child: welcome.

THE PRINCE. How do you, lady mother? [*He kisses her hand*].

THE KING [*solicitously*] Madam: are you well wrapped up? Is it wise to come into the cold air here? Had they better not bring a brazier and some cushions, and a hot drink – a posset –

THE QUEEN [*curtseying*] Sir: beloved: dont fuss. I am very well; and the air does me good. [*To the Prince*] You must cheer up your father, my precious. He will fret about my health when it is his own that needs care. I have borne him eleven children; and St Anne be my witness they have cost less looking after than this one big soldier, the greatest baby of them all. [*To the King*] Have you put on your flannel belly band, dearest?

THE KING. Yes, yes, yes, my love: do not bother about me. Think of yourself and our child –

THE QUEEN. Oh, leave me to take care of myself and the child. I am no maternal malingreuse I promise you. And now, sir sonny, tell me all your news. I –

She is interrupted by a shrill trumpet call.

THE KING. What is that? What now?

John of Gaunt, who has been up to the town gates to see the fun, runs in excitedly.

JOHN OF GAUNT [*bending his knee very perfunctorily*] Sire: they have surrendered: the drawbridge is down. The six old men have come out in their shirts with ropes round their necks.

THE KING [*clouting him*] Sssh! Hold your tongue, you young devil.

THE QUEEN. Old men in their shirts in this weather!! They will catch cold.

THE KING. It is nothing, madam my love: only the ceremony of surrender. You must go in: it is not fitting that these half naked men should be in your presence. I will deal with them.

THE QUEEN. Do not keep them too long in the cold, dearest sir.

THE KING [*uxoriously waving her a kiss*] My love!

The Queen goes into her pavilion; and a group of noblemen attendant on the King, including Sir Walter Manny and the Lords Derby, Northampton, and Arundel, issue from their tents and assemble behind the chair of state, where they are joined by the Black Prince, who stands at the King's right hand and takes charge of John of Gaunt.

THE KING. Now for these swine, these bloodsuckers. They shall learn — [*shouting*] Fetch me these fellows in here. Drag them in. I'll teach them to hold me up here for twelve months. I'll —

The six burgesses, hustled by men-at-arms, enter in their shirts and halters, each carrying a bunch of massive iron keys. Their leader, Eustache de St Pierre, kneels at the King's feet. Four of his fellow victims, Piers de Wissant, Jacques de Wissant, Jean d'Aire, and Gilles d'Oudebolle, kneel in pairs behind him, and, following his example, lay their keys on the ground. They are deeply cast down, bearing themselves like condemned men, yet maintaining a melancholy dignity. Not so the sixth, Piers de Rosty (nicknamed Hardmouth), the only one without a grey or white beard. He has an extraordinary dogged chin with a few bristles on it. He deliberately separates himself from the rest by passing behind the royal chair to the King's right and planting himself stiffly erect in an attitude of intense recalcitrance. The King, scowling fiercely at St Pierre and the rest, does not notice this until Peter flings down his keys with a violence which suggests that he would very willingly have brained Edward with them.

THE KING. On your knees, hound.

PETER. I am a good dog, but not of your kennel, Neddy.

THE KING. Neddy!!!!

PETER. Order your own curs: I am a free burgess and take commands from nobody.

Before the amazed monarch can retort, Eustache appeals to Peter.

EUSTACHE. Master Peter: if you have no regard for yourself, remember that our people, our wives and children, are at the mercy of this great king.

PETER. You mistake him for his grandfather. Great! [*He spits*].

EUSTACHE. Is this your promise to be patient?

PETER. Why waste civilities on him, Master Mayor? He can do no worse than hang us; and as to the town, *I* would have burnt it to the last brick, and every man, woman and child along with it, sooner than surrender. I came here to make up the tale of six to be hanged. Well, he can hang me; but he shall not outface me. I am as good a dog as he, any day in the week.

THE PRINCE. Fie, fellow! is this a way for one of thy degree to speak to an anointed king? Bear thyself as befits one of thy degree in the royal presence, or by Holy Paul —

PETER. You know how we have borne ourselves in his royal presence these twelve months. We have made some of you skip. Famine and not you, has beaten us. Give me a square meal and a good sword and stake all on a fair single combat with this big bully, or his black whelp here if he is afraid of me; and we shall see which is the better dog of the two.

THE KING. Drag him to his knees. Hamstring him if he resists.

Three men-at-arms dash at Peter and drag him to his knees. They take his halter and tie his ankles and wrists with it. Then they fling him on his side, where he lies helpless.

THE KING. And so, Master Burgess —

PETER. Bow-wow-wow!

THE KING [*furious*] Gag him. Gogswoons, gag him.

They tear a piece of linen from the back of his shirt, and bind his mouth with it. He barks to the last moment. John of Gaunt laughs ecstatically at his performance, and sets off some of the soldiers.

THE KING. If a man laughs I will have him flayed alive.

Dead silence.

THE KING. And now, fellows, what have ye to say to excuse your hardy and stubborn resistance for all these months to me, your king?

EUSTACHE. Sir, we are not fellows. We are free burgesses of this great city.

THE KING. Free burgesses! Are you still singing that song? Well, I will bend the necks of your burgesses when the hangman has broken yours. Am I not your overlord? Am I not your anointed king?

EUSTACHE. That is your claim, sir; and you have made it good by force of arms. We must submit to you and to God.

THE KING. Leave God out of this! What hast thou or thy like to do with God?

EUSTACHE. Nothing, sir: we would not so far presume. But with due respect to your greatness I would humbly submit to your Majesty that God may have something to do with us, seeing that he created us all alike and redeemed us by the blood of his beloved son.

THE KING [to the Prince] Can you make head or tail of this, boy? Is he accusing me of impiety? If he is, by God –

EUSTACHE. Sir, is it for me to accuse you of anything? Here we kneel in the dust before you, naked and with the ropes on our necks with which you will presently send us into the presence of our maker and yours. [His teeth chatter].

THE KING. Ay: you may well tremble. You have cause.

EUSTACHE. Yes: I tremble; and my teeth chatter: the few I have left. But you gentlemen that see our miserable plight, I call on your generosity as noblemen, on your chivalry as good knights, to bear witness for us that it is the cold of the morning and our naked condition that shakes us. We kneel to implore your King's mercy for our wretched and starving townsfolk, not for ourselves.

THE KING. Whose fault is it that they are starving? They have themselves to thank. Why did they not open their gates to me? Why did they take arms against their anointed king? Why should I have mercy on them or on you?

EUSTACHE. Sir: one is merciful not for reasons, but for the love of God, at whose hand we must all sue for mercy at the end of our days.

THE KING. You shall not save yourself by preaching. What right have you to preach? It is for churchmen and learned divines to speak of these mysteries, not for tradesmen and usurers. I'll teach you to rebel against your betters, whom God has appointed to keep you in obedience and loyalty. You are traitors; and as traitors you shall die. Thank my mercy that you are spared the torments that traitors and rebels suffer in England. [Rising] Away with them to the hangman; and let our trumpeters summon the townspeople to the walls to take warning from their dangling corpses.

The three men-at-arms begin to lift Peter. The others lay hands on his five colleagues.

THE KING. No: let that hound lie. Hanging is too good for him.

The Queen hurries in with her ladies in great concern. The men-at-arms release the burgesses irresolutely. It is evident that the Queen's arrival washes out all the King's orders.

THE QUEEN. Sir, what is this they tell me?

THE KING [*hurrying across to intercept her*] Madam: this is no place for you. I pray you, retire. The business is one in which it becomes you not to meddle.

THE QUEEN [*evading him and passing on to inspect the burgesses*] But these gentlemen. They are almost naked. It is neither seemly nor sufficient. They are old: they are half frozen: they should be in their beds.

THE KING. They soon will be. Leave us, madam. This is business of State. They are suffering no more than they deserve. I beg and pray you – I command you –

THE QUEEN. Dear sir, your wishes are my law and your commands my duty. But these gentlemen are very cold.

THE KING. They will be colder presently; so you need not trouble about that. Will it please you, madam, to withdraw at once?

THE QUEEN. Instantly, my dear lord. [*To Eustache*] Sir: when his Majesty has ended his business with you, will you and your friends partake of some cups of hot wine in my pavilion? You shall be furnished with gowns.

THE KING [*choking with wrath*] Hot w–!

EUSTACHE. Alas, madam, when the King has ended his business with us we shall need nothing but our coffins. I also beg you to withdraw and hasten our despatch to that court where we shall not be held guilty for defending our hearths and homes to the last extremity. The King will not be baulked of his revenge; and we are shriven and ready.

THE QUEEN. Oh, you mistake, sir: the King is incapable of revenge: my husband is the flower of chivalry.

EUSTACHE. You little know your husband, madam. We know better what to expect from Edward Plantagenet.

THE KING [*coming to him threateningly past his consort*] Ha! do you, Master Merchant? You know better than the Queen! You and your like know what to expect from your lords and rulers! Well, this time you shall not be disappointed. You have guessed aright. You shall hang, every man of you, in your shirts, to make mirth for my horseboys and their trulls.

THE QUEEN. Oh no –

THE KING [*thundering*] Madam: I forbid you to speak. I bade you go: you would not; and now you shall see what I would have spared you had you been obedient. By God, I will be master in my own house and king in my own camp. Take these fellows out and hang them in their white beards.

The King takes his place on his chair of state with his arms folded implacably. The Queen follows him slowly and desolately. She takes her place beside him. The dead silence is very trying.

THE QUEEN [*drooping in tears and covering her face with her hands*] Oh!

THE KING [*flinching*] No no no no NO. Take her away.

THE QUEEN. Sir: I have been always a great trouble to you. I have asked you for a thousand favors and graces and presents. I am impatient and ungrateful, ever asking, asking, asking. Have you ever refused me even once?

THE KING. Well, is that a reason why I should give and grant, grant and give, for ever? Am I never to have my own way?

THE QUEEN. Oh, dearest sir, when next I ask you for a great thing, refuse me: teach me a lesson. But this is such a little thing. [*Heartbroken*] I cannot bear your refusing me a little thing.

THE KING. A little thing! You call this a little thing!

THE QUEEN. A very very little thing, sir. You are the King: you have at your disposal thousands of lives: all our lives from the noblest to the meanest. All the lives in that city are in your hand to do as you will with in this your hour of victory: it is as if you were God himself. You said once that you would lead ten kings captive to my feet. Much as I have begged from you I have never asked for my ten kings. I ask only for six old merchants, men beneath your royal notice, as my share of the spoils of your conquest. Their ransom will hardly buy me a new girdle; and oh, dear sir, you know that my old one is becoming too strait for me. Will you keep me begging so?

THE KING. I see very well that I shall not be allowed my own way. [*He begins to cry*].

THE QUEEN [*throwing her arms round him*] Oh, dear sir, you know I would die to spare you a moment's distress. There, there, dearest! [*She pets him*].

THE KING [*blubbering*] I am never allowed to do anything I want. I might as well be a dog as a king. You treat me like a baby.

THE QUEEN. Ah, no: you are the greatest of kings to me, the noblest of men, my dearest lord and my dearest dearest love. [*Throwing herself on her knees*] Listen: do as you will: I will not say another word: I ask nothing.

THE KING. No: you ask nothing because you know you will get everything. [*He rises, shouting*] Take those men out of my sight.

THE PRINCE. What shall we do with them, sir?

THE KING [*flinging himself back into his seat*] Ask the Queen. Banquet them: feast them: give them my crown, my kingdom. Give them the clothes off my back, the bread out of my mouth, only take them away. Will you go, curses on you.

The five burgesses kneel gratefully to the Queen.

EUSTACHE [*kissing her hand*] Madam: our ransom shall buy you a threefold girdle of gold and a cradle of silver.

THE KING. Aye, well, see that it does: see that it does.

The burgesses retire, bowing to the Queen, who, still on her knees, waves her hand graciously to them.

THE QUEEN. Will you not help me up, dear sir?

THE KING. Oh yes, yes [*raising her*]: you should be more careful: who knows what harm you may have done yourself flopping on your knees like that?

THE QUEEN. I have done myself no harm, dear sir; but you have done me a world of good. I have never been better nor happier in my life. Look at me. Do I not look radiant?

THE KING. And how do I look? Like a fool.

JOHN OF GAUNT. Sir: the men-at-arms want to know what they are to do with this fellow?

THE KING. Aye, I forgot him. Fetch him here.

The three men-at-arms carry Peter to the King, and fling him down. The King is now grinning. His paroxysm of tears has completely discharged his ill temper. It dawns on him that through Peter he may get even with Philippa for his recent domestic defeat.

THE QUEEN. Oh, the poor man has not even a proper shirt to wear. It is all torn: it is hardly decent.

THE KING. Look well at this man, madam. He defied me. He spat at me. There is no insult that he did not heap on me. He looked me in the face and spoke to me as if I were a scullion. I swear to you by the Holy Rood, he called me Neddy! Donkeys are called

Neddy. What have you to say now? Is he, too, to be spared and petted and fed and have a gown from you?

THE QUEEN [*going to Peter*] But he is blue with cold. I fear he is dying. Untie him. Lift him up. Take that bandage off his mouth. Fie fie! I believe it is the tail of his shirt.

THE KING. It is cleaner than his tongue.

The men-at-arms release Peter from his bonds and his gag. He is too stiff to rise. They pull him to his feet.

PETER [*as they lift him groaning and swearing*] Ah-ooh-oh-ow!

THE KING. Well? Have you learnt your lesson? Are you ready to sue for the Queen's mercy?

PETER. Yah! Henpecked! Kiss mammy!

THE KING [*chuckles*]!!

THE QUEEN [*severely*] Are you mad, Master Burgess? Do you not know that your life is in the King's hand? Do you expect me to recommend you to his mercy if you forget yourself in this unseemly fashion?

PETER. Let me tell you, madam, that I came here in no ragged shirt. I have a dozen shirts of as fine a web as ever went on your back. Is it likely that I, a master mercer, would wear aught but the best of the best to go to my grave in?

THE QUEEN. Mend your manners first, sir; and then mend your linen; or you shall have no countenance from me.

PETER. I have naught to do with you, madam, though I well see who wears the breeches in this royal household. I am not skilled in dealing with fine handsome ladies. Leave me to settle my business with your henpecked husband.

THE QUEEN. You shall suffer for this insolence. [*To the King*] Will you, my lord, stand by and hear me spoken to in this tone by a haberdasher?

THE KING [*grinning*] Nay: I am in a merciful mood this morning. The poor man is to be pitied, shivering there in his shirt with his tail torn off.

PETER. Shivering! You lie in your teeth, though you were fifty kings. No man alive shall pity Peter Hardmouth, a dog of lousy Champagne.

THE KING [*going to him*] Ha! A dog of Champagne! Oh, you must pardon this man, madam; for my grandmother hailed from that lousy province; so I also am a dog of Champagne. We know one another's bark. [*Turning on him with bristling teeth*] Eh?

PETER [*growling in his face like a dog*] Grrrr!!!

THE KING [*returning the growl chin to chin*] Grrrr!!!!!!

> *They repeat this performance, to the great scandal of the Queen, until it develops into a startling imitation of a dog fight.*

THE QUEEN [*tearing the two dogs asunder*] Oh, for shame, sir! And you, fellow: I will have you muzzled and led through the streets on a chain and lodged in a kennel.

THE KING. Be merciful, lady. I have asked you for many favors, and had them granted me too, as the world, please God, will soon have proof. Will you deny me this?

THE QUEEN. Will you mock my condition before this insolent man and before the world? I will not endure it.

THE KING. Faith, no, dearest: no mockery. But you have no skill in dealing with the dogs of lousy Champagne. We must pity this poor trembling fellow.

THE QUEEN [*angrily*] He is not trembling.

PETER. No, by all the saints in heaven and devils in hell. Well said, lass.

> *He nudges her, to her extreme indignation.*

THE KING. Hear that, dearest: he calls thee lass. Be kind to him. He is only a poor old cur who has lost half his teeth. His condition would move a heart of stone.

PETER. I may be an old cur; but if I had sworn to hang the six of us as he swore, no shrew should scold me out of it, nor any softbosomed beauty wheedle me out of it. Yah, cry baby! Give her your sword and sit in the corner with her distaff. The grey mare is the better horse here. Do your worst, dame: I like your spunk better than his snivel.

THE QUEEN [*raging*] Send him away, sir. He is too ugly; and his words are disgusting. Such objects should be kept out of my sight: would you have me bear you a monster? Take him away.

THE KING. Away with him. Hurt him not; but let him not come into the Queen's presence. Quick there. Off with him.

> *The men-at-arms lay hands on Peter, who struggles violently.*

PETER. Hands off me, spaniels. Arrr! Grrr! [*As they drag him out overpowered*] Gee-up, Neddy. [*He finishes with a spirited imitation of a donkey's bray*].

THE KING. That is how they build men in Champagne. By the Holy Rood I care not if a bit of him gets into our baby.

THE QUEEN. Oh, for shame! for shame! Have men no decency?

> *The King snatches her into his arms, laughing boisterously. The laugh*

spreads to all the soldiers and courtiers. The whole camp seems in a hilarious uproar.

THE QUEEN. No no: for shame! for shame!

The King stops her mouth with a kiss. Peter brays melodiously in the distance.

Cymbeline Refinished

A Variation on Shakespear's Ending

WITH

Foreword

Composition begun *c.* 3 December 1936; completed December 1936. Published in the *London Mercury*, February 1938. First collected in *Geneva, Cymbeline Refinished, & Good King Charles,* 1947. First presented at the Embassy Theatre, Swiss Cottage, London, on 16 November 1937.

A Captain   *Patrick Kinsella*
Philario   *Mario Francelli*
Posthumus   *Geoffrey Toone*
Iachimo   *George Hayes*
Belarius   *Earle Grey*
Arviragus   *Philip Geddes*
Caius Lucius   *Norman Wooland*
Cymbeline   *George Woodbridge*
Imogen   *Joyce Bland*
Guiderius   *Gordon Edwards*
Pisanio   *William Devlin*

Period – Britain under the Roman Occupation.
First Century B.C.

ACT V   *A Rocky Defile. A Wild Evening*

FOREWORD

The practice of improving Shakespear's plays, more especially in the matter of supplying them with what are called happy endings, is an old established one which has always been accepted without protest by British audiences. When Mr Harley Granville-Barker, following up some desperate experiments by the late William Poel, introduced the startling innovation of performing the plays in the West End of London exactly as Shakespear wrote them, there was indeed some demur; but it was expressed outside the theatre and led to no rioting. And it set on foot a new theory of Shakespearean representation. Up to that time it had been assumed as a matter of course that everyone behind the scenes in a theatre must know much better than Shakespear how plays should be written, exactly as it is believed in the Hollywood studios today that everyone in a film studio knows better than any professional playwright how a play should be filmed. But the pleasure given by Mr Granville-Barker's productions shook that conviction in the theatre; and the superstition that Shakespear's plays as written by him are impossible on the stage, which had produced a happy ending to King Lear, Cibber's Richard III, a love scene in the tomb of the Capulets between Romeo and Juliet before the poison takes effect, and had culminated in the crude literary butcheries successfully imposed on the public and the critics as Shakespear's plays by Henry Irving and Augustin Daly at the end of the last century, is for the moment heavily discredited. It may be asked then why I, who always fought fiercely against that superstition in the days when I was a journalist-critic, should perpetrate a spurious fifth act to Cymbeline, and do it too, not wholly as a literary *jeu d'esprit*, but in response to an actual emergency in the theatre when it was proposed to revive Cymbeline at no less sacred a place than the Shakespear Memorial Theatre at Stratford-upon-Avon.

Cymbeline, though one of the finest of Shakespear's later plays now on the stage, goes to pieces in the last act. In fact I mooted the point myself by thoughtlessly saying that the revival would be all right if I wrote a last act for it. To my surprise this blasphemy was received with acclamation; and as the applause, like the proposal, was not wholly jocular, the fancy began to haunt me, and persisted until I exorcised it by writing the pages which ensue.

I had a second surprise when I began by reading the authentic last act carefully through. I had not done so for many years, and had the common impression about it that it was a cobbled-up affair by several hands, including a vision in prison accompanied by scraps of quite ridiculous doggerel.

For this estimate I found absolutely no justification nor excuse. I must have got it from the last revival of the play at the old Lyceum theatre, when Irving, as Iachimo, a statue of romantic melancholy, stood dumb on the stage for hours (as it seemed) whilst the others toiled through a series of *dénouements* of crushing tedium, in which the characters lost all their vitality and individuality, and had nothing to do but identify themselves by moles on their necks, or explain why they were not dead. The vision and the verses were cut out as a matter of course; and I ignorantly thanked Heaven for it.

When I read the act as aforesaid I found that my notion that it is a cobbled-up *pasticcio* by other hands was an unpardonable stupidity. The act is genuine Shakespear to the last full stop, and late phase Shakespear in point of verbal workmanship.

The doggerel is not doggerel: it is a versified masque, in Shakespear's careless woodnotes wild, complete with Jupiter as *deus ex machina*, eagle and all, introduced, like the Ceres scene in The Tempest, to please King Jamie, or else because an irresistible fashion had set in, just as at all the great continental opera houses a ballet used to be *de rigueur*. Gounod had to introduce one into his Faust, and Wagner into his Tannhäuser, before they could be staged at the Grand Opera in Paris. So, I take it, had Shakespear to stick a masque into Cymbeline. Performed as such, with suitable music and enough pictorial splendor, it is not only entertaining on the stage, but, with the very Shakespearean feature of a comic jailor which precedes it, just the thing to save the last act.

Without it the act is a tedious string of unsurprising *dénouements* sugared with insincere sentimentality after a ludicrous stage battle. With one exception the characters have vanished and left nothing but dolls being moved about like the glass balls in the game of solitaire until they are all got rid of but one. The exception is the hero, or rather the husband of the heroine, Leonatus Posthumus. The late Charles Charrington, who with his wife Janet Achurch broke the ice for Ibsen in England, used to cite Posthumus as Shakespear's anticipation of his Norwegian rival. Certainly, after being theatrically conventional to the extent of ordering his wife to be murdered, he begins to criticize, quite on the lines of Mrs Alving in Ghosts, the slavery to an inhuman ideal of marital fidelity which led him to this villainous extremity. One may say that he is the only character left really alive in the last act; and as I cannot change him for the better I have left most of his part untouched. I make no apology for my attempt to bring the others back to dramatic activity and individuality.

I should like to have retained Cornelius as the exponent of Shakespear's sensible and scientific detestation of vivisection. But as he has nothing to say except that the Queen is dead, and nobody can possibly care a rap whether she is alive or dead, I have left him with her in the box of puppets that are done with.

I have ruthlessly cut out the surprises that no longer surprise anybody. I really could not keep my countenance over the identification of Guiderius by the mole on his neck. That device was killed by Maddison Morton, once a famous farce writer, now forgotten by everyone save Mr Gordon Craig and myself. In Morton's masterpiece, Box and Cox, Box asks Cox whether he has a strawberry mark on his left arm. 'No' says Cox. 'Then you are my long lost brother' says Box as they fall into one another's arms and end the farce happily. One could wish that Guiderius had anticipated Cox.

Plot has always been the curse of serious drama, and indeed of serious literature of any kind. It is so out-of-place there that Shakespear never could invent one. Unfortunately, instead of taking Nature's hint and discarding plots, he borrowed them all over the place and got into trouble through having to unravel them in the last act, especially in The Two Gentlemen of Verona and Cymbeline. The more childish spectators may find some delight in the revelation that Polydore and Cadwal are Imogen's long lost brothers and Cymbeline's long lost sons; that Iachimo is now an occupant of the penitent form and very unlike his old self; and that Imogen is so dutiful that she accepts her husband's attempt to have her murdered with affectionate docility. I cannot share these infantile joys. Having become interested in Iachimo, in Imogen, and even in the two long lost princes, I wanted to know how their characters would react to the *éclaircissement* which follows the battle. The only way to satisfy this curiosity was to rewrite the act as Shakespear might have written it if he had been post-Ibsen and post-Shaw instead of post-Marlowe.

In doing so I had to follow the Shakespearean verse pattern to match the 89 lines of Shakespear's text which I retained. This came very easily to me. It happened when I was a child that one of the books I delighted in was an illustrated Shakespear, with a picture and two or three lines of text underneath it on every third or fourth page. Ever since, Shakespearean blank verse has been to me as natural a form of literary expression as the Augustan English to which I was brought up in Dublin, or the latest London fashion in dialogue. It is so easy that if it were possible to kill it it would have been burlesqued to death by Tom Thumb, Chrononhotontho-logos, and Bombastes Furioso. But Shakespear will survive any possible extremity of caricature.

I shall not deprecate the most violent discussion as to the propriety of meddling with masterpieces. All I can say is that the temptation to do it, and sometimes the circumstances which demand it, are irresistible. The results are very various. When a mediocre artist tries to improve on a great artist's work the effect is ridiculous or merely contemptible. When the alteration damages the original, as when a bad painter repaints a Velasquez or a Rembrandt, he commits a crime. When the changed work is sold or exhibited as the original, the fraud is indictable. But when it comes to complete forgery, as in the case of Ireland's Vortigern, which was much admired and at last actually performed as a play by Shakespear, the affair passes beyond the sphere of crime and becomes an instructive joke.

But what of the many successful and avowed variations? What about the additions made by Mozart to the score of Handel's Messiah? Elgar, who adored Handel, and had an unbounded contempt for all the lesser meddlers, loved Mozart's variations, and dismissed all purist criticism of them by maintaining that Handel must have extemporized equivalents to them on the organ at his concerts. When Spontini found on his visit to Dresden that Wagner had added trombone parts to his choruses, he appropri-ated them very gratefully. Volumes of variations on the tunes of other composers were published as such by Mozart and Beet-hoven, to say nothing of Bach and Handel, who played Old Harry with any air that amused them. Would anyone now remember

Diabelli's vulgar waltz but for Beethoven's amazing variations, one of which is also a variation on an air from Don Giovanni?

And now consider the practice of Shakespear himself. Tolstoy declared that the original Lear is superior to Shakespear's re-handling, which he abhorred as immoral. Nobody has ever agreed with him. Will it be contended that Shakespear had no right to refashion Hamlet? If he had spoiled both plays, that would be a reason for reviving them without Shakespear's transfigurations, but not for challenging Shakespear's right to remake them.

Accordingly, I feel no qualm of conscience and have no apology to make for indulging in a variation on the last act of Cymbeline. I stand in the same time relation to Shakespear as Mozart to Handel, or Wagner to Beethoven. Like Mozart, I have not confined myself to the journeyman's job of writing 'additional accompaniments': I have luxuriated in variations. Like Wagner dealing with Gluck's overture to *Iphigenia in Aulis* I have made a new ending for its own sake. Beethoven's Ninth Symphony towers among the classic masterpieces; but if Wagner had been old enough in his Dresden days not only to rescore the first and greatest movement as he did, but to supply the whole work with a more singable ending I should not have discouraged him; for I must agree with Verdi that the present ending, from the change to six-four onward, though intensely Beethovenish, is in performance usually a screaming voice destroying orgy.

I may be asked why all my instances are musical instead of literary. Is it a plot to take the literary critics out of their depth? Well, it may have that good effect; but I am not aiming at it. It is, I suppose, because music has succeeded to the heroic rank taken by literature in the sixteenth century. I cannot pretend to care much about what Nat Lee did in his attempts to impart Restoration gentility to Shakespear, or about Thomas Corneille's bowdleriza-tion of Molière's *Festin de Pierre*, or any of the other literary precedents, though I am a little ashamed of being found in the company of their perpetrators. But I do care a good deal about what Mozart did to Handel, and Wagner to Gluck; and it seems to me that to discuss the artistic morality of my alternative ending without reference to them would be waste of time. Anyhow, what I have done I have done; and at that I must leave it.

I shall not press my version on managers producing Cymbeline if they have the courage and good sense to present the original word-for-word as Shakespear left it, and the means to do justice to the masque. But if they are halfhearted about it, and inclined to compromise by leaving out the masque and the comic jailor and mutilating the rest, as their manner is, I unhesitatingly recommend my version. The audience will not know the difference; and the few critics who have read Cymbeline will be too grateful for my shortening of the last act to complain.

AYOT SAINT LAWRENCE,
December 1945

ACT V

A rocky defile. A wild evening. Philario, in armor, stands on a tall rock, straining his eyes to see into the distance. In the foreground a Roman captain, sword in hand, his helmet badly battered, rushes in panting. Looking round before he sits down on a rock to recover his breath, he catches sight of Philario.

CAPTAIN. Ho there, signor! You are in danger there.
    You can be seen a mile off.
PHILARIO [*hastening down*] Whats your news?
    I am sent by Lucius to find out how fares
    Our right wing led by General Iachimo.
CAPTAIN. He is outgeneralled. There's no right wing now.
    Broken and routed, utterly defeated,
    Our eagles taken and the few survivors
    In full flight like myself. And you?
PHILARIO.   My news
    Is even worse. Lucius, I fear, is taken.
    Our centre could not stand the rain of arrows.
CAPTAIN. Someone has disciplined these savage archers.
    They shoot together and advance in step:
    Their horsemen trot in order to the charge
    And then let loose th' entire mass full speed.
    No single cavaliers but thirty score
    As from a catapult four hundred tons
    Of horse and man in one enormous shock
    Hurled on our shaken legions. Then their chariots
    With every axle furnished with a scythe
    Do bloody work. They made us skip, I promise you.
    Their slingers! [*He points to his helmet*]
    – Well: see their work! Two inches further down
    I had been blind or dead. The crackbrained Welshmen
    Raged like incarnate devils.
PHILARIO.   Yes: they thought

We were the Britons. So our prisoners tell us.

CAPTAIN. Where did these bumpkins get their discipline?

PHILARIO. Ay: thats the marvel. Where?

CAPTAIN.   Our victors say
Cassivelaunus is alive again.
But thats impossible.

PHILARIO.   Not so impossible
As that this witless savage Cymbeline,
Whose brains were ever in his consort's head,
Could thus defeat Roman-trained infantry.

CAPTAIN. 'Tis my belief that old Belarius,
Banned as a traitor, must have been recalled.
That fellow knew his job. These fat civilians
When we're at peace, rob us of our rewards
By falsely charging us with this or that;
But when the trumpet sounds theyre on their knees to us.

PHILARIO. Well, Captain, I must hasten back to Lucius
To blast his hopes of any help from you.
Where, think you, is Iachimo?

CAPTAIN.   I know not.
And yet I think he cannot be far off.

PHILARIO. He lives then?

CAPTAIN.   Perhaps. When all was lost he
    fought
Like any legionary, sword in hand.
His last reported word was 'Save yourselves:
Bid all make for the rocks; for there
Their horsemen cannot come'. I took his counsel;
And here I am.

PHILARIO.   You were best come with me.
Failing Iachimo, Lucius will require
Your tale at first hand.

CAPTAIN.   Good. But we shall get
No laurel crowns for what we've done today.
    Exeunt together. Enter Posthumus dressed like a peasant, but wearing a
    Roman sword and a soldier's iron cap. He has in his hand a bloodstained
    handkerchief.

POSTHUMUS. Yea, bloody cloth, I'll keep thee; for I wish'd
Thou shouldst be color'd thus. You married ones,
If each of you should take this course, how many
Must murder wives much better than themselves

For wrying but a little? O Pisanio!
Every good servant does not all commands:
No bond, but to do just ones. Gods, if you
Should have ta'en vengeance on my faults, I ne'er
Had liv'd to put on this: so had you sav'd
The noble Imogen to repent, and struck
Me (wretch) more worth your vengeance. But, alack,
You snatch some hence for little faults: that's love,
To have them fall no more. You some permit
To second ills with ills, each elder worse,
And make them dread it, to the doers' thrift;
But Imogen is your own: do your best wills,
And make me blest to obey! I am brought hither
Among the Italian gentry, and to fight
Against my lady's kingdom: 'tis enough
That, Britain, I have kill'd thy mistress. Peace!
I'll give no wound to thee. I have disrobed me
Of my Italian weeds, and drest myself
As does a Briton peasant; so I've fought
Against the part I came with; so I'll die
For thee, O Imogen, even for whom my life
Is every breath a death; and thus unknown,
Pitied nor hated, to the face of peril
Myself I'll dedicate. Let me make men know
More valor in me than my habits shew.
Gods, put the strength o' the Leonati in me!
To shame the guise o' the world, I'll begin
The fashion, less without and more within.

He is hurrying off when he is confronted with Iachimo, battle stained, hurrying in the opposite direction. Seeing a British enemy he draws his sword.

POSTHUMUS. Iachimo! Peace, man: 'tis I, Posthumus.

IACHIMO. Peace if you will. The battle's lost and won.
Pass on.

POSTHUMUS. Do you not know me?

IACHIMO.   No.

POSTHUMUS.   Look closer.
You have some reason to remember me
And I to hate you. Yet we're sworn friends.

IACHIMO. By all the gods, Leonatus!

POSTHUMUS.   At your service,

Seducer of my wife.

IACHIMO.   No more of that.
Your wife, Posthumus, is a noble creature.
I'll set your mind at rest upon that score.

POSTHUMUS. At rest! Can you then raise her from the grave?
Where she lies dead to expiate our crime?

IACHIMO. Dead! How? Why? When? And expiate! What mean
    you?

POSTHUMUS. This only: I have had her murdered, I.
And at my best am worser than her worst.

IACHIMO. We are damned for this. [*On guard*] Let's cut each
.   other's throats.

POSTHUMUS [*drawing*] Ay, let us.
    They fight furiously. Enter Cymbeline, Belarius, Guiderius, Arviragus,
    Pisanio, with Lucius and Imogen as Fidele: both of them prisoners guarded
    by British soldiers.

BELARIUS [*taking command instinctively*] Part them there. Make fast
the Roman.
    Guiderius pounces on Iachimo and disarms him. Arviragus pulls
    Posthumus back.

ARVIRAGUS. In the King's presence sheath your sword, you lout.

IACHIMO. In the King's presence I must yield perforce;
But as a person of some quality
By rank a gentleman, I claim to be
Your royal highness's prisoner, not this lad's.

LUCIUS. His claim is valid, sir. His blood is princely.

POSTHUMUS. 'Tis so: he's noble.

CYMBELINE.   What art thou?

POSTHUMUS.   A murderer.

IMOGEN. His voice! His voice! Oh, let me see his face.
    [*She rushes to Posthumus and puts her hand on his face*].

POSTHUMUS. Shall's have a play with this? There lies thy part [*he*
    knocks her down with a blow of his fist].

GUIDERIUS. Accursed churl: take that. [*He strikes Posthumus and*
    brings him down on one knee].

ARVIRAGUS. You dog, how dare you [*threatening him*].

POSTHUMUS. Soft, soft, young sirs. One at a time, an't please you.
    [*He springs up and stands on the defensive*].

PISANIO [*interposing*] Hands off my master! He is kin to the king.

POSTHUMUS [*to Cymbeline*] Call off your bulldogs, sir. Why all this
    coil

About a serving boy?

CYMBELINE.   My son-in-law!

PISANIO. Oh, gentlemen, your help. My Lord Posthumus:
 You ne'er killed Imogen till now. Help! help!

IMOGEN. Oh, let me die. I heard my husband's voice
 Whom I thought dead; and in my ecstasy,
 The wildest I shall ever feel again,
 He met me with a blow.

POSTHUMUS.   Her voice. 'Tis Imogen.
 Oh, dearest heart, thou livest. Oh, you gods,
 What sacrifice can pay you for this joy?

IMOGEN. You dare pretend you love me.

POSTHUMUS.   Sweet, I dare
 Anything, everything. Mountains of mortal guilt
 That crushed me are now lifted from my breast.
 I am in heaven that was but now in hell.
 You may betray me twenty times again.

IMOGEN. Again! And pray, when have I e'er betrayed you?

POSTHUMUS. I had the proofs. There stands your paramour.
 Shall's have him home? I care not, since thou liv'st.

IMOGEN. My paramour! [*To Iachimo*] Oh, as you are a gentleman,
 Give him the lie.

IACHIMO.   He knows no better, madam.
 We made a wager, he and I, in Italy
 That I should spend a night in your bedchamber.

IMOGEN [*to Posthumus*] You made this wager! And I'm married to
 you!

POSTHUMUS. I did. He won it.

IMOGEN.   How? He never came
 Within my bedchamber

IACHIMO.   I spent a night there.
 It was the most uncomfortable night
 I ever passed.

IMOGEN.   You must be mad, signor.
 Or else the most audacious of all liars
 That ever swore away a woman's honor.

IACHIMO. I think, madam, you do forget that chest.

IMOGEN. I forget nothing. At your earnest suit
 Your chest was safely houséd in my chamber;
 But where were you?

IACHIMO.   I? I was in the chest [*Hilarious sensation*].

And on one point I do confess a fault.
I stole your bracelet while you were asleep.
POSTHUMUS. And cheated me out of my diamond ring!
IACHIMO. Both ring and bracelet had some magic in them
That would not let me rest until I laid them
On Mercury's altar. He's the god of thieves.
But I can make amends. I'll pay for both
At your own price, and add one bracelet more
For the other arm.
POSTHUMUS.   With ten thousand ducats
Due to me for the wager you have lost.
IMOGEN. And this, you think, signors, makes good to me
All you have done, you and my husband there!
IACHIMO. It remedies what can be remedied.
As for the rest, it cannot be undone.
We are a pitiable pair. For all that
You may go further and fare worse; for men
Will do such things to women.
IMOGEN.   You at least
Have grace to know yourself for what you are.
My husband thinks that all is settled now
And this a happy ending!
POSTHUMUS.   Well, my dearest,
What could I think? The fellow did describe
The mole upon your breast.
IMOGEN.   And thereupon
You bade your servant kill me.
POSTHUMUS.   It seemed natural.
IMOGEN. Strike me again; but do not say such things.
GUIDERIUS. An if you do, by Thor's great hammer stroke
I'll kill you, were you fifty sons-in-law.
BELARIUS. Peace, boy: we're in the presence of the king.
IMOGEN. Oh, Cadwal, Cadwal, you and Polydore,
My newfound brothers, are my truest friends.
Would either of you, were I ten times faithless,
Have sent a slave to kill me?
GUIDERIUS [shuddering]   All the world
Should die first.
ARVIRAGUS.   Whiles we live, Fidele,
Nothing shall harm you.
POSTHUMUS.   Child: hear me out.

Have I not told you that my guilty conscience
Had almost driven me mad when heaven opened
And you appeared? But prithee, dearest wife,
How did you come to think that I was dead?

IMOGEN. I cannot speak of it: it is too dreadful.
I saw a headless man drest in your clothes.

GUIDERIUS. Pshaw! That was Cloten: son, he said, to the king.
I cut his head off.

CYMBELINE.   Marry, the gods forefend!
I would not thy good deeds should from my lips
Pluck a hard sentence: prithee, valiant youth,
Deny 't again.

GUIDERIUS. I have spoke it, and I did it.

CYMBELINE. He was a prince.

GUIDERIUS. A most incivil one: the wrongs he did me
Were nothing prince-like; for he did provoke me
With language that would make me spurn the sea
If it could so roar to me. I cut off's head;
And am right glad he is not standing here
To tell this tale of mine.

CYMBELINE.   I am sorry for thee:
By thine own tongue thou art condemn'd, and must
Endure our law: thou 'rt dead. Bind the offender,
And take him from our presence.

BELARIUS.   Stay, sir king:
This man is better than the man he slew,
As well descended as thyself, and hath
More of thee merited than a band of Clotens
Had ever scar for. [To the Guard] Let his arms alone,
They were not born for bondage.

CYMBELINE.   Why, old soldier,
Wilt thou undo the worth thou art unpaid for,
By tasting of our wrath? How of descent
As good as we?

GUIDERIUS.   In that he spake too far.

CYMBELINE. And thou shalt die for 't.

BELARIUS.   We will die all three:
But I will prove that two on 's are as good
As I have given out him.

CYMBELINE.   Take him away.
The whole world shall not save him.

BELARIUS.   Not so hot.
First pay me for the nursing of thy sons;
And let it be confiscate all so soon
As I've received it.
CYMBELINE.   Nursing of my sons!
BELARIUS. I am too blunt and saucy: here's my knee.
Ere I arise I will prefer my sons.
Then spare not the old father. Mighty sir:
These two young gentlemen that call me father,
And think they are my sons, are none of mine.
They are the issue of your loins, my liege,
And blood of your begetting.
CYMBELINE.   How? my issue?
BELARIUS. So sure as you your father's. These your princes
(For such and so they are) these twenty years
Have I train'd up: those arts they have as I
Could put into them; my breeding was, sir, as
Your highness knows. Come hither, boys, and pay
Your loves and duties to your royal sire.
GUIDERIUS. We three are fullgrown men and perfect strangers.
Can I change fathers as I'd change my shirt?
CYMBELINE. Unnatural whelp! What doth thy brother say?
ARVIRAGUS. I, royal sir? Well, we have reached an age
When fathers' helps are felt as hindrances.
I am tired of being preached at.
CYMBELINE [to Belarius]   So, sir, this
Is how you have bred my puppies.
GUIDERIUS.   He has bred us
To tell the truth and face it.
BELARIUS.   Royal sir:
I know not what to say: not you nor I
Can tell our children's minds. But pardon him.
If he be overbold the fault is mine.
GUIDERIUS. The fault, if fault there be, is in my Maker.
I am of no man's making. I am I:
Take me or leave me.
IACHIMO [to Lucius]   Mark well, Lucius, mark.
There spake the future king of this rude island.
GUIDERIUS. With you, Sir Thief, to tutor me? No, no:
This kingly business has no charm for me.
When I lived in a cave methought a palace

Must be a glorious place, peopled with men
Renowned as councillors, mighty as soldiers,
As saints a pattern of holy living,
And all at my command were I a prince.
This was my dream. I am awake today.
I am to be, forsooth, another Cloten,
Plagued by the chatter of his train of flatterers,
Compelled to worship priest invented gods,
Not free to wed the woman of my choice,
Being stopped at every turn by some old fool
Crying 'You must not', or, still worse, 'You must'.
Oh no, sir: give me back the dear old cave
And my unflattering four footed friends.
I abdicate, and pass the throne to Polydore.

ARVIRAGUS. Do you, by heavens? Thank you for nothing,
brother.

CYMBELINE. I'm glad you're not ambitious. Seated monarchs
Do rarely love their heirs. Wisely, it seems.

ARVIRAGUS. Fear not, great sir: we two have never learnt
To wait for dead men's shoes, much less their crowns.

GUIDERIUS. Enough of this. Fidele: is it true
Thou art a woman, and this man thy husband?

IMOGEN. I am a woman, and this man my husband.
He would have slain me.

POSTHUMUS.   Do not harp on that.

CYMBELINE. God's patience, man, take your wife home to bed.
You're man and wife: nothing can alter that.
Are there more plots to unravel? Each one here,
It seems, is someone else. [*To Imogen*] Go change your dress
For one becoming to your sex and rank.
Have you no shame?

IMOGEN.   None.

CYMBELINE.   How? None!

IMOGEN.   All is lost
Shame, husband, happiness, and faith in Man.
He is not even sorry.

POSTHUMUS.   I'm too happy.

IACHIMO. Lady: a word. When you arrived just now
I, as you saw, was hot on killing him.
Let him bear witness that I drew on him
To avenge your death.

IMOGEN.   Oh, do not make me laugh.
  Laughter dissolves too many just resentments,
  Pardons too many sins.
IACHIMO.   And saves the world
  A many thousand murders. Let me plead for him.
  He has his faults; but he must suffer yours.
  You are, I swear, a very worthy lady;
  But still, not quite an angel.
IMOGEN.   No, not quite,
  Nor yet a worm. Subtle Italian villain!
  I would that chest had smothered you.
IACHIMO.   Dear lady
  It very nearly did.
IMOGEN.   I will not laugh.
  I must go home and make the best of it
  As other women must.
POSTHUMUS.   Thats all I ask. [*He clasps her*].
BELARIUS. The fingers of the powers above do tune
  The harmony of this peace.
LUCIUS.   Peace be it then.
  For by this gentleman's report and mine
  I hope imperial Cæsar will reknit
  His favor with the radiant Cymbeline,
  Which shines here in the west.
CYMBELINE.   Laud we the gods,
  And let our crooked smokes climb to their nostrils
  From our blest altars. Publish we this peace
  To all our subjects. Set we forward: let
  A Roman and a British ensign wave
  Friendly together: so through Lud's town march,
  And in the temple of great Jupiter
  Our peace we'll ratify; seal it with feasts.
  Set on there! Never was a war did cease,
  Ere bloody hands were wash'd, with such a peace.